GARRY LINNELL covered Australian football for *The Age* newspaper and *The Times on Sunday* during the game's most turbulent period in the 1980s. A former sports editor of *The Age*, he has covered a variety of international sport, including the 1992 Barcelona Olympics, the 1990 Auckland Commonwealth Games and a cricket tour of India. Aged 31 and married with two children, he is now a features editor at *The Sunday Age*.

FOOTBALL LTD

The Inside Story of the AFL

GARRY LINNELL

IRONBARK
Pan Macmillan Australia

First published 1995 in Ironbark by Pan Macmillan Australia Pty Limited
St Martins Tower, 31 Market Street, Sydney

National Library of Australia
cataloguing-in-publication data:

Linnell, Garry, 1963– .
Football ltd: the inside story of the Australian
Football League.
Includes index.
ISBN 0 330 35665 8.

1. Australian Football League – History. 2. Australian
football – History. 3. Sports sponsorship – Australia.
I. Title. II. Title: Football limited.
796.336

Typeset in 11/13 Sabon by Post Typesetters
Printed in Australia by McPherson's Printing Group

All photos courtesy of *The Age*.

CONTENTS

Acknowledgements   vii

Chronology   ix

Prologue   xv

1. The End of Innocence   1

2. A Legion of Sworn Enemies   17

3. All the President's Men   36

4. The Power of the Presidents   53

5. The Changing of the Guard   79

6. The Swans' Song (I)   91

7. Preparing for Expansion   118

8. The Beer Wars   127

9. The New Frontier   143

10. The Television Wars   160

11. The Players in the Trenches   194

12. The Bad Buck Bears (I)   216

13. Once Upon a Time in the West   243

14. The Battle for the Cathedral   260

15. Good Old Collingwood Forever   277

16. Marriages of Inconvenience   289

17. Like No Other Business They Know   312

18. The Bad Buck Bears (II) 321

19. The Swans' Song (II) 331

20. The End of the Cold War 345

21. Football Ltd 362

Epilogue 371

Sources 380

Bibliography 384

Index 387

ACKNOWLEDGEMENTS

First, a confession. I'd like to apologise to all those workers in sports stores over the years who have spied me lurking next to the football rack. I know it must have looked strange when I kept leaning over to sniff them but I just couldn't help it. I love the smell of a new football. I can still remember when, at the age of 10, my father brought home my first spanking new ball. It was a bright red Sherrin, signed by Des Tuddenham, and when I pulled away its plastic wrapping, a rich, leathery odour hit me like a punch. I was immediately addicted and have been ever since. The only consolation is that there are thousands of others like me, too; grown men who spent their childhoods sleeping with their footballs, never wanting to let them go. You probably see us occasionally in sports stores. We're the ones wearing dark glasses trying not to look suspicious. Show some understanding next time you see one of us. We need it.

This book had its origins back when I was a boy and in love with the game of Australian football. Like millions of other kids I was entranced by it. What was better than flying over your mate's back to take a big grab? What could possibly compare to the feeling of the ball leaving your boot and sailing perfectly through the goals?

It wasn't until I became a sports writer with *The Age* in the early 1980s that I discovered there was another game going on. It was, in many ways, just as tough as the one out on the field. And it was far more brutal. As the decade progressed, the Victorian Football League underwent the most turbulent transformation any sporting competition in this country has experienced.

This is a book about those changes. It is not the official history of Australian football. It does not concern itself with what took place out on the field. Instead, I wanted to take a look at why the game changed. How, in less than a decade, did the VFL go from being a 12-team, suburban-based competition into a national league spanning the continent and generating turnover of more than $150 million?

While documents and newspaper clippings were invaluable during the research of this book, most of the information was gleaned from more than 130 interviews during 1994 with the men who were responsible for those changes. To all those who gave up their valuable time and memories, I thank them. This is their history and, far removed from the dry minutes of board meetings, it is the only one available.

I owe a large debt of gratitude to Geoff Slattery who, just when the book threatened to overwhelm me, plucked me out of the abyss and guided me through a tough period. I could not have written it without him.

Many others also contributed in special ways. The editor of *The Sunday Age*, Bruce Guthrie, showed patience when my mind wandered off at times, as did my body when an interview had to be conducted. His devout belief that a good story is one about people permeates this book. Thanks to Jason Steger, too, for putting up with my grumpy moods and helping to lighten them. Caroline Wilson, the best all-round journalist I know, provided invaluable perspective and encouragement.

Above all, however, I owe my family who put up with the strange, obsessed figure in their midst who never shaved on weekends, locked himself away in a room for hours on end and whose mood swings matched Melbourne's infamous weather.

This book is for my wife, Suellen, and my daughter, Georgia.

And for my son, Kirk. May he grow up to love the smell of a leather football in the morning.

Garry Linnell
February, 1995

CHRONOLOGY

1858: Scotch College and Melbourne Grammar School play first recorded match of Australian football.

1877: Victorian Football Association begins competition.

1896: Eight Association Clubs break away and form the Victorian Football League. A year later, the system of six points for a goal and one point for a behind is introduced.

1919: Melbourne joins VFL.

1925: North Melbourne, Hawthorn and Footscray admitted to VFL.

1928: The 'Australasian', in its 28 April edition, notes that 'Money speaks all languages in football in these decadent days.'

1940: Player and staff payments reduced by 50 per cent because of World War II.

1962: VFL buys 200 acres in market garden area of Waverley in plan to build its own stadium.

1966: Ross Oakley injures knee in second semi-final and is unable to take place in St Kilda's historic premiership victory over Collingwood.

1970: VFL Park opens on 18 April.

1973: VFL Players' Association formed in December. League administration moves its headquarters to Jolimont offices.

1975: Colour television introduced to football. League forms its Properties Division to market and licence VFL-approved merchandise. North Melbourne wins first premiership.

1977: Allen Aylett elected as president of the League in February. Jack Hamilton takes over as general manager a month earlier.

1980: 'Big-business era' ushered in by lunchtime meeting of four prominent club presidents: Lindsay Fox, Bob Ansett, Ian Rice and Wayne Reid.

1983: League's player rules thrown into turmoil after Swans rover Silvio Foshini successfully challenges regulations in Supreme Court. Jack Hamilton, Ron Cook and Dick Seddon travel to United States to investigate player rules and finances. The 'McKinsey Report' recommends an overhaul of the League's administrative procedures. VFL Task Force subsequently appointed to investigate and recommend changes. Attendances drop for first time in years.

1984: John Elliott and group of club presidents meet secretly throughout year planning to form a breakaway 'super' league. Task Force recommends restructure of League administration. Aylett's role as president abolished. Jack Hamilton appointed first full-time chairman of the VFL commission. Peter Scanlon, Graeme Samuel, Dick Seddon and Peter Nixon appointed part-time commissioners. League introduces salary cap on player payments, effective 1985. Grand Final is played at MCG after compromise deal worked out between VFL and the Melbourne Cricket Club.

1985: Commission releases seminal report on football's future strategy. Clubs agree to a licencing agreement legally forcing them to abide by the League's rules. Sydney Swans become first privately-owned club after being sold to Dr Geoffrey Edelsten.

1986: League contracts Carlton and United Breweries and Bond Brewing as 'joint' sponsors of competition. Jack Hamilton announces retirement. Ross Oakley appointed chairman of the VFL commission. Alan Schwab appointed executive commissioner. Clubs agree to expand competition to 14 teams the following season, admitting the Brisbane Bears and the West Coast Eagles. VFL awards Broadcom rights to football coverage for following five years.

1987: The ABC secures rights to broadcast the season, but loses them to Channel 7 in a five-year, $30 million deal late in the year. Eagles finish eighth on ladder with 11-11 record. Bears finish 13th (6-16).

1988: Dick Seddon resigns from commission and is replaced by former North Melbourne official and player, Albert Mantello. West Coast reaches finals in second season. Ownership crisis at Sydney Swans. Consortium of prominent business identities join forces to buy the club.

1989: In July, League holds summit of clubs in Hobart to discuss future direction of competition. League decides to change name at end of season to Australian Football League. Proposed merger between Footscray and Fitzroy fails after public rally raises more than $1.3 million to save Footscray. League reaches agreement with State Government and Melbourne Cricket Club on construction of a new stand at the MCG to cost an estimated

$140 million. New deal will secure future of the Grand Final at the ground for almost 40 years.

1990: Gold Coast businessman Reuben Pelerman buys the cash-strapped Brisbane Bears after the collapse of the chain of companies operated by Christoper Skase. Collingwood ends 32-year drought by winning premiership. Jack Hamilton killed in car accident. Port Adelaide makes rebel bid to join AFL competition, but thwarted after League clubs vote for the admission of a side sponsored by the South Australian National Football League.

1991: Competition enlarged to 15 clubs with admission of the Adelaide Crows. A bye is introduced during the home and away season and a final six operates for the first time. Grand Final is played at Waverley due to construction work at MCG. Peter Nixon steps down as part-time commissioner, replaced by Michael Carlile.

1992: Resentment among clubs over commission's handling of several issues leads to appointment of insolvency expert David Crawford to investigate and report on commission's structure and relationship with the 15 clubs. Peter Scanlon announces intention to retire as part-time commissioner. Reuben Pelerman steps down as owner of the troubled Bears and club reverts to traditional, member-based structure.

1993: Clubs accept Crawford report recommending clubs effectively hand over almost all their powers to a restructured commission comprising up to eight members. John Kennedy elected chairman. Other members of the new commission are Colin Carter, Ron Evans, Terry O'Connor QC, John Winneke QC and Graeme Samuel. Ross Oakley appointed chief executive officer. Alan

Schwab dies in a Sydney hotel room in mysterious circumstances on 18 June after being sent to help restructure the Swans following failure of private ownership.

1994: Clubs vote to expand competition to 16 clubs with admission of the Fremantle Dockers in 1995. League releases five-year business plan.

PROLOGUE

SEPTEMBER, 1966.
Channel 7 commentary box, Melbourne Cricket Ground.

ALAN 'Butch' GALE: Oooh Michael, you might be right! This could be a draw!
MIKE WILLIAMSON: I tipped this! . . . Twenty-six and a half minutes gone. There's the throw-in. Morrow comes in. Thompson gets the tapdown. Taken by Baldock. Baldock drives in to centre half-forward. They set themselves. No mark to anybody. Hill comes out with it. Stewart has it. Stewart runs in to Morrow. A handpass . . . across to Cooper. Cooper drives it forward. It's a mis-kick!
TED WHITTEN: PLAY ON!
WILLIAMSON: Has it been marked?
GALE: NO! He's going to bounce it. Poor Potter. Look at him . . .
WILLIAMSON: These players are so weary!
GALE: This is madness! They're all on the ball!
WILLIAMSON: There they go. Up goes Mynott. He gets the tap down. Potter has it. He can't break clear. It's taken by BREEN . . . IT'S A POINT! IT'S A POINT! ST KILDA IN FRONT! ST KILDA IN FRONT!
WHITTEN: How long have they been playing, Mike?
WILLIAMSON: They have been playing . . . if my hands will stop shaking I can see the watch . . . twenty-seven and a half minutes . . . twenty seven and a half minutes. There's the kick-out. Up they go. Nobody able to break clear. Across it goes here towards Hill. Hill tries to handpass to Henderson. He's tackled by Morrow and we find the ball being driven forward. It's at centre half-forward for St Kilda. MYNOTT! He'll be paid the mark!

WHITTEN: SLOW IT DOWN! SLOW IT DOWN!

WILLIAMSON: Yes, he's taking your advice all right, Ted. Can the Saints hang on and win their first ever?

WHITTEN: THEY'VE GOT IT!

WILLIAMSON: Oh! Golly me!

GALE: Mynott with the ball. He comes up. It's going to be a good long kick . . .

WILLIAMSON: That's a magnificent kick. It's a ripper. They set themselves. Up they go! And we find a magnificent mark taken by Waters again. He goes across the face of goal. He kicks to that flank position on the outer side. They set themselves . . .

EVERYONE: WHOAH!

WILLIAMSON: There's a break! Tuddenham . . . a break. Tuddenham kicks to centre half-forward. They set themselves. And a mark to Bob Murray! A mark to Murray. Twenty-eight and a half minutes gone.

WHITTEN: HIT THE BOUNDARY LINE!

WILLIAMSON: Twenty-eight and a half gone. There's Murray's kick to the wing position on the outer side . . . THERE'S THE SIREN! ST KILDA HAVE WON IT! THEY'VE WON IT! LOOK AT THIS! . . . OH WHAT AN EMOTIONAL SCENE THIS IS . . . WHAT EMOTION! I sincerely trust you've enjoyed this, really I do. You'd be hard to please if you didn't enjoy this. St Kilda! Their first ever premiership! A magNIFIcent effort from everybody out there today. Look at this!

GALE: By one point, though, Mike. A magNIFIcent effort by both teams. I'm shaking. I don't know how you feel but this is the most emotional thing I think I've ever seen in my life.

WILLIAMSON: Butch, I've just put the lighted end of the cigarette into my mouth. This has been a mag-NIFicent grand final. Alf Potter, are we on direct still? Oh golly, they shouldn't miss this, really. This is magnificent. Emotional. Great. What a game. What . . . a . . . game, that's all I can say.

That's all they could ever say. It was a great game. A great game. And the 1966 grand final had been the best ever, hadn't it? Mike Williamson, Alan 'Butch' Gale and Ted Whitten up there in the commentary box calling the game, more than 101,000 people crammed into the Melbourne Cricket Ground watching it and millions more who would talk and romanticise it for years to come. Oh golly. It was such a great game.

Ross Oakley was there that day, sitting in the grandstand watching the Saints march in. He had a wonderful view, too, even if the large, muscular figure of Carl Ditterich squashed in next to him sometimes partly obscured it.

St Kilda, the perennial loser, the club that was always going nowhere, had finally gone somewhere. It was the last Saturday in September. Barry Breen's wobbly punt kick had gone through for a behind, breaking the deadlock with Collingwood. Then the siren had sounded. The Saints had won their first flag. And high in the stands, Oakley looked on.

Ditterich was a young man with a temper and the strength of two decent pub brawlers. And he'd done it again. The tribunal had suspended him, forcing him out of the biggest game of the year and what would have been the biggest game of his life. He would never get the chance to play in a premiership team. The Saints would never be that good again.

It was the same for Oakley. He'd had to fight hard just to get this far. Every time he seemed on the verge of getting somewhere, of finally establishing himself as a consistent and reliable player, his body had let him down.

There'd been a broken leg. Crook knees. Torn hamstrings. An opponent had even punched him in the face one afternoon, lacerating the cornea in one of his eyes. The bastard hadn't even been reported. The umpire simply paid a free kick down field.

He had done his knee again the season before and some had doubted whether they would see him back at the club. Surely, that was it. But Oakley had persisted. He worked hard over the summer, sweating it out when everyone else was at the beach.

Laps. Sprints. Weights. And he'd proved to himself and the others that he could come back. Again. He played right through 1966 and finally it seemed to be going right. And then came the second semi-final. The knee went again.

There was a newspaper photographer standing on the boundary line when they carried him off. Just before they carted him up the race to the rooms the camera snapped, forever capturing that anguished face contorted with pain.

But even then he didn't feel bitter. Just disappointed. It was a cruel game, everyone who played it knew that. You could watch an opponent fluff the easiest chance and immediately you would be at his side, making snide remarks in his ear, trying to put him off his game because you always took any opportunity to gain that edge. But deep down you knew it could, and probably would, happen to you, too. And when it did, you accepted it.

So as he sat at the MCG watching the team hold aloft the premiership cup, the cup he, too, should have been holding, he felt torn. Should he feel happy for the team? Or should he let that empty feeling in the pit of his gut continue to grow?

He should have been out there, running the victory lap alongside Breen, who would forever be mythologised as the player whose wobbly, errant kick won a flag for the Saints.

He should have been out there in the centre of the ground, with the winter sun low on the horizon, hugging Baldock, slapping Ian Stewart on the back, lifting little Rossy Smith into the air.

He should have been there.

The game had given him so much, and he had given it so much of himself. He felt elated and disappointed and happy and damn it, he felt this strange emptiness, too.

But he didn't feel bitter. Not yet, anyway. There would be plenty of time for that later.

It began with little things. He had played all year, busting a gut for the club, and only missed the preliminary final and the grand final because his damn body had given up on him again. And yet, when the club decided to commemorate the historic season with a team photograph, he wasn't included.

Usually, the full list of senior players was paraded in front of the camera, all striking the familiar pose, standing stiffly and awkwardly, arms folded across chests, wearing artificial smiles. But not this year. Not in 1966. Only those who were out on the ground would have their mug shots recorded for posterity. It was as though the whole year had been for nothing.

There were other things, too. But what really upset him, what really bugged the hell out of him, was an end-of-season celebratory team dinner at a Chinese restaurant down in Acland Street, St Kilda. Neither he nor Ditterich was invited.

Oakley seethed, but said nothing. 'Sorry mate,' he was told. 'There's just not enough room.'

Of course not. Space was tight. Chinese restaurants were like that in the '60s. Hemmed in. Barely enough room to lift your chopsticks or, if you were a true Australian, your fork. Checkered red tablecloths and pale yellow walls. Besides, how on earth could they squeeze him in with all those club officials already having reserved their seats, ensuring a bit of the glory rubbed off on them? It was always the way.

Two days before the dinner they rang Ditterich. 'You're in,' they told him.

Oakley's phone rang a day later. 'Someone's just pulled out,' he was told. 'There's a place for you now.'

He thought about it for a moment. Chinese food. Cold beer. Champagne. Mates from the club. It would be a great night, a night for talking to old friends and being a part of the team again.

'Stick it up your arse,' said Oakley. 'I'm not coming.'

He sits high in the grandstand again but the view is different. He stops talking for a moment and stares out of the window at

the cobweb of overhanging power lines and the maze of rail-
way tracks below them. It is early in the morning. He likes to
be in the office before everyone else. There are no phones ringing, no lawyers, no-one wanting to close a deal or open one, no
reporters ringing for a quote. Just him working quietly and
running the Australian Football League from its offices high in
a new stand at the MCG.

He stares and blinks, the noise of a train hurtling toward
Richmond station dragging him forward 30 years.

Yes, he admits, sitting back in his seat, both hands clasped
tightly together. He should have ended his career then, at the
end of 1966. Anyone could see there was no point in going on.
Even though medical science was making enormous advances,
knee reconstructions were still in their primitive stages. There
was no guarantee of a full recovery. Hell, there was no guarantee you'd ever run freely again, that you'd ever get the
opportunity to kick the footy around in the backyard with
your kids.

But he had to go back, give it one more try, go through it all
once more. It was as though he had to prove he hadn't wasted
all those years, that something could still be salvaged.

He made it back. It was a reserves match in 1967 out at the
old Brunswick Street Oval, one of the last of the truly old-
fashioned league football grounds. A grassy bank in the outer,
an old wooden grandstand with the change rooms beneath it.
The trams rattled past the ground on their way into the city.

It wasn't long before his knee began to swell, puffing up like
a dead toad-fish out of water. It was hard to bend it. Finally, he
agreed it was over and the realisation hit him.

It wasn't worth it, was it?

'Reconstruction surgery in those days wasn't great,' he says,
a wry smile appearing beneath the thickness of his moustache.
'Not many came back. I thought there was more to life than
walking around with a busted knee for the entire future.'

There was, too. He would go to work at BHP and earn a

reputation as a feisty combatant. Later, he would run one of the country's largest insurance companies before being head-hunted to return to the game and oversee the most tumultuous period of change it had experienced.

And what changes had been wrought.

No-one ever said it was just a game anymore. It had altered so much since he'd limped away as a player. On the field the game—the one old blokes maintained had no peer—had evolved into a blur of constant motion, of hardened bodies built for speed bouncing off one another. The players had skills and knowledge no-one had even dreamed of in the 1960s. They still required the basic components of human endeavour the sport had always demanded: courage, the ability to overcome despair, hand and leg skills, a cool mind that could think strategically, even under the most intense pressure. But it was as though all those abilities had been multiplied tenfold. Even the ball had changed, its red leather covered in advertising logos.

Off the field things had moved even faster. The old grand-stands and grassy hills had given way to concrete, plastic and glass. When a player flew for a spectacular mark above a pack in one of the features peculiar to the sport, he was no longer outlined against a blue or grey sky. The horizon was cluttered with superboxes and corporate signs.

Entrepreneurs had been drawn to the game, stunned by its bright lights and promises of instant fame. Politicians had used it as a punching bag in their typically hollow attempts to curry favour with the public. Australian football had been beaten, dragged, bloodied and abused for many years.

It was an easy target because many times it deserved to be punished, to be reminded that it was the people who had made the game what it was; they had embraced it as passionately as a love affair. They just never understood why that love was sometimes not reciprocated.

Oakley had experienced it all, too. They had pilloried him

for years, hurling the worst obscenities at him. He had survived two attempts to oust him. There'd been death threats, security guards around the clock at his home to protect his family, anonymous and obscene phone calls. He had even suffered the worst abuse the game could produce.

He wasn't a 'football person', some of his enemies within the game had whispered. He didn't know and understand how it worked. They thought he was too cold, too impersonal, too . . . too businesslike.

But for all his weaknesses and strengths, for all the bold moves he had pulled off and the ones he had failed miserably at, they couldn't make it stick.

Sitting in his office, with all its trappings of his role as chief executive of the Australian Football League—the big desk with its piles of contracts and confidential legal documents, the leather briefcase, the bookshelf, the art deco table and chairs for guests—he stares straight into the eyes of a visitor.

He had been a player once. He knew what it was like. The game might have changed. It might be almost unrecognisable now as the one he once knew so intimately. But he had played the game.

And he knew, as so many others had discovered over the years, that despite all the changes one thing had remained constant. The game didn't care who you were or what you had done for it. It just didn't care. Some days it let you feel on top of the world. Other days it left that empty feeling in your gut.

They were right. Football was a great game. A great game. But now, it was more than even that.

It was also a business.

THE END OF
INNOCENCE

He loved football. He liked cricket, too, but by the end of summer he was always counting down the days before the football season began. By March, those days had started shortening and everything in Melbourne seemed to change colour; the leaves on the trees turned brown, the grass was restored to its greenness after a summer of heat. The papers were filled with football talk. Kids were out in the street once more kicking footballs end-to-end, trying to stand on one another's shoulders to emulate their weekend heroes.

Ronny Joseph was a typical Melbourne kid. He and his two best friends would often camp out overnight at the Melbourne Cricket Ground just before a Test match and then sneak in through a hole in the fence early in the morning to get a seat in the Members' Stand right on the boundary. But it was football that really sent the blood pumping through his veins.

Joseph loved South Melbourne. It was a club that appealed to his sense of the underdog. South had won a flag in 1933, lost the next three consecutive grand finals and rarely looked like challenging again. They were battlers, always promising a little but always overwhelmed by opponents who were tougher, brasher and more skilful.

And, like any kid, not even Ronny Joseph could remain optimistic. How many times had it happened? Instead of going to the Lakeside Oval to watch South get trounced by a more fancied opponent, he would accompany his best mate, Neil Hudson, to the Punt Road Oval, just a drop-kick away from the heart of the city to watch Richmond flay another hapless club.

At half-time the scoreboard attendants would put up the scores from the other grounds. Joseph would look up eagerly, squinting through the haze of a late autumn Saturday afternoon, to see how South was faring. And there it was. They were up by several goals and a murmur would spread through the crowd. South? Winning?

That was enough for Joseph. The guilt weighed too heavily. He would say goodbye to Neil and hotfoot it over to the Richmond train station. There, he'd catch the next train to Flinders Street. Then followed another train trip, this time in an old-fashioned, two-carriage train down to the Albert Park station. Then he'd bust his heart and lungs by running all the way to the Lakeside Oval two miles away, sprinting through the gate with just five minutes remaining in the match.

He would pause for a brief moment, catch his breath and scan the scoreboard.

South would be losing by six goals.

In 1963 Ron Joseph was in his final year at Trinity Grammar and was wondering what he would do with the rest of his life. Deep down there was nothing he could think of but a career in football. He didn't have the playing skills some other kids had but a life in club administration sounded exotic.

His father, Ray, was an accountant who viewed his son's ambitions with more than just a touch of distaste. 'He didn't see it as the most profound of occupations and ambitions,' Joseph would recall 30 years later. Still, Ray Joseph was well-acquainted with his son's obsession. So he was not surprised when, on a night in early September 1963, young Ron slipped out of the house and disappeared into the night.

They had all been listening to the Brownlow Medal count on the radio, one of the great nights on the calendar of the

Victorian Football League. The Brownlow was the game's highest individual prize, awarded to the fairest and best player in the competition. And even though it was judged by the umpires, those neutral men dressed in white who suffered more abuse during their careers than a non-drinker in the front bar of a waterside pub, it was still taken very seriously.

Minutes before Joseph slipped out of the back door he had heard the final vote read out proclaiming Bobby Skilton the Brownlow Medallist for 1963. Skilton had won the medal back in 1959 as a 20-year-old. Now here he was again, his reputation as the competition's best player underlined once more. Finally, Joseph had something to celebrate. South Melbourne might have broken his heart on more than one occasion, but it had produced a champion.

Ron Joseph just had to see Bob Skilton.

Skilton lived just a suburb away in Moorabbin and while it was still a long hike at that time of night, Joseph was oblivious to time or distance. Nothing really mattered except football. In the darkened streets he finally found Skilton's home. Joseph opened Skilton's front gate and, only ever so tentatively, knocked on the door.

The champion opened it.

'Congratulations, Bobby,' Joseph said, extending his hand. Skilton smiled and returned the gesture.

'Ummm,' said Joseph. 'I was just wondering if I might borrow your jumper so I can wear it to school tomorrow?'

Skilton paused, then nodded. He disappeared up a corridor and returned a few moments later with a red and white guernsey. Joseph's eyes bulged. He looked like a pilgrim who had just seen the Holy Shroud of Turin.

He thanked Skilton and disappeared into the night clasping the champion's number 14 jumper so tightly he didn't think he'd ever let it go. He wore it to school the next day like a badge. All those afternoons when your spirit was broken, when the train journey home seemed to go on forever, when football grabbed you by the collar and shook you so hard you felt its pull for days afterward . . .

It was all worth it.

The following year Ron Joseph left school and shuffled his way through a job with a sales company. It was dull work and Joseph, after he'd finished poring through the daily newspaper sports pages, would often turn to the employment section looking for a way out.

One morning he spied an advertisement for a position as assistant secretary at the North Melbourne football club. Here was an opportunity too good to pass up. Months before he had decided against applying for the same job at Richmond, a club with a rich tradition that was harder to infiltrate than a Masonic lodge. The Tigers, Joseph had been warned, were a strictly Catholic club. Good Catholic boys would always be ahead of him on the list.

At North he impressed the selection panel with his knowledge of the game and his passion for its traditions and myths. Here was a young man, they decided, who would go places. Perhaps sometime down the track he might be valuable in transforming a luckless club into a power in the Victorian Football League. One day he might even help them win The Flag.

Joseph got the job. He was 18 and told them he was 20. He would smile later when he learned that four of the five men on the selection panel were Catholics. He had arrived. He was finally a part of the game. In those days the assistant secretary was lumbered with the worst jobs. Football liked to think it was an egalitarian sport where one and all were equal. But on the totem pole of the game he was down there on the bottom. Still, it didn't worry him. If you wanted to learn the trade of football administration, of knowing how to recruit players, of learning where the money went and where some of it was hidden, it was the only way.

Besides, Joseph was a young bloke, the same age as many of the players around the club.

Within just a handful of years, he would form a close alliance with one of the club's greatest players. And the two of them would help turn football upside down for decades to come.

His wrist was broken and they had rushed him into the dressing room to treat the pain. His hand was bent at right angles to his arm and as a jab of morphine slowly began to take effect he looked up to see a newspaper reporter standing near him.

'Is this it?' the reporter was asking. And through the haze of the drugs and pain Allen Aylett made a decision.

'Of course it bloody is,' grimaced Aylett. It was 1964 and after 220 games in a career notable for its achievements, there wasn't any point going on. Lying on a rubdown table in a room filled with that perfume of Australian Saturday afternoons— the pungent mixture of linament and sweat—he reluctantly conceded his time was up.

No-one would think any less of him for choosing to go out this way, for he had been a courageous player. He had proved himself a real man and if the football world approved of anything, it approved of real men.

Football was a bloke's world and it was the same whether you played at the pinnacle of the game with a VFL club or in a small country town team where the players wore frayed jumpers. Where a hunched-over elderly man called Bluey, who wore a hearing aid and a wide-brimmed hat, served as timekeeper and never missed a week.

Football had always been that way. The blokes played it hard and got together afterwards to drink large amounts of beer and talk about their prodigious efforts out on the field. And their women? They served the food and waited for their men to finish so they could drive them home and put them to bed in the early hours of Sunday morning.

Little changed as you progressed from the bush leagues to the big league. During the 1970s and '80s out at Waverley, the League's giant, unloved concrete stadium, you would always find the players' women waiting outside the dressing rooms after a match. There were no women allowed in the rooms, of course. That was a man's place. So they would wait outside in the cold corridors on freezing Saturday evenings long after the game had finished.

It was a culture laden with testosterone, a culture filled with stories of the game's heroes and villains. Every football club had a player with the biggest penis mankind had ever seen. Every football club had a bootstudder or trainer who'd played back in the '30s and '40s and who could recite the same refrain, it seemed, almost word for word.

'You know,' the old men with their wrinkled faces would say with a knowing nod, 'I played back when the game was a real man's game. There were blokes who'd refuse to leave the ground when they were injured because they preferred to play on with broken necks and their arms hanging out of their shoulder sockets. True.'

But Allen Aylett was not your typical footy bloke. While he well understood the culture of the game, he also wanted it to be something more. He wanted Australian football to firstly spread throughout the country and then, perhaps one day, take on the world. Footy, he would say, was a game that had it all. And for a time, Allen Aylett was a man who had it all, too.

Aylett was five years old when his father enlisted with the army. By the time he returned from World War II in 1946, his son was almost 12 and had grown quickly. Sam Aylett had been a barrel maker with Carlton and United Breweries. He resumed that role when he returned and set about rediscovering his old life. In the middle of it was a boy who had learned quickly how to earn a little pocket money. He also found a boy consumed by sports.

The young Allen Aylett was a typical working-class kid of his time. He carted cases of fruit and vegetables around the streets of his neighbourhood for money. In Brunswick, a blue-collar Melbourne suburb with narrow streets and rows of houses squashed up against one another like commuters on a crowded train, the kids played cricket and football under the glow of the street lamps until exasperated parents finally dragged them inside. They raced sticks down flooded gutters. They went to the league football match on a Saturday afternoon whenever they could to barrack for their favourite team. They went home that night and dreamt of playing in the big time.

By the time he was an adult, there were kids in the crowd who went home at night and dreamt of becoming another Allen Aylett. Recognised as one of the game's best players, Aylett had leaped from the junior ranks of North Melbourne right into the company of the game's elite; tough men who applauded a skilful feat by an opponent with an elbow planted behind the ear. He was fast and balanced, with good hands and anticipation. He became the captain of his team and played for his state. It was typical of Aylett. Being one of the pack had never been enough. He always had to rise above it. Even as a young boy self-conscious of his working-class environment, he had never settled for anything except first place. It was something he seemed to have inherited from his mother Marion, a strong-willed woman who raised her children virtually single-handedly through the war years and who had encouraged young Allen to succeed at anything he pursued.

Aylett was the same as a player, always going that extra yard. It was as though he always needed others, as well as himself, to know that he was the best around. In his early teens he had been self-conscious of his working-class origins and the fact that he came from what was, then, the wrong side of town. It was a common enough reaction. And even though he outgrew it, the desire to prove himself never left.

It wasn't long after his retirement as a player before Aylett, a dentist with an entrepreneurial bent, began rising through the football administration ranks with the same speed he had shown as a player. Within a year of his retirement he was on the North Melbourne committee. By 1970 he was the vice-president, running a dental practice and a newly-opened chain of 'Mr Chips' fish and chip takeaway shops. In 1971, at the age of 36, he became the youngest president of a Victorian Football League club. If anyone had any doubts about his willingness to change things, they quickly vanished.

North Melbourne had been one of the ugliest and least successful clubs in the competition since it had joined the League in 1925. The team always seemed to be hanging on somewhere down near the bottom of the ladder; good players tended to move to other clubs and even its home ground at Arden Street, set on the edge of a once-working class area that was now being transformed into a light industrial zone, was hardly what you would call picturesque. It stood in the shadow of a giant gasometer, with a standing area in the outer and wooden grandstand that had seen better days.

Quickly, however, Aylett set about changing the culture at the club. He encouraged new faces at board level and cajoled and pressured others until they came to accept his view. Football had to change, Aylett told them. The game was becoming more of a business so its officials should also move with the times. With Ron Joseph by his side and an astute numbers man and former club captain, Albert Mantello, for added support, Aylett introduced 7am planning meetings and the club began actively recruiting corporate sponsors. It introduced the concept of the grand final breakfast. It is still the place to be on grand final morning, even for prime ministers and opposition leaders.

Aylett, too, was a brilliant schmoozer. If you were new at the club he would vigorously shake your hand and let you know you were more than welcome. Other club officials enviously watched him host pre-match lunches where every club sponsor would be named, welcomed and treated like royalty. They quickly learned to follow his lead.

And, more than any other club, North began taking advantage of the League rules, bending them slightly here, quietly breaking them there like everyone else and finding any loophole it could in order to improve its position. Aylett wanted nothing less than a premiership and within four years he had secured North's first, in 1975. It was due largely to the club's ability to exploit a new rule introduced by the VFL where players of more than 10 years' experience were free to sign with another club without a hefty clearance fee.

He did it, too, with Ron Joseph by his side. Joseph was the trusted lieutenant, the man who took Aylett's philosophy and turned it into reality. By the end of 1977, the pair had helped engineer two flags for North. By then, Aylett had already moved on. There was a bigger field to conquer: the VFL was waiting to be transformed.

Like any love affair, the passion eventually wanes. And for Ron Joseph it had begun fading by the middle of the 1970s. Other club general managers, the men who found themselves competing against Joseph for talent around the country, sometimes wondered how he had lasted so long.

With his stocky build and rounded cheeks, Joseph was a fretter. He would sit in his office, his desk strewn with paperwork, and scratch his curly-wavy hair whenever he grew perplexed. Which, by the mid-70s, was more often than he'd wished.

He was a perfectionist who became increasingly frustrated when others failed to meet his exacting standards. Those days as a kid, those wonderful days when football was such a magical place, were long over. At the end of 1974, North had made the grand final but lost to a more experienced Hawthorn side. The defeat devastated Joseph. How could they lose? He had put a side together that should have won The Flag. How could it have happened?

'I'd been working my arse off,' he would say years later, still scratching that greying curly hair. In fact, he was exhausted. Ron

Joseph didn't just work for North Melbourne. He lived for the club. He woke in the morning, showered and drove straight to work. Fourteen hours later he climbed back into his car, grabbed something to eat on the way home and then slept before repeating the same thing day after day, week after week. Even when summer arrived, when the football season had stopped for breath, Joseph kept going. Sometimes it was his busiest period. There were recruits to settle into a strange and bewildering city. And the greatest player in the world was still out there in the bush somewhere, kicking bales of hay over haysheds, just waiting for Joseph to drive by, spot him and sign him up.

At the end of 1974 he locked away the recruiting for the following year and quit. Of course, they would talk him back to the club after a few months. It would be a pattern that would repeat itself down over the years. Joseph would work himself to exhaustion, resign, disappear for a few weeks and then be coaxed back to Arden Street.

In 1975 he would eventually return to North in time to see that hard work pay off when the club won its first flag. But during his absence, other clubs went after him.

First came Collingwood. The Magpies were an institution that hadn't won a flag since 1958. But the club still proudly proclaimed itself as the most famous sporting club in the country and few could argue. All they needed was a flag and Joseph, decided president Ern Clarke, was the man to do it for Collingwood.

'I didn't think I should go there, out of loyalty to North,' Joseph would say with a shrug. 'But I got caught up in being feted and taken out to dinner.'

They introduced him to a board meeting one night and Joseph immediately noticed the different culture at Collingwood. It was steeped in the past and ghosts wandered its corridors. 'I went to the board meeting and they all sat down and it's like they ring the bells—you move either to the left or the right.'

At North, Joseph had never even seen a show of hands. Still, he sat there quietly, made polite conversation and they appointed him.

The next morning he rang and said he would not be reporting to work.

Later that year, a young entrepreneur called Craig Kimberley, who would go on to build a giant jeans empire across the nation, asked Joseph if he was interested in a job with South Melbourne, that old club that sometimes had made his heart soar and, more often than not, left him feeling miserable on so many winter afternoons.

He spent six weeks at South before leaving and, in that time, lured the triple-Brownlow Medallist Ian Stewart over as coach and the talented player John Rantall from North. But he had not been prepared for what he found in the books once Kimberley's reform group had swept to power after a controversial and bitter election.

South was in financial trouble. Joseph, who was already missing North again, decided he had to ring the VFL's general manager, Eric McCutchan, and report the news.

McCutchan was an old-style administrator, hailing from the days when general managers were known as secretaries and clubs operated on not much more a shilling. Such was his position and status that Joseph had never worked up the courage to call him Eric.

'I'd always called him Mr McCutchan. But somehow I decided this was so important that I had to call him Eric.

'I finally worked up the courage and rang and said 'Look, Eric, this club's in serious financial trouble.'

'And you know what he said? He said: "I understand what you're saying. The League office is closing for the Christmas holidays. It'll be reopening on the 17th of January. We'll talk to you then."'

But by the 17th of January, Ron Joseph was long gone. He was on his way back to North.

On the 2nd of February, 1977, Allen Aylett became president of the Victorian Football League and Ron Joseph, of course, played a role.

Aylett was elected as the surprising successor to Sir Maurice Nathan, the last of a breed of older men who occupied the role. Like many who had sat at the head of the boardroom table before him, Nathan had been widely seen as a part of the Melbourne Establishment. One of the factors in his appointment had been his perceived close ties with the Liberal Government of the day and the hope of the clubs that he might be able to nurture a closer relationship between the League and the politicians.

But Nathan hardly sat comfortably with the stuffy traditionalist stereotype consigned to him. In the last couple of years of his presidency he had come to the view that the game was changing and that, as the face of corporate Australia changed, so too would the needs of the VFL. Aylett had just the track record to qualify. He had taken charge of North and dragged it into the modern era. Why couldn't he do the same for the competition at large?

There was no disguising the fact, either, that Aylett knew how to sell a product, whether it was his dentistry practice, a football club or himself. In a sport which believed the game was strong enough to promote itself and was so arrogant and confident of its standing among the people that words like marketing were looked upon with disdain and bemusement, Aylett's beliefs were bound to attract attention. And in 1977, when the vote was tied between Aylett and his opponent for the presidency, a former vice-president of the League, Phil Ryan, Nathan held the casting vote. Would it be Ryan, a solid and respected man who would undoubtedly maintain the traditions of the game? Or would it be Aylett, who represented a break with the past? Aylett had feared there might be a last-minute push for Ryan who, he felt, offered the game stability but little vision or willingness to change. He and his supporters had needed to work extremely hard just to garner enough votes to secure a tie. But Aylett's hunch was wrong. Nathan scribbled Aylett's name on his ballot and the outsider assumed the presidency. At the end of the meeting, Nathan put his lit cigar to the ballot papers and watched them burn. It would be a symbolic act. The League had dispensed with the past and an uncertain future lay ahead.

On one night leading up to the vote, Joseph sat outside Aylett's house in Moonee Ponds and talked to the man he had worked alongside for so many years.

'Do you really know what you're getting yourself into?' he asked Aylett. 'They'll fight you when you get there. They'll resist you. You won't have the same loyalty you've had at North. If you're going to stick around, you'll have to develop your own political base.'

And, warned Joseph, he would find that having the League's general manager, Jack Hamilton, among his support staff would not be the same as having a loyal club manager about the place.

By 1984, Aylett had been president of the VFL for eight years, his days at North were long gone and Joseph's words that night outside his Moonee Ponds home had rung true.

Aylett knew his League was in deep trouble. The era of his presidency, when it seemed he and the game could do no wrong, was over. And, as he liked to point out to those around him, he had seen it coming for a long time. After all, he had been known as a man of vision and men of vision could always see the bad along with the good. Wasn't it Aylett who had warned the clubs as early as 1980 that their apparent success was really a mirage, that unless they somehow put a halt to their profligate ways the years to come would see them plunged into poverty and uncertainty?

'The VFL has a choice,' he had warned. 'It can demonstrate that it is able to undertake effective self-regulation of its affairs or, on the other hand, it can allow football hyperinflation to increase in an unrestrained fashion. This latter alternative would be to the long-term advantage of no-one, including the players.'

But who had listened? Very few. Everyone was too busy spending.

Aylett's problem was that while the clubs appreciated his flair for marketing and his enthusiasm, they also wondered sometimes whether he lived in the same world they did. After all, he was always rabbiting on about this national league idea of his, that Australian football should expand its horizons and look outward, escape from its tribal Victorian origins and become Australia's truly national game.

But to some clubs, Aylett never seemed to know when to leave well enough alone. Why, just a few years before, he had stood up at an official dinner to mark the start of another season and launched into one of his 'I have a dream' speeches. As he spoke passionately about teams in Brisbane and Sydney, about a national competition dominating the Australian sports scene, everyone had nodded knowingly at one another.

Sir Keith Macpherson, the chairman of *The Herald and Weekly Times,* whose company provided the League with much-welcomed sponsorship dollars and free advertising through its blanket coverage of the game in its newspapers, fell asleep at the table.

To some, Aylett seemed a man possessed. But even his critics agreed that his enthusiasm could be infectious. One year in the early 1980s he pushed for a seminar to be staged for all club administrators and delegates in Surfers Paradise. Not surprisingly, most clubs approved of the idea, congratulating Aylett on his stroke of genius. Who would vote against the chance to spend a few relaxing days in the Queensland sun? Six weeks before the seminar, Aylett approached Fitzroy's director, Leon Wiegard.

'Leon,' he said. 'I want you to speak to everyone on memory training each morning.'

Wiegard, who knew as much about memory training as the next man, declined politely. Aylett insisted, giving him three books on the subject. It was an idea that had gained popularity in the United States and Aylett had decided it was time Australian football learned about it, too.

So Wiegard, who told Aylett that the last book he had read had been *Biggles in Borneo* and that he still hadn't finished it, followed Aylett's instructions. By the time the seminar began, he was briefing club delegates each morning on how to best retain the information they would be pounded with throughout the day.

By 1984, if Aylett and Hamilton were not the most unpopular men in Victoria, the only ones more disliked were serving time at Her Majesty's Pentridge Prison in Coburg. A year before, Aylett had climbed the podium at the end of the Grand Final to award the victorious team, Hawthorn, its trophy. As he was introduced to the crowd a chorus of booing began in the members' section, that genteel bastion of Melbourne's Establishment. You could not say, however, that Aylett failed to unite people from all backgrounds. It wasn't long before the entire crowd of 110,332 had joined in the chorus; a sustained, unprecedented noise that ricocheted around the arena for what seemed an eternity.

Even the clubs that had once supported his push for change had turned on him. Collingwood had launched its own, highly secret investigation into Aylett's association with the League, his role of president of the National Football League—the game's national umbrella body perceived largely as an extension of the VFL—and his expenses incurred on trips as president of both organisations.

Other clubs were also disenchanted with Aylett. By early 1982 the Geelong president John Holt had come to the belief that Aylett had fallen in love with the presidency. Holt had been one of the key figures in Victorian football called to the

Old Melbourne Hotel in 1977. There, he had found Aylett and Joseph in the midst of some serious number crunching. Holt was a key figure in the equation.

'Will you support Allen for the VFL presidency?' Joseph asked Holt.

'Well, I'm a man who believes a man should only do that job for three or four years,' replied Holt, before turning to Aylett. 'Allen,' he asked, 'Is that the sort of time frame you'd be looking at?'

Years later, Holt would recall Aylett nodding in agreement. The Geelong vote was wrapped up. But as the years passed, Holt watched Aylett become more obsessed with the position. Three years passed. Then four. By 1982 Aylett had been in the post for six years and was showing no sign of relinquishing the role. The owners of American baseball clubs had a term for it: commissioneritis. They had watched their own men fall in love with the top job and seen how hard it was for them to walk away from it. Even in 1984, with the rumblings of discontent among a small but powerful number of clubs and a remarkably antagonistic attitude among the public, Aylett would remain captivated. By then, Holt had departed the scene. Aylett was still around. But not for long.

As the 1984 season moved toward its finale, Aylett was no longer the young, fresh-looking VFL president he had been way back in 1977. While he prided himself on being fit and healthy—his 4am starts to the day and all-night working sessions were legendary—the pace had quickened, the burden had grown heavier and it was beginning to show. Those who saw him regularly noticed that bags were beginning to form under his eyes.

And now, even further pressure was being applied. There was talk among the clubs that John Elliott, one of the country's wealthiest and most ambitious businessmen, was plotting to form a breakaway national competition.

A LEGION OF
SWORN ENEMIES

(Tuesday, 4 September, 1984. 7.30pm)

The apocalypse had arrived the year before. The flames from hell had roared up the sides of the hills, sucking all the oxygen out of the air. The trunks of old gum trees had blistered in an instant. And that crackling sound, which grew louder by the minute as the flames fed on anything alive, made it seem as though the whole world was burning.

When it finally ended it looked like someone had thrown a black blanket over the landscape. The place had been transformed. A carpet of ash had replaced the undergrowth. Trees which had stood erect and tall were bent and black.

Now, a year later, the yellow arcs of headlights exposed the grotesque, twisted outlines of those trees as the cars began the final climb up the mountain toward the old mansion. It wouldn't be long before the grim products of the Ash Wednesday fires were completely hidden from view. A fog was rolling in and the weather updates on the radio suggested it would get thicker.

They were on their way to stave off an apocalypse of their own making. The general managers and presidents of most of the clubs of the Victorian Football League had agreed to make the hour-long journey from Melbourne to find out whether one of Australia's most prominent businessmen could save them. He had a plan, he had told them. That night at Mt Macedon he would reveal how football could be saved.

Inside the mansion the lights were on, several open-hearth

fires were burning fiercely and the kitchen was filled with activity. 'Sefton', set in 23 acres and hidden from Mt Macedon Road by thick cypress and holly hedges, had been built in 1908 by the Baillieu family, one of Australia's richest clans. By 1982 it had been bought by the giant pastoral and brewing company, Elders IXL, which used the property as a function centre and weekend retreat for its executives. It had been fortunate to survive the previous year's fires, suffering only the loss of a gardener's cottage.

In the early 1980s, such was the luck of Elders and its driving force, John Elliott.

Anything Elliott did seemed to work. For a man who took many chances he possessed a remarkable amount of luck. Perhaps because of that, he had grown used to getting his own way. Failures had been few. Ever since he had taken over the small Tasmanian jam maker Henry Jones IXL and used it as a vehicle to conquer the corporate scene, Elliott had charged ahead.

But there was one place where he had discovered that his influence and power counted for little. Who would have thought that football would show the disrespect it had? And how dare it?

Elliott was the president of Carlton, and the Blues were just about the best damn club the competition had seen. They sought and demanded success. When other clubs sought solace by consoling themselves with a finals spot, nothing less than a premiership could console the Blues. By the 1980s they had come to stand for everything a professional football club should: a sound administration, a powerful group of sponsors and corporate supporters, the best gymnasium facilities money could buy and the best players money could buy, too.

Without Carlton, the League would have been in enormous trouble. The Blues had a big following among the Victorian public. They attracted almost as many people through the admission gates as Collingwood. The team played an attractive game. It was filled with well-paid, skilful and courageous players. By 1984, they had already secured two premierships since the start of the new decade and looked set to dominate the rest of it. And just as importantly, with Elliott's arrival as president the year before, the club had further enhanced its standing in the business community.

But the president was unhappy. He thought the game was being run in a mediocre fashion by Allen Aylett and Jack Hamilton. To Elliott, both men seemed to be trying to outdo one another, always jockeying for position, always squabbling.

He could have lived with that. After all, such things were hardly a rare event in the corporate world. But what really annoyed Elliott was a greater sin committed by Aylett and Hamilton. They were only paying lip service to Carlton.

They would have to be taught a lesson.

'The way they exercised their power was they would go to the weak clubs and push things through,' Elliott would say many years later. He was sitting in his office in Collins Street, the business centre of Melbourne and the natural habitat of the city's Establishment. He was puffing away on another ever-present cigarette. Elliott didn't just draw gently on a cigarette. He sucked on it so hard that at times the whole cigarette seemed to have turned to ash in seconds.

Every so often he would squint out the window. Was it the smoke in his eyes that made him screw up his face or the memory of those clashes with the old Victorian Football League? It must have been the smoke. Elliott was a man of few regrets.

'They had a fairly socialist agenda. Equality of everything. We felt there was a system where they would take more and more. But the bottom club was getting as much money as us and we'd just won a couple of flags. Everything was a *fait accompli* when we got to the board table. We were having no say whatsoever in the place.'

Elliott had also grown increasingly alarmed at the state of

the game. He was not alone. The VFL had just endured one of its worst years in 1984, losing the confidence and support of the Victorian public. The financial state of many of its 12 clubs was parlous after an orgy of spending over the previous two decades.

To the president of Carlton there was only one solution. Elliott had taken it upon himself to begin a drive for change. And on a cool night in the Victorian countryside in 1984 he hoped to send Australian football on an irreversible course toward a national competition.

One by one they arrived.

There was Ian Wilson, the president of Richmond, a man skilled in the cloak-and-dagger politics of the game. Wilson was one of the tough guys. He headed a club that for years had helped shape and influence the many enormous changes the game had seen. Like Elliott, he also had Aylett in his sights and had done so for years. He didn't like Aylett's flashy style and the way the president had turned the game's central administration into a power base. And whenever an opportunity arose, Wilson was ready to take a swipe. Wasn't it he who had been on the phone to one League official earlier in the year, snooping around trying to get details on Aylett's expenses?

Another Melbourne businessman and Elliott conspirator, Greg Sewell, was also there. Sewell was president of Essendon, another of the powerful clubs. Dick Seddon, a lawyer and chief executive of Melbourne, had also come along. He'd been among the first to hear of Elliott's secret plans and had made sure he was involved, not because he thought it was a good idea, but because no-one was going to be organising anything without him at least knowing what was taking place. Particularly if that club happened to be Carlton. No-one trusted the Blues. They were always out for themselves and whenever they offered you a deal you studied it closely looking for the catch. Even then, sometimes you only discovered it when it was too late.

And then there was the president of Collingwood, Ranald Macdonald. He'd been the first person Elliott had approached at the start of the year. He was the last to arrive and apologised as soon as he walked in the door. He had lost his way and been forced to stop at a farmhouse for directions.

When they had all arrived, Elliott welcomed them to Sefton and gestured toward the dining room. He wanted to get them in an unfamiliar location. He'd ordered plenty of good wine and food. He wanted to have the whip hand. He wanted it to be one of the most significant meetings experienced by Australian football in its 130-year history.

John Dorman Elliott was not regarded as a subtle man and his face had a lot to do with it. Fleshy and broad, it boasted as its main feature the nose of a boxer. He had played footy with Old Carey Grammarians and in 247 games had clearly dispensed with the idea of subtly avoiding the tackles of his opponents.

Charge in head first. The aggressor will always take the prize. That seemed to be Elliott's maxim and it was based on an old football law: always be the first man to the ball. Dictate terms. Force others to catch you.

It was the Elliott business creed, too. After taking over Henry Jones IXL in 1972, he'd targeted vulnerable companies, relics of the 1970s struggling into a new era with outdated managements and techniques, and swallowed them. Expand, expand, expand. Elliott and his management team had voracious appetites and little seemed to sate them.

So football puzzled him in late 1983 when he finally agreed to take on the Carlton presidency, having refused it four years before. The rules of the outside world were rarely found in football. It was a self-contained universe of its own where few natural laws seemed to operate. When it came to football administration, the first to make a move did not necessarily take the prize. Naturally, Elliott felt uncomfortable. What in hell was going on?

He had discussed his concerns with Carlton's general manager, Ian Collins, soon after taking office. Elliott had a lot of time for Collins. He, too, was a schemer and pragmatist who got the job done and who was fast developing a reputation around the League as a man as tough at the bargaining table as he had been on the field. That suited Elliott perfectly. He would need men he could trust if he was to make his mark on this bizarre world.

Collins had been a back pocket player for the Blues in the 1960s and was a typical defender of his era. He had a soft, boyish face with a high forehead that rarely changed as he grew older. Lacking the skill and flair of some of his higher-profile team-mates, he had compensated by developing what became known in the game as a pair of educated elbows. Where others could dodge and weave their way through a crowd, Collins aggressively eliminated the variables head-on.

It was a frugal existence, but then he never considered himself an artist anyway. His style had never been captured better than on one wintry Melbourne afternoon. Bobby Skilton, Ron Joseph's boyhood hero and one of the game's most decorated and revered players, had been scrapping for the ball at the base of a pack, desperately trying to lift his hapless South Melbourne against the strength and toughness of Carlton. Finally, after what seemed an eternity, the man they called 'The Chimp' emerged through a forest of hairy, muddied legs with the ball, thinking he was in the clear.

Those who saw Skilton play claimed he possessed a unique sense of awareness, of always knowing where everything was on a football field at any given time. But on this miserable day, when his boots and socks felt like lead weights and the leather ball seemed to grow heavier by the minute, his intuition deserted him briefly. It was enough for Collins to collect him, leaving him bloodied.

Clearly Collins was a practical man. He also shared his president's doubts about the stability of the game and where it was heading. Here they were, a powerful club in the scheme of things and yet their voice could rarely be heard at the board table. And there was also the matter of money, too.

At the end of each year, the income from the season was divided equally among the 12 clubs. Elliott would pinch the bridge of his nose, usually with a lit cigarette in one hand and wonder why clubs like Carlton, Collingwood and Essendon, who lured the majority of paying customers through the gate, were not compensated for their drawing power when the poor clubs at the bottom of the ladder, caught in a vicious cycle of no-money-no-players-no-crowds-no-money, received the same dividend.

That cycle extended into every niche of the competition. The same teams were making the finals every year, the others seemed simply to be along for the ride to make up the numbers. It was a competition that had become boring, predictable and stagnant. Occasionally one of the lower clubs would reach for greatness and grab it, but it was only a fleeting moment. Despite their parochial interest, Collins and Elliott believed that structurally the League required a significant amount of renovation.

So in early 1984 the pair had hatched a plan they believed would rectify the situation.

Elliott called Ranald Macdonald, a prominent figure in the Melbourne Establishment who had made his name as managing director of David Syme and Co, publisher of the Melbourne broadsheet newspaper, *The Age*. Elliott told him he had a few things on his mind and asked to meet him at the Elders office in Prahran. Gradually others became involved: Essendon's Sewell, Richmond's Wilson and Seddon at Melbourne. Michael Standish, Elders' corporate lawyer, was summoned and asked to supply a legal opinion on whether clubs like Carlton could leave the VFL without repercussions.

And Collins set to work on the complicated task of constructing a proposal for a national football competition that would, a few months later, turn into a detailed 48-page document called 'A proposal for reconstructing the existing competition to make it viable for the long term.' It was a long-winded title. But these were men, after all, who had opinions and liked to share them with others.

A cancer had been working its way through the Victorian Football League for many years and the victim, along with close friends and lovers, had been having a hard time coming to terms with the news.

Since 1896, when the Victorian Football League was formed, the men in charge of each of its clubs had jealously guarded their fiefdoms. Each week they met at the boardroom table and argued well into the night over the smallest and most obscure points of order.

'I'll never forget one of my first VFL board meetings,' recalled Bill Kerr. Appointed managing director of the West Coast Eagles in the late 1980s, Kerr arrived at VFL House for a meeting of club directors expecting the evening to be filled with discussion on the future of the competition, its financial problems and strategies for coping with a new, professional era.

'They spent what seemed like hours debating the colour of socks worn by players,' Kerr recalled.

While collectively they supposedly controlled the game and made decisions to guard its future, each club was a small nation, suspiciously patrolling its borders and always on the lookout for the slightest incursion by the enemy. And the enemy was always one of the other 11 clubs. The game was in a constant state of flux; alliances changing almost weekly. Two clubs forged an understanding until one began trying to steal the other's best player or gain a financial advantage.

And just like anywhere else, football had discovered that it was not immune to the changes going on elsewhere in society. Those days when victors cheered their losing opponents from the field in recognition of their efforts were long gone. A new era demanding a more professional approach had arrived, but the clubs were still burdened by the baggage of the past. It was the old quandary; go forward, or maintain the status quo?

By the late 1960s and early 1970s there was no choice. Losers were just as likely to be booed from the field and humiliated by crowds who demanded far more.

Cautiously and awkwardly, the clubs had embraced the concept of becoming more professional, more business-like. Suddenly, by the 1980s, there were bank managers willing to loan them large amounts of money and corporations were just as eager to have their name associated with a piece of Melbourne culture. These were the 1980s, after all. Bank managers were no longer the dour number-crunchers of the past. The Victorian Football League had become a small but relevant analogy for Australia at large. It was an orgy of spending, a hedonistic period when each club's existence was predicated on its ability to survive the year and win The Flag.

The Flag. Grown men, who had been to war and seen mates blown to pieces, who had raised families and launched successful business careers, could be reduced to tears by The Flag. In their corporate offices they were tough and brutal operators. They took decisions which affected the lives of many of their workers. They subscribed to the free market and the laws of the concrete and perspex jungle. But put them in a football environment and common sense departed. Footy did strange things to many of them. They did things in football that would have earned them a nasty rebuke from shareholders and possibly the boot.

The Flag. To be the man who secured a premiership for his club would guarantee immortality. There would be more acclaim, more publicity than any successful corporate takeover could give them. Shares, pension packages and a place in Who's Who could be gained by anyone who knew how to play the corporate game. But The Flag was different. John Elliott and men like him had achieved many famous victories in business. But they didn't have a Flag. And in the late 1970s and early 1980s, the desperation of many men to obtain it had methodically laid the mines which began blowing Australian football to pieces.

By the time Elliott's dinner at Mt Macedon began, the shrapnel was flying everywhere. After reaching a peak in 1981, VFL attendances had been dropping each year. The public had quickly grown disillusioned with a body that had increased admission prices by an average of 17 per cent a year, well ahead of an average inflation rate of 10 per cent. The obsession of winning The Flag, now driven by escalating player payments, meant that players seemed to start each year in a different coloured jumper. The game was no longer showing loyalty to its lifeblood, the supporter, and so the supporter had decided his or her allegiances would be better served elsewhere. It seemed the game, too, had forgotten that the supporter of the 1980s was not the same person who walked through the admission gate 50 years before. Then, blokes used to enjoy going to the footy on a Saturday afternoon, having a few beers, watching a game and getting away from the missus and kids. But who in the 1980s wanted to stand, cold and wet, on a crowded embankment with the bitter stench of urine and beer floating by just to get a glimpse of a footballer who, in all likelihood if he showed anything decent during the season, would waltz off to another club the following year?
Well, some did. They were the romantics. There were not many of them left, but they clung stubbornly to the old ways. Football for them was the last remnant of another age. They were vocal; they wrote to newspapers, called talkback programs, denounced the ever-increasing presence of businessmen in the game, demanded that The Game return to its old ways. Why can't at least one thing stay the same? Why does everything have to change? Football was the one thing in your life that was never supposed to alter as you aged. It was always there; the same

anticipation at the start of another year, the same anguish, heart-break and triumph. Hadn't you ever wished as an adult that you could slip back to a time when you were six or seven years old? When there were no such things as bills and mortgages? When the only uncertainty was how late you could stay up on a Friday night? When childhood was such a safe place?

Football had been just that. A safe place. A haven. The annual rhythms of the sport, its tempo and mood swings, had hardly altered. But reality couldn't be held at bay forever. Between 1972 and 1980, player payments had leapt an incredible 1826 per cent. In comparison, the average weekly wage had grown from $97.30 to $270, an increase of 262 per cent. By the time of Elliott's meeting, the Victorian Corporate Affairs Commission had completed a lengthy investigation into the financial state of the 12 League clubs and discovered that at least five of them were technically bankrupt and another three were close to it. In 1972, 1867 spectators had been required through the gate to pay the average VFL player. When the '80s began, that figure had rocketed to 13,422 spectators.

And what did they see? A game that seemed to have lost any sense of where it was headed. There were lawyers and accountants taking it over. The buck had replaced the ball as the game's object. And every time some new disaster appeared, and it seemed a week did not pass without one, the VFL made confident noises that the worst was behind it. Several studies had been undertaken and all had pointed to deficiencies in the League's decision-making processes. Some streamlining of the administration had begun to be implemented. A task force, bringing together members of business, politics and football, had been appointed to investigate the broad direction of the game. But nothing could disguise the fact that the competition would always be endangered as long as the clubs themselves continued to have the ultimate say in the running of the game.

They had shown enough to prove they could not be trusted.

By the time the 1984 season began, Elliott and Collins' plan was developing well. Collins had flown to Perth and held secret talks with several clubs in the West Australian Football League. He received a warm welcome. Unlike South Australia, which strongly distrusted anything coming out of Victoria, the West Australians were sick and tired of having their competition plundered by the richer marauders from the east, annually losing their best players to fatter and more attractive contracts. So, if a national competition gave them the opportunity to retain their own players and further boost their support base by getting in before other WA clubs, then well and good. Collins then flew into Adelaide and received the response he was expecting. Most of the South Australians were as cold as ice. Still, he believed there was enough interest in both states to keep the project going.

Standish, too, had supplied Elliott with the legal advice he'd been wanting. There was nothing to stop Carlton and others breaking away from the VFL to form their own competition.

As the year progressed, word inevitably leaked among the clubs. Elliott and Collins were up to something and hadn't bothered approaching them. Typical, wasn't it? The rumour had it that a national league was being formed and only a select few would be invited to join. By May, calls were being made to Carlton. Denials were issued before Elliott confirmed that yes, some talks had been held. A plan had been worked out, he admitted. But it was dependent on the VFL being unable to sort out the mess which it called its decision-making processes.

That seemed to be enough. The issue died away. Behind the scenes, however, nothing changed. Collins kept adding up the figures, Elliott kept talking to the clubs he trusted. Finally they decided the rest of the competition should be told. The property at Mt Macedon would be the venue.

By the time representatives of nine of the 12 clubs were seated and the entree had been served, Elliott began briefing them. The time had come for change, he said. And it was going to happen whether most of them there liked it or not.

Elliott had thought the setting and the tone of the meeting would be enough to convince those attending that he was deadly serious and that the future of the game was in their hands. But as the evening progressed and he went into the details of his proposed national league, some of those present began shifting uncomfortably.

It was time to break away from the VFL and form a national competition, Elliott told them. The old days and their old ways were over. But if you wanted your club to join this new expanded league—and which club could afford not to?—there would be no room for anyone who couldn't pay their way.

Elliott, typically, pulled no punches. He began his proposal by saying the underlying reason for the preparation of a national league was due to 'the fact that all major and minor Australian football league competitions are facing critical financial instability . . . all are experiencing a crisis situation.

'Many root causes can be put forward as to why the present clubs are so financially unviable but the real cause is that in the present climate of attempting to achieve success in the short term, expenditure has outstripped income.'

No-one disagreed.

'There has been very little, if any, responsibility being accepted by club directors,' noted Elliott. They were, he said, 'usually in office for a limited period at the whim of the parochial club member. These members are, in the main, only interested in one factor: on-field success.'

There were other reasons, too, ones which all the clubs had seen developing for years but had done nothing about. Spectators were now more cautious about where they spent their money, said Elliott.

The attitude of players and their loyalties to clubs had changed too.

'The introduction of player agents, the trading of players between clubs and the willingness of players to readily swap clubs for personal gain has been highly inflationary. Many of the players who place themselves on this market are the "fringe" league footballers.'

The rules of the league were antiquated and had failed to keep pace with the changing game.

'The rules and regulations can be challenged by players and clubs under the Trade Practices Act. However, on the other hand, players are excluded from the Workers' Compensation Act and every effort is being made to exclude them from the Health Act.'

But the major problem, the one which all those at the dining table knew only too well, was money and an increasing lack of it. Since 1982, Elliott said, the deterioration in the financial solvency of the clubs had been alarming.

All of the clubs represented this night, he said, had 'shown no restraint in player payments . . . paid excessive transfer fees . . . allowed VFL expenditure to escalate year by year . . . allowed VFL staff to increase . . . allowed VFL marketing to grow without due control and direction . . . allowed the VFL to accumulate $42 million in assets through club finances and then allowed the articles of the League to be worded so that no club had any equity in the assets . . .'

On it went, a comprehensive and lengthy listing of the faults and illnesses which plagued the competition. No-one and no club was spared. But underlying it all was a strong anti-VFL flavour. Aylett and Hamilton were unloved at Princes Park, Carlton's home ground, and Elliott, along with those presidents closest to him, particularly Macdonald, were keen to push that line.

Finally, Elliott got to the nub of the matter. The VFL, he said, was at the crossroads. And there were only two options: retain the current 12-team competition or go national.

And really, there seemed no choice. 'To survive as the current League competition, it appears as if it will be necessary to re-organise financially 50 per cent or more of the existing teams,' he reported to the meeting.

'If this re-organisation does not take place voluntarily and with the financial backing of the VFL, then it seems inevitable that the Corporate Affairs (Commission) will be forced to investigate and perhaps wind up some of the clubs and instigate action against some of the club directors.'

The threat of legal action against some of the very men in the room was a well-used scare tactic. But it never failed to raise the odd eyebrow. And Elliott was not averse to playing on the emotions of those at the table opposite him.

According to the Elliott vision, the new national competition would be run with strict financial criteria in place. All 12 of the Victorian clubs would be invited to join, along with two each from WA and SA. But not all would make it. Each club applying for membership would have to prove it had a net worth of at least $250,000 with the ability to maintain that over time. With about half of the Victorian competition technically bankrupt, Elliott believed they would end up running a competition of no more than 12 teams, with just seven Melbourne-based clubs competing.

Matches, instead of being scheduled for a Saturday afternoon, would be played throughout each weekend, along with Friday and Monday night games, to prove more attractive to a commercial television network and maximise media revenue. A draft system would be introduced to maintain a controlled market for the transferring of players; a four-man board of management would control the game, with its chairman acting as the full-time Football Commissioner. Even with a 14-team competition, the Elliott-Collins plan estimated that 'a substantial positive cash flow could be earned', with the fledgling competition earning a total revenue of $45 million in its first year. This would compare to the VFL's total income—its 12 clubs included—of $37.5 million in 1984.

Dr Kevin Threlfall was president of Geelong, a club representing the satellite city 75 kilometres south-west of Melbourne and generally regarded as a sober, traditional club bordering on the conservative. He had gone to the dinner because 'you had to know what was happening. If you didn't know you were left out in the dark.'

Like several in the room, Threlfall was sceptical of Elliott's plan and his motives. Why hadn't he brought the issue up at the VFL board table instead of this cloak-and-dagger business?

Earlier in the evening Elliott had approached Threlfall outside the dining room. He was, he told Threlfall, planning to set up a special sub-committee of those here tonight. They would be called 'communicators' who would help keep everyone up to date with the latest events. That made Threlfall even more suspicious. What was Elliott's real agenda?

To those seated near him, Threlfall had been looking increasingly uneasy as the dinner and discussion progressed. Eventually, looking worried as the fog rolled in, he made his apologies. 'I'll have to get going. It's getting foggy out there and I've got a long trip home.'

Ron Joseph, who was representing his president, Bob Ansett, who was overseas on business, found himself perched next to Elliott at the table. God, he thought. What must this look like? He had known very little of the plan before this night, but now it must have looked like he was Elliott's right-hand man. He shifted uncomfortably. Whenever Joseph grew nervous or found himself in a strained or serious atmosphere, he had an uncontrollable urge to laugh.

When Threlfall announced he was leaving in order to miss the fog, Joseph felt it beginning. The whole meeting, supposedly called to decide the fate of one of the country's longest-running sporting institutions, was close to degenerating into farce. His body began shuddering as he fought, unsuccessfully, to control a wave of laughter beginning deep in his belly. Even hours later, his mind kept wandering back to the nature of Threlfall's departure, forcing him to giggle. He felt self-conscious, knowing others were looking at him. But he just couldn't help it.

Sitting near Elliott, Collins raised his eyebrows in amazement. Had all this been happening on the football field, he would have dealt with it quickly and quietly. Christ, it was all so bloody typical. He knew what the clubs were like. Here they were, trying to debate its future and people were worried about the fog? It had all been much simpler when he was a player.

Later that night Collins drove Joseph and Dick Seddon back to Melbourne. The fog was thick, speed was not recommended and so there was plenty of time for conversation. Joseph and Seddon were strongly of the view that it was time for all the secrecy to end.

'We have to tell Mick (Aylett) and Jack Hamilton,' urged Seddon.

Joseph agreed. It was fine for things to be kept quiet in the planning stages, but now that the time had arrived for action the League should be officially informed. A few weeks before, Ansett, who ran the growing Budget rent-a-car business, had met Elliott and Collins at Carlton and United Breweries' Bouverie Street office. They had outlined their plans for a breakaway competition. Ansett, a long-time proponent of expansion, had listened with interest. But he had reservations. Why go outside the VFL, he had asked? Let's get going with a national competition, for sure. But let's use what's there already.

Collins was trapped. His first loyalty, of course, was to his club and Elliott. Why bother telling the League anything? Its officials had had their chance. But Joseph and Seddon persevered and made it clear they would go to the League no matter what Collins thought.

It was in the early hours of Wednesday morning when the trio finally arrived home. But they hardly slept. By 10 o'clock that morning, all three were sitting in Jack Hamilton's office in Jolimont watching his craggy face drop as they told the general manager and his president that football was about to change.

At 5pm that afternoon the VFL board convened for a regular meeting of directors. Also at the meeting as observers were David Mandie, Bob Miller, Neil Busse and John Kennedy, four of the five members of a task force appointed by the League to investigate the competition's flaws and the way the League looked after business.

Aylett opened the meeting by welcoming the task force and then revealed he had been briefed by various club representatives that a meeting had been conducted the previous night at Mt Macedon. Aylett said the issues raised at Mt Macedon were virtually the same being considered by the task force.

Some discussion followed among the directors. Who had been invited to the meeting? Who hadn't? Who did Elliott and his mates think they were deciding on the future of the game outside the boardroom?

Noted the official minutes of the board meeting: 'After further discussion it was resolved that the Victorian Football League Board of Directors take no action in relation to the meeting of club representatives, but that the President informally convey to those involved that the document prepared and considered at such meeting be made available to the directors, clubs and task force for consideration.'

Elliott and Collins went back to their proposal, refined it, enhanced several recommendations, including one which would involve the setting up of a 'commission' to administer the game and submitted it to the task force.

Within three weeks, on 1 October, the task force handed down its report. Its findings were an indictment on the League and the way the central administration and its clubs had run the game for years.

Its chief recommendation was that the League should create a new board of management, comprising an executive commissioner along with four part-time commissioners who would be designated separate areas of responsibility: legal; finance; business and marketing; industrial relations and public relations. The clubs, after considering its ramifications, accepted it.

It was the first step in a series of many that would radically transform the game of Australian football. It would be the beginning of the end of the power of the clubs, the ones which had formed the VFL in the first place. It would cause a significant shift in the game's balance of power. It would create change, change and more change.

But it wouldn't alter one thing. John Elliott and many of Australia's other prominent businessmen would continue to wield great influence on the sport.

Football was the latest game in town.

3
ALL THE PRESIDENT'S MEN

In a game and a business where a man's character was often assessed by the strength of his handshake, Jack Hamilton had the firmest in town. The only comparable experience was putting your hand in a vice and tightening it quickly. But while the handshake had become a trademark, the first impression Hamilton left on a visitor was his face.

It looked as though it had been hewn from wood or stone by a caricaturist with a chainsaw. It was a face dominated by a large nose and a head of sweeping hair that always seemed to hang down close to his eyes. There were crags and crevices, lines and creases, truly a remarkable face which had been used to the fullest by its owner in the preceding 50 years. And, as Aylett and Hamilton had become increasingly unpopular with the public over the years, it was Hamilton's face which came to be depicted as the face of the VFL.

In the sports section of one of Melbourne's three daily newspapers of the time, there was a running joke among the sub-editors responsible for designing each back page. When the VFL announced admission price increases, a photograph of a wickedly grinning Hamilton would accompany the text. If prices failed to go up, a sour and glum looking Hamilton peered out from the back page. The message was hardly subtle.

The League was money-hungry. It devoured everything in

front of it. Too often, it was the wickedly grinning visage which greeted readers over their breakfast table.

'My kids were 15 before they found out my first name was Jack . . .' was one of his favourite lines. '. . . they thought it was Bloody.' It was followed by a cackling laugh that, no matter how often you heard the joke, forced the listener to laugh along.

But by 1984 there was not a great deal of laughter echoing around VFL House. People driving past the offices in Jolimont would sometimes lower a window and scream an obscenity at the blurred brown brick building which housed the League's administration. It was a tough time for all who worked inside it. Greg Durham, the League's secretary and one of its key finance men for more than a decade, would assume a different identity at weekends or when socialising, telling people at parties who asked him his line of work that he was an accountant. It saved time. It saved arguments.

Hamilton, however, was hardly one to shy away from an argument. He was, after all, an old defender from Collingwood who played during the 1950s, a period of the game anyone who could remember it fondly recalled as a wonderful era. The game still had its virginity intact back then. Television and its remarkable influence was still only a curiosity when introduced in 1956. People got their information from the radio and newspapers, men wore long overcoats and felt hats and coached others to play the game hard. Some played it unfairly, too. But they still gathered for a beer after the match.

Hamilton played his first senior match with the Magpies in 1948. A year later he joined the VFL administration as a junior clerk and never left. For those who worked with him, he was a difficult man to assess. Possessing a quick and dry sense of humour, he could turn quickly on a vulnerable target with a sharp tongue. He was a hard task master and if you were pleased with something you had achieved, you usually had to be satisfied with the knowledge of a job well done, for Hamilton rarely handed out praise. Perhaps it had something to do with his long apprenticeship, waiting in the wings of the conservative McCutchan, whose reign as general manager lasted 20 years, and wondering whether it would be himself or Ralph Lane, the finance secretary, who would succeed McCutchan. Hamilton eventually won the post, but his rivalry with Lane remained until the latter bowed out of the League's administration in November, 1983.

Hamilton was a tough old bastard from a generation of tough old bastards. If his education was lacking and he sometimes failed to understand the intricacies of the rapidly developing business side of the game, he made up for it with sheer bluff.

In late 1983 the League had been under enormous pressure. The state government had been pillorying the VFL for threatening to play its grand final the following year at Waverley, moving it away from its home at the MCG. There had been other legal problems and the marketing side of the game, something which Hamilton believed defied understanding, had grown at a fantastic rate. His desk was piled high with documents.

On the day of the office Christmas party which ushered in a welcome holiday for everyone, the League's finance director, Mike Tilley, walked up to the third floor to wish Hamilton a merry Christmas and all the best for the new year.

Tilley, who had been in the job for three months after being recruited from the accounting firm Arthur Andersen, had been leading Hamilton through many of the documents in recent weeks. Lately, they had piled so high the general manager could barely be seen. But when Tilley walked into Hamilton's office, his desk was bare.

Tilley was dumbstruck. He stepped forward incredulously. Not a single scrap of paper could be seen on the huge desk. And sitting behind it was a rather self-satisfied Hamilton.

'Jack, where's it all gone?' asked Tilley.

'It's all been taken care of,' replied Hamilton, dismissing the question with an abrupt wave of the hand.

Impossible, thought Tilley. 'Where are all the contracts I need you to sign?'

Again, Hamilton dismissed the question. Tilley knew not to take it further that day. Tilley suspected he knew what had happened. Hamilton had simply put a bin at one end and then swept the desk clear. It was the only plausible theory. It was the end of an old year, after all. And hadn't Jack told him once before that if someone never bothered him with a problem within three or four days of raising it, he regarded it as no longer a problem?

If some of his business methods were hardly the sort of thing condoned by the wheeler-dealers of Collins Street, those men with their university degrees and business school diplomas, then Hamilton never showed concern. And what he lacked in education, he more than compensated for with nous and the cunning of a street-smart operator.

Hamilton was a man who had his own moral code. Few people knew that he smoked. He believed that sporting administrators should not be seen smoking and would never allow himself to be photographed with his favorite pipe in his hand.

Unless you were near his office, or happened to walk into the small room nearby with its wash-basin and shower and smelt the pungent aroma of pipe tobacco, you would not have known he smoked.

And it was a topic you rarely brought up with him. Tilley tried it once. 'How long have you been smoking, Jack?,' he asked one afternoon.

Hamilton grunted, then barked at him. 'What do you want?' he asked, staring coldly at him. Tilley quickly moved on to another subject.

He was an intimidating figure and many quickly came to think Hamilton was indestructible. He grew on just about anyone who worked with him or even against him. When the Victorian Labor government was at war with the League and using it as a public whipping boy, the Premier, John Cain, and Aylett developed a personal animosity which went far beyond the borders of a political disagreement. But Hamilton? The government loved him. Besides the fact that he seemed to them to be a typical 'Labor Man', they liked his sense of theatre and humour.

Perhaps they also admired him for another trait. Hamilton was one of the game's best politicians. Perhaps it had something to do with the manner in which he became general manager. Soon after he won the job on a vote of all the club directors, close friends assumed he had made a decision that he would never allow himself to be placed in such a vulnerable position again.

He knew where many of the bodies were buried at the clubs and understood, perhaps better than anyone else, the shifting loyalties and machinations of the 12 League clubs. Others, too, marvelled at his use of the telephone. He had never met one he didn't like and Hamilton used the phone to develop a remarkable network of supporters and contacts throughout the country. It seemed every country and metropolitan league official had, at one time or another, received a call from Hamilton. Sometimes it was just a gentle inquiry, an innocent call to check on the league's progress and any potential problems which he, as general manager of the VFL, could help them solve. With his renowned sense of humour, Hamilton made them all feel like mates. And all that groundwork would one day pay off.

Since 1977, Hamilton and Aylett had complemented one another brilliantly.

'Jack and Allen were a great team for a long time,' Ron Joseph would recall one morning. He was scratching his head, as usual. 'Jack's greatness was his job of running football day to day. He did that very well. Jack knew that a game still had to be played. Jack could keep the competition going while Allen pursued this vision he had.'

The papers would dub them the League's 'dynamic duo'.

In their early years, most believed they got along famously. But those who worked with them closely always sensed an underlying distance between the pair. Some thought both were competing for the right to be the League's public face, although why anyone would want that role defied belief at the time. While they appeared to get along well at meetings and whenever they were discussing strategy, they rarely socialised.

By 1984, however, Hamilton was privately criticising Aylett. He would express frustration if Aylett kept a taxi waiting downstairs for any length of time, believing it to be an unnecessary expense at a time when the two men were encouraging the clubs to show restraint. He wondered, sometimes aloud, whether it was right and proper for the president of the VFL to be making so many phone calls, lobbying this club or that. Surely it was the job of the general manager?

If Hamilton had begun falling out of love with his president, Aylett was hardly enamoured of his general manager. Aylett would occasionally express annoyance to those around him that Hamilton seemed content to get by day by day, that he had no driving vision for the future and that it was fortunate that he, Aylett, was at the helm because no-one else seemed prepared to take a chance.

Under Aylett's presidency, the VFL had experienced the fastest growth of any sport in the country. Always pushing, always exhorting everyone on to further heights, Aylett was like the coach of a club.

VFL House, which housed the game's central administration, was populated by many of his hirings. In fact, it was one of the most colourful collections of employees in town.

John Hennessy had been one of them. Aylett had urged the appointment of a corporate planner back in 1979. He'd seen the way the game was heading and wanted someone with expertise to help put in place a structure that could help the competition better cope with its growth pains.

But a corporate planner? In football? The move had surprised many of the clubs. Many who worked at VFL House also failed to understand Aylett's thinking. Surely corporate planning was the province of its then company secretary, Ralph Lane? Even a decade later, Hennessy's role would perplex many.

'Aylett was pushing him along at a million miles an hour, Jack was trying to slow him right down and Ralph kept telling him to get stuffed,' was how one former administrator recalled the office chemistry.

Hennessy resigned from the VFL in March, 1984, but he would be remembered for years to come. Had he been a quiet, retiring man then Hamilton and others might have regretted his departure more than they did. But Hennessy was not a retiring sort of bloke. Hired from the Gas and Fuel Corporation, he joined the League with an academic background and what some regarded as an attitude and sense of humour to match it. Some of those who worked with him never quite got it. He liked practical jokes. When he learned that he had earned the sobriquet 'Egg Man'—it had something to do with the belief that Hennessy was quite intelligent, a bit of a bookworm and so, in that great Australian tradition, was an 'Egg Head'—he broke several eggs over the head of the League's enraged media director, Ian McDonald, at an office Christmas party.

Hennessy had also shown a courageous attitude to authority which, in the conservative world of football, did not go down well either. As a cricketer with the district club side Prahran, he decided to run for club president. He was writing a thesis at the time for a university course and its thrust was the vulnerability of sporting clubs to takeovers.

Here, he thought, was a wonderful opportunity to put his theories to the test. The man he opposed, Bob Parish, was an Australian cricketing institution, an influential figure at Victorian level who was also chairman of the Australian Cricket Board. He had managed Australian teams on an Ashes tour as well as a trip to the Caribbean. He was a man of high standing. You didn't mess with Bob Parish. You didn't even think about it.

Yet here was Hennessy, a tall man with a long, bouncy stride, standing against him. Parish won. But in a tribute to Hennessy's disarming manner, he created a fluster. Those at the club still remember the election quite warmly. Old supporters, many of whom had not been seen around for years and who could barely walk, they were so old, miraculously turned up on the night to ensure Parish retained his position. The VCA changed its eligibility rules as a result of Hennessy's campaign to ensure that prominent officials could never have their positions threatened again.

Hennessy's experiences at Prahran, however, were nothing to what he encountered at the League. As corporate planner he was responsible for trying to put together strategies that would take the game into the future. One year, after several months of hard work, he released a plan that outlined a ground rationalisation scheme.

Ground rationalisation had become one of football's obsessions. The League had believed for a long time that it was pointless for every club to have its own home ground. The rental costs were a burden and there was usually little funding available to improve facilities for a public that was demanding comfortable seating and clean, hygenic toilets.

Clearly there were too many ovals being used by VFL clubs. Hennessy's recommendations included the relocation of several clubs to grounds they could share and thus save money.

Ten years later, a wide grin would work its way across Hennessy's face. He was sitting in his office in Port Melbourne. Well, sitting was not exactly the word. Every few minutes he would lurch out of his chair and bound across the room to a whiteboard. Grabbing a pen, he would begin frantically drawing a graph or a chart to explain his theory on the game. Then, abruptly, he would be back in his seat, grinning.

'As long as you had the support of Allen and Jack you could do whatever you wanted,' Hennessy would say. But not when it came to moving clubs.

His ground rationalisation was logically sound. But Hennessy was dealing with a League built not so much on logic as emotion. He was vilified. A recommendation that the old Lakeside Oval, South Melbourne's home ground, be dispensed with drew an angry response from South. Copies were leaked to the press. The clubs were outraged. Never mind, thought Hennessy. At least it was a report backed by the League.

He had not, however, counted on the political cunning of Hamilton. With the League under attack, Hamilton's defence of the controversial blueprint began to wane. Publicly he stopped referring to it as a League-sponsored report.

'Jack started calling it the "Hennessy Report",' Hennessy would recall. And that smile grew ever larger.

But as far as Aylett was concerned, Hennessy was the perfect man for the job. The president had deliberately called for the establishment of a corporate planner's role in a bid to change the thinking at VFL House and Hennessy tried his best.

'You could see the whole system was wrong,' he said. 'It just wasn't sustainable in the format it was in. It had grown too quickly, too fast. But no-one really knew how to change it.'

At one stage, as a wave of paranoia swept the offices as leak after leak kept hitting the press, Hennessy went to Hamilton and Aylett with a plan.

'Listen,' Hennessy told them one day as they expressed frustration over yet another leak, '. . . we just don't know who's listening to any of our conversations. Or how they're doing it.'

Hennessy thought it prudent to cover all bases. So, with Aylett and Hamilton's approval, a security firm was called in to sweep VFL House for bugs.

But the best example of Aylett's driving ambition for the VFL was typified by a small, wiry character who boasted a sharp eye for a deal and a buck. A week barely passed without him entering Hamilton's office or calling him with a new idea to make money.

Some actually wondered what Jim McKay enjoyed best; the financial reward for making a deal or the act of cutting the deal itself. Whatever it was, McKay had displayed exemplary form in both categories during the eight years he had been involved with the League. Within a few years, his love for the deal and its outcome would see his star rapidly wane with the League, before blinking out completely.

But his impact on the game was enormous and, in many ways, he had helped change and influence the game just as much as Aylett and Hamilton had throughout the late 1970s and early 1980s.

McKay first worked closely with the VFL in the mid-70s when the advertising company he worked for, the world-wide firm of J. Walter Thompson, took over the VFL account. The League was still taking its first tentative steps into the corporate sea and decided the agency could best look after its needs. Jimmy McKay was instantly their man. He had begun his working life in the mail-room at GTV-9 straight out of Glenroy High School. It did not take long before those above him recognised he was not destined to sort mail for the rest of his life. McKay was an operator in the truest sense of the word. He moved up quickly, seizing any opportunity which came his way and turning it to his advantage. In 1972 he'd been a co-organiser of the Sunbury pop festival. He eventually went on to produce several football and variety programs for Channel 9 before moving into advertising.

The then-president, Sir Maurice Nathan, recognised that his League's image could do with some help. Within the administration, concerns had begun mounting by the middle of the 1970s that the game's almost hypnotic hold on the Melbourne public was loosening. There was a new generation of Victorian emerging that would enjoy more leisure time than any before it. It had a higher disposable income. The car was no longer the luxury it had been 20 or 30 years before; it was now a necessity. And soccer, that foreign game played by dagos, wogs and all those other people who ate strange-smelling food and gesticulated wildly with their hands, had begun to grow in popularity.

In fact, soccer, known as football in just about every corner of the globe except the southern states of Australia, was quickly emerging as a threat to the Australian game. In 1974 the national team, the Socceroos, made the World Cup finals for the first time. Schools were showing a greater interest in including it in their physical education curriculum. And the kids' parents were hardly complaining about it either. After all, soccer was a safer sport. There were fewer injuries. You could remain relatively clean for a whole match. You didn't come home with scraped knees, puffy eyes and scratches down your back.

Australian football, thought McKay, was a game being viewed increasingly by teenagers as an older people's sport. It was where your father and his friends went on a Saturday afternoon.

McKay saw many possibilities for the game. In fact, from a marketing and corporate exposure point of view, it was uncharted territory. He began by promoting the idea of clubs advertising their sponsors on jumpers and shorts. But it was hard work convincing League clubs that a whole new world awaited them, that sport could be a part of that bigger business community.

Nathan and McKay kept pushing. In 1976, the VFL set up what it grandly called its Properties Division. Styled blatantly and unashamedly on the Properties Division of the National Football League in the United States, the VFL version, propelled by McKay, quickly became the League's third largest source of revenue. VFL Insurance had been set up and began making instant inroads into the insurance arena, using discounting and saturation advertising.

McKay was like a kid in a lolly shop. So many things to do, so much money just waiting to be made. With VFL Insurance carving a niche for itself, he had another idea. Why not introduce VFL Travel? Supporters could book package holidays using an agency boasting the League's identity. It was just so easy and he had the field to himself. So first he began a round of interviews with prospective travel agencies, assessing which ones could best suit the League's needs and identity. It quickly became apparent that Jetset, one of the nation's leading agencies with a strong attachment to Ansett, was the best option.

McKay made his recommendation to J. Walter Thompson and they were just as delighted. Ansett, after all, was a much-valued client of the firm. But a week after McKay made his recommendation, Jetset switched its allegiance to the rival airline TAA. The deal was under threat immediately. McKay was told J. Walter Thompson had to resign the account after what, he learned later, was a call from Sir Reginald Ansett to one of the advertising agency's chief executives demanding the VFL account be dropped.

McKay was angry and reluctant. Drop the football? He was on to a good thing. This, after all, could be his meal ticket. So he called Nathan, who by now he had got to know quite well, and made his pitch. 'I don't have a lot of money,' he told Nathan, 'it's only me and my secretary. But if I quit J. Walter Thompson will you give me the VFL account?'

According to McKay, Nathan agreed to back him by giving McKay $10,000 up front—50 per cent of his first year's retainer. Nathan might have suspected that his decision would have repercussions for the game. But it is almost certain he failed to realise just how far-reaching an effect the 28-year-old McKay's involvement would have on the game of Australian football.

Within 12 months the Properties Division sat just behind gate receipts and television rights as the game's biggest source of revenue. In 1977, revenue for the division amounted to about $300,000. A year later it was more than $500,000. In 1979, more than $1 million flowed in.

Licencing was the game and McKay and the League began exploiting it to the hilt. You could have a VFL-endorsed breakfast, with cereals and bread on the market carrying the League's logo. There were household products, trinkets, school books, the League's own brand of football. Babies could wear VFL-approved bibs. On it went. For McKay it was a particularly lucrative trade. In 1980 his company was paid $155,000 commission by the League, based on the 20 per cent cut it took from all deals it negotiated. It was indeed a good year for McKay. The trade magazine *Advertising News* named him its Marketing Man of the Year.

If, under Nathan, there had still been some caution exercised when it came to marketing the game, then under Aylett it was thrown to the wind. If the threat of soccer was to be fought off and the Australian game well and truly branded on the minds of the sports-going public, then the president and his marketing man would proceed as fast as they could.

But they needed a strategy. How could they change the game's image? Football had to become a trendy sport, where trendy, groovy people felt they had to go on a Saturday afternoon and watch a match. It began with a study of the media. Every newspaper, radio and television journalist was surveyed as to which team they followed. Television personalities were approached and asked for their club allegiances. An enormous list was compiled. Then the League began inviting those television personalities to matches and awarding them special status at the pre-game luncheons. McKay aimed to deliberately engineer a new hype about the game. He wanted Don Lane, the host of a popular night variety show, to go on air and say, 'Hey folks, went to the football last Saturday. Did I have a great time or what?'

Merchandising gimmicks, like scarves in their favourite team colours and even jumpers, were sent to the television stars. The League ran a competition in conjunction with *The Herald and Weekly Times* which gave away cars, house and land packages and other expensive prizes. It was claimed at the time to be the world's largest newspaper promotion. But what came out of it was far more lucrative for the League and McKay. Everyone who entered the competition—more than 100,000—had to supply their address, age group, which team they followed and other valuable data. It was a gold mine. Fed into the computer, the list proved enormously valuable to the League for years to come. Out of it came many things, including a junior supporters' club, with a sponsor of course, designed to attract younger children to the game. It became known as the Kellogg's Junior Supporters' Club. As part of its television rights deal, Channel 7 screened a 30-minute program each Sunday morning. Members of the club, aged between six and 14, could attend five matches for free by showing their membership card. By targeting such a young audience the VFL believed it could set in train the habit of a lifetime. And, of course, with the junior club boasting a phenomenal membership of about 30,000 by the early 1980s, it could also offer potential sponsors an extremely valuable and lucrative audience. A good and loyal VFL Junior Supporter would do the right thing and urge Mum and Dad to buy VFL-endorsed products.

By the 1980s McKay was in clover and the credo was clear. 'The more VFL logos which are seen,' he said one day, 'the more sponsorships we'll get, the more merchandise we'll approve and the more endorsements we'll give. That means the more the VFL makes.'

The League's attendances were climbing. A survey had shown that a remarkable 39.3 per cent of all Australians were 'interested' in the VFL competition.

More importantly, the League had established itself as the premier winter sporting code. In the northern states, rugby league was struggling for acceptance. Its administration had allowed the game to wander aimlessly. Matches were one-sided, violence on the field was endemic and the crowds had dwindled. Australian football, meanwhile, was surging ahead. It had even made its first tentative step on the path to a national league by moving the debt-ridden South Melbourne to Sydney and redubbing them the Sydney Swans. The code had a focus and was developing a strong corporate identity. Aylett was positioning the game to a point where his own dreams could be realised. And many of those assisting him, including McKay, were being rewarded handsomely for their efforts.

But by early 1984 McKay's handlers were beginning to wonder whether he required a new leash. Hamilton would introduce him to someone new with the words '. . . and this is Jim McKay, our marketing man . . .'

Hamilton would pause for a moment as the new man shook McKay's hand. '. . . and you'd better count your fingers,' he would add, chortling.

Everyone liked Jim McKay for the money he brought to the League and its clubs. But not everyone liked the way he did business. There was a theory among his critics that McKay knew how to make a deal, but could only do it once. That he burned too many people. Years later, when the League moved into the 1990s and embarked on another round of trying to sell the game overseas, it would encounter a trail of network executives in various countries who had all encountered McKay at some time in the past and who no longer wanted to hear the words 'Australian football'.

By 1984 word had begun getting back to the VFL that many of its licencing subsidiaries were unhappy with their treatment at the hands of McKay's Active Marketing. With his contract up for renewal in October, the League decided to put its marketing contract up for tender.

During the process it sought the advice of Kevin Luscombe, known in Melbourne as a specialist adviser on marketing affairs. At 8.30am Wednesday, 8 August, a special meeting of the League's marketing committee was convened to hear presentations from the two firms which had tendered for the rights to manage the League's marketing affairs—Westwood Rogers Marketing Pty Ltd and, of course, Active Marketing.

But before representatives from both firms were allowed in to make their presentation in front of Aylett, Hamilton and senior representatives of 10 of the 12 clubs, an interim report was presented to the meeting containing the 'observations' of Luscombe.

Only one of the two tenderers, Luscombe reported, had specifically answered the League's brief. It was Active Marketing. Perhaps this was understandable, said Luscombe, given the company's familiarity with League operations.

But there was, he noted, a substantial variance in commission rates. McKay was proposing a remarkable 23.5 per cent which, to those present, was regarded as extravagant compared to his present 20 per cent and particularly up against Westwood Rogers' offer of 12.5 per cent. 'The rationalisation of the 23.5 per cent was not detailed in Jim McKay's submission and this should be fundamental,' said Luscombe. 'The obvious missing ingredient in all these submissions is an over-riding marketing strategy. The focus is on returns, costs and promotional events.'

Luscombe agreed with the League's growing belief that it should bring many of its marketing operations back 'in-house . . . for strategic direction and management control. The tenders should be for licencing and some part of endorsement marketing only.'

Then, just before the presentations began, a lively discussion ensued among many of the general managers present. 'It was submitted by some general managers that the League's image was not enhanced by the alleged aggressive and perhaps harsh manner in which Mr McKay approached and dealt with potential licensees,' recorded the minutes of the meeting.

'It was further noted that it appeared to be the view that once licensees had been contracted, there was insufficient servicing and follow-up contact made by the League's marketing division, operated by Active Marketing Pty. Ltd.'

Finally, the presentations began. Bruce Westwood and Keith Rogers of Westwood Rogers gave a solid presentation which honed in on McKay's perceived weaknesses. The League's failure to properly service its licensees was costing it substantial sums of money. It was also their belief that there appeared to be 'a degree of inaccessibility' to existing VFL-endorsed products at retail level. A failure to meet consumer demand, recorded the minutes of the presentation, had effectively encouraged the sales of pirate merchandise in major retail outlets.

McKay was aware of the criticisms levelled at him and his company. In his presentation he concentrated on Active Marketing's successes, pointing out that the NSW Rugby League marketing division was netting just $6,000 a year, providing a dividend of a paltry $500 to each club. To suggestions he had not adequately serviced existing marketing licensees, McKay claimed the drop-off rate was below five per cent over the previous two years.

When asked about his proposed 23.5 per cent commission rate, McKay 'conceded that he would be prepared to negotiate at around 20 per cent.' But to go lower would mean unprofitability. There had to be a bottom line. And Jim McKay could always find it.

Eventually, McKay won a watered-down agreement with the League. But the events of 1984 and the attitude among many of the club general managers served as signposts for a new direction.

Everything was moving forward. They just had no idea where they were going.

4

THE POWER OF
THE PRESIDENTS

Like any politician worth his salt, John Cain kept a diary. At the end of each week during his tenure as the Premier of Victoria he would sit down and record his impressions of the week. There were plenty of them, too. There were the factional deals that so riddled his Labor party; the intricacies and byzantine nature of them could leave you breathless or just plain confused. There was the battle to control the economy and fights with the unions. And of course, the ever-present public opinion polls.

There was also another issue which cropped up with some frequency in the diaries of John Cain in the early to mid-1980s. His government was at war with the Victorian Football League and was relishing the opportunity to sink its boots into a sporting administration all too ripe for a public kicking.

The Government knew a winner when it saw one. God knew there were few easy point-scoring opportunities around for politicians. By arguing the case 'for the people' against the greedy, money-hungry League, Cain's government could not lose.

The main issue was the League's ambition to play its Grand Final at its own ground at Waverley. It wanted to expand the stadium's capacity but would continually be frustrated by State and local government planning laws. The League also wanted to play football at the MCG on Sundays. Sport was changing and the way people went and watched it was also shifting. If Cain would allow soccer matches and other sporting codes to use the MCG on Sundays, why not the VFL?

Football passionately believed it contributed a great deal to the state. Its finals series attracted tourists from around the country. It created jobs and poured millions of dollars into the economy. And it was tired of being treated shabbily at the MCG by the Melbourne Cricket Club. The VFL wanted to control the ground on grand final day and receive a far greater percentage of the gate. If it didn't, it always had Waverley.

But following the election of Cain and his party to government in 1982, the Waverley-MCG row became more than just a political issue. Cain and Aylett couldn't stand one another. It was a deep-set personality conflict. They were two very different men. Cain was a lawyer who had been in politics for some time. He knew when to cut his losses and understood that compromise was always part of any political equation.

Compared to Cain, Aylett was politically naive. He had his vision of the future and it didn't allow any room for those damn politicians.

'At first I could speak to Cain, but I soon found him unreasonable and not too interested in football's problems,' Aylett would say later. 'He appeared to be more concerned with votes.' He sounded surprised.

Barely a week passed during the early 1980s when Aylett and Cain were not at each other's throats in the papers, lambasting one another for being selfish and inflexible. Aylett didn't trust Cain while the Premier didn't like what Aylett and the clubs were doing to football.

Cain's attitude towards the League was not just a handy, overnight conversion because there were votes to be won. The Premier was an old-fashioned traditionalist when it came to sport. He didn't fully understand why football was changing and experiencing its extraordinary growth pains. Why did the VFL always want to make money? What was wrong with 12 teams running out on the field each Saturday afternoon and playing one another as they had for most of the century? Why expand into Sydney? But even if he did comprehend the reasons for the changes, he remained suspicious about the men who controlled the game and their motives.

Cain had not been in office for long in 1982 when he sat down in late July to record his impressions of another week. He had gone to the football the previous Saturday, he noted. Aylett had been there and 'pestered me again about the proposal to extend VFL Park. The VFL is quite obsessed about the thing and determined to teach the MCC a lesson and take the grand final away from that ground.'

Cain stayed on after the match to attend a function. Also there was the president of St Kilda, trucking magnate Lindsay Fox, and the president of North Melbourne, Bob Ansett.

The presence of two of Australia's leading businessmen set Cain thinking. He was still wondering about it when he addressed his diary for the week.

'When you see these people responsible for key positions in the administration of League football, it makes you wonder what League football is all about,' Cain observed.

'The success of the club and the VFL seems to be an extension of their own ego and become a prestige thing with them. The spectators and players and everything else associated with the game appear to be just part of the power play that goes on.'

Cain, a veteran of Labor Party politics, had seen some of the best schemers in action. But even he seemed in awe of the intrigues and politics of the men who controlled the game of Australian football.

He was the son of a truck driver and sly grog operator in Richmond, who hardly set his school alight with academic brilliance. But Lindsay Fox didn't care much for that. He had a degree in street smarts and it would take him a long way.

After buying a second-hand Chevrolet truck and delivering

soft drinks in the early 1950s, Fox was successful enough to own and operate five by the end of the decade. He was also trying his hand at League football as a ruckman with St Kilda. Too slow and lacking the ability of many of his opponents, Fox was honest about his talent. 'I was a hack,' he would say quite often years later. 'In 1961 Allan Jeans (embarking on the first of a 16-year coaching career with the club) told me I had no future in the game and I agreed.'

But there was a big future in trucking. Fox, through a combination of hard work and being in the right place at the right time, quickly established a transport empire. Securing contracts with companies like BP, Coles, Dunlop and Woolworths, his fleet grew to more than 1000 trucks by the time he took over as president of his old club in September, 1979.

St Kilda had seen better days, but there weren't many of them. The Saints, despite boasting a potentially huge membership base in Melbourne's southern suburbs, rarely capitalised on that potential. After winning their only flag back in 1966, the club had only been back to the grand final once more, losing to Hawthorn in 1971 by seven points. Since then the Saints had deteriorated. By the end of the 1970s a cycle of failure had set in. The club had the smell of a loser. It was losing a lot of money, its players were not regarded as the most disciplined collection of footballers in the League and its home ground at Moorabbin seemed to add to the club's sense of loss. It was a small ground with a shabby outer and the men's toilets seemed to be forever blocked.

Fox had been told by a senior club official during 1979 that the Saints were in debt by about $150,000. Fox brought in the internationally respected Arthur Andersen and Co. to conduct a search and report. The club official had been overly optimistic. The company discovered St Kilda had a net deficiency of $1.6 million. There were creditors all over the place. Fox was amazed his old club was still operating.

So he addressed a board meeting. 'You're $1.6 million

down,' he told the subdued directors. When Lindsay Fox spoke, people listened. His sentences were rarely punctuated with an 'ummm' or a nervous 'aaah'. He was forthright and damn right. Combined with his sizeable physical presence, that fleshy balding head and squinting eyes, people rarely argued with him.

'The easiest way to fix it is for each of you to write out a cheque for $230,000 . . .' he told the board, '. . . or resign.'

They resigned. Fox brought in a new board and began negotiations with the club's banker, ANZ. Five corporate sponsors were signed up. One creditor agreed to have money owed to it transformed into sponsorship. All Fox thought he had to do now was get his club some decent players.

Fox was adamant things would change at St Kilda. 'Personally,' he told everyone when he took over, 'I hate failure. And I hate losing. If changes have to be made, I'll make them.'

It didn't take him long. The season was only a few weeks old in 1980 when Fox witnessed an incident that made his blood boil. During a match against Hawthorn at St Kilda's home ground at Moorabbin, two St Kilda defenders ran into one another. Had it happened on the other side of the ground, it might not have made such a big impact. But they collided right in front of the entertainment area and Fox was watching. He went home that night sulking, his mood hardly improving when the incident was replayed on television.

The following morning Fox summoned several key board members and club officials to his weekender at Portsea, the holiday retreat for Victoria's well-heeled. It was a painful call for many of them. Vice-president Graham Huggins was staying at Ocean Grove on the other side of Port Phillip Bay and the chairman of the club's match committee, Roger Head, was staying a little further down the coast at Anglesea.

But within an hour a decision was reached. Coach Mike Patterson was out. Fox didn't believe Patterson was a leader.

What Fox wanted, and what the club needed, was a leader more than anything else, a man who would instil discipline and fire in the belly of the players. He wanted them to revere some-one. Carlton's legendary champion Alex Jesaulenko accepted the job. Huggins and Head left Fox's private beachfront in a speedboat and then caught the ferry back to Queenscliff in time for a late lunch. If they hadn't realised then, they knew now. Lindsay Fox didn't muck around.

Many other football club officials were very wary of Fox. It wasn't so much that he was a new boy who thought he could run the game the way he ran his business. It was his demeanour that put many off. Fox, they thought, was too smug for his own good. He made out as though he knew it all. And he also seemed to show no interest in working for the good of the game. He was too interested in making a success out of St Kilda.

But if others were wary of Fox, the feeling was hardly recip-rocated by the St Kilda president. Fox just didn't have much time for many of his contemporaries in football.

'King Solomon had it right,' he would say many years later, comfortably wrapped in a large leather chair. It was a strange conversation because Fox looked so comfortable and so con-tented that he barely moved a muscle in almost an hour. He just sat there and stared while a question was asked, occasionally allowing a smile to cross his face just to let you know he was still breathing. You wondered who was the one being observed.

His office was a place even young kids could enjoy. Large model trucks sat on coffee tables and window sills, symbols of the empire. Fox believed history contained many lessons, and the legend of King Solomon contained a large kernel of truth about football officials.

'Two women claimed a child they had was theirs,' he recited, staring straight at his visitor without blinking. 'Solomon pulled out a sword and said, "I'll give you half each." One woman said, "It's not my child." King Solomon gave that woman the child. The one that was prepared to have the baby cut up had no real interest or concern.'

Finally he blinked and looked out of the window. 'Too many football administrators were there for their own benefit . . .' he said. '. . . and not of the club.'

Fox would have one of the greatest impacts on the game of football in the 1980s. His actions would force the League to revise its rules and realise finally that it was not immune to the forces of change in the world around it.

It was not as though football had not been warned, either. Right from the start Fox had made it clear that he intended to apply the very principles he abided by in business to the game.

By the 1980s, many presidents of VFL clubs were no longer former captains of their clubs, but captains of industry, men who had made their mark on Australia's corporate scene and who saw their elevation to a football presidency as some kind of reward. Most were men of sizeable egos who boasted strong opinions and were familiar with getting their own way. Yet put them together and their renowned business sense sometimes seemed to desert them. Football had a strange hold on everyone.

The new era was officially ushered in at the Toorak home of the socialite and Carlton president, Ian Rice, on 17 April, 1980. Over a two-hour lunch, four influential men got together to discuss what they saw as football's most significant problems and how they could change them.

Joining Rice was Fox, Wayne Reid, the debonair president of Melbourne and Bob Ansett, the fast-talking chief of Budget Rent-a-car and newly-appointed president of North Melbourne.

They were, said Fox later, 'just new boys discussing what the game is all about.' But it wasn't so much what the game was about that interested them. It was what the game wasn't about that concerned them.

They were, said Rice, 'all involved in private commerce as

heads of private industry and all friends.' Rice, until his appointment following the controversial resignation of George Harris, had hardly been known to haunt the club's dressing rooms. But he was the president of Carlton and the club had rarely boasted a titular head who did not have an opinion or two he liked to share.

The VFL, said Rice, was 'taking away the free enterprise of the clubs.' Big Brother, he feared, was taking over football.

'Maybe that is a good thing, maybe it is bad; but it is certainly not the way our country is run and it is not the way we are used to running our businesses.'

Fox wanted all zoning regulations scrapped and no restrictions on recruiting. Ansett wanted a 'free enterprise system'. Predictably, the arrival of the new breed of president was viewed suspiciously by the old guard.

Ansett had been made aware of the suspicions of his involvement in the game a few weeks before the lunch. He had been on the phone with Jack Hamilton and the League general manager had been in one of his less-than-subtle moods.

'The collective experience of all of you is two hours and 20 minutes,' he said.

Well, thought Ansett, that might have been true. But look at the collective experience of the VFL. In almost 90 years, what had it achieved, except extend the administration's power over the clubs?

When news of the lunch meeting at Rice's home leaked to the press, Ansett stepped forward and offered his views. 'The VFL should be accountable to the clubs. Well, in my experience the clubs are accountable to the VFL. How the hell does that happen?

'I would hope that out of that meeting, with four fertile minds, we could come up with some alternative to the schemes proposed by the VFL.'

Ron Tandberg, recognised as the country's premier cartoonist, summed up the fears about football's new direction and the motives of the men who were taking control. In *The Age* newspaper, he drew a cartoon of Fox, Rice, Reid and Ansett hunched over a table covered in cash.

A football bounced past them.

'What's that?' asked Rice.

Ansett was a marketing man whose mission in life, apart from being successful in business, was to make the customer happy. He had taken a good look at football when he was approached by North to become president and saw that the needs of the game's customers were being ignored. Football had always attracted support and had never really had to work at it. Ansett thought it could improve its approach.

With his broad American accent and, for its time, bizarre theories on treating the customer like a king, Ansett was another newcomer viewed suspiciously in football's little world. He was one of the first breed of 1980s entrepreneur and his breeding was impeccable. His father, Sir Reginald Ansett, had been one of Australia's most influential businessmen, capable of calling a federal minister and getting things changed if he didn't like them.

Sir Reg's marriage to Grace had broken up in the early 1940s and she took her two sons with her to the United States. Bob Ansett was eight when he left Melbourne. He was 32 when he returned in 1965. In between he had served in the US Army, played American football and studied business administration on a scholarship at the University of Utah.

He set about applying what he'd learned to the car rental business, an industry which, in Australia, was floundering. Only three per cent of Australians at the time rented cars. Within a couple of decades that figure would climb to 20 per cent, boosted largely by the hard-sell, up-front style of Ansett.

He had also become involved with North Melbourne as a sponsor and had watched as Aylett, his lieutenant, Ron Joseph, and a band of willing followers guided the club from obscurity into one of the game's powerhouses. But when they approached him to become president in 1979, he'd made it clear it would be on his terms. There would be no unwieldy board of directors dominated by old players. He wanted the club restructured and he would get his way.

But his ambitions didn't just stop there. If North was to move into the 1980s and continue as a strong club, the competition itself would need to change. Ansett declared his hand early. He showed little regard for the social niceties of the time. Bland statements and cliches were not for him.

Why shouldn't the VFL become a national competition, he'd ask. Why couldn't clubs be privately owned? Wouldn't that solve many of their financial problems?

As Ansett asked his questions, others began to ask their own. Who was this bloke with the American accent? Who was he to tell them how to run this great game? Who did think he was?

Within two years they were asking the same questions of Ranald Macdonald. But the new president of Collingwood had been extensively briefed on what to expect. Nothing he encountered, then, surprised him.

'When the presidents look each other in the eye and you consider behind the scenes what they are doing to you and your people are doing the same thing, it's a pretty surprising relationship,' he would observe a few months into the job.

'After 100 days I'm not thinking I've got all the answers, or even a few of them. Unless the presidents get together and work intelligently with the VFL executives to work out where the game is going, I just can't see us getting anywhere.'

Macdonald had risen to power at Victoria Park on the strength of a campaign to return the club to its rightful place as Australia's most popular and successful sporting organisation. Within a handful of years, the Magpies, under the direction of Macdonald and his 'Magnificent Seven' takeover group, would end up right on the brink of bankruptcy.

Chesborough Ranald Macdonald was one of the most influential men in Victoria and, for a time, in the country. Some of those close to him regarded him as a bit of an anachronism, a decent, hard-working, well-meaning chap transported from the playing fields of 1920 Eton to the crueller corporate world of the 1970s and 1980s.

He was educated at Geelong Grammar, the cradle of the Australian Establishment, where he was a schoolmate of Kerry Packer. Macdonald's father, Hamish, was killed in Java during the war and his Scottish stepfather, Colonel E.H.B. Neill, wore a monocle and a red carnation.

A second cousin to Rupert Murdoch, Macdonald was the great-grandson of the founder of *The Age* newspaper, David Syme. He was elevated to the role of managing director of *The Age* at 26 when, according to legend, he asked Oswald Syme for a job as promotions manager. Macdonald's rapid speech startled Syme so much he thought Macdonald was asking for the managing director's job. He got it.

He had a style few others possessed or could keep pace with. Les Carlyon, a former editor of *The Age*, would observe that 'Ranald is capable of holding three conversations simultaneously while working on an idea of his own with the felt pen that is his talisman and signalling instructions to his frantic secretaries with the free hand, all the time half-hidden behind a volcanic eruption of reports, magazines, newspapers, scribbles, schedules, schemes, the half-baked and the just-thought-of.'

Always a Collingwood supporter (at Grammar he'd had to put up with the ribbing of his peers who, as many of the well-heeled did, barracked for Melbourne), Macdonald had been the up-front spokesman for the New Magpies during their 1982 takeover campaign. The club had been struggling that season on and off the field and would record a loss of almost $400,000 for the year. This, thought Macdonald, was ridiculous. Why was the most famous sporting club in the land, one which inspired more passion and loyalty among its supporters than any other, in such a precarious position? Why had it failed to win a premiership since 1958?

The New Magpies swept to power. Almost immediately the club embarked on an unprecedented buying spree and within months had spent more than $1 million on six players. But by then the club's board had fallen victim to football's usual malaise, riddled with factions and murmurings of discontent.

Allan McAlister was the club's treasurer. A short, stocky man, he had never played the game at elite level and he felt that several other members of the Collingwood board ignored him because of that. But McAlister had an ace up his sleeve. When the club went searching for a new coach at the end of the 1982 season, a list of candidates was drawn up. McAlister went to Macdonald and told him he believed he could secure the best of them all: John Kennedy.

Football people revered Kennedy. He'd made his reputation in the 1980s, transforming Hawthorn from an easy-beat side into one of the competition's toughest clubs. They played a hard brand of football and Kennedy coached them that way, too. He was a shrewd tactician with a roaring, thundering voice that could put the fear of God into veteran players as well as the young recruits. And for a club that needed to drag itself back up, he would have been perfect.

McAlister had known Kennedy for some time. He rang him one day and asked if he'd be interested in the Collingwood coaching position. Kennedy indicated he would and the pair began discussing the possibility of such a move.

McAlister reported back that Kennedy was effectively in the bag. The deal was set.

Then, just before McAlister finalised the deal on behalf of the club, he received a call at home one Sunday morning. One of the board members was on his way to Adelaide to sign up South Australian coach John Cahill. McAlister made a series of furious calls to try to stop the deal. But it was too late.

He rang Kennedy, embarrassed and humiliated, and apologised for leading him down the garden path.

McAlister was surprised that Kennedy was not as angry as he had expected. But then, Kennedy had been around football clubs long enough to know how they took care of business.

It was an incident in 1984 which typified Collingwood and the League's staggering progress through the 1980s. Soon after taking office, Macdonald had been involved in a clearance wrangle over the club's former coach, Tom Hafey, who'd been sacked by the previous administration. Macdonald would not allow him to go to another club unless the Magpies were compensated.

'We've got to do what must be in the best interests of Collingwood,' he announced, 'and there is precedent for it. Give us a nice big ruckman.'

A nice big ruckman. For more than a century, football club officials and coaches had searched the land for a nice big ruckman and more often than not they had failed. Mae West rarely found one in Hollywood and Australian football clubs had the same problem. A good big man was hard to find.

The ruck was one of the most mythologised positions in the game. A contest began with the bounce of the ball and there was a theory that whoever controlled the ball once gravity began pulling it back to earth would control the game itself; because of the sport's aerial skills, a big man with long arms would get to the ball first.

There was also the matter of his size. One of the rituals of Australian football takes place shortly before the first bounce when the teams take to the field. Once there, they perform a warm-up lap and undergo several routine stretching exercises. It happens from the big national League right down to a bush game where utes and trucks ring the oval. But the players are doing more than just warming up. They surreptitiously eye one another, checking out the size of the other team, their strengths and speed. It was moments like those when games could be won and lost before a ball was bounced.

So a big man was good to find. And Macdonald and his Collingwood board wanted one.

Their search took them to Melbourne, Dick Seddon's team and a club which had not won a premiership for 20 years. When Seddon had arrived at the club to take charge as executive director in 1980, he discovered that all the film footage of the club's greatest moments was in black and white. The era of colour had arrived but the Demons had accomplished nothing since 1964, the year of their last premiership under the tutelage of the game's most legendary coach, Norm Smith.

Melbourne had been one of the game's most dominant clubs of the 1950s. Perceived as a team of silvertails whose players came from wealthy homes and had enjoyed a private education, Melbourne's fall from grace after 1964 had hardly brought a tear to the eye of its opponents.

Seddon had barracked for the club as a young boy growing up in Ballarat and when he moved to Melbourne and set up a successful law firm specialising in corporate and securities work he continued the affair. He became a member of the Redlegs, an influential coterie supporters group. Then he took charge of the club's legal affairs before accepting the role of executive director for what he thought would be a short, three-year term.

He stayed almost five and during that period attempted to drag Melbourne from what he called the horse-and-cart era into the 1980s. When he joined, Melbourne had no bank account of its own. It was not even incorporated. Years of subservience to its cricket counterpart had turned it into a quaint anachronism in a League where most of its opponents were already embracing Aylett's new corporate philosophy. One of the first things Seddon set about doing was luring Ron Barassi, now the master coach, back to his old club.

He finally achieved this at the end of 1980 in a complicated deal which signalled that the Demons had unharnessed the horse and cart. Melbourne, which had finally been incorporated, released its annual report to members on 3 December that year with a short statement by the club's president, Wayne Reid, that the club had paid $239,833 for a 100 per cent interest in two companies. They were Vigee Pty Ltd and its wholly-owned subsidiary, Sixty Eight HFA Pty Ltd.

Few members were aware that the two companies were closely linked to Barassi. Another connected company, Vigee Holdings Pty Ltd, had been previously known as Ron Barassi Holdings Pty Ltd.

Seddon structured the deal so that Melbourne could buy Vigee Pty Ltd, a company which owned the 'options' on the coaching and a half share in the advertising services of Ronald Dale Barassi. Over three years, Barassi was to be paid about $80,000 in what was seen as potentially a tax-free deal.

Seddon relished the politics of football and his fertile imagination and knowledge of corporate law soon manifested itself in other areas. Melbourne became the first club to list its players as assets. In the same report as the Barassi transaction, the club's balance sheet labelled its players as 'intangible assets' based on the value of their contracts. The players were listed under net assets totalling $1.6 million. The report also showed that the players had been paid $502,966 for their services in the 1980 season.

'They are assets,' said Seddon, defending the move. 'Every time a player is transferred we get paid, or if we recruit a player we pay.'

While the practice of listing players as assets was discontinued in the late 1980s, very soon every club was copying Seddon's lead. By 1984, he had been around long enough to know when he saw a good deal in the wings. And when Ranald Macdonald came looking for a nice big ruckman, Dick Seddon was waiting.

Glenn McLean was a young man going places in 1983. Recruited by Melbourne from VFA club Sandringham, the 22-year-old ruckman was handsome and quick and showed enough on the field to convince his peers he had a big future.

His form was excellent in 1983 and at one stage he held on to the No.1 rucking position, despite the presence in the team of the Brownlow Medallist, Peter Moore. But a year later that form would lapse and suddenly the only place Glenn McLean wanted to go was Collingwood.

McLean complained that he was not given a fair go in the ruck, spending much of his time in the reserves. When he made the senior side, he found coach Barassi stuck him in the back pocket or played him off the bench, hardly a glamorous position for such a young man out to impress the football world. When Collingwood showed interest, he responded. How could he not? Here he was, languishing at a club that, despite Seddon's best efforts, was destined not make the finals again while Collingwood, the most famous sporting club in the land and destined to play off in the preliminary final in 1984, wanted him.

Melbourne did not share Collingwood's enthusiasm for McLean. While the Demons believed he had talent, they wondered whether his heart was fully in the game. He seemed to show more interest in rock music and playing the guitar. He was hardly on good terms with Barassi.

To be on bad terms with Barassi was to know it. One of the game's most decorated players, he was at the centre of one of its most seminal moments when, in 1965, he handed in his Melbourne jumper, simultaneously breaking the hearts of thousands of children with the number 31 sewn on the back of their jumpers and duffle coats. Barassi switched to Carlton, which he coached to a famous comeback premiership victory in 1970 over Collingwood.

Barassi was a hard taskmaster. He had proved that during a successful coaching stint at North Melbourne. He was in the

Kennedy mould; a tactician who played as many games with his players' minds as he did with the opposition. He was not averse to humiliating a man in front of his peers. In fact, it was one of his favorite techniques. Cock up in front of your mates, went the Barassi credo, and pay the penalty.

Seddon rightly assessed that Collingwood was desperate for a big man. Its stock of quality ruckmen was thin and the Magpies were showing strong signs of life. He also knew that the Collingwood board had been spending up big.

McLean had not signed an official contract with Melbourne for the 1984 season, but the club believed it still had a legally-binding agreement with him for three years, which would see him earn $32,000 in 1984, with $2000 annual increments for the following two years. As well, incentive payments of $5000 were assured if he finished among the top three vote-getters in the club's best player championship. Seddon once even paid McLean $3000 to paint his house, even though it was still years away from requiring a fresh coat. He wanted the young man to know where his bread was buttered.

But Collingwood nagged away at McLean and got him to sign a three-year contract. Melbourne hit back in May by issuing a Supreme Court writ, asking for a trial and calling for an injunction to restrain Collingwood from 'inducing or procuring' McLean to break his agreement with the Demons. As they waited for a date for a hearing, the Magpies played McLean in their reserves team. Seddon denounced them for the move. 'McLean will be the loser in this and will end up in the wilderness.'

A counter-writ was issued on 5 June by McLean, asking the Supreme Court to order the VFL to clear him to Collingwood. With the League reluctant to act—its memories of a Supreme Court case the previous year involving a player called Silvio Foschini were still vividly etched in the minds of Hamilton and Aylett—the matter dragged on. All the while Melbourne stood firm. It would not give McLean a clearance unless Collingwood paid handsomely.

By the end of June, Macdonald and his board were under pressure. They had promised supporters they would see McLean regularly in a Collingwood guernsey and a deal had to be secured, no matter how. The board authorised Macdonald to pay Melbourne up to $120,000 for a transfer fee for McLean.

Seddon demanded $180,000 and refused to budge.

The stalemate ended when Macdonald agreed to the fee, signing a cheque for $60,000 of his own money. It was a sizeable contribution and Melbourne officials would remember it fondly for years.

'He put in $60,000 of his own money,' Seddon would say with a big smile many years later. 'His own cheque . . . Here he was, giving $60,000 which would be a major sponsorship at any other club and he couldn't tell anyone or get any credit from his club because he'd gone against his own board.'

Macdonald should have left it in the bank. Just 18 months later, in January 1986, Collingwood terminated McLean's services. His League career was over after just 44 games.

Soon after, McLean briefly explored the possibility of returning to Melbourne. 'I had a talk with Melbourne, but I realised I wasn't fair dinkum about football,' he said.

He left to embark on a career in rock 'n' roll and was never heard from in football again.

Following the Toorak luncheon at the home of Ian Rice in 1980, secret get-togethers among the presidents became the rage. There were now more businessmen getting involved as the clubs, eager to embrace the corporate world, courted company executives as a way of attracting more business.

Many of the meetings achieved little. 'They used to have wild parties and lots of cigar smoking and puffing,' one former club president would recall sarcastically years later.

On June 16, 1982, the presidents got together and, for one of the few times in memory, agreed on a common alternative. There was just one hitch. What they agreed upon was illegal.

They met at the offices of Geelong president John Holt in Albert Park. The 11 presidents and Melbourne executive director Dick Seddon (substituting for club president Sir Billy Snedden) were sitting around the table pouring out their problems to one another. It began dawning on several of them that perhaps they could no longer trust themselves to run the game of Australian football. They were too fragmented, too distrustful of one another to ever form a decent, workable partnership.

They had all heard a presentation by Allen Aylett just a few days before, urging them to work together for the good of the game, to combine their strengths and ensure football could face the hurdles likely to arise in the near future.

The meeting in Holt's office was a start. They would all agree on a complete review of the way the game was structured. The international consultancy firm, McKinsey and Co., would be called in and asked to review the game's direction and its structure. And almost all would agree in the meantime to a 'hands-off' arrangement in a bid to stem the flow of players going to court to win clearances.

Too many players and their managers, went the argument, were taking the legal road. So they agreed, in apparent defiance of the restraint of trade laws, to scale down the trading in players.

But could such a truce last? Could they trust one another?

The situation was clearly out of control. Something had to be done. Surely, argued some of the presidents, the Templeton-Moore situation could not be repeated.

A young lawyer named Jeff Browne had been enjoying significant success in recent years managing the affairs of several leading players and taking clubs to court when they refused to clear their players to another club. Now he was out hawking two of the game's most celebrated players—Kelvin Templeton and Peter Moore. A figure of $500,000 was being touted. The clubs, which had allowed men like Browne to manipulate them and play upon their fears, wanted to put a stop to it.

According to evidence Fox would give in court less than a

year later, the meeting in Holt's office resolved that all the clubs should be compensated for not chasing the players they normally would have been pursuing. A delegation was dispatched to VFL House. One of the delegates was Fox.

He told Aylett and Hamilton about the meeting at Holt's office and what decisions had been taken. He then issued the demand to the League on behalf of the clubs. Six million dollars, please. Half a million for each club. Organise it for us and we'll guarantee to keep the competition under control.

'There was no way known that could be done in terms of financial prudency,' the League's former company secretary, Greg Durham, would recall years later. 'But as always in football you're looking for compromise.'

The compromise was that the League would set up the Club Development Fund. It replaced the old ground development fund, which had seen a levy on each cash-paying patron go toward improvements on grandstands, toilets and other public facilities. Every club at the start of the following year was given $100,000 up front and, in order to meet the payments, the League increased admission prices yet again. The public would once again be asked to pay for the follies of the clubs.

Over the next three years the clubs would be guaranteed payments of more than $120,000 until the $500,000 figure was reached. But this wasn't enough for some clubs. They went out and negotiated $500,000 loans. The League's development fund payouts then went straight to the banks to service the interest of the loans.

The grand plan, however, would fail. The initial payments were made without a dollar being raised by the fund. That, estimated the League, could be recovered by the operation of the fund over the next few years. But the decline of the game's popularity soon put a halt to such ideas. The scheme was weighted on the expectation of cash-paying adults continuing to flock to the game. They didn't. By 1984 attendances were dipping alarmingly. And in effect the League's debt would grow by $3 million.

But few of the clubs seemed to mind at the time. They would worry about those problems tomorrow. Today there were flags to be won.

When they left Holt's office they all thought much had been achieved. But they hadn't counted on Lindsay Fox.

Hadn't one of them already hit the nail on the head? At another of the president's get-togethers that year, Melbourne's Sir Billy Snedden had been trying to broker a peace deal among several warring clubs. St Kilda was one of them.

'Come on Lindsay,' urged Snedden in the crowded room as the rest of the group looked on half amused. 'Show some heart, will you?'

'Don't be stupid, Billy,' piped up one of the presidents from the back of the room. 'You know he hasn't got a fuckin' heart.'

He was wrong. Fox did have a heart. It was just that where other clubs were concerned, it was made of ice. In March, 1983, in a crowded room of the Supreme Court, Lindsay Fox showed them all how cold it could be.

Silvio Foschini was living proof of the great Australian dream. His mother and father had made the trip to the new land from Italy 21 years before and now their son was one of their adopted country's best footballers.

Playing for South Melbourne at the age of 17, his introduction to senior league football had been brutal. In only his third senior match he was knocked unconscious. He had also been forced to quit Mazenod College, where he had studied for his Higher School Certificate, because he would not play for the school team, preferring to concentrate on his more lucrative league career.

He was a gifted player with an uncanny knack for kicking goals from difficult angles. With his confidence up, few could stop him. Foschini was like the steel ball in a pinball machine, ricocheting off opponents, darting through gaps, bouncing off bumps. But when South Melbourne moved to Sydney in 1982, Foschini didn't want to go. There was plenty of interest in him among other Melbourne-based clubs. Lindsay Fox's St Kilda impressed him most.

Foschini entered into an agreement with Chester Tucker, a well-known supporter of the Saints. The deal, worth $193,500 over four years, was designed to by-pass the League's anti-poaching laws. It stipulated that Foschini was to play football as directed by Tucker. It was enough for Silvio Foschini, who signed and then asked the Supreme Court to declare the League's rules invalid and a restraint of trade. The Swans had refused to clear him to St Kilda. Fox decided he would risk being declared a pariah and launch the inevitable challenge on the rules.

The case began in March 1983 as a new season started. By the time Fox was called to the stand on 22 March, he was in no mood for niceties. He wanted Foschini and was sick of being forced to run a football club on principles at odds with his belief in a free market.

At the meeting at John Holt's office the previous year, Fox told the court, a secret deal had been struck that clubs would not play footballers cleared by a court. The agreement had been kept secret, he said, because those at the meeting knew it was illegal and almost definitely a restraint of trade.

'At the time my club was looking for $500,000 because we had entered a scheme of arrangement at the end of the 1981 season,' Fox told the court. 'We were looking to clear the debt to our players and $500,000 could cover that situation.

'John Holt took the chair and related the problems of Templeton and Moore. He then went on to highlight the financial problems with the clubs and said there had to be some move by which stability and saneness would come into the stupidity of running around with the huge cost of players and transfer fees, when in essence most of the clubs were broke.'

Fox, having decided he was already on the road of no return, decided to go the full distance.

'During the meeting it was agreed any player cleared through the courts would not be played by any clubs. Eleven of the 12 people representing clubs were in total agreement. One, because of his legal background, was not prepared to vote . . .

'Dick Seddon (a solicitor) was adamant that this was part of a restraint of trade, it had some interest associated with the Trade Practices Act and accordingly it was illegal, and he was not prepared to put his name to such a situation. However, he understood the implications of it, and would respect in principle the result . . .'

Fox went on to tell the Supreme Court that, shortly after the meeting in Holt's office, he and two other presidents had gone to VFL House and told Aylett and Hamilton of the decision. 'They didn't want to know anything.'

In fact, just a few weeks before the court hearing, Fox said he had been at a birthday party in Bendigo and Aylett had asked him about the deal. 'My response was that the agreement was null and void. It had been an attempt to get some stability into the League but it finished up being quite farcical.'

A few weeks after his court appearance, Fox and Foschini won their landmark case and the League's rules were thrown open.

But it was hardly the end of the farcical player swapping that would haunt the League for much of the decade.

Several years before, a West Australian footballer named Brian Adamson had ended up in the High Court in a battle to gain a clearance from Western Australia to the Adelaide club Norwood. During the case, Mr Justice Murphy labelled the football zoning and transfer regulations of the time a system of feudal serfdom. It would be a common phrase uttered by the courts in the years to come as judgment after judgment continued to erode the legal standing of football's player rules.

But the League and its administrators acted slowly. While

everyone acknowledged the inevitability that one day the rules would be thrown out completely by the courts, little action was taken when it came to planning a response and a course of action. When Fox gave the nod for St Kilda to proceed with a Supreme Court case in a bid to win the services of Foschini, the League was caught with its pants down.

The Supreme Court ruled on Friday, 15 April, 1983, that the VFL's rules and regulations were in restraint of trade. Foschini, said Mr Justice Crockett, was entitled to play with St Kilda.

The next day Foschini ran on to VFL Park in a St Kilda jumper to take his place in the team to play Geelong. The Saints had another surprise in store for League administrators, who had spent the previous night grappling with the court decision. Running on to the ground was another former Sydney Swans player—Paul Morwood. Under the League rules, Morwood remained tied to the Swans. But St Kilda's legal advice suggested that following Mr Justice Crockett's decision, there were now no rules. The clubs, which had skirmished and battled one another in various attempts to get around the game's laws, now had what many thought they wanted: anarchy.

They didn't like it. St Kilda was instantly ostracised by the football community as it hastily constructed a standby set of regulations to get the competition through the rest of the season. Aylett and Hamilton were present at the pre-game luncheon when the news raced through the crowd that Morwood was on the field in a St Kilda jumper. 'What have you done to us?' they asked Fox. 'I'm just trying to look after the club,' he replied.

Fox was typically defiant and unrepentant. 'I was born with pressure,' he said. 'I've had no sleepless nights.'

Around the rest of the League, however, there were quite a few sleeping tablets being passed around. But for all his intentions, Lindsay Fox would not succeed.

St Kilda would finish on the bottom of the ladder again at the end of 1983, its fourth consecutive wooden spoon.

Why did football continue to defy businessmen? At almost every club which boasted a prominent identity as its president, the financial situation failed to improve.

The year after he threw the game into turmoil with the Foschini case, Lindsay Fox's St Kilda was again in trouble. In December, 1981, the club had entered into a scheme of arrangement in a bid to repay debts of $1.45 million. The scheme had been granted a five-year moratorium in which all debts would supposedly be paid off.

By the middle of 1984 the Saints were in no position to reach their target. They had suffered an operating loss of $94,000 the previous season and, with just two years left before the pay-off deadline, there was no way the scheme would succeed.

Instead, the club chose to offer its creditors up to 22.5 cents in the dollar. One of the two administrators appointed to oversee the scheme of arrangement was David Crawford, an emerging light in the insolvency field.

'If the creditors reject this as an alternative, then they are going to have to make a decision whether they want the St Kilda Football Club to liquidate,' Crawford said in 1984. 'If the club goes into liquidation it is just like any other company. It will be wound up and the assets realised.'

While trade and general creditors were offered just 7.5 cents in the dollar, the club's football creditors, including a significant number of former players, were given the option of taking 22.5 cents. To many of them, it was still a paltry offer, considering the years of service they had given the club.

One of them was perhaps the club's most legendary name from its glory year back in 1966. Barry Breen had given outstanding service to the club. True, the Saints had allowed him to continue his career until he reached the 300-game milestone. But hadn't he also repaid that debt by the blood and sweat of a career spanning a remarkable 18 years?

While no-one was happy accepting such a huge cut in the money they had worked for and been promised for so many years, the players and Allan Jeans, their premiership coach, would eventually agree to the deal. For many of them it would leave a bitter taste and a telling reminder that football was sometimes a brutal game. Like so many had discovered in the past and would continue to experience in the future, football didn't care who you were.

Breen was owed $75,000, the most among the players. He received little more than $3,000.

Ten years later, it still hurt.

'It (football) has given me a couple of beltings,' he would say one morning with a subdued voice. 'And I've probably had as good a run as anybody. I did just about everything I set out to achieve except win a best and fairest. Now, you look back. St Kilda players were the only ones not to get paid. All the problems the clubs have had since; the Swans, the Bears, Fitzroy . . . everyone still got paid.'

The players, Breen said, had agreed to the repayment scheme 'because we wanted to save the club. We could have put the boot in and said "get stuffed" and put the club into liquidation.

'But there is no recognition of the fact that we did it. I didn't get a letter from Fox saying thanks very much. There's no acknowledgment of it at all in any shape or form at the club, no acknowledgment of the sacrifices I made and the sacrifices made by a whole lot of other people owed lesser amounts. That always irks.'

The presidents had tinkered and toyed with the game, but was it any better off? Fox had, through the scheme of arrangement, saved the club from disappearing. The scheme saved it almost $1.3 million, money it could never have found. But along the way people had been hurt.

There were lessons to be learned from this, Breen lamented. 'I always say to people look, don't get bitter at the football club. Reserve your bitterness for the people who made the decisions.

'People in footy clubs always change. Only the club stays the same.'

5

THE CHANGING
OF THE GUARD

Allen Aylett was running out of time.

The 1984 season had finally dragged to a close when Essendon defeated Hawthorn in front of the smallest crowd at a grand final in almost 30 years. It was a significant rebuff to the League and the game itself. Who would have thought a few years before that only 92,685 people would bother showing up for the greatest game of them all?

The match itself had contained all the magic and excitement the game was known for, with Essendon staging a brilliant 60-point last quarter to defeat a side many regarded as the best since the Melbourne powerhouses of the 1950s. It was a victory, too, for Essendon's coach Kevin Sheedy who, more than anyone else, was intent on staging a revolution of his own on the field. For most of football's history, players had pretty much stayed in their nominated areas. Backmen stayed in the defensive half, they punched the ball away instead of going for the big spectacular mark and they were usually among the slowest and least skilful players on the ground. The centremen and wingmen were slotted into the speedy category, while the forwards were the flashy, strong type. Everyone wanted to be a forward.

Perhaps it was because he'd been consigned to the backline in his days as a player with Richmond that Sheedy was prompted to exact a little revenge. His philosophy was simple but revolutionary. Every player on the field, he believed, should be capable of playing in just about any position. He wanted a machine with interchangeable parts. You're a backman with little speed but you know how to use your elbows in a crowded pack? Work on it son, was the Sheedy creed. I want to see you kick goals.

There were other coaches who were also changing the game, too. Men like Carlton's David Parkin and Fitzroy's Robert Walls were constantly pushing it forward, demanding more speed, more power. But by far the biggest influence on the game's evolution was Sheedy. And just like Aylett and others in the game who had pushed for change, Sheedy found few people dared trust him.

But that was all right. There were flags to be won.

Yet a dismal year, perhaps the worst experienced in the League's history, was hardly over as the strains of the Essendon club song carried through the Melbourne air that night. There were still three months left in 1984 and they would prove to be among the most momentous anyone cared to remember.

Elliott's push for a breakaway league had eventually been headed off, at least for the following year. But even the most blindly loyal True Football Person could see that it would eventually happen. It was no longer a question of whether your club had the best recruiting staff anymore. So what if you had a decent centre half-forward who could kick a bag of goals each week? You were nothing unless you had money.

During the year, Michael Tilley, the League's new finance director, had compiled a confidential report on the VFL's financial crisis. He found that in the previous year the League and its 12 clubs had lost a combined $1.9 million. Six clubs— Geelong, Sydney, Fitzroy, Footscray, Collingwood and St Kilda —were technically bankrupt at the end of that season and the word 'crisis' was regularly being bandied around VFL House.

The 1984 season had seen little, if any, improvement. And Aylett's standing among the most influential clubs had continued to slide.

Men like Richmond's Ian Wilson had always disliked Aylett's handling of the job. One day Wilson had rung one of the League's key financial men asking for information on Aylett. Collingwood, too, was out there looking for some dirt.

Even Hamilton, the ultimate football politician, had endured a tough year. For a while there it had seemed Elliott's planned breakaway league might mean the end for him. And there had also been an in-depth and highly damaging investigation of the League's administration by *The Age* newspaper. One of its reports had claimed there was a high level of dissatisfaction with the VFL administration over Hamilton and Aylett's style of management.

Within days of the report a pledge of loyalty was circulated among the staff at VFL House. Each employee's name was typed on a sheet of paper, with an empty space next to it for a signature. Needless to say, each employee asked to sign complied enthusiastically.

No-one, however, asked Hamilton to pledge his loyalty to Aylett. He could not have signed his name to any such plea.

Throughout the early 1980s the League had been inundated with reports into its financial problems. There had been the report by McKinsey and Co., which had been invited to study the League's decision-making processes for a fee of $80,000 following a meeting of the club presidents back in 1982.

At the same time, mindful of how history would view his presidency, Aylett decided to produce his own report. He wanted something recorded for posterity.

'It is not hard to conclude,' he wrote, 'that unless our structural problems of player payments, player transfer regulations, grounds, club finances and the overall viability and structure of our competition are looked at seriously, and some real, on-going solutions are found, our present competition will not exist in its present form for much longer. Experience overseas has shown it is relatively easy for a professional sporting organisation to run into financial difficulties. We still have the opportunity not to make the same mistake.'

Aylett went on to recommend the formation of three independent commissions: a structure and finance commission would investigate private ownership and the introduction of new teams to the competition; a players commission would produce a workable system of player transfers and a method of ensuring player payments would rise in line with the cost of living; and a grounds commission would produce a long-term strategy for ground use in the competition and the long-thorny question of playing football on a Sunday.

But as Aylett suspected, his report was soon overshadowed by the McKinsey report. In a memorandum to the club presidents which accompanied the report, McKinsey came up with few surprising observations. But it hardly refrained from skirting around the issues either.

'The League today faces a financial crisis and increasing external pressures,' it said. 'At the current rate of growth in revenues and expenditure, the consolidated annual losses of the League could be as high as $5 million per year by 1984 . . . The financial crisis and deteriorating external relationships have developed because the management structure and decision-making processes of the League are inadequate for the game as it exists today and even less appropriate for its long-term development.

'The central representative body, the VFL Board, has never had a clear and abiding authority from the clubs to make binding decisions for controlling and developing the game. Hence, it does not have the authority to make decisions on methods of arresting the League's financial decline and the possible collapse of some clubs. The urgent challenge for the League is to develop a management process that creates the authority needed to solve the current financial crisis and make the critical decisions for the long-term future of the game.'

To meet that challenge, McKinsey and Co. recommended the

League should change its organisation structure, appoint independent task forces to address major issues and establish a 'VFL Commission' whose role would be to help resolve deadlocked decisions.

Everyone agreed with the sentiments contained in the McKinsey report. By October 1983, the League had established a task force to investigate and make recommendations on several key areas affecting the competition, including the number of teams in the competition, their location and private ownership. Within the next 12 months the task force, comprising John Kennedy, the managing director of the James Richardson group, David Mandie, a former Richmond defender, Neil Busse, the managing director of Safeway, Bill Pratt and Bob Miller, the member for Prahran and a state government appointee, also examined the decision-making processes of the League.

In August it had handed down an interim report criticising the League's decision-making processes. And in October, it delivered its recommendations.

The task force's second report contained few observations that were new. It had all been said many times before: the League's decision-making processes were deficient; the League was seen as secretive and insensitive to the needs of the supporter; the club directors, as part-time officials, faced conflicts of interest; the skills required in an organisation the size of the VFL were not there . . .

On it went. But this time the clubs did something remarkable. They took notice.

The task force had recommended that a five-member commission be set up to independently run the game, freeing the clubs to pursue their dreams of The Flag without the added burden of making decisions on the sport's future with one eye on their own prospects.

The report was presented to the clubs in the first week of

October. Aylett then headed overseas to Ireland in his role of National Football League president. The Australians were once again to play a series of 'Tests' against their Irish counterparts, once more under composite rules. Aylett had been in Ireland just a few months before, accompanying a schoolboys tour, and had quickly found out why politicians only ever travelled overseas when they were secure at home. The phone had constantly rung with supporters back in Melbourne telling him of the latest plotting; of Elliott, Macdonald and Wilson out to get him.

'I think it was a personality thing more than anything else,' Bob Ansett would say a decade later. 'Allen went through a period where he got a Rolls-Royce and it looked in the eyes of others that he was . . . there was always a strong respect for him. It was just the negative way he was doing things.'

In October in Ireland Aylett began to hear word that Hamilton was moving against him.

Aylett still wanted to stay in football. He knew the game was hanging precariously and the events of the next 12 months would have a big say in its future direction. And he hadn't been through everything over the past seven years just to disappear quietly from view now.

Aylett would claim later that one evening in Ireland he called Hamilton to keep abreast of the latest football news. Aylett suggested that, given the inevitability of the commission being formed in time for 1985, he could well become its chairman while Hamilton would occupy the post of full-time commissioner.

'I haven't decided what I'm going to do yet,' replied Hamilton, according to Aylett. 'I am not committing myself to you. I will wait and see what happens.'

But Hamilton already knew what was about to happen. During Aylett's absence he had opened a meeting of the marketing committee by declining to sit in Aylett's chair. 'That's the death chair,' he'd called it. Almost immediately an Aylett supporter at the meeting phoned the president in Ireland to relate the latest incident.

By the time he returned home, it was clear to Aylett that he no longer had the numbers for the job he wanted. Jack Hamilton might not have boasted a formidable education, but he could certainly count.

On 7 November, the clubs appointed a sub-committee to investigate the task force's recommendations. Two weeks later, Hamilton was officially appointed the game's first full-time commissioner. By then it had also become clear to Aylett that he would not even be given one of four roles as part-time commissioner of the game.

Hamilton had made it clear to the sub-committee interviewing candidates that he didn't want Aylett around and most members were inclined to agree. A process of change had begun. And by dispensing completely with Aylett they could send a strong signal that a new era was about to begin.

'It was clear to us all on the panel that he would have wanted the job,' Ansett, the chairman of the panel, recalled. 'But it was also clear that he would have accepted the job of part-time commissioner . . . (but) we felt that it needed a new break, a new direction. With it becoming increasingly clear that Jack would be the full-time commissioner, it just couldn't work with Allen as a part-time commissioner. It just wouldn't work.

'Jack was a bit of a politician in his own way. I always had a lot of respect for him. He was more of a traditionalist than Allen and slower to move . . . his general communication skills could have been better. There was a fair bit of criticism and justly so.'

A week before the sub-committee recommended the four men it believed were capable of joining with Hamilton to save football, Aylett announced his resignation as president.

'It's time I went,' he announced. 'It would be wise to break the Aylett-Hamilton partnership. If I have to bear the cross and be the scapegoat for the public image change, then that's okay by me. While I can admit to a degree of disappointment and some hurt, I have never been one to worry about the past . . .'

They were brave words but they still failed to mask the bitterness and disappointment. Aylett had sacrificed much for football. He had driven himself to the point of exhaustion many times. And he was right about being the scapegoat. If anyone would bear the blame for what happened to modern football in the years to come it would be Aylett.

As usual, the clubs and their administrators would willingly nail anyone to the cross at any opportunity. As long as it wasn't themselves.

The sub-committee set up to recommend four new part-time commissioners to join Hamilton was fully aware of the limitations of the new commissioner. Ansett was aware of internal criticisms at VFL House about Hamilton's communication skills and recognised he would need as much support as he could get.

When the four new men were announced to the press at VFL House on 12 December, no-one was in any doubt that football was about to undergo significant changes. Football writers looked at one another incredulously when the names were released. Peter Scanlon? Graeme Samuel? At least everyone recognised Peter Nixon, a former Federal Government minister. And everyone knew Dick Seddon, who had quit as Melbourne's executive director a fortnight before.

But Scanlon and Samuel? What did they know about football? Surely this was another sign of the encroachment of business into the game.

Graeme Samuel knew very little about football and absolutely nothing about its politics. But he knew a lot about many other things, particularly corporate and takeover law.

He had agreed to join the commission at the urging of Lindsay Fox. The pair had met years before when Fox struck a deal with Courage Brewing. Impressed by Samuel's analytical mind, Fox later asked him to crunch a few numbers for St Kilda on whether it would be worth the club becoming privately owned.

But if Fox was one of the few people in football to know of Samuel, there were plenty of people in the bigger world outside who knew of him.

That world of the Australian business scene was a small, club-like place where you couldn't deal for long without bumping into a familiar face. And Samuel had contacts. He had joined the law firm Phillips Fox and Masel in 1969 and had become a partner within two years, a remarkable ascension in such a short space of time. Awarded the firm's corporate practice, he had been sent to London to work with a merchant bank to gain more experience.

By the early 1980s, merchant banking had lured Samuel away from the law firm. He took over as corporate adviser with Hill Samuel Australia, which would later become the Macquarie Bank. There he met John Gerahty, another man completely unknown to football who would play a strategic role in its affairs by the end of the decade.

Samuel was a player. The only black mark in his copybook was a word that seemed to accompany him whenever his name was raised—arrogance. Samuel had an aggressive, in-your-face style and while no-one doubted his brilliance in getting the job done, they sometimes wondered whether he could have done it in a softer fashion.

Samuel, who had advised on some of Australia's biggest corporate takeovers during the early 1980s, and who would go on to play a pivotal role in helping BHP stop Robert Holmes à Court's takeover attempt in 1986, was aware he had a problem. But he would never quite work out how to solve it. Years later he would admit it was a negative trait.

'I've had this in almost every walk of life,' he would say. 'If you could tell me how not to be arrogant and to get the thing done, I'd do it.'

Of all the part-time commissioners, Samuel would be the only one to last the distance into the mid-1990s. It was typical of his style. He had come into the game knowing little about it, and understanding even less its bizarre politics, alliances and personalities. But he would work hard at it. And in the end the football world would give Samuel grudging entry into the world of football administration. They would treat his comments and decisions with the same amount of distrust and suspicion they accorded anyone else.

Peter Scanlon was also a big name on the corporate scene. He was one of the original 'gang of four' who, in concert with John Elliott, Bob Cowper and Richard Wiesener, helped create the industrial giant Elders.

He had met Elliott while studying commerce at Melbourne University. A year below Elliott, he served eight years at Heinz, becoming the group's general manager for marketing, before Elliott introduced him to the gang taking over the jam maker Henry Jones IXL.

Elliott had pushed for his inclusion on the commission after a former colleague of Scanlon's at Heinz had raised his name with the sub-committee as a likely candidate.

The sub-committee immediately warmed to Scanlon, particularly when Ansett interviewed him over a cup of coffee. Scanlon, decided the sub-committee, was a genuine Football Person. And while they needed someone with strengths in the marketing area, his football background would certainly help win him support among the clubs.

Scanlon had grown up in a football household. He had loved and followed the game all his life. His father Jack had been captain-coach of the VFA club Coburg and a day rarely passed without the game cropping up in conversation around the dinner table. Scanlon went on to play amateur football and kept following the game from a distance as he set about establishing a sizeable personal fortune.

When he was approached to join the commission he was aware the game had lost its way, but he had no idea by how much. He thought the game no longer knew what it stood for, but he had been around football long enough to understand how it had happened.

When he took up the position on the commission, he discovered a competition that had been changing in pieces for many years. But everyone had been too concerned with the latest change; no-one had gone back and looked at all the changes in a historical perspective. Perhaps they did not have the time. Many of the people in the game were volunteers. They barely had enough time to get the most basic of tasks completed.

Scanlon could see many more changes were required before the VFL could be taken off the critical list and nursed back to health. Along the way he, too, would be welcomed into football's brotherhood. And perhaps more than anyone else, Peter Scanlon would, for some time, become the most feared man in the game.

Peter Nixon's talents were well-known. He was one of politics' hard men, the sort of man sent by the party leader to get a job done. But even he would be astonished at times by the ferocity of the bickering within the game. But if he ever had a problem, he only had to look as far as Dick Seddon.

The four names nominated by the sub-committee were accepted with little dissent. But predictably, the clubs were not prepared to give away entirely the power they had held for more than 80 years. Ignoring a recommendation by the task force that the commission be totally autonomous, it was instead appointed for 12 months and had no power over which clubs could be excluded or included. The board of directors maintained control over policy and strategy of the competition.

It was, noted Aylett, a halfway house. 'I believe in change and more independent thinking by people not aligned with club parochialism,' he said, not for the first time. 'The really hard decisions should be made by people with independence.'

As the commission soon discovered, there were plenty of

hard decisions to be made. And as they prepared to take over in their official roles in February, 1985, one of the first hard decisions was already looming: the possible sale of the Sydney Swans.

It would be the first serious test of the commission's business acumen and talent. Its performance would leave a lot to be desired.

6

THE SWANS' SONG (I)

Barry Lyons was a stranger in a strange land. For years he had lived in a comfortable little world where there were rules and laws to be obeyed and people to be respected.

But as he sat in a Westpac bank office receiving a stern lecture from a branch manager his old world seemed far away. Maybe he had just been dreaming? All those years of working in public utilities like Telecom and Australia Post; safe, protected environments where people did weird things, like paying their bills on time. They even signed agreements and stuck to them.

And now here he was, just a few months into a job in football administration with the old South Melbourne club. And already he was being reprimanded on how badly his club was being run. Terrible, muttered the bank manager. How could people be so irresponsible when it came to money?

Lyons stared back at the man. Irresponsible? No. Just wait, he found himself saying to the bank manager. Have patience, please. The club is about to move permanently to Sydney, to capture foreign territory, to carve out a historic place in Australian football's promised land.

Lyons fed him the hype. And finally the manager handed over what he wanted: a cheque for $500,000. It was near the end of 1982. Most of the players had not been paid for the season and, having played 11 of their matches in Sydney, were growing increasingly bitter and cynical. The club's plans to shift the players permanently to Sydney in the coming months would receive a significant boost if its players could have some spending money over Christmas.

So Lyons clutched the cheque tightly as he caught a tram back to the club's office. Everyone gathered and stared at the cheque as though it was a holy relic or even a premiership cup, something the Swans had not seen since 1933. Had anyone seen a sum so large?

Lyons gave the cheque to the office boy to deposit in the club's local bank acocunt. The kid stuffed it into his leather jacket and disappeared as Lyons and a weary-looking Swans accountant sat down and began the happy task of writing cheques to the players.

Within 30 minutes the kid was back in the office looking sheepish. Somewhere as he made his way on his motorbike to the bank, the cheque had fallen out of his jacket, fluttering away forever in the breeze.

The accountant simply stared at the kid in disbelief. Lyons picked up the phone and dialled the bank manager who, just a couple of hours earlier, had been lecturing him on the financial irresponsibility of the club.

'Um, we've lost the cheque . . .' Lyons said. 'Do you think you could cancel it and give us a new one?'

More than 10 years later, a wry tone would work its way into Lyons' voice. 'That didn't sort of enhance our reputation,' he observed.

Just what was a man like Barry Lyons doing in football? He had been involved with amateur clubs for years. And when a man he had worked with at Australia Post called John Hennessy joined the VFL as its corporate strategist, Lyons' interest increased. Football administration. It sounded like a dangerous undercover job compared to the staid, predictable world of Telecom.

Hennessy tipped him off in late 1982 that a job was available with the Swans and he should ring the club's general manager, Brian Dixon, the former Victorian minister for sport.

Lyons won a post as administration manager and joined a club that was rapidly heading into an abyss of the League's making. At the end of 1981, the VFL board had agreed to a request by the South Melbourne Football Club that it play its 11 home games in Sydney the following season. The move sparked a bitter and very public fight between the club's staunch supporters and those like Allen Aylett, who believed the dream of conquering the entire country was now within reach.

In 1980, Hennessy had prepared a confidential 34-page report titled 'The Sydney Solution—VFL at the crossroads.' The report, which recommended the establishment of a team in Sydney, forecast that a Sydney-based club could earn a surplus of $750,000 after its first three years and that average crowds would increase from 17,500 in the first year to 20,000.

The League had cautiously tested the market in Sydney over a number of years, scheduling up to four games a season by 1979. There were several reasons behind the move, one of them being fears that the Victorian market was close to saturation point in the race for sponsorship and corporate dollars. As well, unless the League went national, or at least moved into the lucrative Sydney market, it could not hope to increase the value of its television rights.

And there was also football's empirical belief. It was a variation on the colonial notion of white supremacy. Australian rules was the best game in the world. It was the right game. Therefore, everyone in the country would embrace it if only they were given a chance. Besides, what opposition was there in Sydney anyway? The rugby league, that untidy game played by men with necks thicker than their heads, was struggling by the end of the 1970s, beset by financial and image problems. In fact, no-one really understood why football had died away in the country's biggest city. At the turn of the century the game had been all the rage. But by the time of World War I it had all but disappeared.

Aylett had never disguised his desire for a club in Sydney. But not everyone inside League headquarters shared his dream.

When it became obvious that South Melbourne's financial problems were not going to improve—its plight was exacerbated by being located in a suburb filled with an ageing and unshifting population—the League had begun seriously investigating the Sydney option.

Company secretary Ralph Lane was asked to crunch the figures on the Sydney market. 'I was asked to do some projections on what their income might be and how they'd fare up there, and when I did, it didn't show a very good or satisfactory position at all.'

By 1982 the die was cast. South Melbourne became the Swans and the 'new' club, boosted by a $400,000 loan from the VFL, was launched at an extravagant party at the Sydney Opera House. The League and its president had seen the future of the game and its name was expansion.

As usual, when a job needed to be done, Aylett used a man he could trust to get the job done. Graham Huggins, the former St Kilda president and a close number-cruncher for Aylett, had paved the way in Sydney, examining the marketing opportunities and logistical problems needed to be overcome for a VFL club in the country's largest city. And then another trusted colleague, Jim McKay, visited the Swans players at a training session at the old Lakeside Oval just weeks before the club was relaunched in Sydney. And as usual, Jimmy McKay was selling hard.

He looked the players in the eye and told them the move to Sydney could see them become overnight sensations. 'I told them that if they played their cards right they could establish their futures to a degree they could never have imagined. They will be the only major team in the largest football competition in Australia, playing in a city of four million people. In Melbourne, 300 players all have to compete to become famous.'

The Swans went on to win 12 games in 1982 and at one stage looked a chance to play in the finals before their form dropped. But there was one bonus. The club overpowered North Melbourne in the final of the League's night championship series, capturing the $105,000 first prize. The future, it seemed, was assured.

But off the field the outlook was not as appealing. It was clear very early in the year that the League's optimistic projections were just that. By early July, the club had already asked for a deferment of its first repayment of $150,000 on the $400,000 loan and had begun lobbying the other 11 clubs to accept a reduction in their guaranteed $20,000 for making the trip north to play matches.

The club's board was also in turmoil. One of its directors, Kevin Campbell, resigned after authoring an internal report that warned the club was on the verge of bankruptcy. Campbell believed that low gate returns (the Swans were picking up less than $8000 a game), the cost of being a club effectively based in two cities and an escalation in player payments had all contributed toward the club's financial plight.

'. . . the South Melbourne Club Ltd is a production-oriented organisation with no marketing expertise and little interest in financial controls,' he wrote.

But no-one listened. Instead, Campbell was attacked from within and resigned to save the club another internal upheaval. Despite all the comforting noises emanating from Aylett and Hamilton, the world at large was not welcoming Australian football with open arms.

'Dear Sir,' wrote Brian Dixon, the Swans' executive director, in a letter to the credit manager of CIGS Nominees on 2 December 1982.

'The club is presently experiencing liquidity problems. As a result of these problems, the directors of the club are unable to discharge the debt owing to you immediately, but propose to do so within the forthcoming six months.'

It was a familiar letter in the lead-up to Christmas and Barry Lyons wondered what in hell he had got himself into. The club was beset by financial difficulties and Dixon was not winning any friends either as he set about the difficult task of convincing the players they all had to shift to Sydney the following year if the club was to make a success out of the move.

Within six months Dixon had been sacked and Lyons took over as general manager.

It was a difficult year. The novelty of a VFL side had faded for the fickle Sydney public and attendances slumped by 40,000. A scheme of arrangement for creditors was introduced. The League ploughed even more money into the club, with loans totalling almost $1.5 million. In May the VFL effectively took control of the club, appointing a new eight-man board. Six of the eight would be VFL administrators, including Aylett, Hamilton and his deputy, Alan Schwab. Only two members of the previous board—Michael Edgley and John Keogh, were retained.

The newspapers were filled with endless speculation on the future of the club. Administrators with several other clubs began murmuring about the long-term viability of the Swans. How much more money could the League expect to put into the club, just to keep its vision of a team in Sydney alive?

Aylett remained undaunted. Was there no end to his unbridled optimism? With the Swans' debts estimated at almost $2 million, he went on the offensive. He claimed that by 1992 there would be two teams playing out of Sydney.

'I don't think it's out of the question because of the great spectator appeal of Australian football,' he said. 'And of course, as a by-product we're going to see unbelievable increases in sponsorships and properties and TV rights like we see now in the US and other parts of the world.'

Watching events in Sydney closely in 1983 was John Elliott and his company Elders. They had already done some preliminary sums. Could they buy the Swans? They would need to pay out $1.6 million in debts, buy 1800 members' tickets at $40 apiece and were looking at another five or six million to inject into the club over the next five years to make it a going concern.

Preliminary discussions were held with the League. But in the end the plan was dropped. Elliott would move on to Carlton. But he would not forget the Swans. And in 10 years' time he would renew his interest in taking over the club.

Could the Swans be saved? By 1984 the signs finally became encouraging. The team won six of its first nine games and seemed to be on its way to the finals. The financial problems had eased and Sydney people were once again taking notice. By round 10, more than 26,000 people crowded into the Sydney Cricket Ground to see the side take on Carlton.

Lyons couldn't believe it. The Swans were the flavour of the month. At the traditional pre-match luncheon, staged to appease sponsors and prominent members, it seemed almost everyone in Sydney was present. 'Every freeloader in Australia was there jumping on the bandwagon,' Lyons would recall later.

Politicians, celebrities, television personalities; they were all there. Among them, too, was a quietly-spoken and shy doctor with an entrepreneurial bent. His name was Geoffrey Edelsten and he had become a regular at Swans matches. He owned a string of medical clinics around the city, all of them notable for their 24-hour service, plush reception and waiting areas and a piano in the lobby.

Edelsten had bought two special membership tickets at $5,000 each. Normally, businessmen who bought such tickets paid for the ticket at the start of each season. But Edelsten struck a deal with the club to pay his membership fee in instalments of about $900 a month. It was an arrangement that struck Barry Lyons as slightly peculiar. People who could afford to buy such high-priced tickets rarely needed to put them on lay-buy.

Lyons was, of course, happy to take Edelsten's cash in whatever way he could. But the method of payment struck him as bizarre, given the doctor's reputation for wealth. It was a subject that Lyons and Huggins discussed regularly.

'It did indicate to me that he wasn't exactly flushed with cash,' Lyons would say. 'Huggins and I used to be quite happy. But we talked about it. How unusual it was.'

Still, what did it really matter? Money was money, after all. And the Swans were on a winning streak, weren't they? But as usual, trouble wasn't very far from the club.

They lost the game against Carlton, copping a hiding of 52 points. Then they lost the following week to Essendon. Then Melbourne beat them. And St Kilda.

It was a remarkable slide. Barry Round, the club's veteran ruckman, was dropped after 314 games. But he did not take it quietly. He would not play in the reserves, he announced. He was retiring. And then coach Ricky Quade was bundled off to hospital with a reported bleeding ulcer. Rumours flooded the game. The club denied them. Truth in football was a regular casualty.

Barry Round and Quade were locked in a personal dispute that went far beyond the borders of the game. It culminated in the week of Round's axing from the team. At training on the Thursday night, an incident between the pair left Quade with a blackened eye. Within days Quade resigned. Round was eventually restored to the senior side late in the season but by then it was too late.

The Swans had gone nowhere again. Clearly, if a club was to survive and succeed in Sydney, something extraordinary had to take place.

During 1984, as the Swans began their slide to 10th place on the ladder, Bob Pritchard was in Toronto working on behalf of

Kerry Packer. Pritchard was a marketing man and worked with the Packer-owned PBL which, among other things, controlled the marketing of Australian cricket. He had been involved in the packaging of cricket following the end of Packer's World Series Cricket revolution in the late 1970s and now he was in Canada helping to produce a rock video clip.

PBL's main interest in the project was a 3-D camera which it believed could revolutionise the television industry. Also involved in the project was a company called Concert Productions International. One of its partners was Bob Ballard, the part-owner of a couple of Canadian professional sporting teams.

Pritchard went along to several baseball games with Ballard and they got to talking about the Australian sports scene. It was completely different from the US, Pritchard explained. For instance, there was no private ownership of clubs.

Ballard was surprised. He believed club sport went nowhere. Private ownership and stock ownership, he told Pritchard, was the only way to go. The Dallas Cowboys franchise in the National Football League would become an example Pritchard would use to bolster his argument over the next decade. In the early 1960s, 'America's Team' had been worth $200,000. Within 20 years, the value of the franchise had leaped to $200 million. Why couldn't the same thing occur in Australia, asked Pritchard, albeit on a smaller scale?

The discussions with Ballard had a pivotal effect on Pritchard. They would, within just a few months, prove to be the catalyst that would trigger one of the most remarkable periods in Australian sport.

There was no better example of the separate species of mankind known as Marketing Man than Pritchard. He was a flashy dresser with a love of chunky jewellery. His hair was always carefully in place; he wore the most fashionable suits. And when he began the hard sell, few people could withstand the onslaught without succumbing.

He arrived back in Sydney from his Toronto trip armed with a 25-page proposal of why private ownership of a sporting team could be a tremendous investment. Ballard had written most of the document himself and it argued strongly for the privatisation of sporting clubs. Bob Pritchard was a convert. And he had someone in mind. Surely Kerry Packer, Australia's richest man, could spare a few million dollars? All Pritchard had to do was find a club.

One afternoon in November, 1984, Barry Lyons was taken to lunch at a pub in The Rocks in Sydney by a couple of sportswriters. It was a farewell of sorts. The League had just appointed a former South Australian football administrator, Don Roach, as the club's executive director and Lyons, feeling hemmed in, had resigned and intended returning to Melbourne. He'd had enough of football administration for the time being and the year just finished had been extraordinarily long. The problems between Round and Quade had only added to the pressure.

While they were having lunch, Lyons was introduced to Pritchard, who was there on separate business. They got talking. Lyons had been wondering for some time what it would cost to buy the Swans. He'd even made the odd call to see whether there was enough interest in the business community to put together a package to buy the club. Given its debts, he figured it could be bought for a song. He outlined his theory to Pritchard and found a willing listener. Bob Pritchard had just found what he had been looking for.

But Packer wasn't interested. Pritchard's proposal had been sent to the Boss and he sent word back that it did little to excite him. Pritchard remained undeterred.

He had been reading the papers and, like most people, had seen Geoff Edelsten's name crop up on more than one occasion. Edelsten was in the midst of changing the way the medical profession marketed itself to the public and his flamboyant approach had, naturally, attracted the media.

Pritchard and Edelsten went back a long way, but hadn't seen one another for almost 20 years. Back in the 1960s, Pritchard had tried launching himself as a pop singer. While he failed to go on and become an Australian music legend, he did record a single, 'Pretty Girl'. The song was produced by Edelsten, who was then just 23 and producing records as a side-interest. Pritchard would forever remember him as the man who took a chance on his musical career. Now he wondered if Edelsten was prepared to take another.

The doctor was interested. They talked about how much it might cost and Edelsten rang Lyons to ask him about the true financial position of the Swans and the process they might face if a bid was made.

But neither Edelsten nor Pritchard knew anyone at VFL House. Lyons was going back to Melbourne so he would be of little use. And then Pritchard remembered the name of a guy he'd come across a few times in the marketing world. Jim McKay. He was still working with the League and, from what Pritchard had heard, making a handsome amount of money. He knew everyone, too. Maybe he could help.

In early December, McKay flew to Sydney and had breakfast with Edelsten and Pritchard at the Regent hotel. There, the trio hatched the genesis of a plan that would transform the Swans and that would, eventually, prove to be one of the greatest financial disasters in the history of the game.

Just like the Swans, Edelsten had experienced a tough 1984. His medical centres had achieved a lot of publicity and his reputation as a millionaire-cum-entrepreneur was also growing. But he had significant problems, too. And one of them earlier in the year was a disgruntled patient who had been harassing him for some time.

Edelsten wanted to get the patient off his back. At about 10.50am on Sunday 15 April, Edelsten spoke to his young wife, Leanne, on his car phone. She was at home at their

16-room mansion in Dural. Unbeknown to either of them, their conversation was being taped by Rex Beaver, an electronics buff who lived in Sydney's western suburbs and who had made a habit of taping people's conversations on mobile telephones.

Leanne asked Edelsten if he had spoken to anyone for advice.

'Yes, I did. And he was the one that said that he thought that he (the disgruntled ex-patient) was very dangerous and odd and um, I ought to get someone to bash his brains out.'

'Head beaten around, broken nose and broken arm and broken leg.'

'Yeah, that's right.'

'So that he's out of action for a little while.'

'Um.'

'So that he'd think twice about it.'

'Mm'

'Will he do it?'

'Pardon?'

'This bloke?'

'Oh, this bloke will do it for ten grand.'

'I don't know.'

'Maybe if I asked him he wouldn't charge you ten grand.'

'Oh I think he would.'

'You think?'

'Well, I helped him, em, he just said he doesn't drop his price for anybody and that's it. He said "I'm a professional—it's my livelihood."'

'Beating people up? Is that all he does?'

'No. He kills people.'

'Does he?'

'Yeah. Nice young fella. But ah, I think he's a professional killer.'

Edelsten had, in fact, met this professional killer earlier in the year when he operated on him to remove a tattoo. The man was Christopher Dale Flannery and he was due to be tried for murder. But three days before the trial was scheduled, Edelsten operated on Flannery. That night, Flannery was admitted to hospital and his trial was subsequently adjourned to later in the year when, two days into the trial, the jury was directed to enter a verdict of not guilty.

It was not the only unsavoury episode from Edelsten's past. In 1977 he had invested a large sum—reportedly $500,000—in the Centrefold night-club in George Street. But it opened without obtaining a liquor licence and eventually the enterprise crashed. One company associated with the venture petitioned Edelsten for bankruptcy, alleging it was still owed more than $100,000. But following an out-of-court settlement the bankruptcy petition was withdrawn and soon after Edelsten went to the US to try his hand on the West Coast.

Even there it seemed Edelsten had a hard time keeping business out of court. One of his companies, Preventicare Inc, was involved in litigation in the Superior Court of California and Edelsten had $US935,000 awarded against him.

He stayed in California for only 18 months before returning to embark on his dream of building a medical empire the likes of which had never been seen in Australia. By 1984 he had achieved a great deal. But there were signs that his image was not all it was cracked up to be. Barry Lyons had seen that when Edelsten began his payment scheme for a membership ticket.

Despite the allegations that would come later, Edelsten was a devoted follower of Australian football. He had grown up in Melbourne and followed Carlton as a boy, living close to the ground. When his business and medical career began to improve, he had also sponsored Carlton's cheer squad, the Bluebirds.

Yes, being associated with the Swans as its new owner would undoubtedly assist his business profile, particularly with his plan to expand his medical empire into Melbourne. What better publicity could one hope to attract in Victoria than being associated with a footy club?

By the time the new VFL commission was in place, Edelsten, Pritchard and McKay had put together a proposal to buy the club and lodged it with Jack Hamilton. Within days the news had been leaked to the press and then, a week later, it seemed everyone wanted to buy the club.

Basil Sellers, a Sydney businessman with close links to the new part-time commissioner, Peter Scanlon, had declared his hand. Sellers would be crucial in driving the price up. Behind Sellers was an impressive array of business talent including another Scanlon associate, John Gerahty. And then one of Melbourne's leading businessmen, Richard Pratt, also decided to put in a bid.

The race was on. Pritchard, Edelsten and McKay met to discuss strategy. Edelsten would recall years later that he paid McKay $50,000 as a consultant and he would be worth every cent. Through him the trio would attract other key football identities. Allen Aylett would become a consultant following his departure from the VFL.

The Edelsten camp was not averse to paying well. In the coming 12 months, Pritchard would negotiate a lucrative deal with Edelsten. 'I was on a good screw,' he would admit with relish a decade later. His tax bill alone would amount to more than $180,000 in just one year and the doctor would also buy him a two-door Mercedes coupé for $125,000.

Pritchard had a lot of time for Edelsten, although he says he was unaware at the time of the doctor's financial and legal problems. But both he and McKay realised that Edelsten's flamboyant image would need to be massaged and hyped even further if they were to beat the more solid, conservative bid of the Sellers group.

'He was already a flamboyant character, but he wasn't getting the press we thought he needed,' Pritchard would say later. 'The only thing people in Sydney understand is, if you like, "flash trash". We decided we'd market the hell out of Edelsten as a personality.

'Within three months he became a superstar. The deal was essentially that he'd put in the money and I'd run the marketing and then he'd do what he was told.'

Pritchard was still with PBL, but now the task of winning the licence to own the Swans became a full-time occupation. The phone never stopped ringing and when it did, Pritchard and McKay were dialling out, rustling up the numbers, calling the press. McKay, because of his close links to the League, kept a much quieter profile, leaving the public statements to Pritchard and Edelsten.

Pritchard: 'As soon as Dick Pratt stuck his hand up, I think we must have had three weeks solid of sending out faxes saying what does a Melbourne guy know about a Sydney team? We pushed that barrow as hard as we could. Funnily enough, no-one came up with the fact that both Edelsten and I came from Melbourne.'

Everyone was told to think pink. The media were invited to look at Edelsten's latest 'pink car.' It was 'mink-lined', Pritchard boasted to the hacks. He made sure no-one got close enough to feel it. Fake fur was fairly easily identifiable once you had it in your hand.

They would double-park Edelsten's car outside the Regent, outside a night-club, outside anywhere where it might attract publicity. There was talk of a pink helicopter. There were other largesses, most of them figments of the fertile imaginations of Pritchard and McKay. The media lapped it up.

Clearly, Pritchard could not keep working with PBL. The company took him to lunch one day in an effort to keep him, telling him that private ownership of a football club would never work. And then they laid the heavy bit on him.

'It's still not too late to change your mind,' a senior PBL executive told Pritchard. 'One of the things with Packer is that once you leave, you LEAVE. Don't think you'll be able to come back.'

Why would Pritchard want to come back? He was on a good

thing. He and Geoff Edelsten were going to win the licence to run the Sydney Swans. They'd turn the club into a profitable operation, everyone would make money and the club would be successful for the first time in more than 50 years. What could possibly go wrong?

Jack Hamilton's secretary put the call through to the new commissioner. It was the Monday before Easter, a traditionally busy time in football, and Hamilton was just a few months into his new role. Already there was a mountain of paperwork building on his desk. And it wasn't like the old days, either. There was no sweeping the stack into the bin. These new commissioners, particularly Scanlon, were sharp businessmen. They didn't miss much.

On the phone was David Wilson, an investigative reporter with *The Age* newspaper. Wilson told Hamilton that the paper had been given several sensitive documents relating to Edelsten which it could not publish but which might have an impact on Edelsten's bid.

Hamilton was interested. There had, of course, been rumours circulating about Edelsten ever since he announced his bid. But the commission had no way of knowing whether those rumours could be substantiated. Hamilton told Wilson to meet him behind a tree in a nearby park.

A tree? Wilson was bemused. He was unaware it was a favourite meeting place of Hamilton's, particularly when he didn't want anyone else to know what he was doing.

There, along with another executive from *The Age*, Hamilton read the documents and, alarmed, agreed to get the commission together to look at them.

Hamilton then spoke to a lawyer for *The Age*, Peter Bartlett, regarded as one of the finest defamation lawyers in the country. Bartlett had discussed the issue with Wilson and the paper's editor, Creighton Burns. Was it in the public interest to let the VFL see the documents?

They'd eventually agreed it was. Bartlett and Burns were extremely conscious of the need for confidentiality. Had Edelsten known what was transpiring, he could have taken legal action. So a meeting was set up for Good Friday when the city was deserted. They would meet at Bartlett's office at Gillotts (now Minter Ellison), a firm of solicitors in Collins Street.

The new commission arrived and after a briefing from Burns on the need for confidentiality, Wilson spoke for more than 30 minutes, outlining the nature of the material.

The documents were wide-ranging and damaging. Among them was the transcript of Edelsten's conversation with Leanne about Flannery. There were crime intelligence reports from the Bureau of Criminal Intelligence, fed by federal police operatives in California during Edelsten's 18-month sojourn on the west coast of the United States.

None of it, however, was in a publishable form and little could be substantiated had Edelsten been tackled in court. Peter Nixon aggressively questioned the three newspaper representatives. Hamilton asked the odd question. And the rest of the commission sat quietly, read what was in front of them and then left, having barely said a word.

A month later, and just four weeks before the clubs voted on which bid to accept for the Swans, Wilson rang Hamilton and asked him where the commission stood. Hamilton was adamant. He'd been shocked by what he had seen. There was no way Geoff Edelsten would become the first man to privately own an Australian football club.

Wilson was confident enough, on the basis of Hamilton's briefing, to go with a strong story headlined 'Edelsten bid for Swans doomed; Sellers to get the nod.'

But what Jack Hamilton thought and wanted wasn't necessarily what would happen anymore.

Throughout May and June of 1985, the bidding process for the Sydney Swans dominated football talk. Who would buy the

Swans? Would it be Edelsten, the flamboyant entrepreneur? Or Sellers, the 'mystery' man who rarely spoke publicly and provided little information on his bid or the members who made up his consortium?

There was a good reason behind Sellers's low profile. He had withdrawn from the race. As Edelsten kept upping the ante, Sellers kept going back to his figures. There was simply no way the club could break even, he believed, if a buyer had to pay that much up front. By now, Edelsten was 'offering' $6.3 million, a ludicrous fee which, in reality, was worth only $2.7 million in hard cash. The rest would come in development funding and other payments already scheduled for the next five years.

Sellers had contacted Scanlon, who was by now emerging as the most influential figure on the commission. To those around him, it seemed Hamilton had already aligned himself closely to Scanlon and was relying on him more and more for advice and guidance.

Sellers told Scanlon he was withdrawing. Fine, said Scanlon, who knew a sound business decision when he saw one. Just do the commission one favour: don't tell anyone you've withdrawn.

The League still wanted to milk Edelsten for as much as it could get. It had already commissioned the firm of Touche Ross to investigate his financial condition and whether he did indeed have the money he claimed. If that report gave him the thumbs down, or if new information came to light indicating Edelsten was an unfit and improper person to control the club, they could always go back to Sellers.

After the meeting on Good Friday, the commission had decided it needed more advice and had asked Hamilton to approach the Victorian police commissioner, Mick Miller. According to commission members later, Miller had told Hamilton to ignore the documentation shown to them by *The Age*. The Bureau of Criminal Intelligence had files on many people, he said. But much of it could be hearsay. You could only go on what you had at the time.

The commission, however, found itself in an awkward position. Scanlon and Samuel had both disqualified themselves in May when Edelsten claimed they were too closely linked with Sellers. While they continued to have significant input at commission meetings, they could do little publicly when it came to the bidding process. And all around them were the signs that something was definitely not quite right with the doctor.

On 30 May *The National Times* reported that Edelsten was no stranger to controversy. 'He is under investigation by several Commonwealth agencies at present,' revealed the award-winning reporter Colleen Ryan, 'including the Director of Public Prosecutions (who is interested in where Dr Edelsten gets his money); the Australian Federal Police and the Commonwealth Health Department.

'Other Government agencies who have encountered Dr Edelsten include the Australian Taxation Office, which has attempted to wind up two of his companies, and the Corporate Affairs Commission, which has prosecuted five Edelsten companies a total of 10 times in recent years for failure to lodge documents and has four current matters outstanding against the doctor's companies.'

Yet even this was not enough, apparently, for the commission. Pritchard and McKay had decided on a strategy of announcing enormous bids for the Swans in an effort to scare off other suitors. Now, it appeared to have also affected the commission. The clubs were receiving regular letters from Edelsten telling them how he was interested in their welfare. A big fee for the Swans meant more money distributed to the cash-starved Victorian clubs. How then, could the commission recommend against Edelsten?

In early July, Touche Ross reported to the commission that 'we are of the opinion that Dr Edelsten has the capacity to fund the proposed financial committments.'

Edelsten and the clubs anticipating a financial windfall were not the only ones to breathe deeply. McKay and Pritchard were also extremely relieved men. Their front man had been investigated by one of the world's leading financial and management consultants. And if they could find no wrong, then surely the rumours about the good doctor could finally be laid to rest. In the following years, senior League officials would shake their heads in disbelief.

Edelsten's Dural mansion was packed on 31 July. There seemed to be people in every room of the house and the house had a lot of damn rooms. There were reporters and photographers, television cameramen and sound men, publicity flacks and a general assortment of hangers-on.

The phone finally rang. It was Commissioner Hamilton. Congratulations, he told Edelsten. You now own the Sydney Swans.

The champagne flowed and backs were slapped. They'd felt all along they could get up and now all the hard work, the number crunching, the interminably dumb questions from the football press . . . everything had been worth it. The clubs had readily grabbed Edelsten's cash. In the end, the commission had brought a white board into the board room and divided it in two. On the left side it wrote in Edelsten's bid. On the right, Sellers's final bid. It was, of course, no contest.

And now the celebrations were well underway. Pritchard had achieved his dream. Edelsten was now more famous than he could have ever imagined. And Jim McKay had once again added to his reputation as a man who could get things fixed in football.

But about an hour into the celebratory party, Edelsten asked Pritchard to meet him in a bedroom upstairs. They closed the door and sat on the edge of the bed.

The moment would remain forever etched in Pritchard's memory. 'We're sitting there on the bed and he says, "mate, there's something I've really got to tell you. The only problem is I don't have a dime. I have no fucking money whatsoever. So now we have to go out there tomorrow and find someone with the dough."

'I said "Jesus, I've already been through all that".'

Pritchard, however, would not have to endure the agony of finding someone with money to invest in a football club. Instead, they would come to him. He just wouldn't know about it until it was too late.

Edelsten had done business with many men over the years. One of them was a public accountant from Perth, Robert Nichevich. He was the major shareholder in a small public company with the name of Westeq Ltd.

Edelsten had been shopping around looking for an investor to help him expand the medical clinics. During one meeting, Edelsten excused himself. He had to rush off for a meeting concerning the Swans. Nichevich was interested. He introduced Edelsten to two partners, Phillip Grimaldi and Bob Coghill.

By the time Edelsten was due to make his second instalment of $250,000 to the VFL on 5 September, Westeq had agreed to fund it. The doctor had at last found what he'd been looking for.

At least, that is what he thought. But Westeq, which had only joined the stock exchange in 1983, had visions of something much more. Grimaldi, Coghill and others drove a hard bargain with Edelsten. In return for their money, his shareholding in the venture would be slashed. The first thing Pritchard, who had set up a company called Powerplay to run the enterprise, knew about Westeq was when he was called to a meeting in the office of Grimaldi.

'I got called into his office one day and I'd never met him before and he said 'We're the new owners of the Swans' . . . I went from 25 per cent to 5 per cent in two and a half minutes,' he would say later. 'They told me they still wanted me to stay

111

as chief executive, but that Geoff was not going to have much to do with the club. He'd be a figurehead.

'They were all accountants. They weren't keen on all the Edelsten stuff. The idea was to float the thing and raise money. They didn't like the idea of pink helicopters . . .'

While his shareholding had been cut significantly, Edelsten remained undeterred. He was the public face of the Sydney Swans. And the club would still need him if it hoped to be successful. And besides, not even the VFL Commission knew who really owned the Swans.

Bob Ansett, the North chairman, had taken the call from Edelsten and was mildly surprised that the new owner of Sydney wanted to drop by the Budget office in Melbourne for a coffee and a chat.

He arrived one afternoon. The pair exchanged pleasantries before Ansett asked him the purpose of the visit.

Edelsten reached into his bag and pulled out a cheque book. He scribbled away without saying anything and then handed it over to Ansett.

The cheque was written out to the North Melbourne Football Club. It was for $1 million. Ansett had seen a variety of opening gambits in business before. But nothing like this.

'This is nice,' replied Ansett. 'What do you want? Budget? North Melbourne?'

'I want the Krakouer boys,' smiled Edelsten. Jim and Phil Krakouer, two Aboriginal brothers from Western Australia, were gifted footballers who had set the League alight in recent years with a combination of skill and an uncanny ability to always be in the right place at the right time.

But no-one would have suggested they were worth anywhere near $1 million. Ansett declined. Some of his closest advisers at the club would say later it was the worst decision he ever made, but Ansett had his reasons. North was experiencing financial problems and, while $1 million would have easily solved them, it could also have ripped the soul out of the club. He needed the Krakouers more than money at that time. Without them, he could not have marketed the club at all.

Marketing. It was now the buzz word around the League and other clubs were starting to take notice. Even though most of them sneered at what they regarded as Pritchard's crass publicity stunts, there was a realisation that football clubs could promote themselves much better than they were doing. But first they had to make sure they stopped the doctor from signing up their best players.

There was money to be burned. Every player agent and manager in the country was on the phone to the Swans, putting out the feelers to let them know their players were interested in moving north if the dollars were right.

At times it seemed as if every decent player in the competition had been approached. And Edelsten had moved quickly too. The most influential player manager in the competition was Jeff Browne. The new Sydney owner moved quickly to get on his good side before Browne became a problem for him. For the past three or four years Browne had wreaked havoc in the League, taking clubs to court and negotiating expensive deals for his players. Some had cottoned on quickly. Dick Seddon had paid him a retainer at Melbourne to ensure he did little to the detriment of the Demons.

Browne supplied Edelsten with a list of well-known players he should consider recruiting. Not unexpectedly, some of Browne's players were also on the list.

Gerard Healy was a key player in the Melbourne side. He was on a surfing holiday in Katherine when he rang Browne to check developments. Browne suggested he catch the first flight to Sydney.

There, after Healy had been kept waiting for what seemed like ages, Edelsten breezed into the room with a large black box. The box kept ringing. Inside it was a mobile phone. It was a constant accessory of Edelsten's and seemed to go everywhere with him. At one memorable VFL board meeting, Edelsten had left the box sitting in the corner of the room and sat quietly as the meeting progressed. The box began ringing. And kept ringing.

Eventually, Hamilton summed up the driest voice he could muster. 'Doctor,' he drawled, 'Your box is ringing.'

Edelsten offered Healy the fee of $350,000 for three years, $110,000 more than Melbourne was prepared to pay. It was an impressive deal and Healy resumed his surfing holiday a contented man. He would be surprised to discover at the end of his career that a close team-mate, Merv Neagle, had earned even more than him, picking up $395,000 for three years, along with a 260ZX Datsun.

But while there were high figures being bandied about, it took some work for the players to turn them into hard cash. At the club's first training session in preparation for the 1986 season, Browne walked into the change rooms and hauled the four players he managed outside. He then walked up to Edelsten and told him they would not be returning until he received some money.

Edelsten was on the mobile phone immediately and his wife soon arrived in an expensive car with a cheque.

Other negotiations were not as confrontational. A young player at the Swans had emerged as one of the best and most exciting forwards in the game. His name was Warwick Capper and big things were predicted for him. Edelsten, too, was fully aware of Capper's potential, but it was not just his footballing potential that interested him. Capper was a charismatic figure, at least on the field. He wore the tightest shorts imaginable and within 12 months Edelsten and Pritchard would make sure they continued to shrink. He had a mane of blond hair and an athletic body that could propel him to great heights above a pack.

Socially, however, the young Capper was inept. He'd always been a quiet kid. His mother could remember taking him out in the car and if they were going anywhere new, like a swimming lesson where he would need to meet strangers, young Warwick would succumb to a dreadful attack of asthma, wheezing like a seal in the back seat.

He was shy and stammered when forced to speak to strangers, his strange, clipped words emerging at a rapid rate. But Edelsten and Pritchard both thought that small problem could be overcome through voice projection training and a little coaching in some social niceties.

Browne represented Capper and had been looking around the League for new opportunities for his young charge. Decent full-forwards were always in short supply and a good dollar could be earned if you knew how to put the ball through the posts. But Edelsten insisted Capper should remain with the club. In 1985 he had been the Swans' leading goalkicker with 45 goals. They would build the side around him if necessary.

Browne met Edelsten in the front bar of the Hilton Hotel. There, they worked out a new and very attractive contract for Capper on a serviette. Edelsten signed it. Done. It was nice doing business with the doctor.

In the end the club would secure seven highly-paid new recruits and would, by varying estimates around the competition, spend more than $2 million to field its side in 1986. That was about twice the club's allowable salary cap and the Swans suffered several fines for breaching it. The heaviest fine was a paltry $20,000. Clearly, the League preferred to look the other way.

The Swans had the players. Now, just as importantly, they had to win over Sydney. How could Pritchard and McKay achieve what four years of perseverance by the League had failed to sustain?

They began by commissioning a survey of 168 Sydney suburbs. They obtained crucial data on socio-economic demographics, the attitude of various communities to different sports; their likes and dislikes. The research indicated one overwhelming point: the Swans were not seen as a Sydney team. Rather, they had been dumped on the city by a foreign code eager to expand but unwilling to spend the necessary time and money to achieve its aim.

So the club set about changing its image. Ticket deals were restructured. Normally hostile Sydney journalists loyal to rugby league were targetted, wined and dined. Almost every magazine in the country was identified and articles were then offered to them using Swans players as key characters. The skipper, Dennis Carroll was a keen golfer. His story was told to a golf magazine. *Modern Bride* was alerted to any upcoming player engagements and weddings. Promotions and giveaways were announced, using television, radio and newspapers. Advertising space was bought in the press.

By the time the 1986 season began, the hard work had already begun to pay off. Crowds rose as the Swans and their publicity-hungry owner became the latest rage in Sydney. McKay came up with the idea of matching jackets for Edelsten and his 'glamorous' wife Leanne. Edelsten's bore the words 'Sydney Swans Owner.' Leanne's said simply 'I own the owner.' It was a ploy that attracted publicity around the country.

Pritchard organised teams of people to call local radio stations during Swans matches, asking for updated scores. Eventually, because of the response, several stations began regularly updating listeners with the club's progress. Even the club's cheer squad was not immune. It became part of the overall orchestrated plan to turn the club into the most exciting event in Sydney. All their banners and accompanying slogans were checked to ensure they fitted in with the organisation's marketing objectives. They were ordered to be brief, clever and preferably, controversial.

Pritchard knew how to work a room and, indeed, a city. Why hold a promotion at a venue when you needed people to turn up? It rarely worked. So the club took its promotions to places where a crowd had already gathered. The Swans were regular features on Sydney's beaches over the summer of 1985–86.

They wanted women, too. They wanted everyone. The team's motif was installed on emery boards and distributed throughout the city's beauty salons. It was another ploy that worked well; by the end of the 1986 season, 34 per cent of spectators would be women, compared to an average of 14 per cent for the rest of the competition.

Sell, sell, sell. Nothing, it seemed, could stop the Swans except the club's time-honoured tendency to self-destruct. And despite the clean-out at the club, the introduction of new players and owners and even the team's relocation to Sydney, someone was always capable of pushing the self-destruct button.

7

PREPARING FOR EXPANSION

By the time the League sold the Swans to Edelsten, the fate of the 11 Victorian clubs had become football's big question. And the fact that people were now asking the question was a significant breakthrough. A decade before, no-one would have dared pose it. The VFL was like the universe, wasn't it? It just went on and on, slowly evolving but never ending. The clubs were invincible, too, weren't they? Who had ever heard of a football club disappearing because it didn't have any money?

The idea had been ludicrous. But by the middle of 1985 many within the game had begun to question how long the orgy could last. They had been spending up big for almost two decades now and the bills were arriving. It looked grim.

As always, there were just as many football people who refused to believe there was a crisis. The facts were palpable and easy to understand; the clubs were in the midst of a financial crisis that could, ultimately, destroy the League. Players were not being paid at some clubs. Yet the True Believers clung to their faith. Football would always pull through, they reasoned. The game was too big to ever be destroyed by such a crass and mundane matter as money. Something would always come along. In football parlance, they believed in the last-minute goal, that fantastic moment when, with just seconds left on the clock and the team down by five points in the grand final, a freakish goal is kicked by the young rookie still too young to shave.

Who would kick that goal for the League? There were no likely candidates on the scene, no gangly, acne-ridden wonder kids just waiting for their chance at glory. The horizon was instead cluttered with the jostling bodies of overweight businessmen in suits and bearing briefcases.

Such was the state of the game. In one corner were the realists; pragmatic men who believed the only means of salvation for the game was to develop clear heads and cold hearts. In the other corner were the romantics and true believers. There was little middle ground. You either believed the game was a self-sustaining entity with the power to always pull through. Or you did not.

By the middle of 1985 even the young VFL commission was experiencing the same debate. Jack Hamilton was a true believer. Like any old player who had survived the tribal Saturday afternoon battles and who had reached adulthood by copping sweet the bumps and knocks of older men, the League was the safest of places. Certainly, Hamilton was aware that several clubs, including his beloved Collingwood, were perilously close to disappearing. Collingwood's chequebook at one stage had been stationed on finance director Mike Tilley's desk. Several of the League's finance directors had paid visits to the club's bankers to reassure and explain to those nervous men the arcane and mystifying ways of the VFL and its methods of income.

Tilley's task was an unenviable one. Even by as early as April of 1985, he had worked his way through enough figures to project that half of the clubs faced another year of losses. In July, he wrote a short but snappy report to the League's board of directors which said that two of the clubs predicting large losses for the year 'are in a VERY weak financial position and an immediate improvment is necessary if they are to survive.'

Hamilton read all the data and understood it. But to some of the men who worked with him on the new VFL commission, he still seemed to believe that the game would continue to survive, no matter what happened.

His faith was as deep and strong as that of a table-thumping country town Baptist minister. And he needed it, too.

Things were certainly perilous at Hamilton's old club. By late 1985 Collingwood's finances were in dire straits, bad enough even for the Magpies' genial and philanthropic president Ranald Macdonald to write to his general manager, Peter Bahen, reminding him that the club still owed him money.

Macdonald had loaned the club more than $200,000 of his own money by then to keep creditors from the door. He was having a difficult time getting it back.

In a letter dated October 22, Macdonald wrote:

'Dear Peter, could I just put on record my position over two aspects of the club's operations.

'Firstly, to confirm that, at this stage, I do not intend adopting the course set down in the letter from my accountant . . . which is that my legal advisers be instructed to serve notice on the club for the payment of monies owing to me. You will recall that the Board agreed that you and the Treasurer (Mr Alan McAlister) would meet in the immediate future to work out what was able to be paid to me of the money owing. The club is already in default of repayments approved by the Board of both the principal and also interest of my short-term loan. I would remind you that the schedule was recommended by the Treasurer and went through the Board . . . I await your advice as to the club's ability to pay . . .

'As regards the overall financial situation facing the club, I believe it is important to record that with the proposed 'million-dollar' sponsor, and on the signing of the licencing agreement, the payment due the club from the sale of the Sydney Swans which, coupled with the League finals and other payments . . . season tickets and other sponsorships allows myself and other directors to feel confidence that the Club is viable.'

Macdonald's optimism was the sort shared by Hamilton and other clubs around the League. Something would always come along.

Not one commission member shared Hamilton's belief in the omnipotence of the VFL competition. For much of the year the commission had spent a great deal of time and effort working on a document it hoped would provide the spark for a new era in the game. The firm of strategy consultants, Pappas Carter Evans & Coop, had been retained to help the commission investigate the competition's problems and analyse a collection of data never before assembled on attendance trends and recreational pursuits competing with the game. One of the firm's partners was Colin Carter, an influential figure with the Geelong Football Club. Footy and business were never far apart.

It had not taken long for the individual personalities of the commissioners to come to the fore and within a few months it became clear that Peter Scanlon had become its most influential member.

To his fellow members he was an impressive man. He would sit quietly at meetings letting everyone else talk, taking down the odd note and watching the body language of those putting forward an argument. Then, when it came time for him to deliver his opinion, he would lean back and characteristically open a sentence with the line 'I might be a bit dumb but . . .'

It was a warning that Scanlon had thought through all the options and was now about to deliver a devastating critique of someone else's idea. In the years to come many of the League's administration officials would cringe and steel themselves for the blistering attack that inevitably followed those words.

Such was Scanlon's impact that his mannerisms would still be recalled in fine detail years later by those who observed him at close range. A former League official would recall: 'He could chop them up using a sophisticated knife in the rib cage . . . I think Jack was overawed by Scanlon and his financial acumen. He liked Scanlon. He had played footy and he saw in Scanlon the same things he saw in himself when he played for Collingwood. He was tough and uncompromising.'

But not all those on the commission were enamoured of Scanlon or even Graeme Samuel. Dick Seddon carried with him the usual lawyer's cynicism of most things. He had known Hamilton for several years and had watched with interest as Hamilton manoeuvred his way into the commissioner's position ahead of Aylett. He saw Hamilton as one of football's greatest political animals, a man who had 'white-anted' Aylett by putting 'the old slippery slide underneath him.'

Now, as the commission's first year developed, he watched Hamilton form a close and admiring relationship with Scanlon. Even Samuel had grown on the crusty old chief commissioner and few had thought that was possible. The two were from different worlds; Samuel the rich, Jewish corporate identity; Hamilton the rugged, coarse Collingwood fullback. But something clicked. Hamilton even bestowed a nickname on Samuel: Harry.

One day Seddon asked him about the origin of the nickname. It was after Harry Beitzel, explained Hamilton, the famous nasally-voiced radio commentator. Talked a lot. Knew nothing. But even Samuel had begun to influence Hamilton as the year progressed and the demands and pressures on the commissioner increased. So much so that Seddon, who believed he and Hamilton were the only two 'true' football people on the commission, found the commissioner siding against him on some issues.

'The problem I had was that Jack would agree with me, but when it came to the crunch at a meeting he'd leave me for dead,' Seddon would say years later, squinting out of the window. Below his cluttered office in St Kilda Road, the leaves on

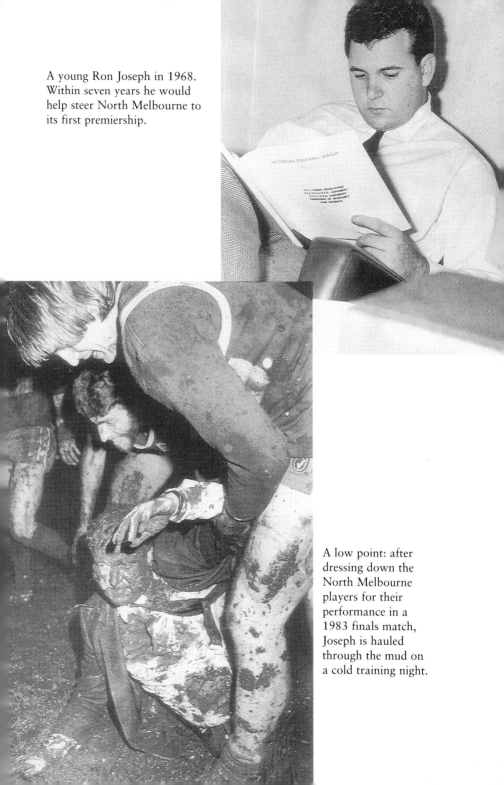

A young Ron Joseph in 1968. Within seven years he would help steer North Melbourne to its first premiership.

A low point: after dressing down the North Melbourne players for their performance in a 1983 finals match, Joseph is hauled through the mud on a cold training night.

Appointed as the youngest president of the Victorian Football League, Allen Aylett presided over one of the game's most turbulent and controversial eras.

The young Allen Aylett at the height of his playing career with North Melbourne.

Ross Oakley is carried from the Melbourne Cricket Ground in September 1966, after injuring his knee in the second semi-final.

Ron Joseph after 30 years in the game: 'I've walked away a couple of times through sheer frustration and tiredness.'

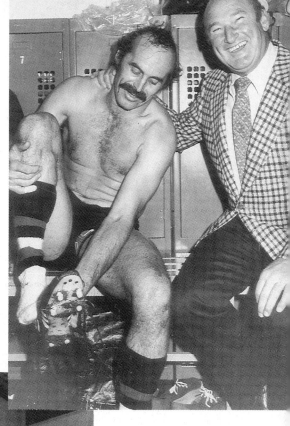

Lindsay Fox (*right*) and one of the game's most legendary figures, Alex Jesaulenko.

Ranald Macdonald (*left*) and Collingwood general manager Peter Bahen. Macdonald's presidency saw him lose more than $200,000 of his own fortune in one of the club's most controversial eras.

Jim McKay's name rarely hit the headlines but his work behind the scenes in marketing football changed it forever.

Jack Hamilton: the League's general manager became its first chief commissioner.

John Elliott and an ever-present cigarette: his secret plans to form a breakaway national league led to massive changes in the way the League was run and, ultimately, its expansion across the country.

1986: Alan Schwab (*left*) disguises his disappointment at losing out to Ross Oakley (*far right*) for the League's top post as a relieved Jack Hamilton looks on.

Ian Collins was one of football's toughest administrators, who moved to the League's central administration following the death of Alan Schwab.

Ian Collins in typical pose. As tough on the field as he was off it, he played in the 1962 grand final with a broken jaw.

Silvio Foschini (*left*) and Mark Jackson: both men had an impact on the game; Jackson for his on-field antics and Foschini for his challenge to the League's player rules.

the trees were turning orange-brown, another sign that another football season was underway. Seddon looked into the distance and the nostalgic smile momentarily disappeared from his face. 'Those other guys had him,' he said, staring straight ahead.

Seddon believed it was too simple to explain away the League's problems just as a matter of greed. You had to understand the game's history, its long struggle to control its own destiny.

Indeed, football had fought many battles to achieve its pre-eminent position by the 1980s. Despite its popularity as the major winter sporting code in the southern states, it had been enslaved to cricket for years. Cricket, which drew far fewer paying spectators, controlled many of the grounds on which football played. It dictated when the football season could begin and when it ended. The game's revolution, said Seddon, only began when football rose up and fought off its oppressors.

'In the '60s all the grounds were controlled by outsiders; councils or cricket clubs,' he explained, sitting back in his seat with his eyes half-closed in concentration. 'It was that struggle where the football clubs wrested control of their stadiums that really had the most profound change on them. It enabled them to build licensed social clubs . . .'

Soon after the social clubs came perimeter fence advertising. Souvenir stands also began to appear. And then television revenues began seeping in too. And because they had money, they had a new way of luring talent to their club. And new talent meant an increased chance of winning The Flag.

'They were really running on the smell of an oily rag up until then,' said Seddon. 'And money, as it often does, corrupts. That's when all good people in footy forgot that they could be competitors on the field but had to work together off the field. They were suddenly running around offering other clubs' players money and inducements.'

At about the same time that football encountered money, it also discovered it was not immune either to the social revolution taking place in the late 1960s. Flower power was a happening thing and even though the youngest football recruit was more interested in a senior game than a protest march, the notion that the individual was more important than the whole began to take hold.

It was, of course, a notion which was anathema to the game and its strict code of unity. How often did coaches, from senior league level down to the little league where eight-year-old boys donned baggy shorts and chased the footy every Saturday morning, drill the idea into their heads? The team is bigger than the individual. Always think how you can help a team-mate. Put your body on the line for the greater good of the team.

Even the law had helped reinforce the idea. 'The principal was that you were always entitled to restrictive rules for the orderly and good management of an organisation,' said Seddon.

But, asked Seddon, what was reasonable and unreasonable? The Foschini case had decided that issue.

The old line that had once separated the football world and its competition had been erased within just a few years. They were competitors on the field and now they fought one another just as ferociously off it, vying for market share and corporate sponsorship dollars.

On an evening in October 1985, the warring clubs came together again around the board table to be reminded once more that their behaviour required a good deal of improvement.

The reminder came in the form of an unpretentious-looking document called 'Establishing the basis for future success.' Immediately and inevitably, the commission's strategy plan aroused controversy. Here for the first time was a comprehensive diagnosis of the disease afflicting the game, along with several potential cures.

Page after page provided irrefutable evidence that the game

was in decline. Importantly, it noted that the greed among the clubs was not the key issue behind the financial malaise. The problem, the commission said, was with a competition still bound by the rules and conditions of the amateur body it had sprung from decades before.

But what to do? Debate had raged within the commission for months over the best course of action. Clearly the VFL had to expand interstate. There was no question that unless it did so within the next couple of years, a budding Kerry Packer-type entrepreneur would come along and stage the same sort of coup endured by cricket in the late 1970s. And by expanding, new teams could be expected to pay admittance fees to the competition. That money would be readily welcomed by the Victorian clubs.

'A small expansion of the competition, with clubs admitted from Adelaide/Perth, is economic and positions the competition to capitalise on new markets in Melbourne and elsewhere,' noted the report.

But first, there were some hard realities that needed to be faced. 'The longer term interests of the competition will be best served by club mergers in Melbourne,' said the commission. 'The commission proposes incentives to encourage this, but the process will be entirely voluntary.'

Several members of the commission already believed at least one, and possibly two, clubs would disappear by the end of 1986. Fitzroy, a club whose officials could not remember a time when they were not strapped for cash, was teetering on the edge. And you could take your pick of the other candidates; Footscray? North Melbourne? Even St Kilda, with that handsome population base south of the Yarra River, could not be ruled out in the extinction stakes.

The commission's decision to tackle the issue of mergers was typical of Scanlon and Samuel. All the commissioners knew the proposal would be unpalatable. It was a little like telling a child that Santa Claus didn't exist. 'Without mergers clubs will go to

the wall, privately owned or not, with acrimony and disillu-
sionment,' noted the report.

Just what was the VFL trying to do to the competition, asked
the average football supporter. They looked at the cold words
on the pages of their morning newspapers and wondered
whether it had all been worth it; all those afternoons spent
huddling on cold, wet embankments supporting a team that
could, if the commission had its way, disappear overnight? This
was a Victorian competition. It belonged to Victorians, not
those damn interstate cities.

The commission argued that expansion was required to 'gain
maximum benefit for the existing competition structure . . . it
gains otherwise unavailable benefits from the strong VFL fran-
chises in Melbourne (through live TV) and Adelaide and Perth
(through attendance and live TV).'

By the end of 1985 the commission gained the endorsement
from the clubs for a secure, three-year term and the agreement
to go forth and begin investigating the possibility of expanding
the competition.

The first half of a remarkable decade was over. The Swans
had been sold to a flamboyant, if eccentric, doctor. A licencing
agreement had come into force, under which the clubs agreed
to abide by the League's rules or risk expulsion. The task force,
which had helped steer football into an uncertain future, had
delivered its final report, which went largely ignored by the
commission and the clubs.

The football world was changing rapidly. In the 1985 annual
report, Hamilton promised there was more to come. 'The coming year promises many difficult decisions for the Commission,
but much excitement and progress along the way.'

Jack Hamilton didn't know it at the time but it would be the
last time a summary of his would appear in the League's annual
report. Within just a few months in early 1986, a series of
events would help convince him that he was not the man to
lead football into a new era.

THE
BEER WARS

Harold Mitchell had just showered and climbed into a pair of warm pyjamas. The fire in the living room was burning fiercely and just above its comforting crackle he could hear the wind and rain whipping through the trees and across the paddocks outside.

It was, he decided, a perfect night. Could there have been a better one? The wintery conditions had appeared as though on cue. It was Saturday evening and another football season was about to begin. Mitchell's team, Carlton, was due to play the opening game of the pre-season competition at Waverley. He had been looking forward to this for weeks. On his 20-acre property deep in Melbourne's outer-east, Mitchell had positioned his ample frame in his favourite chair and sat back to watch the game on his big-screen television.

But Harold Mitchell was showing more than his usual interest in a football pre-season competition. As one of Melbourne's most colourful advertising men and, some suspected, one of its most influential, he had played a significant role in several secret negotiations with the VFL in the previous weeks. His client, the Alan Bond-owned Castlemaine-Tooheys, had just decided to take on its rival, John Elliott's Carlton and United Breweries, on its home turf—Victoria. And there was no better way to fire a direct shot at Elliott than on the football field. It was the only place, some figured, where you were guaranteed a genuine chance of piercing the man's thick hide.

It had begun, inevitably, with the assistance of Jim McKay. No-one could accuse him of slacking off. In fact, despite the criticism levelled at him from some quarters, there were still many who believed Jim McKay was a marketing genius. Here he was, keeping an incredibly low profile but playing a significant role in the Sydney Swans and now he had brought a lucrative new sponsor to Hamilton.

Mitchell, after McKay had done the heavy work in convincing Castlemaine that it should be involved in football, had helped strike a lucrative sponsorship deal with Hamilton that would see the red and yellow of Castlemaine's 'Fourex' label wrapped around the League's goalposts. The negotiations had been controversial from the start. They proceeded to become bitter when CUB, having heard of the Fourex deal, suddenly decided it too, wanted to bid for the sponsorship rights. After much wrangling, a deal was struck and Fourex gained the goalposts. Even better, it was told by Hamilton it could have them during this pre-season competition, the Foster's Cup. It was a key selling point, for a lot of the action in a football game took place in the goal square. The cameras were always ready to zoom in on the small area. It was, more often than not, the scene of triumph or failure.

So Mitchell sat back and let his attention wander during the pre-game introductions. He started paying attention at the first bounce. Almost instantly, he was wrapped up in the game. The ball went down forward and a goal was kicked. The goal umpire waved his flags and the ball was quickly dispatched back to the centre. Mitchell thought something was amiss. But he couldn't quite figure out what it was.

And then it hit him. The ball went forward again. And there it was! The goalposts! Where were the bloody Fourex signs? Christ! What a debacle. What the hell was going on? He sat up abruptly in his chair, the rose colour in his cheeks rapidly spreading to the rest of his face. Craning forward and staring intently at the screen, he thought he could make out a thin white material wrapped around the Fourex signs.

He was out of the chair and had the telephone in his hand before his startled wife could ask what was wrong. By this stage his hands were trembling, his fingers fumbling at the dials. He rang telephone inquiries.

'Get me the number for VFL Park at Waverley,' he barked down the line. 'I want the direct line to the VIP room.' It took forever. Each time he glanced at the television screen it seemed the ball was always in front of the goals. And there were those bloody white goalposts sticking out without a Fourex logo to be seen.

Eventually Mitchell tracked down a number and got through to the room on the third level of Waverley just before quarter-time. Hamilton was called to the phone and answered as though he knew what was coming.

Mitchell lost whatever control he had remaining. He rained abuse on Hamilton, calling him every name he could think of, and then some. While the storm raged outside, it was nothing compared to the one unleashed within.

'Yes, Harold,' was all those at VFL Park could hear Hamilton managing to say. 'Righto, Harold.'

After several minutes, the fire inside Mitchell had hardly abated. 'You just wait there Jack,' he yelled at Hamilton. 'I'm bloody coming out there and I'll see you in the car park.'

'Righto, Harold.'

Mitchell slammed down the phone and, without a moment's thought, stalked off into the dark, cold night in pyjamas and dressing gown. He climbed into his BMW, slammed the door and headed for Waverley.

The bloody VFL. He cursed and railed against the unfairness of it all.

Couldn't they get anything right?

Beer and football. Hadn't the two been made for each other? Australia was a big land, went the commercials. With a big thirst. Full of big men. Big men liked to drink beer. And talk in short sentences. With the beer barons locked in mortal combat for control of the Australian beer market, the fight had inevitably moved into the football arena.

It had begun the year before. Midway through 1985, Alan Bond had acquired Castlemaine-Tooheys in another move so typical of the 1980s entrepreneurs and, in particular, the little round man from Perth who had brought the America's Cup home. He paid a staggering $1.2 billion for the company (just the interest to service his borrowings was estimated at more than $190 million) and immediately signalled his intention to take on CUB, owned by Elliott's Elders-IXL. It promised to be the fight to end all fights.

There were estimates that both companies were spending up to $40 million each a year, just on advertising and promotion. Elders boasted 48 per cent of the national beer market. Bond, with Castlemaine up his sleeve, claimed 42 per cent. In London, Castlemaine had launched an advertising campaign with Fourex, claiming 'An Aussie wouldn't give a XXXX for any other beer' as it targeted Foster's world-wide reputation as Australia's leading export brew.

But if Bond hoped to win the beer war, he had to take it to Elliott in Victoria. As part of his strategy he would even take over as president of Richmond for a short but memorable time, notable for his achievement in mispronouncing the name of the club captain at the annual meeting.

Victoria had the least number of hotels 'tied' to a brewery and he could not hope to chalk up victory without claiming the southern state. And, as his marketing strategists pointed out, there was no better way to make inroads than through football. The League, always on the lookout for more and more money, saw the battle coming and, like the manager of a munitions factory in war time, rubbed its hands gleefully.

What followed, however, was not the pot of riches the game's administrators envisaged. Instead, it became a classic tale of football's clumsiness and ineptitude in the corporate world. Its performance would harm it for years to come. For Jack Hamilton, it was also the beginning of the end.

Harold Mitchell thought Fourex had stitched up a deal with the League right under the noses of CUB. He'd been down this path before, having got involved in a past sponsorship deal between the VFL and the car manufacturer Nissan. He was also familiar with the internal workings of the game, having served on the League's publications board administering, among other things, its highly profitable weekly *Football Record*. And now early in 1986, with a beer war raging around them, Fourex had pulled off the biggest of coups. Oh, the beauty of it all. They could just see the faces on the CUB executives.

On 8 January, 1986, Bond Brewing executives finalised a three-year deal with the League, having been brought to the table by McKay. It was worth just over $2 million and the League's television rights holder, Channel 7, had been approached to give its blessing to the deal. One executive would look back fondly on the deal. 'The package would have given us total Fourex association with the religion,' he said wistfully. 'We would have owned the temple.'

And then something mysterious happened. CUB discovered football was about to strike a deal with its arch-enemy. Suddenly, Mitchell was informed, CUB had prepared a bid. The commissioner had decided it would only be fair to allow CUB to put forward a presentation.

Mitchell was suspicious.

Peter Scanlon had been a director and key strategist of Elders IXL, CUB's parent company. But he quickly absented himself from discussions on the deal, along with Samuel. Mitchell was not alone with his suspicions. There were even those who worked within the League administration who thought the dealing had a peculiar smell to it. Just how comfortable would a man so closely linked to Elliott like Scanlon feel if Elliott's greatest business opponent of the time secured a sponsorship deal with the VFL competition? Several senior executives thought they knew.

By late January, Hamilton was under pressure. Bond Brewing was threatening legal action. CUB was making noises that, given the sponsorship money it already poured into the game through several club deals, along with its long-time association with the game, it deserved to be the corporate sponsor. Under pressure, Hamilton took an uncharacteristic step. He agreed to split the sponsorship.

Carlton and United Breweries was told it had won the corporate sponsorship package. It would also get to sponsor the Victorian side in its interstate clashes, as well as the entertainment at the grand final. It would pay about $800,000 once the package was totalled.

Hamilton then contacted Bond Brewing. Fourex can have the goalposts, he told them, a patch on the umpires' shirts and we'll talk about the rest later on. The fee would be about $700,000, an expensive sum for a company which had finished in second place.

Instead of a three-year deal, each company was offered a one-year contract. And, to avoid any friction in future, they were told a tender process with sealed envelopes would operate the following year.

Then, a few days before the Foster's Cup began, the League's company secretary, Greg Durham, received a call on his office extension. It was Hamilton. Make sure the Fourex signs are on the goalposts by Saturday night, Hamilton told him. We don't want anything going wrong.

Durham was surprised. While he was aware of the dual sponsorship deal which had been struck, he wondered why Foster's would ever allow a rival brand to display its bright red logo on the goalposts during a competition that was, effectively, run for television.

Still, he went ahead and carried out Hamilton's orders. Someone obviously knew what they were doing.

Bruce Siney, CUB's chief marketing strategist, arrived at Waverley in time for the pre-game dinner. He was accompanied by the company's managing director, Peter Bartels. They were looking forward to a meal, a glass of wine and a decent game of footy. But the night hardly got off to a promising start.

It wasn't long before Siney noticed the stark, bright XXXX signs on the goalposts. He blinked for a moment. Surely this was a joke? It wasn't.

Siney spied Hamilton in the room and lurched toward him, his face turning red. He had always suspected that Hamilton regarded him as a polite, endearing fellow. Well, he would fix that.

Hamilton had played fullback for Collingwood during football's tough era. He'd copped plenty of treatment and dished it out, too. But no-one gathered in the VIP room that night, including the old veterans with their craggy faces, could ever recall Hamilton suffering such a public lashing as the one he received from Siney.

Years later the force and violence of Siney's verbal spray would be recalled by everyone in the room. But only snatches of what he said would be remembered. And the man himself would be too polite to recite the actual language he used.

'A deal's a deal, Jack . . . what the hell do you think you were doing? . . . I thought we'd agreed we were going to be sponsors . . . how could you ever come to the conclusion that you could sell a sponsorship to two mortal enemies like this? . . . It's the most ridiculous thing I've ever seen . . . Do something now. Cover it up for, for God's sake . . .'

On it went, a raging storm. And Hamilton stood there, suffering in stunned silence. When it was finally over and Siney had been ushered from the room to calm down, Hamilton walked up to Durham.

Hamilton's face was the colour of ash. Durham, who had always faithfully believed in the invincibility of his general manager, had never seen him like this.

'Do something,' Hamilton told Durham. 'Get rid of them.'

Durham moved quickly. He found the catering manager and they grabbed several tablecloths and raced on to the ground. There, with rain threatening to fall again, they tied the table-cloths around the goalposts, covering the XXXX signs.

And that was what so enraged Harold Mitchell as he sat in the warmth of his country property barely an hour later.

By the time Mitchell was halfway to Waverley, however, it dawned on him that he would look ridiculous stalking through the giant stadium in his pyjamas and dressing gown searching for Hamilton. He pulled over to the side of the road and rang Waverley again. This time he got Durham.

'Go home,' Durham told him. 'We'll work it out on Monday.'

Damn right we will, warned Mitchell. He hung up and rang the mobile number of a Fourex executive who was also on his way to Waverley. They agreed to wait until the following week.

The recriminations seemed to last forever. With Scanlon and Samuel unable and unwilling to help Hamilton extricate him-self from the mess because of their conflict of interest, it was left to Dick Seddon, with his legal expertise, and Peter Nixon.

Peace talks were held, but war occasionally broke out. In one meeting, a snarling Mitchell, more accustomed to the raw real-ity of the commercial world than Nixon, who had spent much of his career in Federal Parliament, turned to the VFL commis-sioner and tried to antagonise him.

'You're nothing but a cattle rustler,' Mitchell said, referring to Nixon's farming background.

Mitchell was stunned by the response. 'He went absolutely

livid. He'd been in the Parliament all his life. He gets to his feet and says 'I object! I object! Withdraw! Withdraw!' . . . he was going crazy. It was a very tense time.'

At another meeting, Seddon joined Hamilton in his office. A large pile of correspondence sat on the desk. Slowly, Seddon made his way through it. There were faxes, documents and slips of paper with signatures everywhere.

'Jesus, Jack,' he'd mutter with each new revelation. 'What the hell is this?'

Hamilton would sit there looking grim-faced, unable even to crack a wry joke about his predicament. In fact, he looked so grim that Seddon at times wondered whether he was on the verge of crying.

A settlement was eventually reached between the two brewing companies after many threats of legal action and accusations. But neither was happy with the arrangement and the manner in which it had been conducted. At the end of the season, neither showed interest in renewing the deal. Fourex hardly rated the sponsorship a success. It had not been told before signing that many clubs and grounds had long-term signage contracts with CUB. At times, only three grounds in the competition would carry the XXXX logo.

CUB, and particularly Siney, had no interest in dealing with what it and he regarded as amateurs. Besides, it copped a hiding from the press and the public after it put on the entertainment display at the 1986 grand final. The traditional entertainment turned into a 15-minute commercial for Foster's, complete with a giant Foster's flag. Everyone was left with a flat taste in their mouth.

For Hamilton, the experience was a rude and ugly encounter with the worst aspects of the commercial world. Those close to him noticed a big change in the man in the following weeks after the pre-season debacle with the two brewing companies. The old zest had gone. This was not the job he had spent his life working for. He was the man who settled problems with the clubs, who dealt with the byzantine politics of the game. This corporate scene was something completely different.

'Jack was a very fair person,' said Mitchell. 'He was a marvellously fair person, but sadly he was too fair for the hurly-burly of the VFL'

Hamilton spoke privately with Samuel and Scanlon at length about his role and whether he was the right man to do it. This, too, was an unusual step for Hamilton. In the past if he had harboured doubts about his abilities, he had never mentioned them to anyone, bluffing his way through it bravely. But now it was clear that he was fast approaching the point where he either closed his eyes and swam out into the deep, or took the safe option and returned toward the comfort of the beach.

Jack Hamilton decided the tide was turning. It was time to head back in.

Jeff Browne had been, in the words of one League official, 'a pain in the arse' for some time. From behind, he looked like any other dark-haired lawyer with a suit. It was when he turned around and exposed his face that he caught an opponent off-guard. He had soft, boyish features that had hardly altered since he had played in Collingwood's under-19 side and later with the VFA team Preston. It was a deceptive look in a world filled with hardened men with jagged faces, because behind the innocent facade lay a sharp operator who was always prepared to push a confrontation right to the edge.

Football feared Jeff Browne during the early 1980s. He held the whip hand and everyone knew it; the clubs, the officials and the players. And Browne knew it. When it came to a contract negotiation, he usually got what he wanted.

His first deal on behalf of a player took place when a friend asked him to look over a proposed contract. It wasn't long before word spread among the players. There was a guy in town who you could trust and who wouldn't sell you out to the club.

By the early 1980s, business was brisk and Browne's law practice was effectively being funded by his football work. It seemed everything he touched he got; the clubs knew the rules were vulnerable to a challenge and Browne had scrutinised them closely. It was because of his growing reputation that he received a call one day late in 1981. It was an accountant called David Shewan who represented two footballers, Collingwood's Peter Moore and Footscray's full-forward Kelvin Templeton. Browne and Shewan compared notes and figured the pair would be worth $500,000 just in transfer fees to any club that wanted to buy them.

Those were the days. The League had anti-poaching rules in force, but they were hard to police. 'I became directly involved and found myself talking to various VFL clubs about this proposition. We'd meet late at night in city hotels,' Browne would recall with a boyish smile years later. 'They'd smuggle the coach in and we'd hold all these secret talks.

'It was a lot of fun but it was silly. It was a boon for what I was doing.' Indeed, Browne was fond of telling anyone who wanted to hear that he was partly responsible for the trail of blood between Collingwood's Lulie Street and Richmond's Punt Road. Browne had seen Ranald Macdonald and his New Magpies coming from a long way off and was well prepared, helping to stitch several deals together which saw Richmond's Geoff Raines and ruckman David Cloke leave Punt Road for the claustrophobic and demanding environment of Lulie Street.

But it was the Moore-Templeton switch to Melbourne that saw Browne move into the big league. 'Melbourne paid it because it didn't want to go court,' he would say, leaning back in the chair, still unable to get rid of his smile. 'Our strategy was that there should be extra money for the players and for the people who put the deal together.'

Within a few months both Moore and Templeton became Melbourne players, joining what would become Ron Barassi's failed five-year plan to rescue the club from years of mediocrity.

Templeton had won the Brownlow Medal in 1980 and was a tremendously well-built athlete; barrel-chested, strong and with powerful legs capable of propelling the ball long distances. But the following year he damaged his knee and was never the same player again. That didn't worry Browne or Melbourne. By 1986, when injuries finally forced him out of the game after earning $85,000 a season, Templeton had managed just 34 games in three years.

The night the Templeton-Moore deal was finally stitched up, Browne, Shewan and the players went looking for somewhere to celebrate. It was all too late, however. In John Cain's Victoria it was hard to find a drink anywhere after 10pm. The quartet settled for hamburgers and cokes at McDonald's instead.

The fact that Browne had become the most loathed man in the game hardly deterred him. He was out to give the League a decent kicking. 'I thought the VFL had been a bit slack over a long period of time . . . poaching rules and high transfer fees, telling a player where he could play because of where he'd been born . . . I thought those views were unjust. A lot of people thought I was out to destroy the clubs and the competition.

'It really got to the point where I was issuing proceedings pretty regularly for players . . . some of them I never even saw. The accountants would ring me up and give me instructions. Something had to give.'

It did.

Soon after the commission was formed, Dick Seddon, the man who had put Browne on a retainer during his days at Melbourne and who knew the damage he could wreak, sounded out Browne about ending his personal Cold War with the game.

He was interested. 'I had found that whilst we were adversaries in court we thought, basically, that we were not all bad blokes. The thing that broke the ice was the decision by the VFL to enter into a licence agreement with its clubs. That's something I'd felt was necessary for a long time.'

Browne was a specialist in franchising and knew the technicalities of the law. The League was adamant that it needed more control over the clubs and a licence agreement—which would involved all clubs signing a document guaranteeing they would abide by the League's rules in order to maintain their place in the competition was the way it could be done.

It was also a way of circumventing the problem of asking the clubs to punish one of their own. If a club transgressed the rules, perhaps by illegally poaching an opposing club's star player, the rest of the League clubs were reluctant to impose harsh penalties. Who knew what club would be castigated next?

With a licence agreement, those problems were no longer an issue.

'Browne came into it because I'd reckoned he was the best sports lawyer,' Seddon would assert with the stern face of a true believer. 'When I went to the commission I brought him with me. (But) It took me 12 months to convince Jack to bring him there.'

'I thought long and hard before going to the VFL,' said Browne. 'I had a pretty thriving business. Edelsten had been pretty kind to me financially . . . financially, had I stayed doing what I was doing, it would have been a better result for me. Everyone was becoming a contact point for me; passing on friends, getting me to do their conveyancing. I didn't have a moral problem in giving the VFL a caning. But when the commission started talking about an integrated labour market control system, that was when I thought "that's what they need to do".'

Browne struck a deal with Hamilton. He would no longer act for, or represent, any player or club. He would act only on behalf of the VFL central administration.

The poacher had turned gamekeeper.

And now one of the League's former gamekeepers had turned feral. Allen Aylett had watched the formation of the commission in late 1984 with scepticism. He had wondered aloud several times about the right of people like Peter Scanlon and Graeme Samuel to administer the game, but for the most part he had remained silent.

He had, of course, hardly disappeared into the background. Besides the consultancy work he had performed for Edelsten, Aylett had also remained as president of the National Football League. The NFL was, supposedly, the governing body of the sport in the country, boasting representatives from all state bodies around the country.

But in reality it was a paper tiger. The VFL attempted to control it and when the other states rebelled and vetoed any VFL proposal, the Victorians went ahead and did it anyway. Still, as the titular head of the NFL, Aylett took the role seriously. And when Hamilton came after him again in late 1985 he decided to fight back.

Hamilton wanted Aylett removed as president and his argument was sound; the VFL's NFL director should be someone affiliated with the League; not a former president. Aylett had heard Hamilton was after him. Indeed, several people had heard Hamilton boasting at the grand final that Aylett would be replaced within the next four weeks. Aylett had been promptly informed of the talk and warned to prepare a counter-attack.

Within a week the battle went public. Just days after the League voted to replace Aylett on the NFL with its executive director, Alan Schwab, Aylett released to the press a letter he had written to Hamilton.

'Dear Jack,' he wrote. 'I received your note last night in which you stated you wanted to give me the opportunity to publicly resign from the position of president of the National Football League of Australia due to pressure of business or because of my involvement in my Sports Consultants business.

'You know this not to be true. I will not be publicly resigning for either of these excuses ... your offer at this stage amazes me . . . I have carried out my duties with all endeavour and under constraints placed on me by you.'

Here, Aylett decided to twist the knife a little. He wanted everyone to know just how powerful Hamilton had become.

'At your direction, I did not send written reports on NFL matters to the commissioners and directors of the League,' he wrote.

'The regular reports were sent to you only. I have not been given the opportunity at any stage to report directly to them. No invitation to do so was even forthcoming . . .'

Finally, the antagonism between the two men was out in the open. Aylett might not have had the weaponry at his disposal to shoot down Hamilton, but he wanted everyone else to know what he thought of the chief commissioner.

Aylett's broadside, however, had little impact. Hamilton still had many friends around the League and, to them, anything Aylett did or said looked or sounded like the antics of a bitter man out for revenge.

The commission had much on its mind. The clubs agreed to extend its powers and its lifespan by a further three years at the end of 1985. But they remained extremely nervous about what was to come. Clearly, men like Scanlon and Samuel had made their views known around the competition; footy faced a slow and cruel death unless it either contracted or expanded. Contraction was an option few wanted to consider, although by 1985 and early 1986 several clubs had begun sounding one another out. All their talks took place at one venue; 367 Collins Street. From his office in the middle of the city, Peter Scanlon had a view of inner Melbourne few could match and it became a favourite venue of several club officials as they occasionally gathered in Scanlon's office to discuss the possibility of merging.

But it was still the least preferred option. As 1986 opened with the hope that the game could pull itself out of the quicksand, many of football's Lords were coming to the view that the only way to go was national.

One advantage was the extra cash. A couple of new teams would have to pay a licence fee to join the competition and new money would be warmly welcomed. But expansion also held many uncertainties. After 90 years, few savoured the possibility of a Western Australian or, even worse, a South Australian team joining the competition and winning The Flag. What would that do to almost a century of tradition? The most vehement opponents of the expansion push claimed it would threaten the very fabric of Victorian society.

No-one, however, could supply a clear answer. As usual, footy managed to overshadow the international cricket season that summer as the debate began to warm.

Within League headquarters, a great deal of number-crunching was taking place. Could the VFL expand into other states? Was the country ready for a national league? And would there be enough money around to fund such an enterprise?

9

THE NEW FRONTIER

It was one of football's unwritten codes of conduct. You could talk forever about what a great game it was; how it could snatch you from that dreary world you lived in and, for a couple of hours, take you to another place where nothing really mattered except what 36 young men could do with a red leather ball.

But you never talked about the other side of football; its dark side where it picked up people, built them up and then suddenly dropped them from sight. The greatest of games could also be the cruellest. You had to have a big heart to succeed because sometimes it seemed the sport itself didn't have one at all.

Years after football's most important decade was over, a young man would sit in his trendy Camberwell town house and speak the unspeakable. Cameron Schwab was only 31, but he had seen both sides of the game. His father, Alan, had been one of the sport's most fêted administrators. The old man had worked at club level and during the early 1970s was one of the architects behind the rise to power of the Richmond Football Club. Then he had moved to the VFL administration and by the mid-1980s was the game's chief tactician and Hamilton's loyal deputy. But the events of 1986 would trigger a slow deterioration in the man's spirit and play a tragic role in his death seven years later.

Cameron was the younger of Alan Schwab's two sons and

143

had followed his father into football in 1982, picking up a job with the Melbourne club straight from school. The son, it seemed, was destined to follow the father. At Melbourne, Cameron was the office boy but he learned quickly. He was already steeped in the lore of the game. As a boy, it seemed hardly a week went by without the Schwab home playing host to some of the game's greatest names. And even when his parents separated when he was 12, every weekend in winter was spent at the footy.

Cameron joined Melbourne with Dick Seddon and Ron Barassi's five-year plan in full swing. By 1988 he seemed to have fulfilled his destiny, becoming Richmond's youngest ever general manager. By 1994, he was out of the job after the usual bout of club politics. And so he sat there on a black leather couch, raising the subject of football's darker side.

Football takes people, he said, and then it leaves them for someone else. 'What it does is, it not only dumps them, it gives them nowhere to go.'

He shifted uncomfortably. 'As human beings, they can't replace what they had. It happens with footballers. There's no doubt about that.

'I made a pact with myself that I was never going to let footy get to me. I've seen what it's done to people. I've seen so many sad people, people who can't put their heads up anymore because of what footy's done to them.'

In his last days in football, Cameron Schwab's father became one of those sad people. And his fall had its origins in the tumultuous year of 1986.

Hamilton was on his way out but for several months only he, his family, and the other commission members knew it. Then, on the evening of 4 June 1986, the football world was stunned. The commissioner announced to a meeting of the clubs that he wanted to retire and would leave by early October, barely 18 months into the job.

There was complete silence in the meeting for a brief moment as Hamilton outlined his reasons. He told them he had been thinking about retirement since early in the year and while no mention was made of it, the beer war debacle had clearly triggered thoughts of leaving.

By the time he emerged from the meeting to be swamped by the media, football officials were sprinting to any available microphone to record tributes and thanks. But some were also wondering privately about the timing. Why was Jack going now? Here was a League in deep financial trouble, about to move into uncharted territory by expanding interstate and the man who had been at the helm for almost a decade had decided to leave. Some were suspicious. Had Scanlon and Samuel tipped him out? There was little doubt the pair had counselled Hamilton quite heavily in the weeks before. But both men had urged him to stay. Scanlon thought it was far too soon, and the competition in too chaotic a condition, for a change at the top.

But Hamilton made the final decision on his own. He knew his time was up. 'After 38 years there is a pressure build-up,' he conceded, swamped by a battery of cameras, microphones and television lights. 'There is an enormous responsibility heading up the VFL.

'The League is about to enter a new era and I believe the time is opportune for someone else to come in and lead football into the future,' Hamilton said. 'While there may be trying times ahead, I have no doubts that the game is very much alive and well.'

It was a typical piece of bluster by the commissioner, who knew more than anyone else that the game was not well. But he was hardly going to pour a bucket on the business he had served for 38 years either, particularly not at a time when it needed to steady its shaking hand.

Typically, too, he went out with a few gags for the press, that collection of men who had helped forge and protect his image for all those years. How hard was the job, he was asked.

'It's a job any three people can do,' shot back the reply.

Would he take up a position on the board of his beloved Collingwood following his retirement?

'Look, I've just got off Devil's Island. I'm not going to live on Alcatraz.'

On it went. But by the time the press conference was over, the shock of Hamilton's announcement was gone. Instead, there was just one question doing the rounds: Who would the League get to replace him? Alan Schwab was the hot tip. The loyal deputy. A real Football Man. A crafty administrator. He, too, had plenty of support out there among the clubs because he, like Hamilton and other real Football Men, knew how important it was to have the clubs on your side. After all, Schwab had been one of them once and, like all of them, had fought his fair share of battles with the League. At one stage in the late 1960s he had threatened the League that Richmond, one of its biggest drawcards, would withdraw from the competition and start up a new league if it did not meet its demands on player transfer fees. He knew how to play the game.

Schwab was the likeliest choice, but just as quickly as his name cropped up, another rumour surfaced. No-one quite knew where this rumour first originated. It just seemed, like many football rumours, to appear from nowhere. And as each day passed it gained strength. Schwab might not be the man to take football into its brave new world, went the thinking. Maybe it was time for football to go outside into that other world out there, that strange environment where no football person felt safe or secure, and hire a man of corporate standing.

To many of the traditionalists, such a step was unthinkable. Why bother going outside when a man like Schwab, who within a week of Hamilton's announcement had suddenly been praised as a footballing genius, was sitting there waiting for the job?

And Alan Schwab wanted the job. It would be the fulfilment

of a life-long ambition. At the age of 45, he would be the man to take the game into its uncertain future.

There was just one problem. While Schwab had many fans in football, they were not on the VFL Commission. Peter Scanlon and Graeme Samuel, particularly, had another name in mind.

There was the usual sub-committee appointed to come up with a recommendation to replace Hamilton. But the real power and influence remained with Scanlon and Samuel.

Scanlon was sceptical of Schwab's reputation and believed he was not the man to take over the running of the game. He knew the rules inside out, that was for sure. There was a national player draft about to be implemented in the next few months, in time for the national competition. It would be the cornerstone of the new-look League and would, hopefully, restore some semblance of balance to a pathetically lop-sided competition. Schwab had been the man responsible for knocking it into shape.

But where was his business background, the proof that he could handle himself in the corporate world? Was he capable of stitching together a multi-million dollar sponsorship deal and avoid the shambles of the XXXX-CUB debacle? Scanlon thought not and confided to Samuel that someone else was needed. There would be opposition to such an appointment, that was for sure. And Schwab had already made his intentions known. A lot of work would need to be done if Scanlon was to prevent Hamilton's deputy from taking charge.

Schwab had taken Ron Joseph to lunch one afternoon at a swank restaurant around the corner from VFL House. There he outlined his plan. If he won the job he wanted Joseph to be his second-in-charge. Together, the pair of them would knock the game back into shape and prove to the businessmen that pure football people could manage their affairs without the intervention of the money men.

If anyone knew about politics in football, it was Schwab. He had joined the League after a successful career at Richmond and if anyone could survive a lengthy period as general manager of Richmond, he had proved himself a more adept politician than any of those in Canberra. His career had been marked by advances at significant times; at St Kilda he had been a junior official when the Saints won their first flag. As Richmond general manager he'd become one of the most powerful figures in the game; an astute judge of player talent with the added ability of knowing what the next trend in the game would be long before it became apparent to his colleagues.

He also genuinely loved the game. And that appeared to make him fit the criteria Hamilton had announced when he had retired. 'I would hope the person would have an enormous love of the game,' he'd said and no-one loved it more than Alan Schwab.

But his love extended only so far. As the weeks went by following Hamilton's announcement, and speculation mounted that perhaps he was not the odds-on favourite he thought he was, Schwab let it be known that he might be forced to move on, perhaps back to club level as an administrator if he missed out on the chief commissioner's job. It was a veiled threat that served its purpose. Support for Schwab buoyed, particularly among several on the sub-committee. How could they afford to lose someone of his pedigree?

Scanlon put the word around that another candidate should be considered. His name was Ross Oakley. It was not a new name to many in football; for five years he'd been a director at Hawthorn and a familiar face around the traps. But what were his credentials?

Scanlon and Samuel had checked them out and came back impressed. As managing director of Royal Insurance, he had shown the ability to manage a large company and he also had a marketing background. Plus he was an old Wesley boy. In the business world, that counted for something. Wesley was one of Melbourne's most esteemed private colleges. As its old boys moved on into business, they created networks of their own. They kept in touch with one another. They helped one another whenever help was required. Graeme Samuel was an old Wesley boy, too. But the pair had come from vastly different backgrounds.

If Samuel's family could comfortably afford to send him to Wesley, Oakley's could not. His father, Hector, had been one of those brilliant all-round sportsmen. He played cricket for Victoria, amassed a record number of runs for his district club St Kilda, had a single-figure golf handicap and played A-grade pennant tennis.

Hector Oakley had moved his young family from Kyneton to the sandbelt Melbourne suburb of Sandringham and held high hopes that his two sons, Dennis and Ross, would inherit some of his talent. Both did, but it was football at which they excelled, not cricket. Dennis starred at full-forward for VFA club Sandringham.

Hector had worked for BHP and then moved on to Stanley Titan, the tool and wire manufacturer and, while his job as the company's marketing general manager paid well, it was not enough for the family to send Oakley to Wesley immediately.

Oakley was an immature kid for his age, interested in sport and not much else. He drifted into most things and seemed to lack any driving ambition to make a name for himself away from the sporting arena.

His first three years of secondary schooling were spent at Hampton High School. 'It was a real dump in those years,' he would recall. 'We used to have teachers that would leave their teeth at home. We'd jump out the back window and they wouldn't know we'd gone.'

He followed Dennis, his older brother by three years, to Wesley at the start of fourth form, but by the time he was 19 he still wasn't sure what he wanted to do. It had taken him three years to earn his leaving and matriculation certificate and he was in no hurry. By then a League football career was beckoning and St Kilda secured his services.

It was the early 1960s and the Saints were about to embark on the most successful period of their existence. The club, too, had also decided to move from its old home ground at the Junction Oval further south to Moorabbin in 1965. The decision highlighted the common problem facing many clubs at the time; subservient to their cricket club cousins, the football clubs found they had little power over the grounds they played on despite their crowds subsidising the operations of the cricket clubs.

Over the Oakley dinner table many an argument raged over the cricket-football war, particularly when St Kilda moved. Hector the cricket club stalwart, up against a young son who parroted all the footballing arguments.

Ross Oakley moved on to university and then went to work with BHP. There would be a succession of roles from then on, all of them leading Oakley further up the totem pole of business. And he was there, right at the top of his industry, when the telephone in his house began ringing early one morning on 5 August, 1986.

He picked up the phone. 'Greg Hobbs from the *Herald*,' said the voice at the other end.

Oakley went cold. Hobbs was the paper's chief football writer. He could be calling for only one reason.

'I hear you're going to be the next boss of the VFL.' Hobbs told Oakley he had received very strong information.

Oakley's mind raced through a series of explanations, none of them convincing. 'You'd be stupid to print that,' replied Oakley. 'And I want you to remember this: if the story's wrong, I'm going to sue the pants off you because it will damage my commercial career substantially. If it's right, I'll never give you a story again when I get the job.'

Oakley's bluster, however, failed to deter Hobbs. He published and several months later Oakley would hand him the VFL's award for the best news story of 1986.

The word Hobbs had received was dead accurate, and the culmination of several weeks of intrigue and backroom dealing at the highest levels of the game.

Neither Scanlon or Samuel believed Schwab could do the job, but neither of them wanted to lose him. Politically, his departure would be devastating for the commission. There was every chance many of the clubs aligned with Schwab would revolt. Scanlon and Samuel worked within a floor of one another in Collins Street and spent a lot of time debating how to handle the problem. At one stage their discussions became so heated they began shouting at one another. And when they calmed down, they came up with an idea. What if the new commissioner's job was split? Oakley, of course, would have most of the power. But Schwab's role could be sold to the clubs and the public as something almost on an equal standing.

Scanlon had put this idea to several of the sub-committee members. He'd already spoken to Oakley and been impressed by his approach. He also knew Oakley had his reservations. Who would want to surrender a high-paying job with little public profile to become a moving target on the League scene?

Everyone agreed that if Schwab could be talked into staying, then the plan should be adopted. Scanlon rang Schwab and invited him around for a drink one evening. There, Scanlon laid it on the line. He looked Schwab in the eye and told him he wasn't good enough to get the main job, that football could suffer if he was thrown into a role he knew little about. And yet, Scanlon told him, he still had plenty to offer the game and a lot of skills that could complement Oakley's business acumen.

Then Scanlon delivered the punch. If Schwab didn't accept the proposal, Scanlon would resign from the commission the following morning.

Schwab went home and thought about it. He rang Scanlon

the next morning, bitterly disappointed. Yes, he said. He'd take the option offered him.

All that was left was for Oakley to meet with Schwab. Over a coffee, Schwab made one last stab. He proposed that he and Oakley be joint managing directors of the League.

'It doesn't work that way, Schwabby,' Oakley told him. The pair remembered one another from their St Kilda days, but had not seen much of each other since.

'You can call it whatever you like. But there can only be one boss. Someone's got to take the responsibility. Someone's got to have the final say. And I'm not coming if that's going to be the case.'

They talked for half an hour. Eventually, they struck a deal. Oakley believed Schwab had accepted the notion that only one man could wield ultimate power. 'But you can have your head on most things,' he told him.

They agreed to adopt different roles and reponsibilities. Schwab would look after the day-to-day matters of the game; the rules and the scheduling of matches. Oakley would concern himself with the overall picture and strike the deals on the all-important television rights and corporate sponsorships.

The sub-committee made its recommendation to a meeting of the clubs on 15 August. It was promptly accepted. Peter Scanlon and Graeme Samuel had their man. And Alan Schwab, at the age of 45, had just seen his career come to a shuddering halt with little prospect of it ever improving.

The game had claimed another of its own.

If the battle for the commissioner's job was a tough and bruising affair, it had nothing on another stoush that was quickly approaching its climax. The fight over whether the Victorian Football League should expand nationally had reached fever pitch within a month of Hamilton's announced retirement. And it was a fight only football could produce, a heated debate where all the emotions and furies the game incited in those who followed it spilt into the open.

The competition was split between the conservative clubs, who believed expansion would put even greater financial pressure on those clubs already with their backs to the wall, and those who believed a national competition was now the only method of saving the game.

Everyone used whatever ammunition they could find. Fitzroy, which by 1986 was facing debts of more than $2 million, surveyed 700 spectators at a game at Victoria Park. The club's nomadic wanderings had once again seen it move grounds. Now, it was sharing an uncomfortable alliance at Collingwood's home ground. It was like a lamb spending the night in a lion's den. Did the public want a national competition? Predictably, almost 95 per cent said no. It was like the old political adage: never hold a Royal Commission unless you know what the outcome will be. Surveying 700 conservative football fans at Victoria Park and wanting to know if they wanted their League disrupted by change was a little like asking 700 people inside the Vatican if they believed the Catholic Church should merge with the Muslim faith.

But what did that matter? It was the overwhelming 'no' vote that Fitzroy bandied around town. It looked great in headlines and backed up the club's claims that the commission, that group of powerful, yet silent men, were hell-bent on changing the game no matter what the public wanted.

Hawthorn, a club noted for its conservatism, also launched a campaign of its own. 'I wouldn't like to be in the situation where Melbourne people go to the races on grand final day because Perth is playing Adelaide in Melbourne,' warned the club's chief executive, John Lauritz.

Richmond, the club that two years before had actively promoted the idea of a breakaway national competition, also stepped into the fray. In a letter to the League and circulated to all the clubs, Richmond's general manager Kevin Dixon argued that the commission was pursuing a national competition 'irrespective of whether that is the right way for football to go . . .

this club is concerned that no sound, logical reasons have been advanced for a 14-team competition as opposed to a 16-team or 10-team competition.'

To the commission, it seemed as though the entire football world had rounded on it. Even the taciturn and wry Hawthorn coach Allan Jeans, who had coached St Kilda to its first flag back in 1966, broke his normally strict personal code of maintaining the lowest possible public profile by demanding that the commission come clean and give its reasons behind the national push.

Kevin Bartlett, the champion Richmond rover who held the League's record number of games with 403 senior appearances, was also vociferously against expansion and, in his regular column in *The Sun* newspaper, commanded an impressive audience each day. Even two days before the clubs were due to make a decision on whether to award the commission the power to push ahead with plans for a 14-team competition the following year, Bartlett clung to his beliefs like a creationist at a lecture on the theory of evolution.

'Football supporters can take heart,' he wrote on 29 July. 'The national league won't even get off the ground.'

Bartlett based his beliefs on the notion that four clubs would vote against any move for expansion in the following year. The commission required an 8-4 vote to get its recommendation through. But Hawthorn, Richmond, Collingwood and Fitzroy were against it. Others were wavering, too, just waiting to be led.

Why was the commission so hell bent on a national league? It had argued the pro-expansion case strongly in private. Throughout September, Hamilton and his part-time commissioners had lobbied the clubs intensively, arguing that the inclusion of a team from WA would boost television rights revenues by $1.75 million. But publicly, out there where it mattered among the supporters and the media, their performance left a lot to be desired. Football had never required leadership more than now and the commission was failing to supply it.

Hamilton was on the way out, Oakley was on the way in and neither man was in a position to spearhead an attack into the future. And Scanlon and Samuel, the two most influential part-time commissioners? The last thing they wanted was publicity. Scanlon abhorred it. He and Samuel preferred to work in the shadows.

'One thing Peter Scanlon hated was making speeches,' John Elliott would say. 'He wasn't very good on his feet publicly . . . what he was good at was across the table when a deal had to be done.'

It was a bizarre situation. And it dragged on for several months before the clubs met on 1 October, just days after John Elliott's well-paid Carlton team, boasting the best talent money could buy, had succumbed to Hawthorn by seven goals in an anti-climactic finish to the season.

It was the most anticipated meeting in the League's long history. Not since 1925, when North Melbourne, Footscray and Hawthorn had been admitted, had there been a vote to admit a new club.

Outside VFL House in Jolimont, a large crowd of vocal Fitzroy supporters had also gathered, adding to the drama. Besides the pending vote on whether to admit teams from Western Australia and Brisbane, the future of the Fitzroy club was also on the agenda. The Lions had been one of several clubs limping through the 1980s, burdened by a heavy debt and without the corporate backing enjoyed by their wealthier brethren. Their problem was typical of the changing nature of the game. The club had emerged to represent one of Melbourne's toughest inner suburbs. Fitzroy had been staunchly working-class at the turn of the century, its narrow, cobbled streets and rows of thinly-walled terrace houses home to generations of loyal footy supporters.

But by the 1980s Fitzroy was a rootless club. Its suburban home had been gradually transformed into a yuppie kingdom in line with many similar inner-city suburbs around the country. The Lions had become a nomadic side, always on the lookout to share a home ground with another, usually wealthier, club. It had not won a flag since 1944. Now it was faced with an ageing supporter base. As each year passed, the old familiar faces on the terraces and in the grandstand slowly disappeared. There were not many new, young ones replacing them.

The Lions had also been financially shattered by a series of player trades in the late 1970s and early 1980s that left them cash-strapped and vulnerable. Leon Wiegard had inherited the mess when he became chairman. From the start he had sensed trouble. Publicly he maintained the typical attitude of a besieged club official. Problem? What problem? But privately the gregarious Wiegard feared for the club's future. There were only so many times you could appeal to the hearts and purses of the public. In 1985 he had held several talks with Melbourne and its president, Stuart Spencer, about the possibility of the two clubs merging. The talks, naturally, had been held in Scanlon's Collins Street office. The negotiating teams had agreed on new colours, the structure of the board, even a new name: The Melbourne Lions. The chairmen would serve alternate years. But Fitzroy procrastinated over the deal, worried about how it could sell such a proposal to its members. In the end, like so many similar proposals over the following years, it fell apart.

Now things were desperate, but Wiegard thought he had found an answer. Hecron, a local construction company, was offering to buy the club for $2.6 million, effectively paying off its debts and allowing the club to start afresh. There was one catch: the commission was against private ownership of Melbourne clubs, for reasons it had stated clearly in its strategy document the year before. The sharks were circling and Wiegard could see the whites of their eyes. The club had already been targetted by several syndicates vying for the right to the licence to run a team out of Brisbane, and even the Fitzroy players had shown interest in moving north, if only to end the constant pressure and speculation about the club's future.

At one stage the Fitzroy board actually approved an in-principle move to Brisbane. But no-one was really happy with the 5-3 result. It decided to declare it 'a straw vote' only.

Years later, Wiegard would wearily nod his head when prodded about those times. In the long run it would have been better either merging with another club or moving interstate.

'I regret that,' he would say. 'The only thing we could never legitimately offer was hope. We could offer survival. But not hope.'

And what was football without hope? You didn't support a team simply because its colours were nicely co-ordinated. You followed it because you hoped that one day it would win The Flag for you. And Fitzroy had no chance of achieving that. Not in the 1980s. Not when you needed money to win a premiership.

One Sunday morning during the 1986 season, Wiegard had ventured down to club training at Wesley College. Wiegard prided himself on his knockabout manner and his performances as host of the pre-game Fitzroy luncheons were legendary. He called the players together and looked each of them in the eye.

'Well, boys,' declared Wiegard, 'the club's decided it looks as though our future no longer lies here. It looks like Brisbane or Perth.'

The players stared back, stunned by Wiegard's unexpectedly blunt appraisal of the situation.

Wiegard tried to break the ice. 'Anyone here got a preference for where we go?' he asked.

No-one said anything. And then rover Bernie Harris said he would like to see the club move to Perth.

'Why?' asked Wiegard.

'Perth's a six-can trip.' Even at its worst, the game managed to produce a lighter moment.

But on the evening of 1 October 1986, there was little room for levity.

There was a lot on the line, not only for Fitzroy. The commission was also under pressure. It had made clear its intentions: with the South Australians characteristically wanting more time to consider their position, the commission wanted a team from Perth, to be controlled by the game's governing body in that state, the Western Australian Football League, and a club out of Brisbane, to be run by the sports promotor and entrepreneur John Brown. And it didn't want Hecron 'owning' Fitzroy.

It would be a tough fight and, as the meeting progressed, Scanlon and Samuel sensed the mood was against them. Hawthorn's Ron Cook had made his case clear: Brisbane was OK, but there should be a 12-month cooling off period on the question of a team from WA. Who knew what sort of monster the VFL would be creating if it allowed a team of West Australians to play in the competition? Cook feared a Perth presence more than anything. Like every club in the League, his side had boasted its share of players recruited from the west and he knew only too well the large pool of talent one side servicing an entire state could draw upon.

It became clear halfway through the evening that the commission was in trouble. Cook seemed to have convinced enough clubs that another year of waiting and weighing up the pros and cons on a Perth team would not be a bad thing.

Samuel leaned across to Hamilton and told him to call an adjournment for 10 minutes. Then Samuel, Scanlon and Hamilton called Leon Wiegard into a side office. If they could convince him a WA team was a good thing, the vote would be secure.

The three impressed upon Wiegard the value of voting for WA; more than $600,000 dollars was likely to go to each Victorian club as their share of the licence fees. The Hecron proposal would not proceed. Where else was Fitzroy going to get the money it needed to stave off the shadow of the corporate affairs office and its growing list of creditors?

They had Wiegard in a corner. But the Fitzroy chairman was also a handy politician. And he knew the commission was in trouble too. It couldn't afford to lose on this one. The whole concept of expanding the competition required a presence in Western Australia.

Wiegard said he would vote for WA if the League would guarantee bank loans for the club for the following couple of years. 'In front of Jack and Scanlon I was happy to accept it,' Wiegard would recall. 'Even though it was only verbal . . .we needed the money. And we needed that guarantee. That money saved Fitzroy again.'

Over the following years, the Lions would prove to be football's version of Houdini. Time and again they would find themselves in apparently inescapable financial trouble, only to find one saviour or another arriving on the doorstep just in time.

The meeting resumed and a vote was called. Fitzroy approved the commission's recommendation for a Perth side. The deal was done.

And then Ron Cook exploded. 'You've bought a vote,' he shouted at the commissioners. 'You've blackmailed us.'

When the meeting finally broke, Cook was still livid. His club, he announced, was 'absolutely shattered' by the vote. Hawthorn, Collingwood, Essendon and Melbourne had voted against the proposal. But it had been carried 8-4, the narrowest possible outcome.

'I am sick and tired of the clubs' financial problems and how they have cheated on their balance sheets,' cursed Cook.

'They are so desperate for money, but bankrupt people never make the right decisions. How people who have stuffed their own clubs' finances could vote like that in the interests of money is beyond me.'

The commission had carried the day on a national competition. It had got what it wanted. But it had also made an enemy for life. In that, however, Ron Cook would not be alone.

10

THE
TELEVISION WARS

Was Ross Oakley tough enough? Barely a week had passed since he had moved into the game's most senior post and already the question was being tossed around Melbourne. Could he handle the pressures that accompanied being one of the most criticised and ridiculed public figures in the state?

Whenever the questions arose, and Oakley heard it often enough, he had a ready-made response. Of course he was tough enough, he would tell those around him. Those people asking the question hadn't bothered to find out much about his past. Didn't they know he had had to take some bloody tough decisions in the business world? At Royal Insurance he had cut the workforce by 250. Who knew what effect those sackings had had on the lives and families of the people who had lost their jobs? He would have preferred to have kept them on, guaranteeing them and their families a regular livelihood. But something had to be done and the buck had stopped with him.

Of course he was tough.

He'd weathered plenty of storms in business. What about his career at BHP? He had been asked to write a report on the company's plan to recycle its cans. BHP had been trying to prove to everyone that while aluminium cans were recyclable, it was also recycling its steel cans. But Oakley's report revealed otherwise. Hardly any cans had been recycled. Those that had been collected had been dumped at one of the company's steelworks and had kept piling up. They could not be put in the furnaces because of a special brand of tin coating that, in high temperatures, wrecked the furnace.

Noses were put out of joint and Oakley came under heavy attack from other departments. A series of conferences and meetings were held to discuss his report. 'It was me against the lot of them,' he would say years later, his face grim, his chin thrust out aggressively.

The fall-out over the can controversy saw the corporate planning department where Oakley worked split into smaller sections. He soon sensed he had reached a pivotal moment in his career. It was time to move on. He took a senior job with Wynn's, a wine company. Then he was headhunted to go to AAMI, the insurance company. The company was struggling after dominating the car insurance market for years and needed a big win to re-establish itself. It did so with a clever advertising campaign, showing cars out of control plunging through several disasters. They ended up grabbing 10 per cent of the market share off their main rival, State Insurance. Profitability climbed $7 million over three years and soon Oakley had become the managing director. From there he had jumped to Royal Insurance.

Tough enough? Now, here he was heading the Victorian Football League, without a doubt the organisation which controlled Australian rules. Even those in other states like Western Australia and particularly South Australia, where they loathed the VFL for its greed and arrogance and the contempt it displayed toward their own competitions, had to agree.

The VFL was the best competition in the land. Its 12 teams had the best players, the biggest support staffs, the finest resources. Of course, they had the most money too. That was the bottom line. They could pay top dollar. It was inevitable. Any kid who grew up in Western Australia or South Australia and who showed any talent was quickly spirited away to the east, where the bloody Victorians had an annoying habit of adopting him as one of their own.

So had they known what was taking place in the upper echelons of the VFL in late 1986, those South Australians and their brethren further west would have enjoyed a wry smile. The VFL was in deep trouble. It was staring at disaster. And Ross Oakley, who thought he had made some pretty tough decisions in the world of business, was staring straight at it across a table in an office in downtown South Melbourne.

When Oakley joined the League, its public image and financial woes were not the first problems confronting him. More pressing matters needed to be resolved. All the game's major contracts were up for renewal. The VFL needed a new corporate sponsor for 1987. The airlines agreement had expired and a new one was vitally important given the amount of travelling the clubs would be doing the following year. And the television rights agreement with Channel 7 had also ended.

In the season just finished, Channel 7 in Melbourne had paid the League a $3.3 million package for the rights to telecast the game. It was a significant amount for the time but the commission believed that a national competition, with more matches and more opportunities to screen games in prime-time, should guarantee them far more. They desperately needed it. They had pressed hard for expansion, arguing the case for more than 12 months. Increased television rights had been a crucial aspect of that argument. Now they had to deliver.

It wasn't looking very hopeful, not at this moment in the South Melbourne headquarters of Channel 7. Oakley had come down to see the general manager of Seven, Ron Casey. Accompanying him were Peter Scanlon and Jack Hamilton, who had agreed to stay on until early October.

Oakley had seen the portly figure of Casey enter Hamilton's office a couple of times and figured Hamilton was smoothing out the edges on a new television rights deal that had already been under negotiation for some time. Others in the VFL offices thought it strange that Hamilton did not regularly include Oakley in his discussions. But Oakley had let it ride.

Until this meeting at Channel 7 headquarters. The four exchanged pleasantries, then Casey sat back. 'Well, what do you have in mind?' he asked.

Oakley waited for Hamilton to start talking.

'Well,' said Hamilton, nodding at his replacement. 'Off you go, Ross.'

Oakley was stunned. What was he supposed to say? He had no real idea how the TV rights package was put together. In years to come, he would go through the files and still fail to find a signed contract between the network and the League. He was embarrassed and also slightly angry at being dropped deep into it.

He began by telling Casey why the League's television contract should be worth far more in the coming years. Value had been added to the product.

Casey remained unimpressed. Over the years he had forged a close relationship with Hamilton. Now, here was this younger upstart, along with Scanlon, one of those smart money men from Collins Street who had made a killing on the corporate scene, telling him his station was expected to pay far more for the football rights.

Casey thought Oakley, in his attempt to sound knowledgeable, was being overly aggressive. When you looked at the package they were promising for the following year, there wasn't a great deal of live content. Didn't the League realise you needed live football in prime time to make a difference, to pull in the ratings and the advertisers?

Channel 7 offered the League $3.3 million for 1987. There would be no increase.

The battle lines had been drawn. Football was about to embark on the most significant and far-reaching battle it had experienced. When it was finally over, nothing would be the same again. The very few people left who still thought football was all just a game would be forced to change their minds.

FOOTBALL LTD

The sport had embraced television cautiously ever since its introduction into Australia in 1956. That year the game's cathedral, the Melbourne Cricket Ground, was resurfaced and used as the main stadium for the last of what the world would call the 'Friendly Olympics'. The movement was in the process of farewelling the amateur ideal, even though it would falsely lay claim to that ethos for years to come. Television had arrived and was in the process of changing forever the games people played.

While television was a novelty seen mainly in store front windows that year, it had already begun its encroachment into sport in the United States where, by the late 1950s, more than 80 per cent of households boasted a television set.

The world's first sporting event had been broadcast on May 17, 1939, when a baseball game between two American college teams, Princeton and Columbia, was aired from Bakers' Field, Manhattan. But it wasn't until 1951 that the marriage between sports and television was consummated. It took place in front of hundreds of thousands of American viewers; a baseball title match between the Giants and the Dodgers. It was close, exciting and decided in the bottom of the ninth inning with a last-ditch home run. Suddenly, television was not just a vehicle for variety shows. It was almost as good as being there. Sometimes, it gave you a better view than the seat you could afford to buy.

American television network chiefs discovered they were sitting on a goldmine. Sports were relatively cheap to broadcast compared to other programs where the 'talent' had to be contracted and trained. Viewers, the majority of them blue-collar, were sports fans. And, best of all, advertisers loved to be associated with sport. The people who watched American football were largely male, middle-aged and their family's main or sole breadwinner. Therefore, they tended to make the big decisions on what sort of car to buy. Or what brand of beer they drank.

There was nothing to suggest anything was different in

Australia. But with television's arrival, the VFL decided it was best to play it cautiously. And, as with everything, there were some within football who thought the game had moved too quickly.

Fearful of suffering a drop in attendances and just as concerned that the rival Victorian Football Association might jump in ahead of it, the League agreed that during the 1957 season, the three stations—7, 9 and 2—could televise live the final quarter.

The following year, the League earned the princely sum of 500 pounds. But by the end of the season it had begun to harbour strong doubts about the new medium's impact on the game. Attendances fell by almost 150,000 that season and continued to drop in the following two years. The stations weren't that enthusiastic, either. Selling commercial time during the final quarter of a match was a tough task.

But the dwindling crowds were enough for the League. It pulled the plug on television and almost immediately its decision was vindicated. Without that live telecast of the final quarter, crowds rose by a remarkable 360,000 in 1961. The following year, despite the grand final being a sell-out, the League was steadfast: no live broadcast. Instead, any station interested in screening a replay of the game could do so for 600 pounds.

From there, television became an integral part of the game, but only on the stringent terms laid down by the League: no live broadcasts. Replays and panel shows became the standard fare. At one stage in the 1960s, the small percentage of the Victorian population that didn't like football could find no respite from the game on television. Every station, including the ABC, had decided to run replays on Saturday evenings.

But as the years passed, only one station, HSV-7, remained closely aligned with the game. A large part of Seven's image was built around football. It broadcast 'World of Sport', a curious Sunday morning program the like of which had never been seen before or since. For hours on end, old footballers and commentators would sit around yarning about the day's previous matches, interrupted only by the odd guest or competition. A Thursday evening program, 'League Teams', which previewed the line-ups for the coming Saturday matches, would achieve cult status. And then there was the replay. Seven's football coverage lived and died by the replay. If that day's games were close and exciting, it rated well. If not, it still rated. But it needed the tight results.

Oakley wondered why Ron Casey felt so sure about his position. How dare he offer the League the same amount as the year before? At one stage he had even said Seven would not have offered $3.3 million were it not for the starting up of the so-called national competition.

Casey was known around the League as the 13th director of the VFL and, in reality, he had a far greater impact on the game than most of the 12 men who sat around the board table.

To those who worked with him over the years, Casey was a taciturn man who kept his emotions closely checked and his thoughts private. His method of negotiating the football rights used to annoy some of his fellow executives at Seven. Ron Casey did it on his own. No-one else was invited along to sit in on negotiations. They were not informed of what had taken place once he'd arrived back at the office except when it was mentioned casually that 'Oh, by the way, we've got the football for another three years.'

That was all anyone heard until a program director or football producer received a call from League headquarters.

'So, you'll be covering the promotion in the city square, I take it?' the voice from the League would say.

'Excuse me?' would ask the bewildered HSV executive.

'Well, it's part of your deal with us . . . Go and check it with "Case" if you like.'

Why was Casey acting so confidently? Did Seven think it had an inalienable right to broadcast the game? The commissioners sat around the table for hours discussing the problem. They decided to hawk the rights around town. Surely, with a national competition about to begin, the commercial networks would be falling over themselves to gain the rights.

He went to Channel 9. No interest. It was the same at Channel 10. Oakley couldn't believe it. This was football, wasn't it? This was Melbourne, right? What in hell was going on?

Several weeks passed. Time was running out. And then Casey contacted the League again.

He was growing impatient. The League, he told them, had taken too long. Channel 7 would now only offer $3 million.

That was it. The commission met following Casey's revised second offer. Obviously it was unacceptable. If Oakley had not harboured suspicions beforehand, he had them now.

'There's a keep-off-the grass agreement here and the deal's been done,' he said. 'We've got to find another option and see how we can break down this agreement rather than have Seven in control of it.'

The sporting agreement among the networks, Casey would say years later, was never as strong as many thought. 'The sporting situation was never as firm as the agreement on international programs,' he would say. 'That was a well-understood protocol.'

Outside his home in Brighton, a soft rain was falling and Casey's voice seemed to fluctuate in intensity to match it. In his later years he still boasted the same barrel-like physique that had helped give him such a commanding presence during his days in the television industry.

'You bid like fury for a new product but once you had it on air that remained your property, until the new owners came in and that went out the window. Imported programs, there was a definite understanding of keep-off-the-grass. If MGM produced a new program then everyone would go for it. But once you bought it, when it was renewed that program stayed with you.

'The other thing was that sporting rights were getting expensive. Very expensive. So the networks were quite happy to say we'll stay with what we've got. Let's go along with that. The ABC couldn't be in a situation like that because that would have been politically difficult for them.'

More than just politically difficult. Had such a keep-off-the-grass agreement been made public at the time, with all its implications that the networks were acting as a cartel to keep prices down, it would surely have attracted the interest of several Federal Government regulatory bodies, including the Trade Practices Commission.

While the League believed the networks had done a deal by divvying up the major sports among themselves in order to keep broadcast rights from spiralling like they had in the United States, it had not always been so.

In the early 1980s, Seven's dominance had been challenged more than once. At the end of 1981, the 10 Network had put in a substantial bid. The station in Melbourne was then owned by Rupert Murdoch and the powerful media mogul had gone to some lengths to woo the League. Once they collected Allen Aylett at the Moonee Valley racecourse and flew him in a chopper to a luncheon rendezvous.

The Channel 10 presentation to the League was a well-considered document and made a big play at wresting away the rights from Seven. Ten offered $2.26 million a year for three years and promised to throw its considerable influence in the media behind the Swans' first season in Sydney: 'News Limited newspapers will support the full-time introduction of Australian football into New South Wales via its leading morning newspaper *The Daily Telegraph* and its top-selling afternoon paper, *The Daily Mirror*.'

Seven, however, won through with a bid of $2.85 million in the first year, building to $3.42 million by 1984.

That was about the last time there was a decent competition for the rights. When Channel 10 missed the deal, its star football reporter, Rob Astbury, a volatile and highly-strung man, broke down weeping at VFL House. He was not the last person to shed a tear over football's relationship with television.

Now, with the summer of 1986/87 fast approaching, where could the League go? Scanlon had already approached Kerry Packer who, unbeknown to most, was on the verge of selling the Nine network to Alan Bond.

Scanlon told him of the League's plight and looked for advice on what to do with the rights.

'Warehouse them,' Packer told him. 'Don't commit yourself for more than a year.'

Scanlon had reported back to the commission that a long-term agreement, given the turbulent state of the television industry, was probably not in their best interests. And clearly the money wasn't around. But who would want to strike a deal for just a year? Scanlon suggested a small company based in Sydney that fitted the bill perfectly. He knew an outfit specialising in business and marketing videos. While it was a minnow in a sea of sharks, Broadcom had bigger ambitions. It wanted to be a player on the television scene. With Peter Scanlon giving it a push, it had every chance.

It was a voice, observed one of his colleagues on more than one occasion, that sounded like it had come 'from his balls or his feet'. It was deep and rich and almost melodic. Listen to it for any length of time and it had the ability to hypnotise.

Steve Cosser grew up an army brat. The old man, Ray, was on his way up toward the rank of staff sergeant. Margaret, his mother, doted on the young boy. The pair had adopted him when he was just three days old and just another name in a growing list on Britain's state adoption agency.

From the start, Steve Cosser had shown special qualities, including a decent imagination, even more fertile than most of the other nine-year-old boys around him in Yorkshire.

From his bedroom upstairs he would put wires through the ceiling from his stereo and microphone and connect them to a speaker in the kitchen. Margaret would write out requests for songs and slip them under his bedroom door. Then she'd scurry back to the kitchen to hear young Stevie Cosser introduce the music.

He was good. When the family was posted to Cyprus, he conned his way on to the local radio station. By the time he was a teenager he was an announcer on the 'Voice of Cyprus'.

Then they moved to Australia. More opportunities came his way. By the time he had reached his early 20s he was the host of 'AM' on ABC radio, the 30-minute current affairs program listened to avidly by the influential and those who wanted to be. Some mornings he would be there in the studio, shirt half undone, trousers undone. It was due to The Voice, he told those who dared ask. The Voice. Cosser explained it came from the stomach, not the throat. There could be no constraints.

The Voice did a lot of talking in those days. Straight after work at 8.30am he would put on a suit and begin driving all over Sydney to push The Music Company, flogging off pre-taped musical cassettes to restaurants and bars. It wasn't Musak, either. The Voice had the real artists, singing their own tunes. Cosser was the first person to think of it.

It had always been like this. A sharp eye for detail, an even sharper eye for a deal. And his baby face helped him somehow. Few could believe the young man sitting opposite them, caressing them with that rich, velvety voice, was just another operator out there, looking to make a fortune.

It didn't take long, though. In 1982, Channel 10 had lured him across to anchor 'The Reporters', a current affairs program designed by the network to challenge Nine's news supremacy. He arrived to sign his contract accompanied by two lawyers.

They were with him five months later when the show was

axed, guaranteeing him a payout of more than $200,000. That money went back into the business. Things continued to grow. In late June, 1986, the dividend arrived.

He sold his remaining share in the company for $900,000. He was 26 and agreed to stay on to manage the business. The buyers were Broadcast and Communications, a small-time media broadcaster, and Basil Sellers' Linter Group. Broadcast and Communications would eventually be bought by the Linter Group and its name truncated as the new title for The Music Company. Broadcom was born.

For football, it was an important deal. The Linter Group was controlled by a cash cow called AFP Investment Corporation. AFP's deputy chairman was Peter Scanlon.

The Voice flew to Melbourne and drove to Oakley's Mulgrave home early on a Sunday morning just before Christmas, 1986.

'I hear you've been having some problems,' Cosser said as the pair sat down. Oakley gave him an outline of what had occurred.

Cosser told Oakley that while Broadcom could not deliver the League a Victorian station, he had plenty of confidence that the game could be packaged around the company for a price higher than what Channel 7 had been offering.

Within a couple of hours the pair reached agreement. Broadcom would guarantee the League $24.55 million over the next six years, with anything above that to be split 50-50. In the first season, the company would also bring forward about $2 million to boost the first season's payments to more than $5.5 million.

Oakley took the agreement back to the commission. It was ratified.

On Christmas Eve just before 5pm, Oakley put in a call to Ron Casey.

'Ron, I'm ringing to let you know that we've just sold the rights to Broadcom. But I hope Seven can continue to stay involved.'

Casey was mystified. Broadcom? The name rang a bell, but only softly. He hung up and walked over to a filing cabinet. There it was. Some young bloke called Cosser had been to see him a few months before, trying to package a weekend business program.

Casey ran his eye down a list of names associated with the company. He saw two familiar ones: Peter Scanlon and Graeme Samuel. He got straight back on the phone to Oakley.

'This is a pretty funny sort of situation,' said Casey angrily.

'I know all about that,' replied Oakley. 'But they didn't vote.'

Casey hung up, seething. That evening, on the night before Christmas, he stirred restlessly.

Tim Lane had been at the MCG on Boxing Day covering the Test cricket on radio when word began sweeping through the press box that Broadcom, and not Channel 7, had won the rights to broadcast football. For the first time in a while, the ABC commentator felt optimistic.

Maybe now there was a chance.

Lane was the best commentator in town. He was a small, thin man who wore his Tasmanian origins on radio like a badge. He had a smooth, unflustered delivery and a voice suited to the rapid transitions from boredom to excitement experienced so often by the game of Australian football. While Lane was predominantly heard on radio, his was a voice which also carried well on television. But, as he had discovered over the years, when you worked for the ABC it usually meant playing second fiddle to the commercial networks.

He had found that out only too well a few months before. With a new administration in place at VFL House and a national competition about to begin, Lane had sensed that the game was about to undergo significant changes. Could there be an opening there for the ABC, which for years had been treated with contempt by Seven despite its status as the only true national network? Lane wrote to the ABC's new managing director, David Hill, and urged him to consider getting involved in some form.

But no bid was forthcoming. So as he sat at the MCG watching the Test, contemplating the news that football's old boys network had finally been broken, he felt a sense of excitement. Still, he had to remember not to get too carried away. He had been with the ABC long enough.

But a week later he realised something was in the air. He was at the Hanging Rock racetrack on New Year's Day, trying to force his way into the crowded betting ring. He spied a familiar figure trying to do the same. It was John Elliott.

The pair exchanged pleasantries. Lane, a confirmed Carlton supporter, grilled the president about whether he thought the Blues could avoid the humiliation of their loss to Hawthorn in the 1986 grand final and win it the following season. The talk inevitably moved to the television rights. Seven was still adamant it would not negotiate with Broadcom.

'Looks like you might be doing a bit of football this year,' Elliott said, and then went on to mention how the League had discovered the keep-off-the-grass agreement among the networks and how awarding the rights to Broadcom was an attempt to break, once and for all, what the League regarded as the networks' cosy little arrangement.

But Lane would have to wait. It was not as clear-cut as Elliott had been led to believe.

Patience, after all, was an ABC virtue.

In the week between Christmas and New Year the commission, and Oakley in particular, continued to cop a hiding from the clubs, the press and the public. Broadcom? Just what on earth was this new bloke Oakley doing to the game? Finally, the commission hit back.

Ron Cook, the president of Hawthorn, a former vice-president of the VFL and a firm traditionalist, had been sniping at the League for days, mourning the loss of Channel 7. His world was upside down. First there was the decision to go national and allow the Western Australians in. He'd fought a tough fight to prevent that and lost. And now another piece of the game's tradition had gone.

Samuel was on holidays with his family on the Mornington Peninsula. Oakley was on the Whitsunday Islands, trying to get away from it all before the real work began. To those who knew him, he had already been knocked around severely by the constant pummelling from his critics. Some began to wonder just how much longer he would put up with it.

Samuel's patience had run out. He'd had enough of being beaten up. So on New Year's Eve he rang Peter Nixon, an old political headkicker from way back. The pair had been in almost daily contact as the television furore developed. But Nixon noticed a particularly angry tone in Samuel's voice this time.

'This is bloody ridiculous,' said Samuel. 'We keep getting kicked in the head and we're not kicking back. We're losing our credibility.

'You've got to stop it,' demanded Samuel. 'I can't do it.'

Nixon hesitated for a moment. 'You really want to?' he asked, surprised at the vehemence and lust for revenge in a man he considered extremely polite and considered.

'Get out there and kick some arse,' said Samuel.

Nixon rang the television stations with a statement, and one even flew a reporter and camera crew down to Nixon's property near Orbost in Victoria's far east for a quick stand-up interview. He was on the phone to all the papers, lambasting Cook and the rest of the commission's critics.

Channel 7, he said, had not even been interested in tendering for the rights and their application had been 'totally unsatisfactory . . . they are so used to the nod and wink approach that they were very critical of even having to tender at all.'

And as for Ron Cook? 'I'm very disappointed that Ron Cook has seen fit to criticise the VFL the way he has,' thundered Nixon. 'He complains that the clubs haven't been told enough, but there was a meeting before the decision was made which he didn't bother to turn up to . . . I'm sick and tired of his continued criticism of the commission.'

If Cook was surprised by the vehemence in Nixon's attack, Casey was infuriated. Just what was Nixon trying to drive at, he asked himself. Was he trying to say that not all of his and Jack Hamilton's dealings had been above board? It was an insult. And if the League thought it could beat Seven into submission, it had another think coming. Casey's resolve not to deal with Broadcom strengthened.

'We refused to deal with Broadcom,' Casey would recall. 'They couldn't get anyone else interested, either. I must say I lobbied a bit with the others, although it didn't have anything to do with keep-off-the-grass at all. I saw it as being wrong for there to be an intermediary between football and the broadcasters. I couldn't believe the League had someone to negotiate on their behalf. Nine and Ten agreed.'

The Broadcom deal, Casey believed, wasn't just morally wrong. It was evil. And it contained within it the seeds of disaster for all the networks.

'I said it'll start happening with all sports. You'll find the IMGs of the world running everything.'

The International Management Group was the world's leading agency specialising in managing athletes. And by the mid-1980s the mention of its name would bring an involuntary shudder from television and sports administrators.

But if Cook and Casey were none too pleased with the League's unexpected strike, others within the football community found it just as remarkable. There were headlines everywhere following Nixon's attack. Everyone was astonished. The commission, that bunch of deliberately faceless men who treated football more like a business than a game, had hit back.

It had kicked some arse.

Channel 7 was owned by the media giant *The Herald and Weekly Times*. As well as owning the television station, the company also published *The Sun* and *The Herald*, Melbourne's largest selling morning and afternoon newspapers. It also owned radio station 3DB. The company was an immensely powerful institution.

They finally met in the boardroom at the Herald and Weekly Times in late January. The company and Casey had been convinced to meet the League and Broadcom by the managing director of HWT, John Dahlsen, a relative of Nixon's.

The chairman of HWT, John D'Arcy, was a new boy in town. He was from Brisbane, an insignificant Australian rules outpost dominated by rugby league. He had been slightly incredulous the previous year to discover that whenever Collingwood won a match on the weekend, *The Sun*'s circulation rose by an average of 10,000. Wouldn't it have been better, he'd once joked to a League official, for the HWT simply to buy Collingwood and stock it with good players, forever guaranteeing good sales?

D'Arcy had been amazed at the passion aroused around the state over the television deal. In fact, he had been amazed at anything to do with football in the southern states. He'd decided it was probably in everyone's best interests that Seven renegotiate the contract, at least for this season. And after a good deal of time convincing Casey, D'Arcy and his general manager from Seven met the League across the table.

It was a long evening. At one stage D'Arcy called Casey into his office to let things settle down, so heated did the negotiations become.

But by the time everyone left the building in darkness they had struck a deal. Seven would pay $1.5 million for the Victorian rights only. And, as usual, it would broadcast the night competition it had started a decade before. It would be called the National Panasonic Cup.

The Foster's Cup, with all its bickering and posturing over

signage rights and contracts, had been buried with the past. But there were plenty of scars remaining.

The following day Oakley publicly revealed the deal and, for one of the few times in the League's history, the head of the League made a bizarre admission: 'If there's one thing I'll be trying to do in the future, it is to try to take the views of the average supporter into account,' he said.

'It has been an agonising time from that point of view, but I've always been confident there would be live and replay television of matches. I can understand the clubs' concern with the delay and their difficulty negotiating deals with their sponsors . . . it may have been a little bit tight for them in tying down some of those deals.'

But, added Oakley, the majority of clubs had recognised 'that it has been a very difficult environment in locking this away.'

Locking it away? The fun had only started.

It began little more than a month later. Seven had just been sold by Rupert Murdoch to the Sydney-based publishing empire, John Fairfax and Sons.

Casey was one of the first to find out. D'Arcy rang him at home late at night soon after the deal had been struck. It was the worst outcome for Casey. He did not enjoy the cosiest of relationships with his counterpart, Ted Thomas, at Seven's sister station in Sydney and hardly expected it to improve with this latest news.

Casey had been hoping that Robert Holmes à Court, the money-making machine from the west whom he'd shown around the station some weeks earlier, would buy the station. But Fairfax had it—and so had Casey.

'I thought you should know this as soon as possible Ron,' D'Arcy said. 'Channel 7's been sold to Fairfax.'

Casey was prepared.

'I'll be in your office first thing in the morning and I want you to release me from my contract,' Casey told D'Arcy. He wasn't sticking around if Melbourne was about to become the poor relation to Sydney.

The League was an interested observer while all this was taking place. It had already developed a contingency plan in case the unpredictability of the television scene threw up another wild card. And as soon as it heard that Seven had been sold, it put that plan into effect. Oakley ordered Broadcom to make a discreet approach to the ABC and its managing director, David Hill, and ask whether the corporation would be prepared to take over the reins in the event of a Seven withdrawal. The deal could only be for one year. The ABC would, of course, have first rights of refusal on the following year's coverage. But the League, given the instability of the media scene, was not prepared to commit itself to any long-term deal.

Hill hardly needed to be asked twice.

Tim Lane was about to find out that dreams really do come true. But seven months later he would wonder about that and conclude it wasn't a dream come true at all.

Just the worst nightmare he'd ever experienced.

With Casey gone and Seven sold, the station was caught in limbo for several weeks before the deal received the official nod from the broadcasting authorities. Fairfax, waiting for approval to be granted, could not deal with or issue any orders to any of the Melbourne staff. And without the guidance of Casey, the responsibility for planning rested with program director Gary Fenton and finance controller Gerry Carrington.

Fenton kept trying to ring Sydney to see which way the station's new masters wanted to go. He was trying to plan the year's programs and what was the point of doing it now if, suddenly, it all had to be changed within a few weeks? Besides, Seven in Melbourne was now a part of Seven Sydney. And everyone had already seen how networking worked at Nine. The left hand moved only when the right hand issued an order.

Finally, he got through to the office of the general manager, Ted Thomas. Yes, Thomas would see him in Sydney. The next day Fenton gathered his programming schedules, went to the airport and caught a plane north.

Fenton was particularly fond of Australian rules football. Like many at Seven, his career had been forged by the game and its peaks and troughs had matched his. And he, like others around him in Dorcas Street, had played a pivotal role in the game's development.

Fenton had been a handy footballer but never made it to League level, settling for an unremarkable career with VFA club Sandringham. In 1969 he had toured with the unfortunately-named Galahs in one of the first pioneering visits to Ireland to play in a series of composite-rules matches. At that time, and many years on, the administrators boasted visions of Australian footballers playing Tests against Irish footballers, whose free-running Gaelic code most closely resembled the game at home.

When the Irish tour finished, Fenton decided to stay on in Europe and eventually wound up in the United States. For a time he entertained visions of earning a lucrative salary in American football, trying out with the Kansas City Chiefs as a place kicker under the club's legendary coach, Hank Stram. It was the sort of stuff many footballers from all around the world dreamed of. The Americans played a boring, even stultifying, game. Everyone agreed on that. But hey, it was the big league. And wasn't there something in the tale about the little Aussie battler who showed the Yanks just how to kick a footy? What a story. A bunch of poofters who had to wear padding and helmets to play footy being taught the rudiments of ball control by an Aussie.

Many tried and very few ever got anywhere. Fenton was one of them. After more than a year away he decided he'd seen and experienced enough. It was time to go home and get serious about a career.

He picked up a job with Seven and by the mid-1970s was producing the station's promotional commercials. His first close brush with the VFL had taken place just a year or two before North captured its first premiership in 1975 under Ron Barassi and the presidency of Allen Aylett. Videotape technology was still in its infancy then and Fenton had been invited along to one of North's board meetings to show them all about this new contraption, the video machine; how it could be used by the club to show players their weaknesses and to keep an eye on opposition clubs and their on-field tactics.

Of course, the damn thing wouldn't work. Fenton had to sheepishly make a premature exit. But he went back at a later date. The machine finally clicked and eventually North became one of the first clubs to embrace the new technology.

It did not take too long for Fenton's career to climb. Casey had kept a close eye on his development and appointed him sports producer, a position which Fenton suspected would help give Casey greater control over the station and, in particular, its sports division.

By the time Casey left, Fenton was programming manager. And now here he was, flying to Sydney to discover the future of HSV-7. There was already plenty of speculation in Melbourne. Everyone had been waiting for Ted Thomas to flex his newly-won muscle and start making moves. They just wondered who, and what, would be first. It didn't take long for Fenton to realise that Australian football was one of the first items marked on Fairfax's hit-list.

Years later, Fenton would claim he could still recall the small nuances and gestures in their conversation. Thomas would say he could hardly remember even being at the meeting. The Fenton version involved meeting Thomas in his office and immediately getting down to business.

Fenton opened by explaining that it was about time they got together and worked out the scheduling of some of their best programs, just to ensure they didn't clash and a problem develop later.

He suggested the series 'Policewoman', starring Angie Dickinson. What timeslot should it be accorded? 'Yes,' said Thomas. 'I would move that to Thursday.'

Fenton scribbled away on a notepad.

Then he suggested 'The Wonderful World of Disney', the time-honoured, early Sunday evening hour for the kiddies. It was an institution in Melbourne. Seven in Sydney didn't have it.

'I'd drop Disney,' said Thomas.

Fenton stopped scribbling and glanced up. The look on Thomas's face would remain forever etched in his memory. Behind the man's spectacles he thought he saw a strange glint in the eye of the Sydney general manager.

In Fenton's mind, Thomas seemed to be getting some kind of perverse pleasure out of all this. Fenton had had his share of fights with Thomas over the years during some of those interminable network and sister-station meetings that took place annually. Thomas would carry on over the football, asking why he had to broadcast it every Saturday afternoon. But they were hardly vindictive battles which left lasting scars.

According to Fenton, Thomas suggested moving the Disney program to 6.30pm on a Saturday.

'Well, we've got the footy replay at 6.30,' said Fenton.

Thomas looked Fenton in the eye. 'What would you say,' asked Thomas, his open hands moving through the air, 'if there was no football on HSV?'

Suddenly, Fenton had an idea of the full magnitude of what was in store. 'Well,' he replied, instantly on guard. 'I guess if HSV didn't have it we would have to come up with other programs . . . given a lead time of about 12 months.'

'What if it was sooner than that?' queried Thomas.

'Well, we have a contract for football for 12 months.'

'What would the viewers of Melbourne think if there was no football on Seven?'

Fenton shot back the first reply that came to mind. 'Well, they'd be up in arms,' he said. 'They'd be marching in the streets.' At the time, Fenton thought he'd over-exaggerated. He was wrong.

Thomas kept pushing and poking, testing the Melbourne program manager. Eventually, the discussion ended and Fenton packed up ready to go home.

'Well,' said Thomas. 'I'm just posing it hypothetically.'

Sure, thought Fenton. He had just seen the future of television at Channel 7 in Melbourne. He started wondering if anyone else would hire him before the holocaust arrived.

Fairfax officially took over the reins at HSV on 13 March 1987. On the same day, the VFL announced that Seven had withdrawn and the ABC had filled its place, taking over Seven's obligations, apart from the National Panasonic Cup, for slightly less than $1.5 million. The whole episode, announced Oakley, had vindicated the League's decision to appoint Broadcom.

'If we'd given HSV-7 a three-year contract, where would we be now?' he asked. 'We would have to renegotiate a new Australia-wide coverage only days before the opening of the season.'

The rush was on. The first premiership season involving teams from Queensland and Western Australia was just two weeks away. Tim Lane's dream had been realised. Now the hard work began.

Broadcom hadn't expected to be thrust into the role of football broadcaster so quickly. The theory had been easy enough. Sell the rights to those who were already in the business of broadcasting live sporting events.

But with the lack of interest and the schemozzle in Victoria with HSV, the small outfit suddenly found itself plunged into the role of host broadcaster to audiences outside Victoria. It was up to its neck in trouble.

Michael McKay, brother of Jim, had started with Broadcom

just eight weeks before the start of the season. He had developed his standing as a football and sports producer with Seven. While producing the 1986 Australian tennis Open at Kooyong, the phone inside one of Seven's large outside broadcast vans rang. It was Lloyd Capps, the director of Broadcom. He offered him a job straight away. McKay backed off but, after several days of Broadcom coming back to him with a higher figure each time, he finally relented.

Casey, of course, had been angry. In fact, initially, he hadn't quite understood why a talent like McKay would sign up with such a dirty, lowdown outfit like Broadcom. When he left Seven, the pair were barely on speaking terms. One senior Seven executive had been McKay's best man at his wedding. For weeks, because of the frostiness between the two organisations, the pair had not spoken except by faxes written by lawyers.

McKay discovered he would have to earn every last cent of his salary when he arrived in Broadcom's offices in Sydney. He didn't even have an office so he set up a desk and phone in the reception area, a move which bemused Cosser, who began to suspect his new employee with such a fine reputation might be a touch eccentric.

Eventually Cosser hired an office for him up the road which meant every time McKay wanted to photocopy a document, or fax someone an important message, he had to walk back down the street. It was a massive task. Almost every piece of equipment had to be hired. Commentators had to be found and lured from other organisations. And, because Broadcom had failed to raise the sort of money it had expected in its first year, budgets had to be reassessed. It was tight. One afternoon, McKay walked dejectedly back to his office up the street after learning another $200,000 had been lopped from his budget. A drunk veered out of a doorway and took a swing at him. For a brief moment, McKay stood there and contemplated swinging back.

He walked on.

Everything that could go wrong went wrong. The season finally opened, not accompanied by the fanfare and gee-whiz reaction everyone had expected, but with a loud yawn. Even the reaction in Melbourne to another new season, with two new teams, was muted. Things had just changed too quickly. Familiar faces were gone. Fairfax had given Seven in Sydney clearance to wreak havoc and bring Melbourne into line and proceeded to live up to the task. Mal Walden, the newsreader, was sacked. Other programs were axed. 'World of Sport', which Seven claimed to be the longest-running program of its type in the world, was in its death throes.

Of course, ratings for many of the shows had hardly set the world alight. But once they were gone, it seemed everyone had religiously watched them all, not even daring to go to the toilet during an ad break. Melburnians were horrified. Here was just another example of Sydney's brutal ascension to power.

The local papers thundered indignantly at the unfairness of it all. Viewers voted with their remote control devices. By the middle of the year Fenton's worst fears would be realised. The Seven news, once so proudly Melbourne-oriented, was barely registering in the ratings. It was a sad last in its timeslot. The cartoon series 'Inspector Gadget' on the ABC had more viewers.

Broadcom's problems continued. Its cameramen were an enthusiastic bunch. They just hadn't really covered Australian rules that much. In fact, many of them didn't know a great deal about the game. They stayed focussed on the man standing on the mark when the action moved on further upfield.

The company was also feeding its broadcasts through Telecom and Murphy's Law was in full operation. Viewers at home in the northern states would be watching a game, caught up in the excitement, when all of a sudden an old episode of 'The Monkees' would flash on to their screens. In one game out of Melbourne, Telecom mistakenly patched through a race from the Moonee Valley racecourse.

In the opening round, Broadcom's team was due to go live with its first program. The host for that first week, Western Australia's Dennis Cometti, was delayed. The production team turned to McKay.

'You'll have to host this one,' said the director. 'We've only got a few minutes to go.'

'Why me?' asked McKay, as if he wasn't busy enough already.

'You're the only one here wearing a jacket.'

And then there was the opening game at the Sydney Cricket Ground. Broadcom had paid good money for new jackets to be designed for its on-air team. With the Sydney Swans having run on to the ground, the game was just minutes away from starting. The team in the production booth needed to cut to Barry Breen, the former St Kilda player, who was preparing for a live report from the boundary line. But they had to keep holding. His jacket still hadn't arrived from Melbourne.

A Broadcom secretary had been sent to the airport to collect it. She raced to the SCG, ran around the boundary and hurled it to Breen, who buttoned it up. No sooner was it on than he was cued in.

Tim Lane's dream of the ABC as football's main broadcaster, at least in Victoria, had also quickly hit a brick wall. When the ABC flew to Sydney to cover Swans matches, Broadcom had already snaffled Seven's old commentary positions. The ABC boys, already criticised for lacking the polish and sophistication of their commercial counterparts, were forced to operate out of an old radio booth, wearing antiquated headphones.

Technical problems plagued the broadcasts. Sound and vision were sometimes out of synch, forcing the program host, Peter Gee, a polite, well-spoken young man plucked from obscurity to be the front man, to resemble a character in one of those bad kung-fu movies from Hong Kong.

An OB van, urgently required for use in Melbourne, caught fire on the long drive over from Adelaide.

And then there was the hiring of Gary Dempsey as a special comments man out of Brisbane for the Bears' matches. It had seemed like a good idea at the time. Dempsey, a Brownlow Medallist and one of the game's greatest ruckmen, was living on the Gold Coast. What Lane didn't know, however, was that Dempsey had a slight handicap when it came to football broadcasting.

He didn't have a voice. Ruck work was a tough skill and Dempsey had taken too many knocks to his throat. His voice had been reduced to a hoarse whisper. Lane found out about it during the first match they broadcast from the Carrara ground on the Gold Coast. Every time Dempsey strained to be heard, a harsh sound was forced from his mouth. It sounded somewhere between the Godfather with a sore throat and a man who had just swallowed a bucketload of gravel.

It was a tough situation, compounded by the fact that Gary Dempsey liked to talk. Lane tried valiantly as the game progressed. But for the life of him he couldn't find a way to shut Dempsey up. After the first game, Lane waited until he had returned to Melbourne. Then he rang Dempsey.

'I'm sorry Gary,' he said. 'It's just not going to work out . . .'

Each Monday, Lane debated whether or not to tune into the radio talkback shows and decided against it. The ABC was being pilloried by anyone with the slightest allegiance to the game. Suddenly, everyone remembered Seven with great fondness. People would say how much they missed hearing the dulcet tones of Peter Landy and Lou Richards. And at least Seven's cameramen knew how to pan the camera to follow the ball.

The ABC also shouldered the blame for many of Broadcom's problems. A memo by Bob Ansett to the League was strategically leaked to a newspaper, claiming the ABC's coverage was appalling and the League should step in and hastily renegotiate a new contract with a commercial network for the rest of the season. Then David Hill got involved in a slanging match with the VFL. Broadcom had refused its request to broadcast live into Sydney a Swans match against Richmond in Melbourne because of a deal it had struck with the pub-and-club operator, Sportsplay, a subsidiary of the Swans' owners, Powerplay.

The season was just a month old. The League was under fire for the television disaster. It was unhappy with the ABC's performance. Clubs were disgruntled. The public was disenchanted. Oakley's baptism of fire had turned into a guerilla war.

Something, it seemed, had to be done.

Lane was on his way home from covering another Bears match on Monday, 27 April, when he was asked to stop over in Sydney for a meeting about the ABC's football coverage. He arrived in the boardroom to discover the meeting was bigger than he had thought.

David Hill was there, so too was the ABC's football producer Alan Pridmore, Cosser, McKay, Oakley and Peter Scanlon. Hill took a conciliatory line during the meeting, conceding mistakes had been made. He had no choice. It was made clear that the League was dissatisfied with the ABC's performance. In the first year of the national competition it had, quite frankly, been expecting more.

As usual, Scanlon sat back and let everyone have their say before outlining, in what some regarded as a brutally frank manner, what the commission required in order for its relationship with the ABC to improve.

For a start, Scanlon was unhappy with Peter Gee as front man.

'Get rid of Gerry Gee,' he said, deliberately getting the host's name wrong.

It was a comment which particularly rankled with Lane. Years later, he would regret not speaking up straight away in Gee's defence. But Scanlon had the chair and he was a hard man to interrupt.

There was another thing, Scanlon said. Why the hell wasn't Drew Morphett involved in the television broadcasts? It was ridiculous. Here was one of the ABC's most popular sporting commentators and personalities and he'd been sent to the obscurity of the ABC's Siberian outpost, radio.

Scanlon had a point. But Morphett was there for a reason. In February, Morphett had criticised the ABC in a newspaper interview for axing the two football programs he hosted, 'The Winners' and 'The Footy Show'. He was hardly diplomatic in his language.

'For me,' he said, 'the decision highlights the uncertainty of the ABC's future football coverage and the black treatment it is giving its loyal staff members . . . I don't think Kevin Berry has ever seen "The Winners" in his life.'

Berry, the head of ABC sport in Sydney, was on the phone to Lane demanding an explanation about Morphett's comments as soon as he heard about them. The popularity of 'The Winners' was largely restricted to Western Australia. The ABC had decided to replace it with an hour-long general sports program. Even Hill was called in to make a public comment in a bid to defuse the row. Morphett escaped the sack by heading to radio.

But with Scanlon in full flight, the ABC was forced to concede the Morphett move had been a mistake. Hill promised things would improve.

And, it seemed, the meeting did achieve progress. The football budget was expanded, allowing for a third commentator to travel to matches outside Melbourne, finally giving the ABC a chance for a commentator to analyse tactics. The public disenchantment quietened.

Berry, the subject of some discontent in the Melbourne office, was replaced in July. Ratings began to climb. And Lane, after months of stress and restless nights, finally began to sleep a lot more comfortably.

But while things improved, it seemed the game and television were always on the edge of a disaster. They fell over that edge in early September when the ABC and the League concluded a long-running competition for football followers.

It was the night of the big barrel draw on the ABC's Friday night footy show, broadcast only in Victoria. A family of loyal ABC football viewers stood the chance to win a trip to Los Angeles and on to Vancouver for one of the League's overseas exhibition matches. Ross Oakley was to pull the winning envelope from the barrel, concluding the nationally-advertised promotion.

But the first name bore an address from a state outside Victoria. 'Stuff that,' said Morphett, by now hosting the program. 'We can't have a West Australian winning it. Wouldn't it be better if someone at home watching it won it?'

Oakley, bemused by events, then heard the voice of a production crew member. 'Sorry, we've stuffed it up,' he said. 'We'll have to re-draw it.'

So they stopped the show. The cameras were restarted and Oakley dipped his arm into the barrel again. Another name from interstate. Damn.

'Sorry, this tape machine is stuffed,' came the word from the floor again. Oakley shrugged. This was, after all, the ABC. You got used to it. Morphett again said something about making sure a Victorian won the prize.

'Look, this is no good,' said Oakley. By now events had overtaken him. It was like being at the beach when a big wave broke over you. There was no point fighting it. You rode it out and accepted whatever treatment it dished out. 'What we have to do is do the draw, get the person and then you can stuff it up as much as you like. As long as we keep drawing that person out.'

Oakley plucked another envelope from the barrel. This time they got lucky. A Victorian had got up to win the prize. Thank God for that. They'd all started wondering whether they would be there all night.

Oakley wedged the envelope inside the barrel in a corner,

where he could easily reach it again. They rolled the tape and, hey presto, the chairman of the VFL commission pulled out the winning entry, a Victorian.

They even caught it all perfectly on the tape machine.

On the following Monday morning, Lane received a call from Ron Barassi at work. Barassi was a part-time columnist with *The Truth*, a newspaper that existed on a diet of sex, big breasts, massage parlour ads and sport. Barassi said the paper had been tipped off about a 'rigged' barrel draw on the football program and was planning a front-page article. The leak had come from a malcontent on the ABC production floor.

The story was out. *The Truth* splashed it and once again the League was under attack. The laws governing the granting of a raffle permit stated the winner had to be the first drawn. And the League had ignored it.

Within a few days, Drew Morphett was visited by members of the police licencing and gaming squad at the ABC's offices in Elsternwick. 'Mind if we tape the interview?' he was asked.

'Go ahead,' said Morphett, whose friends believed he'd never met a microphone or tape machine he didn't like.

But as the interview progressed, and the police line of questioning grew harder, Morphett suddenly grew wiser.

'Shit,' he announced. 'This tape won't be played in court will it? I'll be hung by the balls!'

Twelve months later, Drew Morphett stood in Prahran Magistrates Court and listened to his words echo around the courtroom. The magistrate, along with everyone else, managed a laugh. And Morphett and the producer, Alan Pridmore, were not hung by their testicles, either. Found guilty, they were placed on a 12-month good behaviour bond. The VFL, as a corporation, pleaded guilty and was placed on a good behaviour bond. In the end, the League paid for all three families drawn from the barrel to travel to the US.

On 24 July 1987, the media circus rolled into town and pitched its tent for another performance. Qintex, owned by Christopher Skase, bought the Seven network from Fairfax in a $780 million deal. Within a few days Skase was in Melbourne, sizing up the poor morale.

If there was going to be an archetypal Eighties Man, it was Skase. As a business journalist, he'd shown an even greater than normal level of interest in the amounts of money the people he wrote about were earning and how he could do the same.

Journalism was never going to sate his appetitite and he was soon out of the blocks. In true Eighties style, he had borrowed big and then borrowed more and within a handful of years he was being fêted, along with the rest of the entrepreneurs doing business around the country.

When Skase bought Seven he was hailed as the network's saviour. And one of the first things he did upon his triumphant return to Melbourne was question Seven's senior executives closely. He declared he wanted to restore HSV as the station most identified with Melbourne.

'So, how do I do that?' he asked.

He was met with a resounding, unanimous chorus. 'Get the footy back.'

Skase set about the task immediately and within three weeks he was standing in Steve Cosser's office in Sydney making a presentation to Oakley and the Broadcom chief. The pair liked what they saw and heard. Skase was a smooth operator. He talked straight, never hedging or attempting to fudge his figures. And what impressive figures they were.

The League was being offered the sort of money it had only dreamed about nine months before. Skase was looking to secure the rights over a five-year period for $30 million. That would be at least $6 million annually, with extra thrown in up front at the start of the 1988 season. The money was effectively double what the competition had earned two years before in the last season before expansion.

Skase's presentation also impressed them for another reason. The other networks had finally started showing some interest in televising the game. Nine was showing what the League regarded as a strong interest for the first time in many years. But, typical of the network, it wanted the best. The Grand Final. The State of Origin series. The Finals. Matches in prime time. As for the real grind, the home and away season, the long slog where the drama of a football season unfolded each year, Nine wasn't interested. It could always flog the rights to the season off somewhere else, probably to the ABC.

It would do exactly that two years later, securing the rugby league rights in Sydney for $6 million and then packaging them off in parcels, eventually making a profit of more than $2 million.

'We don't want that,' Oakley had told a Nine executive. 'The package comes complete, or not at all. It can't be fragmented.'

When Skase finally left after making his presentation, Cosser and Oakley smiled at one another. Over the next two or three weeks, lawyers would be called in to fine-tune the deal. But effectively, they had finally found what they'd been looking for.

The season was finally over and, despite the early problems, Lane was satisfied. There were, of course, plenty of things he would have changed. But he was hardly interested now in looking back. Besides, it seemed all but over for the ABC.

It was the 2nd of October in the week after the Grand Final. Throughout Melbourne there was the usual sense of anticlimax, the sort of mood that always permeated the town at the end of another footy season. It had been a long, hard haul, climaxed by the almost-frenzied activity of September.

It was just after 7am and Tim Lane was driving down his street, returning after one of his early morning runs with a few friends. A keen runner, he had decided to train to compete in that year's Melbourne marathon.

As he drew closer to his home, he noticed a strange car

parked outside. Inside were two men. They got out when he pulled up. One of them was carrying a camera.

They were from *The Herald*, Melbourne's broadsheet afternoon newspaper. The questions began immediately as Lane stood at the front gate. The news was sobering. Seven had, overnight, won the rights to televise the League. How did he feel?

How could he feel? He knew it was about to happen but he still felt all the emotion drain from him. While he had always known it would probably come to this, he had not allowed it to completely occupy his thinking. He'd always held out some hope. He had been patient, as only a good ABC man could be. In fact, the ABC had even taken out an injunction in late September in the NSW equity court preventing Broadcom from concluding any deal over the television rights, arguing that the company had failed to live up to its agreement to give the ABC first and last rights of refusal.

And now, everything Lane had worked for over the past 12 months, all those sleepless nights, the stress, the intensity, the mood swings . . . What had it been worth?

He said he was disappointed and now knew how the staff at Seven had felt earlier in the year when they lost the rights. Then he said goodbye to the newspaper men and walked inside, feeling hollow and exhausted, physically and mentally.

His girlfriend of two-and-a-half years was waiting for him. 'Sit down,' she said. 'I've got something to tell you.'

She was leaving him. The relationship was over.

It took a while for everything to sink in. But when it did, Lane decided he had to get out. He took long service leave from the ABC and disappeared overseas, caddying around Europe for a professional golfer he knew. He would eventually return and resume broadcasting the game on radio. But those close to him saw him come back, inevitably, a different man.

Football had a funny habit of doing things like that to the very people who loved it.

11

THE PLAYERS
IN THE TRENCHES

As the 1980s progressed, it seemed hard to remember a time when football's biggest battles had not taken place in the boardroom. All the politics and the fighting, all the crises and financial problems that seemed to envelop the game every few months had overshadowed events on the field. Surely, at its deepest and most basic level, football remained a game? It was a hard thing to judge for those too close to it. If you wanted to find the true essence of the sport you had to close the door to the boardroom and ignore the deep scarring the decade had created. You had to reach deep into the sport's mythology, revel in its legendary stories and figures. By doing that, it no longer seemed a business.

But was that right? Even the place where it all began—the search for new talent—carried a business edge to it. For it was the search for talented young men who could be used to win football's ultimate prize, The Flag, that had made the game what it was.

That search quite often began like this. On a weekday over summer, a couple of club officials would climb into whoever's car was the most reliable and head off for a week in the bush, criss-crossing the countryside's dusty, unmade roads, negotiating the potholes and the cattle being herded to market.

At some clubs it was called the 'scone run'—a week of knocking on doors of prospective recruits and finding yet another batch of warm scones waiting on the kitchen table just freshly baked by Mum. Veteran clubmen always returned home a few pounds heavier.

The sons of those excellent country cooks were the prize and there were times when, at first glance, only their mothers and knowledgeable talent scouts could love them. They were country kids; pimply-faced, shy in the presence of strangers from the big League, with limbs growing far too quickly for the rest of their bodies. But the word had been passed on to the big smoke by wizened old hands on retainers to the League clubs: these kids could play all right. They had the right stuff. Good hands. Could read the play. Knew when to go for the big grab and when to punch it away. It was an instinctive thing, that. Some kids were born with it. They loved the game with a passion few other things in childhood could generate. They would sleep with their old leather footballs, that aromatic leathery perfume comforting them. And it seemed a year didn't go by when a report reached Melbourne of how one adolescent boy, with a gawky body and soft, birdlike down on his upper lip posing as a moustache, was supposed to be able to kick a hay bale over a wheat silo in his thongs.

It was one of football's rites of summer and few were better at the game of traversing the countryside and signing up promising recruits than Graeme Richmond. With a surname like that, there was only one club he could support in Melbourne. Another of the Tough Old Bastards of Punt Road, Graeme Richmond emerged over more than two decades as the most influential powerbroker at the club and, some said, in the game itself. That he was tough, there was little doubt. For years he had carried a grudge against one of the club's most distinguished presidents, Ray Dunn. It had lasted an inordinately long time. Both men had little time for one another and when Dunn died, the main topic on everyone's lips at the club was whether or not Graeme Richmond would attend the funeral.

He did.

'I wanted to make sure he was in the box,' he would say out of the corner of his mouth to someone later.

Graeme Richmond knew where all the bodies were in football. He knew how to prey on the weaknesses of an opposing club official, how to fête him and stroke his ego, all the while stealing his best player from beneath his gaze. But he had a soft side, too. He could talk about football for hours and his eyes would soften as he sat back in his chair and tell you where he thought the game was heading. And when he did that, you knew that here was a man who knew what he was talking about. Richmond knew where the game was heading because he knew where it had been. Too many others forgot that sometimes. The past was just that; something to be dragged out only over a beer or at a reunion of past players. Richmond, though, knew the game's lore and he cared deeply for it. He made mistakes too. Some of them were magnified tenfold because of who he was. His policies would play a role in bringing the club he loved so much to its knees by the end of the decade. But he was always recognised as a master of many things. And there were many who maintained that it was Graeme Richmond's ability to get a player to sign his life and soul over to the Richmond Football Club that was by far his best trait.

The methods were many and varied. Richmond would pull up in his car outside yet another house on the outskirts of a country town and walk inside with an old leather Gladstone bag in his hand. He'd chat with Mum and Dad, wink knowingly at their young, nervous son and praise in glowing terms his amazing footballing ability.

If the kid hesitated, or Dad said, 'Geez, don't think the lad's quite ready to make the big trip to the city just yet,' Graeme Richmond played his ace. He'd open the bag. It would be brimming with pound notes.

'Well, son,' Richmond would say in that gritted-teeth style of his. 'I'm gunna throw all this in the air and if you sign before the last one hits the floor, it's all yours.'

There was also the Television Ploy. In the early and mid-60s many homes in the bush did not have a television set and Richmond was not slow to use this to his advantage. He'd walk in to a new farmhouse with an assistant—sometimes he brought Captain Blood along with him, and what family could say no to the legendary Jack Dyer, the man reputed to have broken the collarbones of nine opponents during a bone-crunching career with the Tigers? In a solemn fashion, Richmond would undo the box and proceed to set up the television, all the while watching the family's eyes widen. He'd fiddle with the rabbit-ear antennas, adjust the knobs, tap the side of the set and generally make out as though he was a high priest conducting a pagan rite. It was done to get one message across: the Tigers were prepared to go to great lengths to take their son and make a man of him.

But sometimes not even the television set, that technological wonder of progress, could sway the old man to sign over his son. They say when Graeme Richmond heard the word 'no', and knew it had been uttered with the finality of a dogmatic parent, the television set was packed back into its box and it, along with Richmond, had disappeared into the distance, long before the commercial break was over.

Such stories and acts of the talent scouts barely changed over the years. Mum would be given a box of chocolates and find a sizeable wad of cash inside, right next to the soft-centred strawberry-centred chocolates she liked. Dad would find a case of beer on the porch.

And even by the 1980s, the chase for talent still held a hyp-notic hold over the football world. But while such stories became the stuff of legend, Ray 'Slug' Jordon, one of its best practitioners, could hardly be described as one of the game's great romantics. He was short and pugnacious, a big man locked inside the body of a stout rover. He had a brilliant tactical mind too, and could stand on the boundary line at a training session on a cold winter's evening, the goosebumps on his arms sticking out in the frigid night air and cast his eye lovingly over the talent assembled out on the ground.

'See that bugger over there?' he'd bark at you, pointing to some hapless player. 'Lots of talent. Good kid. But no ticker.'

The Slug had a way with words and he also had a way with talented young kids. By the middle of the 1980s, he'd earned a reputation as the best coach of young talent in the League. At North Melbourne he had nurtured a phenomenal number of junior players who went on to star at senior level. But for some reason, Slug never quite made it there himself. The closest he came was at the end of 1984 when, as reserves coach to Ron Barassi at Melbourne, he had the chance to take the reins at the Sydney Swans. The Swans were going through one of their periodic crises, the League had stepped in to manage the club's affairs and it wanted Jordon for the senior coaching position. But Melbourne held him to his contract and after that another senior offer never came his way.

In a way he was a victim of his own brilliance. Slug could coach, club people would say. But could he do the same with veterans as he did with the young, impressionable kids? The young blokes were like putty in his hands. He knew just when to bark at them and when to pat them on the backside and console them if things went wrong. Over a career spanning more than three decades at four League clubs, he would coach four premiership reserves sides.

So Jordon was a valuable partner to have on a scone run and one afternoon he played a crucial role in securing a young man who would become one of the most rugged and individualistic footballers in the country.

Rodney Grinter was a young kid with a man's body and a fearsome reputation in the bush leagues. He played for Katandra West and if his footballing ability was legendary so, too, was his capacity to dish out and handle the rough stuff.

One afternoon, Slug and a bevy of Melbourne club officials sat talking to Grinter about his League prospects. Jordon had decided that here was a young bloke who needed some straight talk.

'Listen kid,' he grunted. 'Ya got nothin' goin' for you. Nothin'. The only thing you can do decently is play football. So come on down and we'll show you how to do it properly.'

'Balls' Grinter made the journey and ultimately earned his life membership with the club, along the way attaining cult status and setting a League record for the number of appearances and subsequent suspensions by the League's tribunal.

The players. They were the heart and soul of the game. Without them football was nothing. They pulled in the crowds each week and the best of them, the true champions, could do something for people that few others in any walk of life could manage; they jolted them out of their mundane lives and took them on a trip for almost three hours. There weren't many things in life that could do that sort of thing for you.

But if the players held the key to the game, and if within themselves they held the power to decide the game's future, why had they been so shabbily treated over the years? And why, after all those years, had they not risen as a group, as their colleagues in sports around the world had done, and demanded a bigger piece of the action?

'The League footballer is the worst paid fellow I know,' wrote Bert Clay, a former Fitzroy footballer, in 1952. 'We are top class entertainers. Why not top class money?'

It was a common refrain that had been muttered many times over the years and in 1984 it received another airing. The VFL Players' Association was angry over the League's refusal to pay penalty rate payments to players competing in two Sunday finals matches and was threatening to boycott both games. While such a threat made tremendous headlines for the newspapers, few, if any, in League officialdom took it seriously.

Would players dare strike and miss the opportunity of

playing in a finals series? The game's history was littered with threats and complaints by players that never eventuated and it always came back to one reason. Footballers were far more interested in getting a game than treating the sport as a workplace. Players were unsophisticated when it came to negotiations and largely uninterested in fostering a spirit of unity. After all, how long would they be around? The best might manage to carve out a career over 10 or 15 years, but many would disappear from view after just a handful of seasons and return to the bush or the metropolitan leagues from where they'd come, satisfied in the knowledge they had made it in the big time.

The League's lords made it their business to ensure it was kept that way. They had enough problems as it was without the players, the people who actually put on the show, getting together and demanding to be treated like any other workers. By 1984, in fact, there were many administrators who, unable to face the truth about their own and their peers' incompetency in matters financial, blamed the players for the mess the League was in. It was a view that had also gained some credence among the public, who had grown tired of watching their favourite footballers switch from one jumper to another each season.

When Michael Moncrieff, the president of the VFL Players' Association, indicated that a boycott might be staged during the finals over the issue of Sunday finals, the collective blood pressure of the League hardly rose. A strike? Sure thing. Go ahead. Let's see how much support you'll get.

In late August, Hamilton met Moncrieff, a 235-game player with Hawthorn, and two other players' delegates to discuss their concerns. According to the minutes of a board of directors' meeting the following week, Hamilton 'had taken the opportunity to correct misconceptions expressed by Mr Moncreiff (sic).' He also pointed out, when told the League had refused to discuss superannuation schemes for players, that the VFLPA had so far failed to make a submission to the League.

You could almost taste the triumphant note of the meeting

when the minutes went on to record that 'these matters would now be discussed at a meeting in October, 1984 after the conduct of the finals series and that the boycott threats made by the Association had now been withdrawn.'

It was another backdown by the players. But if they had fully known the attitude among many of the directors toward them, and the strategies in place to give the VFLPA as little recognition as possible, then perhaps their resolve might have been greater.

Like many things in football in the 1980s, the Silvio Foschini Supreme Court decision in April, 1983, proved to be a seminal moment in the game. Less than eight weeks after the verdict was handed down, and after Lindsay Fox had revealed just how far the clubs had been prepared to go to run Football Ltd by their own rules, Jack Hamilton, the League's vice-president, Ron Cook, and Melbourne's executive director, Dick Seddon, flew out of Melbourne for the United States. The information they returned with would, within just a few years, change forever the way the League and its clubs did business with its players.

The three had been sent to the US following a recommendation by a sub-committee, which included Hamilton, Ron Joseph, Seddon and Neil McPhee, QC, set up to frame new rules for the game. Their mission was to gain as much information as they could on the relationship between players and administrators in American professional sports and the way they conducted their competitions.

It was another sign that Australian football looked first to America instead of Europe for guidance. American football was everything many Australian administrators wanted their game to be. While the game itself was seen as boring and unlikely to interest Australian audiences, the marketing and organisation of the National Football League interested the VFL delegation most. And they wasted no time. Their first meeting in New York was with Don Weiss, the executive director of the NFL. Then, 30 minutes into the meeting, Pete Rozelle, the NFL boss, walked into the room.

Rozelle was a legendary figure in the eyes of many sports officials around the world. He was the all-powerful czar of an empire that generated enormous revenues and others looked at him with more than a hint of envy. An American football franchise in 1983 was worth up to $US50 million. By the end of the decade one would be valued at almost $200 million. Even the owners of the NFL's 26 teams had gasped a year before the visit by the VFL trio when Rozelle revealed the latest television rights deal he had secured for them. It was an extraordinary deal, even by the excessive standards of US commercial television. The three American networks had agreed to pay the NFL $US2 billion over five years, guaranteeing each club $US14 million a season and ensuring the average club would be profitable before gate takings and any other revenue was entered into the equation.

Rozelle had boasted a Midas touch for more than two decades and, even though his league was confronting several major problems by 1983 and he was already fighting a war of attrition with several owners, he was still regarded as the man who could fix anything.

His guiding hand had seen the NFL emerge as America's number one sport. And he had principally done it through television rights, playing off the American networks against one another, securing the best deal possible for his league time and again. But it was not just his marketing flair that had secured the NFL's position. Rozelle stuck to a philosophy that the VFL had examined but never quite accepted: unity. Rozelle's theory was soon dubbed 'League Think' and from the 1960s through to 1983 it had dominated the conduct of American football.

'One of the key things that a sports league needs,' Rozelle was fond of saying, 'is unity of purpose. It needs harmony . . . When you have unity and harmony and can move basically as one, you can have a successful sports league.'

In Melbourne, Aylett had come to the same conclusion in the early 1980s. But his many pleas had fallen on the usual deaf ears as the clubs clawed away at one another, desperately seeking the slightest advantage. 'The great corporate success the VFL has enjoyed over the past five years in terms of popularity, and general expansion of the sport at all levels, is being countered by certain VFL clubs facing intolerable financial burdens,' Aylett wrote in his president's report at the end of 1982. 'We must arrive at a workable consensus on our key issues.'

In 1983, in a more desperate and frustrated tone, Aylett had called for unity again. 'We all have to realise that our future is inter-dependent on each other. We cannot be dependent, nor can we be independent, and survive.'

Weiss and Rozelle gave the VFL trio a briefing on how the NFL operated. What most interested them was the fact that the owners of all teams entered into an agreement to abide by the League's constitution. This was a pet subject of Seddon and interested him greatly. It would, within a year, lead to the introduction of licencing agreements between the League and its clubs.

The VFL trio was also briefed on the NFL draft, the game's method of balancing the competition and making sure no single group of teams managed to dominate the competition for any lengthy period of time. Each year, the best of American college footballers would be eligible to be drafted by the pro teams. The team that finished last during the season would have first pick. The second worst team, second pick.

In a lengthy and highly detailed report given to the League following their return, Seddon, on behalf of the three, noted that: 'All the Americans were amazed that our clubs would continue to tear each other apart and did not appreciate the seriousness of working and co-operating together off the field . . .

'We advised that out of the four potential power bases, namely the VFL centralised administration, the clubs, the Government and the Players' Association, we did not wish to have the Government legislate because we were fearful of

Government intrusion, and we had no need to give the Players' Association any credibility and respectability . . . we desired to keep them fragmented.'

Meeting after meeting, Seddon put forward his idea to various football, basketball and baseball executives that players should receive no encouragement to unionise. 'The common thread that seems to be coming through is that in this modern age unions and associations are inevitable, so if you have one in its infancy you should get hold of it now and mould it to your own best interests rather than let it go into an adversary situation where it will become militant and difficult to control,' he reported.

'My instinct is firmly against any recognition or encouragement of a Players' Association because by doing so you give it strength. However, I could not get one person over here to agree with that concept . . . I would rather keep them fragmented and disorganised as long as possible.'

Following their meeting with Weiss and Rozelle, the three headed off for a visit to the New York Giants football team and its assistant general manager, Terry Bledsoe, who instructed the trio on how their player payment scheme worked and also observed that Pete Rozelle had lost some of his 'piss and vinegar because he had been there so long.' In spite of this, he still thought he was 'very good.'

But it was the National Basketball Association and its executive vice-president, David Stern, which most impressed the three, particularly Seddon. He had met Stern previously and the pair were in the throes of striking up a friendship that would last for years when Seddon was posted to New York for business in 1988. Told about the Foschini case and the rules difficulties the VFL was experiencing, Stern, who was responsible for the business and legal affairs of the NBA, lent the three Australians a sympathetic ear, expressing interest in gaining a copy of the Foschini judgement. He then explained the technicalities of the NBA's salary cap, introduced to place a ceiling on how much each franchise could pay its players and prevent a costly bidding war. In effect, it meant the best teams could not pay their players as much as they would like, while the bottom teams could not spend the small amount they probably preferred.

The three flew home confident they had seen the future of football and its name was basketball. Given that the game's growing critics at home were increasingly critical of the emphasis on handballing, it was perhaps appropriate.

The history of the union movement is one of conviction and Geoff Pryor was, if anything, a man of conviction. He was also a product of his time. For most of the 1960s, football had remained fairly oblivious to the social changes going on around it, stuck in a time warp where the Establishment still ruled and dissenters were few. But there were a handful of men who managed to straddle both spheres and Pryor was one of them.

He grew up just two blocks from Windy Hill, the stark, some said ugly, home ground of the tough northern suburbs club, Essendon. The Bombers were one of the strong sides of the competition, a delicate balance of brute strength and skill that would take them to three grand finals during 1960s, winning two.

It was only natural then that Pryor would be recruited by his local club and in 1965, at the age of 19, he signed up to play in the big time. It seemed to be just another example of the great Australian football dream at work. But Pryor was not just another kid who had realised a schoolyard ambition. Football, he reasoned, would only be around for him for a short time. After that? He was determined to make sure he had a career ahead of him, something to fall back on. As his League career began, he also started studies at Melbourne University which, like many campuses around the country, would serve as the focal point for the challenges to authority by the early 1970s.

It quickly dawned on Pryor, however, that his views were not shared by many of his team-mates. Nothing would have a greater impact on him during his football career than when he watched a young team-mate fall to the ground after wrenching a knee or breaking a leg. The injury then usually signalled the end of a career, or a very lengthy and painful recovery. And more often than not Pryor saw it happen to young men who had given up the chance to pursue a profession in order to chase The Dream. He swore it would never happen to him.

By 1970, Pryor was a five-year veteran of League football and a defender to boot, one of the tougher breed of footballers of the era who were required to blunt the skill of opposing forwards. Playing in defence brought a player few accolades. The papers only ever seemed to write about the glamorous forwards and when your team won, it was always the men who kicked the goals who seemed to win the plaudits.

The start of the 1970 season ushered in a new era. Suddenly it seemed football had discovered there was an outside world and that changes were afoot. Was it possible those outside values and ideas could be applied to football? It began with a pay dispute at Collingwood in February when the captain and vice-captain, Des Tuddenham and Len Thompson, walked out and threatened not to return unless granted significant pay rises. Tuddenham demanded $24,000 over three years, Thompson $30,000 over five years. They eventually returned two months later, stripped of their positions, but having won significant concessions. A year before they had earned $25 a match. When they came back, Tuddenham earned $125 a game, Thompson $105.

Pryor watched the events at Collingwood with interest. Within a fortnight, he and four other senior players had walked out, saying they would not return unless match payments were increased. They had a strong argument.

In the 24 years leading up to the Essendon revolt, footballers had been awarded pay rises totalling $19, while the average male weekly wage had risen by $40. Footballers now had a cause. And while few could be bothered, or had the courage, to flock to it, the League realised it had to act quickly to head off any more disputes. A new match payment scheme as well as a system for rewarding experienced players was introduced. In its first incarnation, a player received an extra $10 a match for every 50 games he had played after the first 50.

It was a victory for Pryor and his team-mates, but it came at a cost. Pryor was viewed suspiciously by the club's administration after that and the feeling was mutual. By the end of the 1970 season, disenchantment had taken over. He quit the game and headed overseas.

Two years later, Pryor was back. But while his break had revived his interest in playing football, Pryor's feelings about the treatment of players and their lack of security when their careers ended had not changed. To opposing forwards he was a difficult opponent; his long arms could punch away an incoming ball and he was a fine reader of the play. Off the field, he would show the same attributes.

On 10 December 1973, the VFL Players' Association was formed. The first meeting was hardly the gathering of left-wing pinko bolshies the League and many club administrators believed it to be. The players were far from being a militant union. 'Our last thought is to strike,' said Pryor, shortly after the Association's first meeting at Albert Park which attracted more than 60 players. 'Players want to contribute to the development of this excellent game.' One of their stated aims was to develop a close relationship with the League. It would, with the benefit of hindsight, prove to be a fatal move. The League quickly developed its own aim. If it had to develop a relationship at all with a players' association, it would be a formal and very distant one.

The association's first problem was that Pryor had moved to Canberra to work and only arrived in Melbourne to play on a Saturday. Whenever he rang the League, his phone calls were rarely returned. Club officials around the competition were stand-offish and suspicious. But unwittingly, they would also help the players in their pursuit of more money as the phenomenal corporate growth of the game in the 1970s and the avarice of those club administrators combined to send it hurtling toward an unknown future.

Pryor was determined to give the players a voice, even if they had to scream until they were hoarse to be heard. When the League abolished the 10-year rule, which allowed a player who had served 10 years or more at any club to move to another without a transfer fee, and which had greatly assisted Allen Aylett's drive to build North Melbourne into a League power-house, Pryor quickly protested.

He was successful in talking to the deputy Prime Minister, Jim Cairns, and the Minister for Labor and Immigration, Clyde Cameron, and told them of the association's opinion that the move was done 'for selfish motives and is not in the interests of players.'

Cameron sent a telegram to the VFLPA claiming the League's move was 'cavalier' and that the players should have been consulted before a decision was taken. While the inter-vention of Cameron had little impact on the League's decision, it showed that finally the players were prepared to co-ordinate and argue their case. It also indicated there was plenty of sym-pathy for the players' plight, particularly at a political level.

Even then, the League was an inviting and vulnerable target for a politician.

By the early 1980s, several footballers were earning income packages in excess of $100,000 and the game of enticing and procuring players was at its peak. It was a fiercely fought bat-tle with few prisoners taken alive. The laws of the game were deliberately flouted as clubs tried to entice players contracted to other clubs to make the jump. Inevitably, the player war attracted sport's version of soldiers of fortune; the sports lawyer. If you were a player of any quality, you didn't talk to your club about payment unless your lawyer/accountant/man-ager was present. Preferably, he conducted affairs on your behalf, letting you get on with the game on the field.

'In this day and age there is no way a player should negotiate for himself,' said one of the League's most outstanding players in 1983, Hawthorn's Leigh Matthews. 'You are usually in a difficult position because most of the people you would be asking for a raise are your friends.

'An agent, whether he be an accountant or lawyer, can get you a much better deal because he is aware of your market value. A player wasn't able to go around and ring up six clubs to find out how much they'd pay if he was available. But an adviser could do it, and this obviously has happened for some time in VFL football.'

It seemed that within just a few short years, player agents were everywhere. Jeff Browne was out there plying his trade and quickly amassing a sizeable income. Others jostled to sign the best players with the highest profiles. But none of them could match Peter Jess for sheer pugnacity and cynicism.

Peter Jess. Even the mention of his name gave some general managers a tight, queasy feeling in the pit of their stomach. He was loathed by some clubs, despised by others and the rest of them simply hated his guts.

The guy seemed to have no respect for the institution he was dealing with; who was he to sneer openly at the manner in which clubs paid their players? Peter Jess, they thought, was not a real Football Person. He did not have the game's best interests at heart.

And besides, they said, he was such a rude little bastard.

'They don't like some little piss-ant suburban accountant making life difficult for them,' he said in his high-pitched voice toward the end of the decade. 'I'm not confrontationist, I'm just blunt.'

Nowhere was his bluntness more evident than in 1984 when Collingwood, locked in a bitter player trade war with Richmond that would wreak havoc on both clubs' finances for years to come, organised a meeting with Jess in a bid to retain three players; John Annear, Phillip Walsh and Craig Stewart.

Jess heard out the arguments put forward by the Collingwood delegation and then leaned back in his chair. It was time to up the ante.

'Can I borrow your head?' he asked one of the Collingwood officials.

'Can you what?'

'Borrow your head,' repeated Jess.

'Why?'

'Because I'm building a rock garden at home.'

Throughout the 1980s, Jess built up an enviable stable of talent. Word spread among the players that here was a man who, despite his unconventional tactics, made sure the club didn't rip you off. He made them sweat for every cent.

They tried every tactic they could devise to stop him. Some clubs banned him from setting foot in their offices. Jess simply sent his player in to negotiate and would wait in the car park. The player would appear every five minutes for further instructions. What annoyed the clubs even more was that Jess knew how to cultivate the press and use the football journalists to his advantage. As a rule, most reporters sympathised with the player in a pay dispute and Jess knew a sure way to their hearts. He gave them colourful quotes and an instant headline. Jess was good copy. The clubs, which preferred to issue dull 'no comments' during contract negotiations, were left looking like penny-pinching misers.

By the 1990s, his influence had waned as other astute businessmen moved into the area but he was still there, slugging it out with the big boys. 'There's no money in this caper and I get my bum kicked from daylight to dusk,' he said. 'What pisses me off is that the football pie is getting bigger and the net return to players is getting smaller . . . Why shouldn't players be well paid? They're the entertainers.'

As usual though, the players were generally unwilling to seize the day. As the Eighties progressed, the physical and mental demands placed on them increased dramatically. There were more games to be played and the coaches, in their quest for success and an edge over the opposition, were coming up with new and more demanding training methods. Afternoon sessions began to appear on the schedule; the summer preparation seemed to start earlier each year. There were even clubs that began pre-season training a fortnight after the grand final.

Many players were still trying to perfect the art of juggling a full-time occupation with football. Besides, what had the Players' Association done for them, anyway? It always seemed to be making threats and then backing down. They paid their dues and what did they get? A monogrammed windcheater. The League and its clubs were just too strong, too powerful.

By 1992, the association had reached a critical point.

It either had to make a stand now, or forever fold its cards and walk away from the table.

Justin Madden was one of the tallest players in the game. At 206 centimetres, he was also one of the sport's most fêted ruckmen; a good big man with a heart to match. He had begun his career in 1980 with Essendon, joining his older brother Simon. But he played just 45 matches with the Bombers before Carlton's Ian Collins lured him across to Princes Park. There, Madden escaped from the shadow of his brother to blossom into one of football's most colourful players. He also boasted a healthy air of cynicism about the game. He understood the media and how it worked better than most players. He had seen how players had been built into heroes and then pulled down just as quickly.

That cynicism had led Madden into the presidency of the Players' Association, taking over from his brother when Simon decided he had had enough of the politics. And Justin Madden was in no mood to fold his cards and walk away.

In 1992, he and Peter Allen, the executive director of the

association, launched a campaign for a collective bargaining agreement with the League. They were seeking minimum wage agreements and greater security for the players. Madden was a disarming union chief. He was a favourite of the crowds and he always seemed to be wearing a broad, cheesy grin that exposed a mouth of sparkling teeth. Behind this easy-going exterior, however, was a man determined to push the League into finally recognising the players' needs and welfare as a collective group.

A few years later, Madden loped into a small Italian bistro in Melbourne, its narrow width exaggerating his height and presence. Heads turned. In Melbourne, Justin Madden was recognised everywhere.

He was sporting his trademark grin too, when he remembered how 'the shitfight began.'

Ross Oakley had told the association the League could not negotiate a collective bargaining agreement with them; they would have to negotiate individually with the clubs. Earlier, the League's lawyer, Jeff Browne, and executive commissioner Alan Schwab, had indicated to the players they were keen to do a deal; at least, that was the impression they had given Madden and Allen.

But in 1992, the League had been in turmoil; several clubs were after Oakley's head and the chief commissioner was in trouble. At the same time, it seemed certain a change in Government was about to take place and Jeff Kennett, the leader of the Victorian Opposition, was making noises about dismantling the state's industrial relations laws.

'He (Oakley) needed to exert some power,' Madden recalled. 'If they'd been seen to be too soft with us they might have been under quite a bit of pressure . . . he wanted to save his scalp and he would have been aware that Kennett was going to dismantle the industrial relations laws.'

The players took legal advice, which suggested they had the power to bargain collectively. What they had to do, however, was prove they were in dispute with the League before the Industrial Relations Commission. With Mordecai Bromberg, a former St Kilda player and now a barrister, running the case for them, they went to the IRC. Commissioner Colin Polites found there was a dispute. It meant the players' argument could now be heard within the arm of the Federal industrial laws. Finally, a victory had been achieved.

The cause gained momentum when a meeting of players at the Radisson Hotel attracted enormous support, with many of the competition's biggest names turning up. 'They didn't have to be there,' said Madden. 'They were the ones who were already being looked after. But with them there it finally proved that we had turned the corner and were in it for everyone.

'We were in the box seat. The League realised it was going to cost them a fortune. Suddenly, we were organised and they were a rabble.'

There was talk of games being boycotted, of players refusing to promote the game's sponsors. Such talk had taken place in the past many times. How often had the association threatened to withdraw players from attending the big gala evening of the year, the Brownlow Medal count, only to give in when placed under pressure by the Lords of the League?

This time however there was to be no meek surrender. The clubs eventually formed a sub-committee to negotiate with the players and a deal was struck; all AFL players would be entitled to a minimum salary of $7500. Minimum base payments of $750 for a senior game and $250 for a reserves match were struck. There were concessions granted on injury payments and compensation for delisted players.

But if the League thought that was the end of it, that by finally bowing a little it had tamed a beast that threatened to turn savage, then it had another thing coming. Another battle was looming that would, predicted Madden, become one of the biggest issues the game had seen.

Full-time professional footballers.

It was the argument that had dismayed Geoff Pryor so many years before; players surrendering opportunities to better their lot in life, or at least putting it on hold, to pursue The Dream. It was all right for the superstars, the Wayne Careys, the Breretons and the Locketts. They earned enough to guarantee their futures. But what of the other 95 per cent?

'Whatever you can potentially do other than football is virtually put on hold,' said Madden. 'Everyone is going to have to make some hard decisions: do we go full-time or do we continue as we are?'

And not many were happy with the status quo: not the coaches who demanded their players be on call at all times; and not the players, who sometimes wondered what a private life was like. But whatever took place in the future, Madden was confident that the old, apathetic attitude toward the Players' Association was over. 'The younger players who are coming through, they're entering a newer system than the one many of us found. There's a draft system, a salary cap on the clubs. These younger kids are more aware of the politics. Not because they want to be. But because they need to be.'

There was another issue, though, that troubled Madden besides the question of full-time professionalism.

How could players learn to cope when the cheering stopped?

'Some people call it sports retirement syndrome,' said Madden. His voice had dropped a level and there was no sign of that cheesy grin. 'It's equated to the death of a close relative or a friend.

'You see it around. People are grieving. People who now sit in the front bar and tell you what a great footballer they were, that's all part of it. And I think it will be significant in the way we players, and the League, look at that.'

Of course, sports retirement syndrome was not solely restricted to Australian football; it could be found right across the spectrum. It was most noticeable in boxing, where fighters raised on the clichéd streets of broken glass, who had enjoyed successful careers fêted by the biggest money men in town, suddenly found no-one came knocking once a career was over.

But in Melbourne, you fell hard if you were a footballer. In the unlikely event that a player went on to win a Nobel Prize for devising a new theory for quantum gravitation, he would still be remembered as the talented half-forward who played 86 games with Footscray.

'It permeates every level,' said Madden wistfully. 'It permeates the pores of your skin. No matter how hard and cynical you are, it becomes part of you. You are Justin Madden, footballer. Or Justin Madden, ex-footballer. It engulfs you and the things you go on to do in life end up reflecting back on your footy career.'

So many in football recognised the problem. 'One of the saddest things in sport, no matter what sport it is, is when the crowd stops roaring,' observed Cameron Schwab one morning.

He had seen many instances of sports retirement syndrome at Richmond. During his time at Melbourne, there had been an extraordinary proportion of people with broken marriages. 'At Richmond, you could pick a team of 1960s and 1970s players who could match it with any team of players who got divorced after their playing careers were over.

'What footy does is, it not only dumps them, it gives them nowhere to go. And as human beings they can't replace what they had.'

That was the thing about footy. If it saw you were down, it didn't always reach out with a helping hand. Sometimes it gave you a kick to go on with. And there would be no better example of that than in the bizarre birth and tumultuous childhood years of the Brisbane Bears.

12

THE
BAD BUCK BEARS (I)

Peter Knights had grown up in a football world so comfortable and so protected that there were times he never realised it could be any other way. A champion with Hawthorn, he had made a name for himself with his long kicking and an exceptional ability to leap over a pack higher than just about anyone else. And if the game loved one thing more than anything else, it was a player with aerial skills. The high mark was unique to Australian football. Every other football code in the world had its exciting moments. Soccer had its charge forward and that rare moment when the ball struck the back of the net; gridiron its 'Hail Mary' pass, a long bomb thrown by the quarterback; rugby league a succession of skilful passes culminating in a try. Every code boasted unique skills. But no other game could make a crowd of 100,000 rise to its feet instantly simply by the single act of a man reaching for the sky.

Knights was very good at it and, with his straw-blond hair and almost perfect physique, he had emerged in the 1970s and '80s as one of the superstars of the game. In fact, many accorded him the same status as another of the game's great aerialists, Alex Jesaulenko.

But there was more to Knights than just his playing ability. He was polite and well-spoken, too. In fact, it was all just a little unbelievable, a little too perfect. Surely it was unfair that one man could have had bestowed upon him so many gifts?

Like any sport, football had always loved a cliché. And every time the name of Peter Knights received an airing, commentators and journalists reached deep for one of their favourite clichés. Knights was 'an ornament to the game'.

He was the sort of bloke everyone knew at school, the bloke who had that funny knack of always being in the right place at the right time. He was at Hawthorn when the club had begun an era of supremacy rarely matched in the history of the sport. Hawthorn had not always been such a force. In fact, there were many times when the club was an incongruity within the suburb it supposedly represented. Hawthorn was the archetypal leafy, very comfortable middle-class suburb in Melbourne's east, but its club had been a loser for almost 40 years since joining the League in 1925. Its ground, the Glenferrie Oval, was sandwiched away in a suburban back street, shaped like a sardine can and more claustrophobic than most of the grounds in the competition.

But by the 1980s, the Hawks had well and truly arrived. They played a vigorous running game, structured by their coach Allan Jeans, that eventually sapped the confidence of the opposition. Some said the Hawks were boring. But it was said more in exasperation at their continued excellence than anything else. No-one would have even dared to think of Peter Knights as boring.

Certainly, by 1989—the final year of the most tumultuous decade in the game's history—Knights would have looked quizzically at anyone who described the game as boring. Since 1987, he had been the inaugural coach of the Brisbane Bears. As one of only two new teams in the competition, the Bears had hardly been expected to emerge quickly as a power in the League. It seemed as though they had been introduced into the competition simply as an afterthought. While all the fights and boardroom stoushes had been staged over the talent-rich states of Western Australia and South Australia, and whether they should gain admission, no-one had even complained about the prospect of a side in Brisbane. Even clubs that had argued long and hard against expansion, citing the rigours and stresses on semi-professional footballers being forced to regularly fly inter-state to play, had been content to welcome a Brisbane team.

Play in Queensland? Sure. The biggest danger would be sunburn.

The Bears had hired Knights ahead of several bigger and proven names in the belief that his Hawthorn grounding would help give the new club stability and a sense of direction. It was as though football people believed that if a player represented a strong, united club under the tutelage of a wise and brilliant coach, that player would absorb all the goodness. It was the next best thing to carrying it in the genes.

It was a move that initially paid off. Under Knights, the Bears won a creditable six games in 1987 and seven the following season. They had been the most trying of times. The club had been dogged by controversy since birth; it had endured the humilia-tion of being virtually ignored by the Brisbane media; been treated shabbily by the VFL commission and scorned by every other club in the land. But what had made it worse for the fledg-ling team was the reality of football in the modern era. The Bears, more than than any other club, including even the Swans, had been forced into a shotgun marriage with big business and, as always seemed to be the case, had come off second best.

And now, as if to show that even its most loyal and perfect subjects were not immune to being punished, football was about to break the heart of Peter Knights.

It was a Tuesday morning in the middle of July, 1989. Just a few days before, the Bears had endured one of their most humiliating defeats, losing to Geelong at their home ground. It was the worst kind of defeat, too; a solid thumping that toward the end made it look as though the Bears were not even good enough to play in the same league. And what had made it even more embarrassing were the circumstances. It had been the club's debut under lights at its controversial home ground at Carrara on the Gold Coast. A national television audience was watching. Under the powerful lights, all the Bears could do was dance hopelessly in the dark.

It had been that kind of year. After two promising seasons, things had fallen in a hole for Brisbane. The clubs down south smiled smugly and said, 'We told you so.' Even Knights, whose close friends believed him to be one of the most honest and optimistic men in the game, had begun to suspect his future employment prospects might lie elsewhere. Still, somewhat predictably, he had figured that, with seven games left in the season, something could be done to resurrect a disappointing year.

Knights had been on his way to a supplementary training session for several unemployed players when the phone rang. Despite three years in Queensland, a significant proportion of the team remained jobless. It was typical of the way the club had been received in the northern state; never quite accepted or welcomed. The Queensland public could hardly be blamed either, not after the way the League and the club's owners had treated them.

The club was asking him to a meeting in the office of chairman Paul Cronin. When Knights arrived, he found Cronin waiting for him, along with the club's chief executive Ken Murphy and football manager Shane O'Sullivan. They looked like mourners at a funeral. Knights was about to be buried.

Cronin opened by talking about the team's recent poor performances and the feeling that it was time for a change.

'I was told sponsors weren't happy,' Knights would say glumly years later. 'They needed to make a change and be seen to be making a change.'

Cronin would himself describe the decision to dump Knights as an agonising one. 'That was not done lightly . . . There were sponsors, coterie group members who had had enough. These people, whose opinions I respected and we all respected in the administration, said something had to be done.'

Cronin told Knights he was no longer required as coach. As

a shocked Knights tried to digest the news, Murphy made a point of saying the decision was not unanimous. Both he and O'Sullivan, who had been close to the coach for the past three years, believed he deserved to at least see out the year.

For O'Sullivan, it was the worst moment in his football career. Short, with brownish hair and a chiselled face, he too, would also get the sack within a few years. But it was the departure of Knights that would always leave him cold whenever he thought about it for years to come. O'Sullivan had seen football's brutal side many times. Indeed, there were many instances when he'd had to deliver the bad news to players that their services were no longer required. It was never pretty, not when you had to tell someone that something they had sweated and worked toward for much of their life would forever be out of their grasp. And here, he thought, as he watched the colour drain from Knights' face, was a man who deserved much better.

Even five years later, sitting in a small, brick office deep in the bowels of another club where he'd picked up a new job, the sacking of Knights would force O'Sullivan's face to drop.

'I got the sack myself, but I reckon when Knightsy got sacked it was the worst,' O'Sullivan would say. 'Pete's an emotional guy and he puts 150 per cent into everything he does . . . Peter's so honest. So honest. Probably too honest for his own good in this industry.'

Knights was devastated by his sacking. He'd always been known for saying the right things and, unlike many others in the game, had always been loath to publicly criticise anyone else in the sport. But by the end of one of the worst weeks of his life, not even Knights could withold some of the venom he felt for those who had held his fate in their hands.

Cronin, he said, was 'somebody who doesn't understand the game . . . It was very difficult to speak about football with Paul Cronin because his thoughts were always that things have got to be achieved no matter what the cost, and generally, they can be achieved, I guess, with money.'

Money. It was the root of all football's problems. The game needed it to survive, but somehow it could never strike the right balance. And the Bears knew more about money, or the lack of it, than any club in the history of the game.

Paul Cronin would tell those around him at the club during its first three years that there was no way the Bears would end up like the 'old, diseased clubs in Melbourne.' They would not go broke. They would not have to rely on handouts from the public to survive.

O'Sullivan, wiser and far more cynical years later, would laugh at that statement. For the first time in almost an hour, his face would break into a grin. Then, just as quickly, the grin was gone.

It had taken almost 100 years for many of the Melbourne clubs to go broke, he explained.

Within three seasons, the Brisbane Bears collapsed with debts of $27 million.

Nowhere was the League's inept and clumsy attempt to expand better illustrated than in the high farce staged in Queensland. If football's gestation period for its new national competition was fraught with controversy, then its birth was just as tough. On the other side of the country, the West Coast Eagles, launched under the auspices of the West Australian Football League, had encountered severe financial problems almost immediately. But at least WA was a footy state.

Queensland was foreign territory. Australian rules was not a sport the natives had taken to their hearts. They liked their rugby league and their blue skies and warm air. Footy was a sport of the southern states where the winters could be cold and the only alternative to going to a match was sitting inside reading the Saturday papers.

But there were some who still believed Queensland could be converted and one of them was an actor who, since 1984, had been preparing the way.

Paul Cronin was one of the most familiar faces on Australian television, particularly during the 1970s when he starred in 'The Sullivans', a phenomenally successful saga of an Australian family living through World War II. Cronin had portrayed Dave Sullivan, the patriarchal head of the family, a man of values and a high moral code who could still enjoy a beer in the pub with his mates after work on a Friday night.

While he would go on to other ventures, Cronin had been typecast for life. He would be forever remembered as Dave and he would not be allowed to forget it. When he emerged in 1986 as the head of one of three consortiums seeking a licence for a VFL club in Queensland, every newspaper article referred to his role in television's favourite family. But Cronin wasn't just an actor using his name to attract publicity for a cause he felt strongly about.

A South Australian, Cronin's father Mick had been ruckman and captain-coach of Jamestown in a SA country league and later for North Adelaide. Paul would often go to the footy and stand on the terraces with his father, accompanied by a packed lunch and thermos.

It was the way of many father-son combinations throughout the southern half of the country and the young Cronin, it would seem, was greatly influenced by the towering presence of the older man next to him. 'He was a very fair man, the fairest man I've ever known,' Cronin would say one morning over a coffee in the restaurant of a Brisbane hotel. Every so often, other diners would cast furtive glances toward him, wondering why Dave Sullivan was breakfasting in Brisbane.

'He was a gentleman; his word was his bond and I hope mine is.' With that statement, Cronin fixed his gaze on the interviewer, staring at him bluntly without blinking. 'He was one of the strongest men I have ever met. He was about my size, but I saw him pick up a bale of bags one day off the trolley and that's something like 400 pounds. I was only young, only a kid, and I figured he was the strongest bloke I'd ever seen. He'd pick up a 180-pound bag of wheat and treat it as though it was nothing. It took me a long time to pick up a 180-pound bag and when I did, I thought I was a man.'

The Cronin creed was clear; strength and gentlemanly conduct were two criteria by which to live your life. But if Cronin enjoyed a nostalgic and romantic memory of football's great days when he could stand and watch the game next to a man he thought was the strongest in the world, it was tempered by the pragmatism of a realist. 'We live in a commercial world and we have to move on,' he'd say. 'I'm as fond as anyone of those days. But they're gone.'

Cronin fell into acting, having moved to Melbourne in the late 1960s as an executive with an engineering firm. By the time the VFL made it known it was keen to move into the Brisbane market, Cronin was ready. He'd been dabbling in real estate for five years, making money and always hoping the opportunity for a Brisbane side would eventuate. In 1985 he'd been granted an audience with Joh Bjelke-Petersen on the issue and the Queensland premier had received him warmly.

Cronin loved Queensland. He liked the way people did business there; it appealed to his belief that anyone could be anything they wanted to be. 'They've created a climate up there in which you can make things happen,' he would say. Paul Cronin/Dave Sullivan, with his square-jawed look and neatly-combed hair, was a self-starter and a fair dinkum Aussie bloke. And he was not handicapped, either, by the prejudices and possessiveness of the Victorian football public when it came to a national competition.

'If football is run on a national basis, it's more attractive for sponsors and the television rights are better,' he announced. 'The potential market is just that much bigger.'

Cronin had first tried to lure the financially-plagued Fitzroy to Queensland. He made several approaches to the club's chairman, Leon Wiegard, including an invitation to his home in Kew to discuss the merits of a move north.

'He was a nice enough sort of fella,' Wiegard would recall years later. 'I took it to the board after he'd taken three or four swipes at me. We met in one of the Elders' offices in Collins Street. Fitzroy was really struggling. We didn't know if our next cheque would be honoured.

'Paul was doing really well. He was making his submission and I thought he was winning the board over until someone asked: 'Why Fitzroy; why haven't you been to any other club?'

'Paul said "well, I've always barracked for Fitzroy." No-one knew. It was a little thing but it never sounded quite right, you know?'

The Lions were a lost cause as far as Brisbane was concerned, but the League had made it clear it was still keen to move into Queensland. Cronin's toughest opponent in the race for a club was John Brown, a prominent sports and business figure. Brown had promoted countless tennis tournaments around the country and had helped install the first corporate boxes at the 1972 Australian Open.

By 1986, when he first heard about the possibility of a VFL side in Brisbane, Brown had been in Queensland for three years. He'd been tipped off by a local journalist and acted immediately. He got on the phone to Alan Schwab. The two had been at school together at Camberwell High and had stayed in touch on an irregular basis since. Within hours, Brown had flown to Melbourne and was having lunch with Schwab at 'Frenchy's', just around the corner from VFL House. By 4 o'clock that afternoon, he was down at Nicabella's Hotel, run by Graeme Richmond. Schwab had told Brown he had to meet 'GR', a man who shared the vision for expansion, particularly into the Queensland market. From there, the pair became close friends and Richmond would play a strategic role in Brown's bid, phoning all the influential Melbourne journalists, wheeling and dealing at the clubs.

The commission liked Brown. They liked his business attitude and the fact that he had already shown he knew how to promote sports events. Plus, he also had promotors and entrepreneurs of the ilk of Michael Edgely and Kevin Jacobsen backing him. The commission, in fact, so liked Brown that it decided to recommend him to the clubs as the licence holder of the new Brisbane team. But the commission, and Brown, had not counted on Paul Cronin showing the sort of business savvy unexpected in a soap opera actor.

Over a two-hour meeting, Cronin lured the Queensland Australian Football League into bed with him. It was a canny move; it meant that Cronin's bid had the support of Queensland's only recognised governing body for Australian football. After the mess in Sydney, the clubs felt safe knowing real football people would be in charge.

At least, that was their public stance. Behind the scenes, however, the Melbourne clubs lusted after something far more important; money. The president of the QAFL, Jon Collins, learned this only too well on a visit to the grand final that year.

In a discussion with a club general manager, Collins was told that up to six Melbourne clubs were in desperate straits. With a $4 million licence fee coming their way, the clubs would prefer as much of it as possible up-front, rather than on a 'drip' system where payments due could take years to arrive. Cronin was making noises that he could pay more than Brown.

Slowly but surely, the numbers began turning against the commission. Allen Aylett, the former president, had lobbied hard for the QAFL-Cronin syndicate and his presence at one stage sparked a bitter tirade against him from Hamilton. But, instead of persevering in its belief, the commission chickened out. To have its recommendation rejected by the clubs would be a savage blow to its standing, particularly in a volatile climate where any error could plunge the game into the abyss. The commission withdrew its recommendation and would forever regret it, along with the rest of the football world. Within a few years, the commission would be forced to support a push within the club to oust Cronin.

What was it about football that attracted businessmen who should have known better? There was little money to be made from the game; even the most financially incompetent could see that. And hadn't the experiences of the Sydney Swans proved it? So what was in it for the likes of men like John Elliott and Lindsay Fox?

If you listened to most of them, their attachment to the game was driven by a pure love for the sport. They cared for it; they wanted it to succeed and stamp itself as the premier code around the country.

'What appealed to me was being associated with a competitive contact sport,' said Bob Ansett, the former president of North Melbourne and another of the 1980s Men Who Fell To Earth. 'Footy appealed to me. It's a physical sport and it had the same business philosophy I had. But when I became chairman I didn't use the club to further my own business career. I needed to be careful. I had a high profile and I wanted to make sure I didn't hurt my profile.

'(But) there may have been some benefits . . . you do rub shoulders with politicians and business people.'

You never heard these businessmen mention the word ego, though. To have your name linked closely to a League club, and preferably a good one, was the final stamp of acceptance in Melbourne. You could raid as many weakened companies as you liked; you could split them up and then on-sell the remaining carcass for twice its value and yet you still wouldn't receive the same plaudits and respect that a club president did.

By late 1986, the entrepreneurs and football were madly in love with one another. Both were adventurous types anyway, so their union was always going to be that much easier. And one of the most promiscuous was Christopher Skase. Here was a man who held to the maxim that bigger was better; Skase was hardly the type to practise business's version of safe sex. What was it he once said about his business credo? 'You don't cut back your expenditure, you increase your income.'

A Melbourne boy not exactly fondly remembered by his old school, Caulfield Grammar, as one of its better students, Skase had moved to Queensland in the eighties to realise a long-held ambition to be successful in business. He had departed Melbourne with a chip on his shoulder too, over the manner in which his home town had kept its distance from a young man who was openly and unabashedly ambitious and determined to succeed.

'I copped the cold shoulder all over town,' he would say. 'I was denigrated and isolated and given no encouragement whatsoever. That has long lived with me, and I will never forget it. The Melbourne Establishment may think what it likes, but they are dying, along with their city.'

And Skase was going to show them, too. By the middle of the following year he would ride into Melbourne triumphantly and be fêted as the man who, by spending $780 million, had saved the Seven network and would restore Channel 7 in Melbourne to its former eminence. He would also ride in and save football by signing up the League to a lucrative television rights deal that would underpin the game's financial security for years to come.

But with Skase there was always a negative to each positive and it wasn't just his taste in clothes—his apparent love of large ties, wide collars and a 1970s-style haircut made him look, at times, like either the perfect candidate to host 'The Price Is Right' or to understudy John Travolta in *Saturday Night Fever*. Skase was about to become the major benefactor of the Brisbane Bears, the club no-one really wanted to know about. Within a couple of years, the League was wishing Skase had not wanted to know about the Bears either.

Skase's arrival on the scene came over one weekend in November, 1986. The Cronin-QAFL syndicate needed to pay the $4 million licence fee within a few weeks and several of its members—some of the most prominent names in Queensland business—had developed cold feet when the crunch came to back their pledges of support with hard cash.

Skase was approached by a solicitor called David Dunn, who acted for Paul 'Porky' Morgan, a stockbroker whose firm had just underwritten the $4 million licence fee in anticipation of a public float of the Bears at a later date, a float that would never materialise. Dunn was aware Morgan could be in trouble unless the club received a substantial injection of funds and, knowing Skase, approached the Qintex chief for help.

Skase was soon on board, using a subsidiary company, Queensland Merchant Holdings Ltd, as his vehicle for his first foray into Australian football. Over the next three years, QMH would provide the club with almost $19 million in loans. And when Christopher Skase's make-believe world finally crashed down around him in November, 1989, the League would discover that the original $4 million licence fee paid to its clubs back in 1986 remained owed to the bank that had supplied it; ANZ McCaughan.

But who was to know what was in store back then? Compared to his other business ventures, Skase's dabbling in the football world was more an exercise in philanthropy than another business venture. But he was hardly a disinterested partner.

'Life is not a dress rehearsal,' he said. 'We're only on Earth once, and if you are in it you have to be in it 100 per cent.'

Under the revised consortium structure, Skase, who had made an initial injection of foundation capital of $550,000, along with several business partners, won seats on the club's board. There were other benefits too. He could renew his old love for the game, rub shoulders with some of football's biggest names and was able to use the club to help promote his burgeoning commercial and property interests.

Politically, it was also a sensible move for Skase. Businessmen like him always needed to stay onside with the politicians and Skase, like other entrepreneurs, shmoozed with the best of them. A sporting connection seemed to round off the *curriculum vitae*. And he was welcomed with open arms by the ruling National Party of the day, even if his name was not exactly revered at first.

At a lavish Christmas party staged by Skase, Bjelke-Petersen had referred to 'my good friend, Christopher SKATES.'

At least he got the first name right. It was always 'Christopher'. 'Chris' had too much of a familiar ring to it. One Brisbane-based journalist would always recall the day Skase was introduced at a media gathering for the Brisbane Bears.

'Paul Cronin was up there with a microphone and he introduced 'Chris Skase',' the journalist recalled. 'Skase took the microphone and the first thing he said was "My name is Christopher. Not Chris." It was obviously a thing with him.'

If there were some benefits for Skase in a move into football, it was also fair for the club to assume it would gain greatly from the marriage of convenience. Who would knock back the opportunity to be linked with Christopher Skase's club? The Queensland business scene could be as sycophantic as any other in the country. Skase was the golden boy; he took chances and he was riding high. Perhaps by becoming a sponsor of the Bears, a little of the Skase magic could rub off.

'Porky' Morgan was one of the few brokers who had dealings with Skase who did not bite off more than he could chew. Perhaps it was Skase's manner that warned him not to swim too closely. In the matey world of Queensland politics and business, the entrepreneur who had gained a reputation as being stand-offish and personally remote stood out like a virgin at a Roman orgy.

'He was not a social guy, not a raging pisspot,' Morgan would say. 'In fact, he was a very intense young gentleman. In the three years he was here, I don't think he had any social relationships.'

Cronin became the hands-on chairman of the Bears, looking after the day-to-day matters, and he would be paid handsomely enough; a consultancy fee of $100,000 a year, regular first-class air travel between Melbourne, Brisbane and the Gold Coast and accommodation at a luxury hotel.

In football parlance, a team that has been down on form and rebounds to win a few games is announced as being 'back in town'. In a month, the Bears had been born into a tough world, staggered for a few weeks and then found themselves a saviour. They were back in town.

And just as quickly as they arrived, they departed.

If you wanted to start a new professional football club in an expanded Australia-wide competition, there were better ways to do it than within the tight and strict parameters given to the Brisbane Bears.

The lead-up to Christmas, 1986, had hardly been a season of good cheer for the League. Its new commissioner, Ross Oakley, was in the sights of several club leaders. Ian Collins and Ron Joseph were two administrators querying Oakley's credentials and track record. A new airlines agreement had only just been reached and the television rights controversy was about to break. Up north, with just eight weeks to go before the start of the pre-season competition, the Bears had no place to call home.

A grab-bag of possible venues had been cited: one day it was Kedron, the next day would see a major development at Boondall. Finally, and with time running out, Cronin announced two days before Christmas that the Bears would move to Carrara on the Gold Coast. Carrara was a ground with a large playing surface; it was, in fact, as wide and long as the game's cathedral, the Melbourne Cricket Ground. It had been used at various times by the QAFL to host the odd State match, but it was a relatively unknown commodity down South.

To turn Carrara into a VFL-standard ground in time for the 1987 season required an enormous transformation. Just 12 months before, a QAFL side had played Essendon at the venue and it had taken 8000 people more than two hours just to get into the ground once heavy rain fell. The Albert Shire had upgraded the access roads since then, but the doubters in Victoria were hardly shy in coming forward and expressing scepticism about the entire Bears venture.

Wasn't the club supposed to be a Brisbane team, not one based on the Gold Coast playing at a venue with temporary seating? The move down to the coast had required the written permission of the League and the QAFL as, under a tripartite licence agreement, the club was supposed to have been based within the Brisbane metropolitan precinct. But given that time was fast running out and that it could not afford the embarrassment of unveiling a national league with one of its new clubs homeless, both bodies had agreed reluctantly to the Carrara switch.

For one year only.

But six months into the Bears' first season, rumours began circulating that the club was destined for the Gold Coast long-term. And by the end of the first season, which saw the club finish second-last on the ladder, Skase was determined not to be moved. After the huge establishment costs, shifting the enterprise back to Brisbane was an unpalatable prospect.

Behind the scenes, a fierce exchange of legal letters went back and forth between the League and the club. The decision to stick with Carrara would become one of the thorniest problems confronting the League. It would see the shotgun marriage between Cronin and the QAFL dissolve into a bitter divorce and see the Brisbane public and media turn their backs on the team completely.

The popular view was that Skase, by now in control of the Seven network, was using his influence with television rights to ensure the Bears remained where he wanted them. What was less well-known was that the club was already on its way to becoming a financial basket case.

'The problem was that at the end of the first year the Bears were effectively $12 million in debt,' said Andrew Ireland. A former Collingwood player, Ireland had moved to Queensland

and picked up a job with the QAFL in the early 1980s. By the time the club was launched, he was appointed the QAFL's general manager and, a few years later, he would become the Bears' chief executive.

Like everyone else at the QAFL, Ireland believed the Bears would never win the hearts and minds of the Queensland public until they based themselves in Brisbane. But with Skase's companies having already put in $12 million in effective loans to the club, the financial argument would win the day.

The Bears had spent heavily. Apart from the original establishment costs, they paid between $2.2 and $2.7 million to other League clubs in transfer fees. Footscray received $270,000 when it traded Brad Hardie and other clubs regularly demanded $100,000 and more for quality players.

And Skase was not moving the club anywhere. Said Ireland: 'Skase just said point blank to the commission 'well, if you want to force me to go to Brisbane I'll walk away from it and you'll have a club that's $12 million in debt in its first year. You try and explain that to the general public.'

The League was not prepared to try. The Bears stayed on the Coast.

It was a decision that even rankled with many within the club. When Cronin finally persuaded the League to make Carrara the club's permanent home, he rang from Melbourne to announce the news. The club's administrative staff were summoned into the board room and, once they had gathered, Cronin broke the news. They were there to stay. A call from Cronin for 'Three cheers for Carrara' hardly had the room reverberating with celebration.

'We didn't have the ability to send him (Skase) back to Brisbane,' Oakley would lament years later. 'The way the contract was written made it almost impossible for them to go back once we'd agreed to go to Carrara. The only other options were the QEII stadium and the 'Gabba. (One day) we had a meeting with the 'Gabba trust, Cronin, the QAFL and the Premier (Mike Ahern). We basically had an agreement that the 'Gabba should be it.'

The greyhound track circling the oval would be removed and, believed Oakley, the ground would be upgraded.

'Next day we get a phone call to say that's not happening. The premier now believes that Skase is putting the money in and he should decide where it's going to be. The 'Gabba's not an option anymore. So our major option had been closed off.'

The city of Brisbane continued to thumb its nose at the club. In the Bears' second season at Carrara, Cronin appeared in a series of advertisements endorsing a plan to construct the world's tallest building in Brisbane. He was featured standing in front of such world landmarks as the Eiffel Tower and the Statue of Liberty and asking why Brisbane could not boast a similar landmark.

It wasn't long before a joke began doing the rounds in Brisbane. 'What's the point of having such a building in Brisbane . . .?' went the gag. '. . . Cronin and Skase would only move it to Carrara.'

In its second year, the club would adopt an aggressive marketing campaign to woo potential sponsors and appease those who had laid down their hard-earned cash to watch a side finish 13th on the ladder again. But there was at least some consolation. The pre-game luncheon at Carrara was the best in the competition and so it should have been. Up to 200 of the club's leading supporters would be wined and dined at an estimated cost of $140 a head, with food being flown to the ground from the Melbourne kitchen of the Victorian society caterer, Peter Rowland. Expensive wines and floral arrangements accompanied the best meals Skase's monopoly money could buy.

The costs continued to mount.

With the club millions of dollars in debt after its first season, a miracle was required in the second year for the Bears to avoid being completely shunned by the rest of the VFL family. They would win seven games in that second season in 1988, which was a little miracle in its own right given the playing personnel and the off-field turmoil. What other club in the competition lacked a decent gymnasium facility? At least at Fitzroy, another financially-struggling club, the coach and his players drove down to the club over summer with their own tool boxes to construct a makeshift gym and racks for the weights.

Brisbane was a fabricated club living in pre-fabricated surrounds and trying desperately to buy itself a soul and a tradition. All the players had were themselves and, while they became a relatively tightly-bonded group, even that feeling of togetherness was sorely tested by the events of their second season.

To those on the periphery of the game, football was a simple affair. The big blokes in the centre battled for the ball, tapped it down to the little blokes who then ran and kicked it down-field to the full-forward. It was the most glamorous position on the field and many believed that you couldn't win a premier-ship without a decent spearhead. Of course, throughout the years, plenty of teams without a star full-forward had won premierships, but that did nothing to dispel the popular notion. Get yourself a man who could kick goals and you were halfway toward having a winning team.

Paul Cronin and Christopher Skase wanted a winning team. Below them, several administration officials believed it would take years before the club became a force in the competition. You couldn't, they confided among themselves, manufacture a team overnight from leftovers. You needed to bring the young kids through, develop a grass-roots structure that would nur-ture and provide a steady stream of talent.

But that was ignoring the business reality of the Bears, too. The club couldn't afford to wait. If they were to find a place in the hearts of the Queensland public, they needed to start win-ning consistently and give the Victorians a fright. So Cronin and Skase agreed they had to find themselves a full-forward.

And they only had to look as far south as Sydney. There, wallowing in debt and controversy, riddled by feuding and political turmoil, were the Swans. By 1988, Edelsten had long departed, squeezed out by the sharp operators of Westeq. He was mired in legal problems of his own and a stint in prison was only a few years away. But at least during his brief tenure he had succeeded in capturing the imagination of the Sydney market. Now, after two seasons of failure in the finals—the Swans had played four finals in two years, bowing out in embarrassing fashion each time—the club was washed up, drained of funds and life. The Swans desperately needed cash. Powerplay was in dire straits. Its investment in Sportsplay, a pub and club satellite television company, was costing it up to $1 million a month and the burden on the Swans as a revenue source was proving insufferable. So when the Bears came looking, the Swans hung the 'For Sale' sign around the neck of their full-forward, Warwick Capper.

Capper had emerged as a star in Sydney and seemed to embody that notion of flashiness Bob Pritchard believed was the only thing guaranteed to win over the Sydney public. While he was still shy when confronted in public by a microphone and prone to utter the game's most absurd clichés at his usual machine-gun rate, he remained the club's most valuable asset. And now, with the coffers once again bare and creditors breathing down their necks, common sense departed the scene.

Cronin had raised Capper's name with Peter Knights early in the year. 'I'll get you a goalsneak,' Knights recalled Cronin promising him. A goalsneak? No-one in footy used the term. It was a phrase you heard in the stands, or around the office coffee urn on a Monday morning. Knights was sceptical. Like most who worked in the game, Capper was regarded as a decent player, but one who was unlikely to improve.

He could take a big grab, that was for sure. And, for the most part, he could kick straight. But the Capper legend had been built around him playing on the Sydney Cricket Ground, a squat, fat ground where just one kick would lob the ball to the goalsquare. There, it was easy for 'Capps' to out-bustle an opponent or fly for an overhead mark.

Everyone knew, however, that you could beat Capper in the open. He hardly ever led for the ball, creating a target for his team-mates further upfield. It just didn't seem to strike him as necessary. He'd never had to do it in the past. And with players like Greg Williams and Gerard Healy capable of winning 40 possessions each a match, what use was there? The ball always came to him.

Knights and his match committee talked it over and believed Capper was not the answer to their problems. But for Skase and Cronin, the blond, suburban boy with the sprayed-on shorts was a guaranteed winner. His marketing potential was huge. The publicity of his move to the Gold Coast would be enormous and who knew what sort of benefits, besides his goal-scoring ability, he could provide the fledgling side?

Knights and O'Sullivan were dispatched to Sydney to meet Capper in the office of his solicitor. The trip interrupted a stint at Port Douglas, where most of the team were staying.

In Sydney, O'Sullivan found himself on the phone to Alan Schwab in Melbourne, who knew only too well the financial plight of the Swans. It seemed the entire competition was facing the same financial crisis it had been staring at four years earlier, and which this so-called national competition was supposed to solve. In Melbourne the usual battles against bankruptcy were taking place, while the interstate sides were floundering financially too. The West Coast Eagles. The Sydney Swans. The Bears. All financial flops.

Schwab was in an angry mood. He felt a strong sense of attachment to the Swans. They were part of the original dream of expansion after all, and to lose them would see the loss of the entire national competition. No Sydney meant far fewer television dollars and corporate advertising, not to mention the devastating loss of face for the League.

Schwab threatened O'Sullivan that life would be made extremely difficult for the Bears if they went ahead and signed Capper. The consequences, he told him, would be dire. O'Sullivan felt uncomfortable. He felt a strong sense of allegiance to Schwab, a man he had always admired and who had given him his start in football, securing his first job with Carlton. There, in the same room, was the determined Cronin. He would get his man and he didn't care what Schwab or the rest of the VFL commission thought. Cronin looked at O'Sullivan at one stage and told him matter-of-factly to inform Schwab that the Bears would be signing Warwick Capper.

They did. In February, Capper somehow managed to extricate himself from those tight red Sydney shorts to make the journey to the Gold Coast. He cost the Bears $350,000 over three years, plus a hefty transfer fee of $340,000. His departure was not without the usual acrimony. It would be one of the final acts of Powerplay. Even the Sydney players, de-sensitised by years of fast-talking marketing men and hype, were shocked and dismayed by the departure of their blond mate. Capper had never been regarded as an intellectual giant among his team-mates, but they loved him nevertheless. When he left, they knew the dream was over. Greg Williams, the Swans' Brownlow Medallist and a prolific possession-winner, had rung Cronin just days before the Bears signed Capper. In a last bid to stop the sale, Williams had warned Cronin the move would be a disaster. Sydney needed Capper, he told him, just as much as Capper needed Sydney. 'If I see you in six months, I'll be saying "I told you so,"' Williams told him.

Had Greg Williams been able to predict Tattslotto numbers with the sort of accuracy he showed with his forecast of Capper's future, he would have been a rich man. In the end, he would become one anyway, moving from Sydney to Carlton and becoming the highest-paid player in the game in the early to mid-1990s. By then, Capper was out of football, his flame extinguished, his name appearing only occasionally in the tabloids as they fed on tales of his private life and a possible movie career that hardly moved at all.

By June, 1988, Capper's presence in the Bears' team had become a bone of contention between Skase and Cronin on one side and the match committee on the other. Football had traditionally obeyed the same sort of rule adopted by democracies: a separation of church and state. The administration ran the club and organised the fund-raising; the playing staff had control over who took the field.

But down on the Gold Coast, deep in the neon heartland of the 1980s entrepreneur, those rules no longer applied. Capper was down on form and looked nowhere near the 100-goal-a-year player he had been in Sydney. He needed to do what players had done for almost a hundred years; drop back to the reserves and regain his old form and confidence. No matter how hard Knights and the rest of the coaching staff had worked on Capper, he just didn't seem able to change his style of game and lead for the ball. Carrara was a different type of ground from the SCG; it was large, with big pockets and flanks, and a man like Capper could get lost in them. He often did.

He had to be dropped, not only for his own good but for the team as well. The other players were losing confidence in him. You could see it in the way they passed the ball and looked for other options up forward. But there was one problem. Skase and Cronin had made it clear Capper and three other players—captain Mark Mickan, Brad Hardie and Roger Merrett—were not to be dropped.

It was a bizarre situation. Surely this was a first; the club's chairman and most influential financial backer dictating team selection policy. At one stage in June, the match committee met and decided to resign in protest, but soon reconsidered.

Even years later, Peter Knights's eyes would widen in amazement at the memory. 'There were four players who I was told were not to be dropped under any circumstances,' he would say. He was back as coach at his old club Hawthorn by then, dressed in a tracksuit and sitting in an office surrounded by the paraphernalia of the modern coach: video recorders, computer, scribbling pads and charts.

The four untouchables, said Knights, 'were assets which had cost the club a lot of money and they didn't want those assets running around in the reserves or the QAFL. Under no circumstances.' As a coach, Knights found himself in an extremely uncomfortable position. 'Not only do you know you can't operate under that, how do you look your players in the eye and expect them to show you respect? They know it's unfair. You just can't have a situation like that.'

With Cronin maintaining a steadfast line against dropping Capper, Knights took the step of going over his head. He rang Skase and then met him to discuss the issue. 'One thing I'd always been able to do was sit down and talk footy with him,' Knights would recall. There had been plenty of those footy discussions in the previous 18 months. Skase had been a big Essendon fan as a young man in Melbourne and liked to talk to Knights and others about some of the Bombers' great players he'd watched as a kid out at Windy Hill. During the Bears' first season, Skase was a regular face at matches and training sessions, but by the middle of the second year he had grown more distant, leaving much of the work with Cronin as he attempted to stop his financial empire from crumbling.

'After we had this discussion, he said if it's got to be done, go ahead.'

Knights would always remember the feeling of relief that swept through him when Skase cleared the decision to drop Capper. 'There was this relief, it was just an unbelievable feeling. I then rang everyone on the match committee with the good news and then I rang Cronin. I got a frosty reception.'

But after that little victory, nothing was ever the same again. Within the club, the battle to drop Capper was seen as a turning point. If such a protracted and bitter fight was required just to send the star full-forward back to the reserves, what hope was there?

Capper's place in the side was not the only time Knights and his match committee encountered pressure from above. Early in 1988, Knights and Shane O'Sullivan had been summoned to a meeting where Cronin and Skase, disappointed with a string of losses, demanded the sacking of five players.

The two football staff argued the case against any sackings, saying it would be bad for morale. Skase and Cronin were steadfast; five had to go. It didn't matter who they were as long as five players were chopped from the list. At one stage, discussions became so lively that O'Sullivan was told he either sacked the players, or faced the sack himself.

A year later in November, 1989, Skase's network of companies collapsed like a house of cards with net debts estimated at up to $2 billion. The Bears were in deep trouble. The club had estimated losses of $27-28 million and now Cronin found himself alone, the proverbial boy with his finger in the dam wall.

This was the sort of situation that brought Cronin's Protestant work ethic and attitude to the fore. He was a man under pressure. With Skase off the scene, every one of the club's critics, both internally and outside, were jostling for position to throw the knives. Cronin, they said, had lacked the necessary commercial and football administrative experience to steer the club through tough times. He had been too interventionist. His style had been too confrontational.

Did Cronin have any friends left in football? If so, they were incredibly hard to find. While the League admired his attempts to hold the club together, it also began wondering how much longer Cronin could afford to remain aligned with the club. With the summer of 1989/90 rapidly approaching, the last thing the commission wanted was another drawn-out crisis that would have the newspapers rubbing their hands together with glee. Barely a summer passed, it seemed, without the commission trying to put out brush fires.

If the criticism hurt Cronin, and there is little doubt it did, it only served to further stoke the fires of conviction. Just three days before Christmas in 1989, as he tried to pull together a new consortium of businessmen prepared to save the club, he answered a phone call at his Melbourne home. He was tired and bitter, but determined to hang on as chairman despite growing speculation he would be ousted in a purge.

'I spent 20 years of my life in the television and film industry,' he said angrily. 'By the very nature of that, there's a critic on every bloody show that you do . . . there's a critic who's got to earn his living.

'That's all he's got to do—knock. And we're very good at doing that in this country—knocking achievers. Achievers and entrepreneurs are directly responsible for the employment of hundreds of thousands of people . . . I don't know what's bloody well wrong with half the people in this business. They sit back, they haven't put their hand up for investment in anything and they just knock, knock, knock. It really makes you sick.'

Everyone, it seemed, was sick and tired of the Bears' predicament. In late January, the players met and decided to go on strike, saying they were concerned over the club's management during the previous three years and would not play unless a sound administrative structure was put into place.

Unbeknown to the football world at large, the commission was fully aware of the decision by the players and it was hardly disappointed with the move. Before they had met, Shane O'Sullivan, the last remaining original football staff member, had received a call from a senior League official.

'He indicated they knew what was up and that they wouldn't be disappointed if things turned out a certain way,' O'Sullivan recalled. 'I was told to set a few things up to make sure Paul (Cronin) and that weren't around . . . they (the commission) saw an opening and they could see that the players and the club could play a role.'

Oakley would recall years later that Cronin had been a good man in a tough and difficult position. 'I found him pretty good. He became very emotionally involved . . . I think everyone felt that it was probably time for Paul to go. But in my dealings with him, I didn't find him as difficult to deal with as some others. He never threatened me. And I've been threatened many times before.'

Under pressure, and with the club teetering, Cronin resigned on 31 January 1990, 24 hours after the players had announced plans to strike. He denied the pressure from the players had forced his hand, citing instead 'influences' from outside the club.

Despite its public stance, the commission had intervened directly in the internal affairs of one of its clubs. Now it had to fix a problem of its own making. First it needed someone with money. And even though the 1980s were over, the famous utterance by the circus promotor P.T. Barnum at the turn of the century still held.

There was a sucker born every minute. And it would not be long before another appeared just around the corner.

13

ONCE UPON A TIME IN THE WEST

He was sitting on the fence outside the brick veneer home, just down the road from the Claremont football ground. It was early in the 1980s and Ron Joseph was in Western Australia again, trying to lure two of that state's most decorated footballers, the Krakouer brothers, to Melbourne.

North's glory days during the 1970s had come to a shuddering halt in the new era and the club was again embarking on a rebuilding program. And who better to lead it than Joseph, the architect of North's cunning strategy back in the 1970s to build itself into a football power?

If he could secure the Krakouers, then maybe more success was not that far away for the Kangaroos. In the meat market of Australian football, the Krakouer boys, Phil and Jim, were prime cuts. They played the game on a different level from everyone else. Some wondered whether they were, in fact, Siamese twins who were separated in the rooms before a game and then joined together again afterward. It was the only near-logical explanation for the way they played. Each knew where the other was on the ground at all times. Phil might back out of a pack with the ball, his back turned to the goals, and kick it over his shoulders precisely to the spot where brother Jim was waiting patiently.

If there was a connection, it was telepathic. A handpass from a huddle of players by Jim would miraculously appear in Phil's hands as he sprinted past. The only thing they lacked in football were big heads. Like many Aboriginal players, the Krakouers were shy men who did their talking on the field. Off it, they nodded when introduced to strangers, rarely initiating conversation.

Which was exactly the sort of predicament Joseph found himself in as he sat on the fence making small talk. With the Krakouers, it was very small talk. They had seen his type before; sweet-talking officials from the big league in Melbourne walking into Perth and thinking they could sign anyone with a simple snap of their fingers. So they made Joseph sweat it out as they sized him up, interpreting his body language and weighing up whether he was as genuine as he claimed to be.

They were still sitting there when a car neared the house. 'Here's Wally Maskell,' said Phil.

Joseph turned a pale shade of grey. Maskell was the general manager of Claremont. What would Maskell do if he discovered Joseph sitting there talking to his two most revered players? Did Western Australia still practise capital punishment? Maskell would skin him alive.

Joseph moved quickly. He dived off the fence and sprinted down the side of the house, hiding in the back yard. Maskell drove past, waved to his boys and kept driving toward the end of the street to Claremont's home ground. When Joseph reappeared a few moments later once the all-clear had been given, he found the Krakouers laughing at the front of the house. They liked this funny little man from Melbourne. For someone not boasting a distinctive degree of fitness, he'd shown a remarkable amount of leg speed.

'That broke the ice,' Joseph would recall. 'They got a laugh out of it and eventually I saw the lighter side of it and we became pretty friendly.'

Joseph would finally capture the Krakouers and take them to Melbourne, where their unique style of football would provide

North with an enormous lift on the field and plenty of problems for perplexed opposition coaches. What it also served to underline was how Victorian football clubs had come to recognise WA as just another stopover on the never-ending search for new talent.

'It was like going to Wangaratta or any other country town,' Joseph would say, smiling at the memory. 'The Western Australians didn't really like what was happening, but they sort of accepted it. Perth football people were always more friendly and realistic. In Adelaide, they were more hard-nosed and they hated us much more.

'When I came out of Perth and flew home, I always knew I was $5000 away from a deal. But when you flew out of Adelaide, you never knew if you were going to clinch the deal.'

For years, Victorian clubs had flown into WA and plundered its greatest football treasures. By the 1980s, the WA clubs could not survive without the constant flow of money in clearance fees from the east. And when that flow finally dried up in the financial crisis that beset the League in the mid-80s, WA realised it was time to raise the white flag and surrender completely. Far better to join 'em if you couldn't beat 'em.

What was it they said about the world's financial system? When Wall Street sneezed, the rest of the planet's financial markets caught a cold.

When Victorian football sneezed, Western Australian football came down with pneumonia.

For years, the eight clubs of the Western Australian Football League had enjoyed an extraordinary love-hate relationship with their Victorian counterparts. Each summer they endured the presence of constant raiding parties from the east. It was as though the Victorians were the worst kind of predatory animal, with little concern for their own environment. Once they had burned and pillaged their way through their own state, giving little thought to future development, they moved west across the Nullarbor to the still-green fields of WA. There they had discovered a bountiful land chock-full of talented kids, kids who might one day help them secure The Flag.

It had been going on ever since the late 1960s and early 1970s, when money had begun swamping the VFL and its clubs. By the 1980s, the WAFL was completely dependent on the Victorian clubs and the high transfer fees they were prepared to pay in order to take home a talented player.

'It was like a cargo cult,' Richard Colless would recall later. He was a member of the WAFL board and later would become the first chairman of the West Coast Eagles and part with $1 million of his own money to kick the venture along. 'The WA clubs just sat around and waited for the planes from Melbourne to arrive and for the money from the VFL clubs to be handed around.

'The WA League was bankrupt. In 1983, seven of the eight clubs were effectively insolvent. It was a disaster.'

Colless's view was a rare one in football; it found agreement everywhere. While West Australians used one hand to raise their middle finger at the Victorians, the other one was accepting wads of cash from them. And no club was too proud or too strong to buck the trend.

Michael Carlile, a softly-spoken president of the Subiaco club during the turbulent early 1980s, had moved to Perth from Melbourne in 1978 when the accounting firm Arthur Andersen and Co. decided his expertise in taxation matters was required out west.

Subiaco was a club which had boasted a colourful history in WA football, but it had also become a typical example of the times; broke and broken by the end of the 1970s, it faced an unlikely future in the following decade. In 1980, Carlile's next-door neighbour, Subiaco president Kevin Merryfield, talked Carlile into being co-opted on to Subiaco's board as the club made a last-ditch bid to save itself from disappearing completely. By the end of the decade, Carlile would move to Sydney and become an AFL commissioner. Before then, Subiaco had been rescued and, under his presidency, won a couple of premierships and put $1 million in the bank.

He was perfectly placed, an outsider working within the WAFL, to see how WA football was surviving only on the generosity of the Victorian clubs and their greed for players.

'While the transfer fees propped up the WA clubs, it wasn't good for football,' he would say years later, borrowing perhaps the game's most well-worn clichés. In the game, things were either 'good for football' or they were 'not good for football'. It was a recognition that the game was supposed to be bigger than the interests of just one club.

It was a nice thought, anyway.

'Victorian clubs were raping and pillaging and taking kids who just weren't ready to play League footy,' said Carlile, a harder note creeping into his soft voice. 'They just weren't ready to go that extra level. But the Victorian clubs went ahead anyway. All these kids ended up doing was playing reserves footy in Melbourne and it did a huge amount of damage to the local competition.'

While Subiaco did not lose as many talented young players as others did, it was forced to surrender to the inevitable and allow one of its champions, Gary Buckenara, to move east and join Hawthorn, a club that saw, prophetically, a brilliant career ahead for the talented half-forward.

'We weren't prepared to sell him outright,' Carlile said. 'So we leased him. We were going to lease him for $70,000 a year. Our intention was that after three years we'd build up a bit of money and then sell him. But they changed the transfer rules and we only ended up with $30,000.'

The transfer rules, which had been set following months of often heated negotiations, had seen the Victorians agree to a minimum transfer fee of $60,000 for any Western Australian player, payable to his club. But by the mid-1980s, with the Victorians suddenly fighting their own creditors from the door, such largesse could not continue. The life support system which had maintained some semblance of hope for WA football was about to be pulled. In the end, it would serve notice on WA football officials that, sooner or later, they would have to swallow their pride and climb completely into bed with the Victorians. Better to prostitute yourself than starve.

By 1986 it was clear to Western Australians that the VFL was about to expand nationally. What role would there be for them? While there was little doubt that a national competition was being devised simply to provide a financial lifeline for the Victorian clubs, WA needed to be involved. If the VFL invited teams from interstate and WA was not involved, it could almost mean the end of west coast football. The best players would simply leave to join the big league, gutting the local competition.

Two years before, Colless and several other leading WA football administrators met with their counterparts in Adelaide, including the president of the South Australian National Football League, Max Basheer. If WA endured an uneasy give and-take-relationship with the Victorians, the South Australians experienced no such trauma. They just hated them.

Certainly, Basheer could meet Alan Schwab or Ross Oakley over lunch and the pair would spend a very enjoyable few hours. But no sooner had they departed than they would be issuing comments lambasting the selfishness and parochialism of one another's competition.

Over the years, the feuding between the two states had reached almost comical levels. They were like two old stags locking horns time and time again over the same old piece of turf. The Victorians wondered when South Australia, that bastion of conservatism that liked to boast it had more churches than any other capital city, would be prepared to enter the 20th century. The South Australians wondered how it was possible that a league with such an arrogant and selfish belief in itself like the VFL had managed to survive so far into the century.

During the meeting with Basheer, Colless raised the issue of a looming national league. Both men were aware of John Elliott's scheming during that season to form a breakaway super league and both had accepted the inevitability of Victorian expansion. Perhaps WA and SA could strike a deal and go in together, ensuring the Victorians did not rip them off or at least cut them off at the knees?

'South Australians can't trust WA,' Colless would recall Basheer telling him coldly during their meeting. 'When push comes to shove, you always side with the Victorians.'

Colless, while not overly surprised at the vehemence in Basheer's tone, was nonetheless taken aback. 'Basheer reckoned we were the running dogs of the VFL,' he would say years later. 'Well, I always found the Victorians, while they were arrogant and lacking vision, were infinitely better to deal with than the South Australians. At least with the Victorians you could strike a deal. They had some flexibility.'

WA decided it was best to leave South Australia alone and by 1986 it had decided to actively pursue one of the two licences the Victorians were prepared to offer.

Right from the start it looked like being a tough fight. There was a strong Victorian lobby actively against WA participation in an expanded VFL. They could see all the chickens finally coming home to roost. After plundering that state's football treasures for so long, the Melbourne clubs could see it all heading back home and uniting to form what could be, effectively, a WA state team. How long would it be before WA ruled the VFL?

But of course, sentiment counted for little when it came to WA's money which, as it turned out, was the same colour as everyone else's. The fact that WA was just as broke as the Victorian clubs was an insignificant matter. By now, Colless had become the prime mover in WA's push to join the League and had begun developing a rapport with the VFL commission, particularly the wily Scanlon.

The WAFL did not have the cash reserves necessary to pay the required $4 million licence fee up-front, a non-negotiable pre-requisite for admission. And that was without taking into account the working capital that would also be required to set up a new team. All up, an estimated $15 million had to be found quickly. It was not a terribly comforting scenario for a local football competition more accustomed to getting by on bread and dripping.

But there was a way. These were the mid-80s and in Perth, like elsewhere around the country, the bulls were charging through the stock market. By floating the club, the football public could buy a share in WA's first VFL team. A company that would hold rights to operate the West Coast Eagles, Indian Pacific Ltd, was born. And like the League's bastard child on the other side of the country, the Brisbane Bears, the birth would be a torrid and difficult affair.

Once again, a new club had been given just a few months to elbow its way into one of the most brutal worlds in Australian sport. And West Coast would be given few benefits, either. If the Bears were given a rough ride, the Eagles would enter the VFL with one hand tied behind their backs. They would only be allowed a list of 35 players. They would have to pay the cost of all interstate travel. And that meant a return journey of 6000 kilometres every second week. The Victorian clubs that travelled to Perth for a game would have their airfares paid for by the League.

First, there was the problem of luring players back home. Many were willing; others began feeling the heat from their Victorian clubs, some of which had signed them to extensive contracts the year before in anticipation of WA entering the competition.

IPL's newly-appointed chief executive, John Walker, began

Graham Samuel: the only remaining part-time commissioner, he has wielded enormous influence on a game he knew little about before being appointed.

Dick Seddon: the former Melbourne administrator was a key commission figure behind the League's controversial introduction of salary caps and player drafts.

Peter Scanlon: the architect of much of the game's changes during the 1980s, Scanlon quit the commission at the start of 1993.

Three of football's most powerful men. Channel 7 general manager Ron Casey, Aylett and Hamilton share a smile after concluding another successful broadcasting agreement in the late 1970s.

Christopher Skase: he was football's white knight when he paid $30 million for the television rights in 1987; his fall from grace left the Brisbane Bears with losses of more than $27 million.

Bob Pritchard (*left*) and Geoff Edelsten: the pair turned football in Sydney into a glamorous sport but their high-spending ways would prove costly for the club.

Paul Cronin: he declared the Brisbane Bears would never end up broke like the 'diseased' clubs in Melbourne.

Collingwood president Allan McAlister advises the Prime Minister and Magpie supporter, Paul Keating, on how to maintain a solid political base.

Warwick Capper in his glamour days with Sydney. Traded to the Brisbane Bears, he would never again recapture the form that made him one of the game's superstars.

Edelsten and his wife Leanne (with tracksuit slogan provided by Jim McKay) discuss events with Swans coach Tom Hafey.

Peter Gordon: the western suburbs lawyer became the AFL commission's arch enemy and carries on a lone battle against the League's administrators.

Peter Weinert (*left*) and Craig Kimberley: the two Sydney owners share a triumphant moment in 1992 when the clubs redirect $1.95 million to save the ailing Swans.

Ross Oakley eight years after becoming football's most powerful administrator: 'It's a business. Of course you do deals.'

Alan Schwab and Ross Oakley confront the press during another controversial moment: by the early 1990s, Schwab's power base had eroded.

Football farewells Alan Schwab for the last time in 1993. Among the coffin bearers is close friend and Essendon premiership coach, Kevin Sheedy (*front, left*).

the first of many odysseys to the east. Walker was an old hand when it came to football politics; before being appointed to IPL, he had served as the WAFL's general manager and was fully versed in the labyrinthine politics of the game. 'I took the view that John was the person we needed,' Colless would say. 'We needed someone in there to go out and get things done quickly.'

The WA football selectors were asked to put together a a potential squad of players

Off the field, the race to raise the millions necessary to fund a League team was charging ahead. Two weeks before the Eagles made their regular season debut, IPL increased its campaign to woo the WA public to its cause by distributing 300,000 prospectuses through a Saturday edition of *The West Australian*. A day before, Colless had put the finishing touches to a sponsorship package with the Burswood Island casino resort worth $1.5 million. Under the deal, the club would receive $1 million up-front for the 1987 season, with the resort guaranteed television exposure and a method of packaging football-related casino trips to WA.

But behind the hoop-la and hype, a concerned note was creeping into Colless's voice. 'We have received good support from football followers and institutions are also showing a lot of interest,' he said as he announced the Burswood deal. 'But we also want the general public to be involved with the Eagles as much as possible.'

The general public, however, did not share Colless's enthusiasm. When IPL was finally listed, it was less than half-subscribed. For a company that had forecast a profit of $1.2 million for its first full year of operation in its prospectus, the response was underwhelming.

The profit forecast had been based on the assumption that the Eagles would finish the season no higher than fifth on the ladder; that an average of 16,000 people would attend home games and that a supporters' club would achieve a membership of at least 8500.

But part of the problem was that Perth's general public either didn't understand what IPL was offering, or thought it was too expensive. IPL had assumed a small investor would be willing to part with $1580. For that, the investor would receive 2000 fully paid ordinary shares, a $500 unsecured note that included an option to a reserved seat at home matches, as well as an $80 subscription to a supporters' club.

Colless had ensured the float was fully underwritten, but there was no disguising the sense of anti-climax around the place. With IPL also committed to giving the WAFL several million dollars in royalty fees as part of its licence agreement, the financial burden was enormous.

'I have no doubt we made some major cock-ups,' Colless would say many years later. 'But so what? Who hasn't?'

By then Colless was living in Sydney and had become the chairman of the Sydney Swans. And from across the continent he'd heard the rustling of pages. The history books, he believed, had been revised a little since he'd left WA. The implication was that he, Colless, had made the wrong call in several critical areas during the formation of the Eagles.

The revisionists, with their hindsight, had also questioned the direction of the club under Colless's chairmanship. Tales abounded of lavish reception parties staged by the Eagles for promotional purposes where French champagne was the rule; first-class air travel was not uncommon among the administration. It was as though the Eagles had read the Edelsten, Pritchard and Jim McKay textbook on how to promote a football club.

'I think everyone went Hollywood,' said Neil Hamilton, who would take over the chairmanship of the club by the middle of the season.

Well, Colless conceded he might have made mistakes. But where had everyone else been when those decisions had to be made, most of them hastily? Besides, he'd put his money where his mouth was, too. A million dollars of his own cash had gone into the Eagles to make sure they flew.

'If someone said to me, "Would you do it all again?" I'd have to say no,' Colless would say.

'Footy sometimes brings the worst out in people.'

Back in the middle of the 1980s, as the game tore itself apart at the seams and the WA clubs faced an uncertain future, a commercial flight from Melbourne touched down on the tarmac at Perth airport.

Among the passengers was a family from Melbourne, disembarking to start a new life in a city its inhabitants claimed, with their usual parochial pride, was the most liveable in the country. It was, they said, the best piece of real estate in Australia.

Bill Kerr knew real estate. It had been his life for more than a decade. Born and raised in country Victoria, his profession had sent him to work in London and now it had sent him to Perth to become that city's managing director of the large property firm of Richard Ellis.

As soon as Kerr's two children stepped on to the tarmac, they performed an impromptu celebratory dance. 'Dad, does this mean we're West Australians now?' they asked as they made their way to the baggage counter.

Bill Kerr smiled. Perhaps.

A few days later Kerr was welcomed to Perth and introduced as the company's new managing director. He thanked everyone and promised them a rewarding future. And then he related the story of his children's question on their arrival.

After he'd finished speaking, two men approached Kerr. Years later, the conversation remained deeply etched in his memory. 'The general thrust of it was: "Listen, you might come to live here and like it, but you can never be a Western Australian. You can consider yourself an adopted one, but if you weren't born here, you can never be one."'

Kerr had just encountered his first taste of WA's peculiar brand of pride and parochialism. Kerr had supported

Collingwood when he grew up in country Victoria and it required a certain sort of fanaticism. His patient mother and father would quite often make a lengthy journey each Saturday night to the 'local' store just to pick up a copy of the late Saturday football edition of *The Herald*. He knew all about the parochialism that football could generate; the passions it aroused and the many heated and irrational arguments it could produce in otherwise sensible people. And as he would discover within a few years, it didn't really matter where you were in Australia when it came to football. The same egos and mistakes could be found everywhere.

Kerr was at a Christmas cocktail party on 30 June, 1987, when Neil Hamilton, a prominent Perth lawyer who had moved into business with the funds manager Pacific Mutual, approached him with a drink in his hand. The Christmas bash was a cute annual event, staged by a firm of quantity surveyors in the middle of the year. Kerr was standing in a corner of the room, nursing a cold beer and keeping largely to himself when Hamilton, whose firm was a client of Kerr's, offered him a job.

'A group of us have just taken up a major shareholding in Indian Pacific and your name is on a list,' Hamilton said. 'Interested?'

The pair chatted for a few minutes and Kerr dismissed the approach, assuming Hamilton would forget the conversation by the next morning. But his phone rang promptly and the offer was open: would he become chief executive at IPL?

Hamilton had just engineered the removal of John Walker as chief executive and was about to become the most influential figure in the club's short history. With the float undersubscribed, Hamilton, Colless and three other businessmen had invested a million dollars each and effectively signed their voting rights to Hamilton.

His first move was to send the firm of chartered accountants, Coopers and Lybrand, into the club to discover the club's financial state. It was not a pretty sight.

'A million bucks had been blitzed and it was heading down the chute,' Hamilton would recall. He was not a man to perform a soft-shoe shuffle around a controversial topic, or hide behind the confusing jargon of the business world. But he also understood the problems that had plagued the club since its inception: the pressure had been enormous, the time constraints ridiculous.

Certainly, he would recall, the promotional side 'was a bit over the top.' But there had also been other factors working against the Eagles. The dark side of WA football had emerged.

With WAFL representatives sharing roles on IPL's board, inevitable tensions had arisen.

'There was this force working against them wanting to keep football back in the 19th century,' Hamilton said. 'I could see these tensions. Dick (Colless) would come back from a board meeting and he'd look like he'd gone 15 rounds.

'Deep down these people didn't really want it to happen and were hoping it wouldn't at the end of the day.'

Such were the tensions that by the middle of the Eagles' first season 'there were no minutes of any meetings because it would all end up in a blue,' said Hamilton.

So Walker was out. Kerr was in. And Bill Kerr realised straight away that the Eagles, stuck thousands of kilometres away from the centre of football power, needed to make friends with the Lords of the League.

One of Kerr's first responsibilities as the new managing director was to fly to Melbourne and face one of football's most serious charges: illegal poaching. Both Walker and Graham Moss, the Eagles' first general manager of football operations, had launched an aggressive recruiting campaign over the months leading up to the unveiling of the Eagles. They had had no choice. They needed players quickly and anyone with a WA background and a decent reputation in the League became their targets. Two of them, Hawthorn players Gary Buckenara and ruckman Paul Harding, had been wooed by the pair while still under contract with their Melbourne-based club.

Before Kerr's appointment, West Coast's defence had been a simple one: the club could not be found guilty of poaching because when the alleged offences took place, the Eagles were not a constituted member of the League. That defence had been ridiculed by the Melbourne clubs, who were after WA blood. It was bad enough they had been forced to allow these foreigners into their competition. But if they weren't going to play by the rules, then they would have to pay. Suddenly, the Melbourne clubs were being very precious. For the past century they had devised every method they could to bend or break the same rules they were now proclaiming had been writ in stone. The Eagles' only mistake, it seemed, was in getting caught.

Kerr believed West Coast had to cut its losses. As he and Moss entered the room to meet the commission, he told Moss to stay quiet. Kerr would do all the talking.

'We put a deal to them,' Kerr recalled. 'We would accept punishment as long as the punishment was reasonable in accordance with the size of the offence. The maximum fine had risen from $30,000 to $100,000. And we were looking at two offences.

'I said there'd been enough trouble over this. My suggestion is that you find us guilty in accordance with the original maximum penalty and we will publicly support that. I put the challenge back to them and not to make a public flogging of a club that was still new and inexperienced in these matters.'

As he left the room, Kerr noticed Peter Scanlon wink at him. Soon after, Ross Oakley appeared. 'Well, Billy,' said Oakley to Kerr. 'We found that irresistible.'

The Eagles were fined the original amount and a close partnership had been forged that would become the envy of most other clubs.

'We wanted to get on well with the VFL commission,' said Kerr a few years later. 'We needed to understand what they were about and how we fitted into the scheme of things.'

Kerr and Hamilton quickly forged a close alliance. Hamilton would look after the club's finances and ensure the club was viable. Kerr, meanwhile, would work on the football side, pressing the flesh with the Eagles' cousins in the east and making sure they had the commission on their side.

'To an outsider, it seemed so simple and straightforward,' Kerr said. 'It wasn't until I got there that I found it was so complicated. Most of the people who were there before us had a huge job . . . money had gone in a lot of directions; mainly promotional items. Part of the operating credo had been "we've just got to get out there and make sure people are aware of it." '

'It wasn't a view I shared. I took the view that something as big and powerful as the West Coast Eagles, well, all they had to do was perform out on the field and the rest would come. The launch of the Eagles had been a Cecil B. de Mille production. It was Disneyland stuff, not the sort of thing most football clubs would do.'

But in order to get the team to perform on the field, the Eagles had to have the players. And, stuck with a playing list of 35, compared to the 52 enjoyed by the rest of the competition, the club was not left with a lot of room in which to move.

Within months, Kerr and the board devised a strategy to pressure the commission and the rest of the competition to relent and allow them to increase their player stock. They flew a reporter with *The Australian*, the country's only national daily newspaper, to Perth and briefed him on their views. Television current affairs programs were also given pro-Eagles material. The underlying argument was simple: if the League commission truly wanted a national league, and not just an expanded Victorian competition, then it had to move swiftly and decisively. One afternoon, Kerr made a three-hour presentation to the commission which he believed was the most comprehensive positioning statement any club had delivered. He showed the commission overhead projections detailing the club's policies and projections for the future. At one stage he became embroiled in a heated argument with Peter Nixon, who wondered aloud why the Eagles deserved special treatment when they were, effectively, a state representative side. But by the end of the presentation, Kerr developed the feeling that the commission had come round to his way of thinking.

The Eagles would eventually win the battle. 'When we got our player list out to 52 we were right,' he would say. 'What we wanted was more depth and that's what we got.'

Under the coaching of Ron Alexander, the club had finished eighth in its first season, winning half its matches and finishing just outside the final five. It wasn't good enough. To Kerr, Hamilton and a growing number of other board members, the Eagles looked too much like a Western Australian side. Accustomed to the sandy, dry grounds at home and playing their usual west coast brand of football, a free-flowing, open style with little of the negative defensive tactics employed by the Victorians, the Eagles had been caught short in the Victorian winter when the grounds grew boggy and you had little room in which to move.

At the end of 1987, Alexander was sacked just one year into a three-year contract and replaced by John Todd. The experience, not surprisingly, would leave Alexander an embittered man. 'I've basically been a players' man,' he would say, 'I don't spend a lot of time with directors. Perhaps that's where I've been at fault.'

Todd was a legendary figure in WA football; a volatile man with a cocktail mix of emotions. He had won the Sandover medal—WA's equivalent of the Brownlow—in 1955 as a 17-year-old with South Fremantle, but a serious knee injury the following season hampered him for the rest of a 146-game career.

As he took over the reins, he was diplomatic in his response to Alexander's sacking. 'I think all coaches feel for each other when this sort of thing occurs,' he would observe. 'But the

game is becoming very, very ruthless and I suppose we have got
to accept the pitfalls.'

A ruthless game? Who would dare think such a thing?

Todd would last just two seasons, taking the team into its first
appearance in a finals series in just its second season. But a disastrous 1989, which left the club 11th on the ladder, ended his
tenure. The Eagles' hierarchy had shown itself a quick learner.
The club was three years old and already two coaches had been
discarded.

They would turn to a Victorian, Michael Malthouse, to turn
them into a powerful on-field force. And from there, the
Eagles' performances on the ground matched their improving
financial efforts off it. By the middle of the 1990s, West Coast
had confirmed every fear held by those Victorian officials back
in 1986. A dynasty had been created. And the chickens were
coming home to roost.

14

THE BATTLE
FOR THE CATHEDRAL

It was the day before the 1983 grand final and dark clouds
pregnant with rain hung oppressively overhead. The air was
thick and hard to breathe. It was a day to remember.

By 10am the Melbourne Cricket Ground had come to life.
Teams of workmen were busy painting patches of its green grass
with the blue and white of the VFL logo. There were singers and
dancers rehearsing for the pre-game entertainment the following day. But without the use of microphones and amplifiers
their shouts, and those of the crews testing the sound system,
were sucked out of the air before they could travel outward.

Jack Hamilton had agreed to give up half an hour of a very
busy day to meet a young sportswriter at the ground. The pre-
text was for a photograph for the following day's newspaper. It
wanted a picture of Hamilton with his trademark face out in
the middle of a ground that, within 24 hours, would be filled
with almost 100,000 people.

But 30 minutes stretched into an hour. Hamilton had walked
across to the ground from his office at VFL House around the
corner, met the reporter and the pair began ambling along the
concourse beneath the stands. It was dark in there, but every so
often a shaft of soft light would penetrate an opening and hit a
point on the opposite wall like the beam from a movie projec-
tor. Occasionally the light would strike an honour roll and
Hamilton would stop and pause to read it before ambling on.

Minutes would pass before he would say anything and the young reporter, slightly in awe of the League's general manager, wondered if he had said the wrong thing. What was wrong with Hamilton? He just seemed content to walk along at this slow, sometimes excruciating pace. There were moments when it seemed his mind was elsewhere.

Slowly it dawned on the journalist. Hamilton's mind was elsewhere. It had gone travelling down the years, back to when he was a player. Back to when the game was a sport and not just a business. By this time they had walked past the back of the Smokers' Stand, the very public face of the Melbourne Establishment, the stand where judges, bankers and their sons came to watch a game and where much of the city's old money sat.

At this point in the concourse you step out of the inky darkness and the sight can take your breath away. There, at the end of a small laneway used to run machinery on to the arena, is the ground itself, surrounded by towering grandstands; the giant concrete behemoth known as the Ponsford Stand to your right, to your left a sweeping vista of the northern and southern stands.

Hamilton stood there for several moments. Then he shuffled slowly to a small gate on the fence and stepped on to the arena.

'What was it like, running out here at the start of a grand final?' asked the reporter.

Hamilton thought for a moment and then replied in a very soft voice. 'You could hear the rumble of the crowd as you began to make your way down the players' race and on to the ground,' he said. 'It made your hair stand on end.

'And then, as soon as your feet hit the ground, the noise just seemed to pick you up and carry you out there. You know, it's funny, but I can never remember the actual feeling of having run on to the ground. It was as though you didn't have to make any effort at all. You just got swept along.'

By now Hamilton was standing out near the middle of the

ground and he sounded like a man relating a mystical or near-death experience. The MCG affected people like that. It was even loved by people who had never been there. Writers waxed lyrical about it and even the athletes themselves who performed on its surface, the cricketers notorious for their cynicism and individualism and the footballers who lacked interest in their own sport's history and traditions, looked on the ground in awe.

The MCG was one of Melbourne's most revered landmarks. Situated on the fringe of the city and set in a lush, tree-lined parkland, it played an important role in the psyche of the city. It had played host to an Olympic Games. Many of cricket's most memorable Test matches had been staged there. In 1959, 130,000 had packed into it to hear the American evangelist Billy Graham preach his unique brand of bible-thumping religion. Internationally it was known as one of the great stadiums, even if by the early 1980s it had fallen into disrepair, an old dame with a few too many wrinkles in her face and a little too much rouge trying to cover the excesses of age.

Almost everyone who had been to the ground could remember their first time; the first sight of a footballer leaping for a ball, the slow rhythm of a Test match, the baying of the yobbos in Bay 13.

Hamilton had memories of it, too. He had played one of the best games of his life out on this arena. The 1955 grand final had seen him judged best afield. Collingwood had lost by 25 points to Melbourne, but Hamilton had been firm and solid in defence. It was a performance he always jokingly slipped into a conversation when September came around each year. There had been no award back then for the best player on the field in a grand final. No Norm Smith medal. 'We might have to look at the possibility of awarding the Norm Smith medal retrospectively,' he'd say.

Of course he loved this ground. It had such a rich and proud tradition. It made heroes out of ordinary people and turned regular heroes into myth and legend. But as Hamilton stood there admiring the view on that day in 1983, he also could not help but remember that it was sometimes an unrequited love.

Within 24 hours he and his president, Allen Aylett, would be viciously booed and jeered by the grand final crowd. Not even the appearance of the Devil at Billy Graham's revivalist performance would have elicited such a response. What Aylett and Hamilton had threatened to do was far worse, in the eyes of many football followers, than any satanic act. They wanted to move the grand final away from the MCG and take it to their own personal hell in a giant and soulless concrete cauldron on the outskirts of the city.

Football had been at war for almost 50 years over the MCG. It had been treated like a servant by the ground's trustees and the Melbourne Cricket Club which ran and operated the venue. And the fight it staged throughout the 1980s, and the eventual peace it settled for, would become one of the game's most important episodes as it tried to salvage something from the wreckage of the decade.

It had always angered football administrators that they could never have complete control over the jewel in their crown; the finals series. The MCG had been built on a piece of Crown land handed to the esteemed Melbourne Cricket Club by Governor LaTrobe in 1853. Melbourne had wanted a ground better than its rival in Sydney and the stipulation was that the land would be used 'for cricket and no other purpose.'

By 1933, state government legislation had awarded control of the ground to a board of trustees 'to be maintained and used as and for a place for playing at cricket and for conveniences connected therewith and when not required for cricket for such other purposes not inconsistent with the foregoing . . .'

Cricket. It was the sport of the genteel and gentle. Australian football had in one sense been created and adopted as a winter pastime for cricketers to stay fit for the summer, and for more than a century it was constantly reminded of its role. Football was a more popular sport in the southern part of the country; its devotees were far more passionate and fervent, and the start of a football season was greeted with more anticipation than the beginning of a summer of cricket.

And when it came to drawing crowds and gate-takings, football was clearly cricket's superior. So why did football have to bow and scrape before the MCG trustees and the cricket club, and hand over more than half the income it generated at the ground, to stage a sport so many people wanted to see?

It seemed unfair. The VFL regarded itself as the official governing body of the game, even though countless other organisations were spread throughout the country. It had the best players, the best teams and attracted the biggest crowds. Therefore, thought the League, it was the game's self-appointed guardian.

The trustees and others linked closely with Melbourne's Establishment, however, had always viewed this uncouth and abrasive sporting code with suspicion. It always seemed to be wanting more and more money. And who said the VFL was the final arbiter of a game that belonged principally to the people? It was a classic case of two diametrically opposed philosophies. The League simmered and sulked for years, but by the 1950s it decided to act.

Kenneth Luke was a former president of the Carlton Football Club who, by 1956, had won office as VFL president. Like many before him, he argued long and hard with the trustees, a group comprising some of the most senior and well-known politicians, business interests and Establishment figures Victoria had known. Sir Robert Menzies became a trustee. Arthur Calwell and the pugnacious former Victorian Liberal premier Sir Henry Bolte would also take on trustee roles at various times. When a push began in the early 1950s for Melbourne to bid for the 1956 Olympics, Luke saw a unique opportunity. Princes Park, Carlton's home ground, could be upgraded to become the Olympic stadium. And after that, it could become football's pre-eminent home. The trustees could go to hell. They moved too slowly and had not realised the critical importance to Melbourne of hosting the Olympics. And it seemed to the League, too, that another opportunity to tilt the balance of power would never come along again. Football would at last be able to control its own destiny.

Never again would the sport have to feel humiliated. Everyone knew how some members of the MCC committee sniggered about their superiority over the VFL; how League officials some years were given a small, cold room deep in the bowels of the ground without even the benefit of a heater to add up their sums and do their paperwork after a game.

But there was one man Luke and the League could not dupe; the Labor Premier, John Cain senior. Thirty years later, his son would carry on the family tradition and put a halt to the game's grand plans to unshackle itself from the yoke of the MCG. In 1954, however, the father ruled. Cain senior viewed the League with as much suspicion as the next man and, like politicians before and long after him, knew a winner when he saw one. Football was the people's game and the people had to be protected from those running the sport. The Victorian government would only support the push to stage the Olympics in two years' time if the MCG was accorded the status of main stadium.

There was no argument.

Football was snookered again.

Or so everyone thought. The resentment and bitterness never went away. It was like a bad taste in the mouths of the Lords of the League. They bided their time and waited for the next opportunity. It came in 1962. The VFL decided to buy 212 acres out in the lush and fertile outer eastern suburb of Waverley. Within five years, construction had begun on a stadium the VFL promised would be the greatest in the southern hemisphere. Set amid the market gardens and dairy countryside of the time, the League had been told Waverley would quickly become the next focal point of Melbourne. Twenty-four kilometres from the city centre, Waverley was going to be the new utopia; a burgeoning suburb where young husbands and wives would raise families and gradually pull the centre of the city eastward.

Luke used a silver spade to turn the first sod in 1966 and the grand plan was under way. By the time it opened on April 18, 1970, VFL Park could seat 70,000 and there were plans to boost its capacity well above the 100,000 mark. But if the MCG trustees were nervous over football's bold move, its fears were tempered when the stadium was finally unveiled to the public. It was a typical example of the giant concrete bowls that had sprung up all over America during the 1960s. The seating in the stands, while more modern and comfortable than that at the MCG, left the spectator too far removed from the action. And while a proposed second tier on the outer stand was supposedly on the way in the coming years, the stadium lacked the atmosphere that soaked out of every wooden splinter and concrete crack at the MCG. There were problems, too, in getting there. Unless you owned a car, VFL Park was a notoriously difficult place to visit. And even those who had cars sometimes wished they hadn't bothered making the journey.

Over the years, the Waverley stadium would gain a notorious reputation for traffic jams, particularly at the end of a big game. There were few outbound arteries to ease the flow and a potential train line near the stadium never eventuated. Despite the League's constant public optimism, the ground quickly gained a reputation as the perpetual bridesmaid, always a distant second to the beloved MCG.

It had come at a cost, too.

When Allen Aylett became president, the relationship between football and the MCG continued to deteriorate. Aylett was everything many of the trustees and committeemen despised; he was one of the new breed of entrepreneurial officials the League seemed to attract. Plus, he was a typically abrasive football person who arrogantly seemed to think the League could do what it wanted.

Aylett had been around football a long time and shared the game's loathing for the 'cricket people'. Didn't they realise what an important asset the game was to Victoria and to their own coffers? No, believed Aylett. It wasn't the VFL that was arrogant. It was those men who occupied the stuffy Long Room at the MCG. They were so bent over with the weight of history and their own self-importance, they had failed to move with the times.

So the new, young president of the League must have taken a perverse pleasure in early 1977 when he invited the media baron Kerry Packer to VFL Park for dinner to watch the first night football match. More than $1.5 million worth of lights had just been erected and the ground was bathed in the glow of artificial light. Outside it was raining, but inside the VIP dining room Aylett was beaming in the presence of one of Australia's most powerful men. The pair had something in common, too. The cricket Establishment regarded Packer and Aylett as their arch-enemies and Aylett was about to provide them with an even greater reason to view the VFL with suspicion.

As Aylett related years later, Packer appeared impressed with the lighting at Waverley. And then, off the cuff, Aylett turned to Packer and said: 'The lights are so good you could even play cricket here at night.'

Packer was in the midst of organising World Series Cricket, the three-year rebellion against the cricketing establishment that revolutionised the game while throwing it into turmoil in the latter part of the decade. He was already looking at Waverley as a possible venue for his 'SuperTest' series featuring the world's best players he had signed. The MCG, of course, that bastion of decency and tradition, would have nothing to do with a man who had disrupted the gentle rhythm of the game simply by flashing wads of cash about in the air. And Waverley was, really, a logical alternative.

Aylett could see Packer was impressed. 'How much do you want for the ground?' Packer asked Aylett.

Aylett took a stab at a figure. '$250,000 a year.'

'That seems fair enough to me,' replied Packer.

'We'd also want some share of the catering and parking,' added Aylett hastily.

'No, $250,000 it is. That's what you said.'

The following morning, an agreement was struck that would see the League reap almost $1 million over the three scheduled seasons of WSC. Aylett and Hamilton had agreed they had to move quickly and secure the deal. The president, after all, had only read an article about Packer that night when he arrived home. It mentioned how he liked to do business quickly and efficiently.

Football was, however, true to form. Soon after, a special meeting of VFL directors was called to discuss the proposal. The League had just won $1 million by renting out its stadium at a time when it went unused for six months. It could easily have ended up with nothing. But still some directors fumed. The first signs were there; Aylett and Hamilton had not consulted them. It was further evidence of how the game was becoming beholden to the central administration. Outside the room, Packer was kept waiting. And waiting. Almost an hour passed before agreement was reached to allow him inside to address the meeting. He had no problems once he got inside; Packer was an imposing figure and his bullish face and striking presence soon had the directors eating out of his hands. Yes, by all means, they kept telling him. Please play your cricket at our ground. We couldn't think of a better arrangement.

Everyone benefitted. The clubs collected money and Dr Allen Aylett was appointed the official dental surgeon to World Series Cricket.

Given the climate, it was probably not such a wise move by the president. He already had a couple of enemies within the ranks; one of them was the hardened president of Richmond,

Ian Wilson. 'I am surprised and concerned at the potential conflict of such a situation,' announced Wilson to the press. 'I will probably write to the VFL complaining about Dr Aylett's association with the television magnate.'

Aylett was nonplussed. 'He was saying that I had used my office to obtain payments from Packer,' he wrote in his autobiography years later. 'What a load of rubbish!'

By the 1983 grand final, Aylett and his League were besieged. A significant number of club presidents were now prepared to support moving the grand final to Waverley, even if the state government carried out a threat to prevent the League from increasing VFL Park's capacity by changing the planning regulations.

John Cain junior had made a stand on the MCG; the grand final would remain there, he told Aylett, and his government would legislate to prevent it moving if necessary. Cain, in fact, had already approached the leader of the National Party, Peter Ross-Edwards, to gain an assurance for the safe passage of such legislation through the upper house if it became necessary.

Aylett's relationship with Cain and the trustees had deteriorated into a bitter personal feud. The League had engaged in a long-running battle to play Sunday football which, under government legislation, it was prevented from doing. And yet it continued to be amazed when Cain would grant permission for international soccer matches to be staged at the venue on Sunday afternoons.

Cain looked upon the League as though it was a collection of religious zealots who refused to listen to logic or reason. When his government again refused to assist with roadworks to Waverley that would have helped the League move ahead with its plans to enlarge its stadium, Cain found Aylett constantly pressuring him to change his mind.

'I met Allen Aylett on a couple of occasions at functions. He went out of his way to raise the VFL expansion proposals with me. One of these occasions was at Government House, the other was at a League football match when he urged me to leave the viewing area after half-time and go to a private room where he wanted to discuss the issue at length. I listened for a time but made it clear to him that I'd come to watch the football and I wasn't prepared to listen to a long and protracted submission in that situation . . .

'I gained the impression . . . that the grand final at Waverley had become an obsession with them and in part it was motivated by a desire to 'teach the MCC and the trustees a lesson' by taking the grand final away from that ground.'

Aylett, as president of the VFL, usually attended all trustee meetings. Trustees normally met on a Friday and in late March 1983, the day before the season began, they sat down to consider a submission from Aylett.

For years the League had been unhappy with the percentage of gate-takings it missed because of its second-class citizen role at the ground. He wanted to see the MCC's share of revenue cut from 15 per cent to 10 per cent. The next day, Melbourne was scheduled to play Collingwood in the opening round at the MCG. Aylett told the trustees that if the vote did not favour the League, he would take the match away from the ground.

It was, of course, a hollow threat. Where would he take it, particularly on such short notice? Sir Henry Bolte looked straight at Aylett. 'Dr Aylett,' he said. 'That's a risk I'm prepared to take.'

A compromise of sorts was reached; the money was to be set aside until a final settlement could be negotiated. But throughout that season, whenever an opportunity arose, Aylett would lambast the trustees and MCC, accusing it of holding back money belonging to the League.

The two sides were like children arguing in a sandpit. Both were intractable, both despised the other and both were determined to beat the other. Shouting matches across board tables were common. Aylett would bitterly complain to anyone who listened that even the government had reneged on several promises it had made; Cain, he would claim, had once promised him that the League could control the MCG for six months of the year, handing it back to the cricket club for the cricket season. If the promise was made, it never eventuated.

But before full warfare broke out, a compromise could always be found. By the mid-1980s, the League had settled for the establishment of its own members' area adjoining the cricket club in the northern stand. But nothing ever seemed satisfactory to both parties.

And while the arguments raged, VFL Park sat out in Waverley, its novelty long faded, a bastard child conceived out of hatred and despair. It would never be completely loved. Within just a few years, even its parents would come close to disowning it.

By the time the new VFL commission was installed, Jack Hamilton detected a distinct shift in mood. There were now clubs saying they preferred to keep the MCG as the home of the grand final. Hamilton loved the ground, but he was even more committed to the League's dream of becoming master of its own destiny. Too much blood had been spilled and too much bad blood had been created for him to concede the dream was over.

As usual, it was Peter Scanlon who began making it clear to Hamilton that Melbourne could not sustain two major stadiums without a cost. Scanlon understood the long-simmering rivalries and the reasons behind the construction of VFL Park. But he, like many others, believed Waverley was fundamentally flawed; the League had been wrongly advised from the start and the ground itself, the way it was designed and built, seemed devoid of atmosphere.

Scanlon would tell associates later that he suspected that the commission's burgeoning pro-MCG stance was another reason behind Hamilton's decision to retire in 1986. If the dream was over, what was the point of carrying on? It was another sign that the times had changed too quickly for Hamilton. The new era still required an administrator to have enormous reserves of rat cunning and there were few in Melbourne or even the rest of the country who could match it with Hamilton on that level. But commercial realities were now even more important. It was time to put aside the feuding of the past.

Ross Oakley was more attuned to Scanlon's view because he came from the same world. Of course, he too understood the passion and resentment football felt toward cricket. Hadn't he had long arguments with his father about the same subject more than 20 years before over the dinner table? Hector Oakley, the cricket loyalist, thought football was just out for money. And his son would defend the game's stubborn stance. Why couldn't football decide where it could and couldn't play its matches? Don't forget where most of the money came from, he would point out.

By the mid to late 1980s a changing of the guard had taken place. The old warriors from both sides had retired and carried their grudges off with them. There was still distrust and suspicion, of course. But the personalities that had driven much of the antagonism were gone. The League found itself enjoying polite conversation with the cricket club. And even that conservative and tradition-bound group of trustees didn't seem so bad, after all.

Within a month of Oakley taking control as chairman of the commission in 1986, he, Scanlon and Alan Schwab met three MCC representatives at VFL House. The minutes of that meeting, which concluded with a commitment to confidentiality, showed how, in just a couple of years, the climate had changed and that the time for sabre-rattling was over.

Under a heading 'Communication', the minutes noted:

'It was agreed by both bodies that a better communication should be developed to ensure that the maximum gain is obtained from the playing of matches in the VFL expanded competition at the MCG.

'Both bodies welcomed the opportunity of conducting ongoing negotiations . . .'

Perhaps it helped that in 1983 John Lill had become secretary of the cricket club and Don Cordner was its president. Lill had been with the ICI company for 24 years in an executive role but wasn't too sure how much longer he wanted to stay. He looked around him and saw decent people being made redundant. The wrong people were leaving and the wrong people were being promoted. When the role of secretary of the MCC was first advertised, he was overseas and didn't notice. But it did not take him long to apply when he returned.

Lill was a tall man, urbane with greying hair and perfectly at ease in the world of the MCC. But he also carried with him little of the baggage of the past. He had viewed the MCC job as a comfortable role giving him the opportunity to combine his love of cricket and football. He hadn't counted, however, on what was to come; that from 1983 onward football would experience the most turbulent and critical period in its development. And he would find himself right in the centre of it.

Cordner, too, would prove to be one of the key players. It helped that he and the new League commissioner, Ross Oakley, got along well and respected one another. The old hatred was beginning to disappear when it came to those who counted.

By 1988, the Melbourne Cricket Club and the Trust was facing a delicate problem. The Southern Stand, completed in 1937, had developed a form of concrete cancer. Workers at the ground would amble around it and discover large chunks of cement lying on the ground. The stand, a sweeping, two-level viewing area that spanned much of the outer side of the ground, was falling apart.

Its condition was regarded as terminal; repair work could be carried out but there was no guarantee the cancer would not reappear elsewhere. It was a shame, but it was also a blessing. The Southern Stand had been the true home of the people for half a century; Bay 13 at ground level had become an institution of its own, playing host to countless generations of bare-chested, beer-swilling Australian men who chanted during dull moments in Test matches and entertained the rest of the crowd with their banners and wit. But as the decade drew toward a close, Bay 13 had deteriorated along with the rest of the stand; the wit and repartee replaced by abuse and profanity.

The stand, too, had never quite kept pace with modern life. The toilet facilities had been abominable for many years whenever a big crowd was present, and food outlets were also scarce or barely worth visiting.

The cricket club and the trust commissioned several reports into the problem. They all reported back that to scrap the stand and build a new one, which seemed the only feasible long-term solution, about $100 million would be required. The cricket club required a partner; it had no chance of raising that sort of cash because it had no assets.

At the same time, the club had commissioned Colin Carter, of the consultancy firm Pappas Carter Evans and Koop, to take a long term look at the structure of the MCC. What should it do to make itself well placed to handle the next 10 or 20 years, particularly given the changing nature of sport? Carter, of course, was closely linked with the League. It had been his firm that had done much of the legwork in preparing the VFL commission's blueprint for the future in 1985. The League heard about the MCC's dilemma and acted quickly.

In early June, an envelope arrived at the MCC addressed to Donald Cordner. Lill, who had been granted permission as secretary to sort through Cordner's mail, opened it and began reading a letter many thought would have been impossible just a few years before. Oakley was proposing a long term arrangement that would see football and cricket share the MCG for 30 years.

From there, things began to move quickly. A tour of overseas stadiums was conducted. Architects and engineers were summoned and by May 1989, detailed plans of the proposed stand were presented to the trustees. There, the plan hit a snag.

John Cain was concerned that corporate superboxes dominated the prime viewing areas. 'The plan proposed that at the two best viewing levels corporate boxes and dining areas would have precluded public seating from these areas,' Cain would recall later. 'I said I thought this was inappropriate and the concept that had been embraced in the Southern Stand for years was that it was the place where the public had access to prime viewing space around a substantial part of the ground. This should be maintained.'

In the old days, Cain's view might have sparked another round of bitter feuding. But everyone, it seemed, had drunk from the same cup of conciliation. The acclaimed architect Daryl Jackson quickly suggested several superboxes could be placed behind two rows of cantilevered seats. The boxes were the key to the new stand; without them and their lucrative income it was unlikely the cricket club could service its substantial borrowings.

In March 1992, the Great Southern Stand was officially opened. It had been completed on time and under budget.

Football's holy war was over.

But no-one had told the old warriors.

Allen Aylett spied a comment in a newspaper by John Cain on the day the new stand opened that angered him. Of course, there wasn't much about Cain that didn't anger Aylett, even after all those years. The war had been fought for too long and the passions had been too strong for the invective and dislike to ever fade completely. And when he saw Cain refer to the League's push during the 1980s over playing a grand final at Waverley as a move 'to teach the MCC and the MCG trustees a lesson,' he responded with a letter of his own.

'How absurd,' opened Aylett. '. . . For 30 years, successive Victorian Governments, including the Cain Government, repeatedly reneged on promises to the VFL to improve the lot of the football paying public who were subsidising the MCG and a raft of other sporting arenas and facilities in Victoria . . .

'Let's get the record straight: the great facilities obvious to football as far back as the 1950s have until today been denied to the world's greatest sports fans, the people of Victoria. Football changed things. Not John Cain.'

Football had certainly changed many things. Some things, however, had not.

15

GOOD OLD COLLINGWOOD FOREVER

They had just spent two days in Beechworth and were on their way to the Victorian country town of Yarrambat to collect the family dog from a kennel. The past three years had been enjoyable ones for Jack Hamilton. Away from the stress of the commissioner's chair, he had been relishing his freedom. He'd also become a columnist for *The Age* newspaper, writing occasional articles on the direction of football.

Like most things he'd done, Hamilton had approached the task of writing cautiously. The last thing he wanted to do was bow out of the game embittered like Aylett, firing broadsides at those in charge. But by 1990 he had been out of the game long enough, he figured, to at least put in his two bob's worth.

He and his wife Joan watched the countryside tumble by on 30 May, 1990, as they journeyed down the Yea Road in their Mitsubishi Station coupé. And then, for one of the few times in his life, Jack Hamilton lost control.

'We were going round a bend,' Joan would later say in a statement tendered to the coroner's court. 'The only thing I remember is the left wheels of the vehicle went on to the gravel shoulder. The car went out of control and Jack tried to correct it but we went back across the road and hit the embankment and the car overturned.

'I remember the car coming to rest and I tried to see if Jack was all right, but he wasn't.'

At the age of 61 Hamilton was dead, his neck broken.

The news spread quickly. By early afternoon, television stations were breaking into their regular programs with reports of a road fatality on the Yea Road. Sombre-looking news presenters informed viewers that early reports from the scene suggested it was Jack Hamilton, the former VFL commissioner, who had died.

By that evening, the football world was in mourning. How could Jack be dead? Here was one man who you thought might live forever. So many people had lived and worked within his shadow over so many years that they had come to think of him as invincible. He was too strong to die, surely. Too tough. Football's best people weren't supposed to go this way. Its legends and heroes didn't just vanish overnight. The game was awash with hunched-over old men who had played during the game's Golden Age, who had worn the bruising hip and shoulder bumps, gritted their teeth and played on when the bones in their fingers were snapped by a heavy boot. They just kept going. And when they were just too old to play the game anymore, when the sad-faced official from the front office finally tapped them on the shoulder and told them it was time to go, they went gracefully.

Every so often the newspapers would carry a small item recording the passing of one of them. They always seemed so incredibly old. They had nicknames that belonged to another era, names like 'Chooka' and 'Bluey', nicknames you never heard bestowed in the playground at school anymore. And they always seemed to go peacefully, too. Their funerals would be well-attended; packed with old team-mates who then headed off to the nearest pub to farewell them and talk about old times again.

Jack dead? The news was shocking. Even those who had

never liked him, whether they were the man in the outer with his ingrained dislike for the League, or some of those who worked with him, were stunned. It was a reminder that everyone was mortal, that we would all go some day. And many of us would not get the opportunity to choose the manner of our passing. Waiting for all of us at the end of life was a yawning black hole ready to suck us into oblivion and it happened to football people, just like it did in that other world out there.

Jack dead? Surely his time hadn't yet arrived. It was like the clock that counted down the seconds during a match. Whenever you needed a few extra minutes to claw your way back, to mend a problem and overcome an obstacle, it always seemed to run just a little bit too quickly.

There was never enough time.

His old No. 8 Collingwood guernsey was draped starkly across his coffin at the funeral. More than 700 people crammed the Uniting Church in leafy Toorak, many of them spilling outside on to the driveways and footpaths. The crowd was a mix of football's old and new; veteran players who had played alongside Hamilton in the 1950s, club officials who had parried and argued with him. They were all there and Hamilton's long-time and trusted secretary, Brenda Testro, observed that Jack would have been pleased; a sell-out crowd and no television, just the way he would have liked it.

At the end the pallbearers carried Hamilton out through an honour guard of old players to the strains of one of the game's most sacred hymns: 'Good Old Collingwood Forever'.

Old rivals, some of them taught in the cradle by their mothers and fathers to loathe Collingwood, joined in the chorus.

The day after Hamilton's death, *The Age* published his final column after consulting with his family. It was an eerie piece of writing that covered one of Hamilton's favourite themes; Australian football's long-running battle with rugby league for the mantle of the most popular winter sporting code in the country.

By the end of the 1980s, rugby league had overcome many of the problems plaguing it at the start of the decade. Allegations of corruption had long since faded and the game's image as a tawdry, brutal sport had been changed almost overnight by a glamorous marketing campaign spearheaded by a television commercial featuring the leggy Tina Turner.

In fact, Oakley and his commission had been lambasted for dropping the ball and allowing rugby league to sneak back under football's guard. Just 10 years before, it had been the VFL that had aggressively campaigned and marketed its sport, daring to storm into enemy territory and announce itself as the new kid on the block ready to take on all comers. Now it seemed that the NSW Rugby League had stolen Australian football's thunder. Under the administration of John Quayle, the sport had re-invented itself. And while its attendance figures were still appallingly low compared to its southern-based cousin, and this was something Oakley and the commission constantly sought comfort within whenever the criticisms flew, it had certainly captured the public's attention. It had secured a healthy television contract. It had the media back onside and rugby league had expanded, too, moving into Queensland, Canberra and country NSW. And its expansion appeared to have been far more successful, and accompanied by far less acrimony, than the League's move to a national competition.

By the start of the 1990s, rumours swept through Sydney and Melbourne that the NSWRL was planning a tactical assault on Australian football. It had already staged the odd exhibition game in Melbourne; now it was looking for something more substantial; a real piece of the action, a team of its own down south.

They were, of course, just rumours. But sport thrived on such whispers and before long it had become accepted as fact.

Hamilton had thought it was time to spring to his game's defence. He had sauntered into the newsroom of *The Age* a few days earlier clasping a handful of notes and revelling, as always, in the number of eyes shifting his way as he strolled through the news reporters' area on his way to the sports section. Hamilton had presence, that was for sure. Even at the age of 61 he looked fit and strong. The knuckle-crunching handshake was still there and that craggy face hadn't changed at all. Except everyone noticed one thing; he looked younger than he had for many years. Retirement and the absence of football's pressures had been good to him.

He was his usual ebullient self on this day. While he had taken some time to agree to write a column, he had taken to the task with relish. And here he was, just a few days before his life ended, brandishing his notes and guffawing over a couple of jokes he wanted to insert. But more than anything, he wanted to make the point that all the doomsayers and critics of the League, all those who believed it was now rugby league that threatened football's standing, were sparring at shadows. Fear not, thundered Hamilton. There was no threat.

'When Sir Francis Drake died, legend has it that he left a drum that was to be beaten in the event that England was threatened,' Hamilton began his final column. 'If the drum was sounded, Drake would return to defend his beloved homeland.

'In the event that Ross Oakley, like Drake, should ever have need to blow his Acme Thunderer whistle to summon the troops to defend our beloved Australian Football against the possible invasion of rugby, I would be there, in the frontline, ready to answer the call.'

No-one doubted Hamilton meant what he wrote. If you were deep in the trenches and under attack, what better man to have at your side than Jack Hamilton? Ironically, it had been Allen Aylett on the night of Hamilton's death who had best summed up his former general manager's passion for the game.

He had been, noted Aylett, football's most charismatic character. 'He was unique. Jack had only three loves in his life and, in order, those were his wife Joan and their three children; Australian football in general; and the Collingwood Football Club.'

Now he was gone. But Hamilton's image of invincibility was such that there were some who believed that if Drake's drum was ever beaten for Australian football, Jack Hamilton would still find a way to answer its call.

The football world said goodbye to Hamilton and at the same time it seemed to be saying farewell to a little of its own history, too.

As if to underline the belief that a new era had begun, Hamilton's beloved Collingwood finally broke its 32-year jinx just four months later, winning its first premiership since 1958, the year Hamilton's playing career finished. Collingwood's drought had become the stuff of legend over the years. It had played in eight grand finals during that time and always lost, sometimes in the most remarkable circumstances.

But now the biggest joke in sport was over. Collingwood had won a flag. It was a dour sort of match, played against an injury-riddled, under-manned Essendon side. If it had not been for the fact that this was a historic victory for Collingwood, then the game could well have been consigned to the record books and not the memory. The club had experienced another tumultuous year; there were never any other kind at Victoria Park. During the season it found itself locked in a controversy over the use of anabolic steroids that would, eventually, usher in the introduction of a random drug-testing program for all footballers.

Collingwood had also become one of the first clubs to be convicted of ticket scalping.

Ticket scalping was a mini-industry in Melbourne during September. Touts somehow seemed to gain access to large blocks of tickets that were normally only made available to the clubs and for years politicians and League officials had investigated the issue without finding a way of solving it.

In the early weeks of the 1990 finals series, the League's then finance director, Greg Durham, received word that a tout in the northern suburb of Lalor was selling large blocks of tickets to the preliminary and grand final.

This time, the League decided it had to act. Durham rang the tout and asked how many tickets were available. 'As many as you want,' was the reply.

Durham asked a young administrative officer, Mark Kleiman, to take $2000 cash and buy a block of numbered seats. The numbers would then enable the League to trace the tickets back to their original allocation.

Kleiman travelled out to a large home and bought the tickets in what he would remember had all the hallmarks of 'a real shady deal . . . I just told him I was a Collingwood supporter and really desperate to be there at the games.'

The tickets were traced back to Collingwood. The man had approached the club asking if he could buy any tickets. The official he spoke to, sensing a good deal and a way of increasing the Magpies' already growing revenue, sold them to him. 'We were fined $50,000,' the club's president Allan McAlister would say a few years later. There was just the hint of a sparkle in his eye and, it seemed, few regrets.

Football was all about breaking the rules. It was like tax evasion; every time the Taxation Department brought down a new set of rules and guidelines, tax experts around the country would study them to find a loophole or a way of bending them.

In footy, you bent the rules and you spent a lot of time finding loopholes. And if you failed to find them, you simply broke them.

Was there a club in the League by 1990 that was strictly adhering to the salary cap imposed upon it by the commission? Everywhere you went, you heard rumours and claims of rorts and money being passed under the table. It was a tradition that went back to the turn of the century when wealthy benefactors of the clubs would look after the most valuable players with a stray quid or two at the end of a game.

But while it was a world rife with rumour, the League had

many problems proving it. Sometimes, too, it seemed to lack the heart to go out after those who were flagrantly breaking the rules.

'The cheating we have done is unbelievable,' one club president would say a few years later. 'The cheating the others do is unbelievable, too. But the way we cheat, we leave the others for dead.'

He smiled a cryptic smile and hinted he might reveal all one day. But he never did. He just asked that his name not be used.

Who would have thought in 1986 that four years later the Magpies would be restored to what they regarded as their rightful role as the most powerful football club in the land? If you ever needed proof of football's cyclical nature, then this was it.

At the start of the 1986 season, Ranald Macdonald's great experiment with the New Magpies was in ruins; players had been asked to take a 10 per cent salary cut in January to enable the club to remain within its salary cap of $1.15 million. They had rejected the request but by April, Macdonald's board had decided to impose a 20 per cent cut in a bid to save $230,000.

Collingwood was in turmoil. The club had a deficit of $2.9 million. A fifth member of the original New Magpies had resigned, leaving just Macdonald and Allan McAlister as the sole surviving members of the board. It seemed too that at least Macdonald was not destined to be at the helm for much longer. Above the rising chorus of those within the club demanding his resignation could be heard the familiar noise of a gallows being built.

In the first week of April, Macdonald was determined to fight it out. Couldn't they understand how he had tried to rebuild the club? At times even his clipped, proper voice could not hide its frustration.

'I didn't realise how much needed to be done,' he'd admitted one night on the phone. It was late in the evening and he'd been fielding calls from an increasingly aggressive media throughout the day. 'I thought it would have been done a lot quicker.'

There was an edge to his voice. He'd begun the conversation in a confrontational tone, angered by what he believed was part of a campaign among the media to see him out. But within minutes he calmed down and sounded like a man viewing the mountain top from its base.

Of course, he said, he would accept the blame for the club's financial situation. Club staff had already been told not to expect salary increases and some had even been sacked as part of a cost-cutting measure. No-one liked to do that. But something had to be done to rescue Collingwood and secure its future. And while he would shoulder the blame, there were many reasons for the club's plight, he said.

'First of all, the projections of the money coming into the club after the last elections were over-inflated,' he said. But there was something else too, something every president of Collingwood had been forced to grapple with; the expectations of the followers and the enormous pressure they created.

'There was such pressure on to get players,' he admitted. 'The supporters were expecting more than just a long-term rebuilding effort.'

In March, 1986, the club had been budgeting for almost $150,000 a week in revenue from sponsorships, sales of membership tickets and corporate box holders. March was always the month of hope in football; the raw reality of the season was just around the corner and it was always promising more than it could deliver. There were no serious injuries; the players were all fit; the coach was optimistic and the cynicism and doubt of the supporters had evaporated in the heat of the summer.

But by the middle of April, losses to Essendon, the Sydney Swans and North Melbourne had seen all the March goodwill at Victoria Park disappear. Membership was down by almost 1,500 and $300,000 of projected revenue appeared to have been lost. The sad story was summed up by the mood of the club's high-priced centreman Geoff Raines. He had been one of the big buys at Collingwood when Macdonald's group rose to power and his transfer from Richmond to Collingwood had been at the centre of a ludicrous round of blood-letting and big-money deals between the two clubs. Predictably, Jeff Browne the lawyer was there in the midst of it.

Years later Browne would shake his head at the memory of it all; the excessive fees, the greed and the rivalry. Had he really been in the middle of it all? 'There was a trail of blood between Punt Road and Lulie Street,' he would say. For both clubs, the trail was so thick that it took years to fade. Raines had refused to accept the salary cut and was about to be traded to Essendon.

Now it was no longer a question of whether Macdonald would remain. It was only a matter of the timing and manner of his departure; would he have to be removed or would he take the honourable way out by his own hand?

Typically, Collingwood made sure it was a day to remember. It was the 14th of April and the club was due to begin training at 5pm. But since early in the morning, rumours had swept the town that something big was about to happen at Victoria Park.

Reporters descended on Victoria Park, huddling in groups outside the ground. The smell of blood was in the air, but no-one realised just how much was about to be spilled.

The club's board had met at Macdonald's South Yarra home the day before to discuss his position and the future of the club. They met again on the 14th at 3pm. Two hours later a statement was issued. Macdonald was stepping down, along with coach Bob Rose. The general manager, Peter Bahen, recruited by Macdonald in 1983 from the Australian Ballet Company, was sacked.

It was a brutal end to Bahen's unlikely stint with football and, like so many before him, he left the game with a bitter taste in his mouth. 'Unfortunately, with everybody screaming for blood, there had to be some bodies,' he said.

Having come from outside the game, Bahen was aware, perhaps more than most, of the long-term damage football politics could do to a man's business reputation. He had gone to Collingwood, he would say, with what he hoped was a very good business reputation.

'To have it destroyed by a football club or the whims of people elected to League clubs is pretty disappointing.'

Leigh Matthews, the former Hawthorn champion who had been apprenticed under Rose to learn the subtleties of coaching, was elevated to the senior coaching position. Allan McAlister, the last of the New Magpies, would become president.

Another rebuilding phase would be put into place. Another round of planning would begin. It would take them more than four years, but eventually the circle would turn again for Collingwood.

The Flag. Was there anything some men would not do to win one?

On that day of the long knives at Collingwood, Bob Rose had hung around the rooms as Leigh Matthews took control of the players for the first time as senior coach. Rose was one of the club's favourite characters, a man who could speak gently and politely, a man who had known both eras of the game but who had managed to make the transition without rancour.

Standing there in the rooms, no longer the senior coach, but destined forever to remain a favourite son, he was asked whether he had any ambition to become president of the club. After all, wasn't it what many club supporters dreamed of becoming? McAlister himself had always imagined that one day he might make it into the social club stand. Even as a young boy standing in the outer at the other end of the ground, he'd always wondered what it would be like to walk through those famous rooms, gazing upon the old black and white photographs of the great Collingwood teams of the past and taking his place as a true member of the Collingwood family.

Was Rose the same? Of course, his place in history was

already assured. But perhaps the presidency interested him?

'That's a job I don't fancy,' he said, an honest smile spreading across his ruddy face. 'I don't want to be president of the club.'

After the events of the day, you knew he was speaking the truth.

Five months after the bloodletting in 1986, Ranald Macdonald fell hard again. The three fitness centres he had invested in had collapsed. His personal fortune was gone. His house would be put up for sale and the proceeds would go to the bank. It had all proved too much; he had been unable to properly manage the fitness centres because of his usual capacity for taking on too much. As well as the gymnasium business, he'd been heavily involved in the planning for Victoria's 150th birthday celebrations. And of course, there had been the Collingwood presidency.

'My personal position is hopeless,' he admitted with his usual candour. 'I'm afraid I'm one of those people who probably takes on too much. If you try to do a lot of things, if you take risks, you are going to have failures. That is the free enterprise system.'

It was also the way of football.

16

MARRIAGES OF INCONVENIENCE

The room was filled with so much love and goodwill that many of the hardened men there wondered whether they were at Woodstock instead of a meeting of all the League clubs. Here they were in Hobart in the middle of 1989 and it seemed all the old rivalries and disagreements had disappeared, replaced by a new spirit of co-operation.

Was it true? The commission had organised the two-day seminar at a five-star hotel principally to deliver bad news: it was no longer prepared to sit idly by and wait for one or two Melbourne clubs to die a slow death. Change had to happen and the commission was prepared to offer incentives to those Melbourne clubs down on skid row. If they merged, their outstanding debts would be paid by the League.

It was a sizeable carrot but nevertheless, had it been offered a few years before, the commission would have been skinned alive in front of a capacity paying crowd at the MCG.

So why was there so little angst? Here they were, the general managers and presidents of the clubs, slapping one another on the back in the bar, laughing raucously in smoke-filled rooms and generally behaving like long-lost mates. The general mood was positive. Football had to move forward. It had been stagnant for too long and all those present in Hobart were partly responsible. Big changes had taken place but they clearly weren't enough. The commission, everyone was saying, needed more support. It was time Oakley was treated like the chief executive he was.

The point was reinforced in presentations made by the commission. Oakley and Graeme Samuel told the clubs they could no longer afford to see themselves playing in an expanded Victorian Football League. They had to view the competition as a national one, otherwise that small-town parochial view would continue to hold them back.

And if that meant a club had to disappear, then so be it.

By the late 1980s, an entire cottage industry had sprung up surviving on rumours of club mergers. It all went back to the commission's original 1985 blueprint which had stated there was no way Melbourne could continue to afford 11 professional football teams. No other town in the world had been able to; there was nothing to suggest it was any different in Australia. That statement was now holy writ. And yet, four years after it was handed down in the form of a stone tablet, all the clubs were still there.

And by the time they all sat down in Hobart, a revolving door had almost had to be fitted to commissioner Peter Scanlon's office in Collins Street. Barely a week seemed to pass without a meeting between officials of two struggling Melbourne clubs. Sometimes Scanlon didn't even hang around; he made the introductions and then left on a business mission, the club officials sitting around admiring the view from his office and wondering whether they should throw 100 years of tradition out of those windows.

But that was about as far as it got. Despite the commission's desire for a merger, something always seemed to get in the way. Usually, and not surprisingly for football, it was an ego or two that destroyed the best-laid plans. Back in 1985 Melbourne and Fitzroy, and then Melbourne and North Melbourne, held merger talks. It had been strongly rumoured that the only reason negotiations fell through was because of an inability of the incumbent club presidents to surrender the right to host a pre-game luncheon.

In Hobart, however, the commission had decided to increase the stake. If the heart sometimes ruled the head, the commission believed it had found something even more powerful that in football ruled both; the wallet. Oakley told the clubs that an incentive would be made available. The first two clubs to merge would have their debts paid by the League. The officials of several struggling clubs raised their eyebrows.

They were all doing it hard. Richmond was on its knees. Nine years before it had won a premiership. Now it was burdened by debts of more than $1 million. Talented players had been allowed to leave and there was no money left to cover their losses. Only a handful of veteran players were left; the rest of them were young kids being asked to do a job they normally would only have been allowed to take on a few years later.

North Melbourne, Allen Aylett's old club, was also struggling. Ron Joseph had finally bowed out too, his last great coup being the signing in 1985 of John Kennedy as senior coach. Kennedy was as close to a living legend that the game possessed. He was a father figure for football, a tall man whose height was concealed by a stooping of the shoulders and a hangdog look on his face that suggested he had carried the weight of the game's problems on his shoulders for many years.

Kennedy hadn't coached since 1976 when he had taken Hawthorn to its third flag under his tutelage. He had first taken the reins at Glenferrie Oval in 1960 following his retirement as a player and, just a year later, steered the club to its first premiership.

Throughout his time he became famous for many things, but two stood out; his habit of wearing a long overcoat and his big, booming voice. When John Kennedy spoke, he thundered. His jowls wobbled and the veins on his neck stood out. But he was successful, and for nine years he had been one of football's most sought-after prizes as a coach.

Collingwood, of course, had come close to signing him at one stage but it had been Joseph who helped deliver Kennedy to North Melbourne in time for the 1985 season. However, the odds were against Kennedy when it came to repeating the success he'd enjoyed with Hawthorn. North had hoped he would instil the same sense of pride and toughness at Arden Street as he had at his previous club. He did that, but the Kangaroos hardly possessed the sort of talent Kennedy had had delivered to him at Hawthorn. By 1989, Kennedy was in his fifth and final season as coach. The club was heading toward ninth position, unable to improve on its fourth-placed finish under Kennedy in his first season.

Off the field, the club was also heading toward another tumultuous period. Chairman Bob Ansett was treading close to bankruptcy and North's public float on the second board of the Melbourne stock exchange had hardly been the success many had hoped it would be.

Down at Moorabbin, St Kilda was still treading water, still losing money and showing little sign of improving its lot in life. Which was a shame, said all those knowledgeable football people. If any club should have been successful, it was the Saints, they figured. Why, the club virtually had the entire south-eastern suburbs of Melbourne to itself. It had always produced exciting footballers and now one of its legends, Darrel Baldock, had returned as coach.

But the Saints also possessed something else; a capacity for mediocrity unmatched anywhere else in the League. It was as though the club was cursed. The only people who liked the club's home ground were its hard-core supporters. Everyone else loathed it; from the toilets that always stank and overflowed on match day to the visitor's showers that were legendary among players for having water imported from the Antarctic ice flow.

Those conditions for the public and the players stood out starkly as examples of where the club had got it wrong. The

Saints had gone through administrative officials like Richmond went through coaches. Rarely had there been any stability and that flowed through the club to the long-suffering players and support staff.

There were two other obvious candidates for a merger in the league; Fitzroy and Footscray. When the commission revealed its 'incentive scheme' in Hobart, Fitzroy's president Leon Wiegard, shifted nervously in his seat. He knew what it signalled; the commission was upping the ante and putting on the squeeze. Pretty soon this talk of merger would become a self-fulfilling prophecy. People would begin to expect the inevitable.

The only club that seemed unsurprised by the carrot unveiled by the commission was Footscray. By June 1989, its board members looked like men on death row listening to the gallows being constructed outside. Nick Columb, the club's flamboyant president who had only won the job at the start of the year, had already held several secret discussions with the commission as early as a month before. The commission had told them then that an incentive package was likely to be announced shortly for the first two clubs to merge. It was in Footscray's interests, nudge, nudge, wink, wink, to be one of those first two clubs.

Several key members of Footscray's board had begun to accept the inevitable.

Hobart, however, was not just the place where the commission hoped to send the League on a path to reducing its numbers. Its members, led by Scanlon, Samuel and Oakley, were keenly aware that if the competition hoped to be regarded as a truly national league, then it needed to dispense with the title of the Victorian Football League.

There had been rumblings among the usual conservative Victorian clubs that too much change had taken place in recent years and that such a drastic move as to change the title of the competition could so disenchant an already-embittered public that the game might never recover.

Rubbish, the commission had answered. But in Hobart, it wanted to put forward a strong argument that the time had arrived for everyone to accept that the game had gone national. And it would continue to expand nationally and, unless it changed its Victorian emphasis, the League would allow other sports like the rapidly emerging basketball and the NSW Rugby League to grab a foothold in markets it was not presently serving.

Where else would the commission go for support than the interstate clubs, and particularly West Coast. Since its decision under Bill Kerr to forge a closer partnership with the commission, the Eagles had become a reliable supporter of the League's drive for a truly national competition.

Now, the commission was calling on the Eagles to again wave the flag. Bill Kerr had not intended going to Hobart. There were others, he felt, who could better represent the Eagles' interests. He was too busy, and the club was in the midst of changing its ownership structure, to make the trip.

But Oakley and the commission were persuasive. 'Come and talk to the clubs,' Oakley asked Kerr. 'We need you there.'

So Kerr went. As he had learned in a very short time, it was best not to offend the Lords of the League.

Kerr paused for a moment and looked around the room. His audience was captivated and attentive. His delivery had impressed almost everyone, even those hardened men from Victoria who thought Kerr was just another flashy cowboy from the West.

He had always been a quick thinker on his feet and today he had to draw upon every little trick he knew. He had arrived in Hobart uncharacteristically unprepared. He had watched the commissioners make their presentations the day before, boosted by the usual assortment of gadgets and paraphernalia common to the boardroom. So he knew he had to do more than just talk off-the-cuff; he had to impress upon the club officials there that it was time for the game to go truly national.

But what could he use? He'd rushed off to the nearest shop and bought a ream of large white paper, the sort butchers leave on the front counter to wrap meat.

He had hastily scribbled key words and phrases on the paper and, during his talk, held them up as he stood in the middle of the room. The technique worked well. Kerr never ummed or aahhed, never looked nervous, even if his gut was churning.

And now, boosted by the warm response he'd received, he was winding up. It was time to deliver the sucker punch.

Holding up his last piece of paper, Kerr pointed to three letters he had scribbled hastily in thick black texta: AFL.

'See those letters?' he asked. Those at the back of the room strained to see.

'If you're going to take this national competition seriously, then you need to change the name of the League,' he told them. 'That's a start and a step in the right direction. Otherwise, do you know what these letters will stand for, and what you'll be remembered as?'

Another pause.

'AFL: All Fucking Losers.'

Kerr finished and sat down. Almost immediately, Leon Wiegard replied to Kerr's presentation.

'You know, that's the best sales presentation I think I've ever heard . . .' Wiegard announced. Kerr smiled graciously from his seat.

'. . . And everyone here should ignore what they've just heard.'

Wiegard got his wish on one point. Within days of the Hobart love conference, where everyone agreed the commission had to be supported, that it was time for the game to grow and extend its reach into every corner of the country, the feeling evaporated.

The club delegates reported back to their boards and they in turn got cold feet and everyone started mumbling about the need to protect the game's jewels: its Melbourne clubs.

It was as though Hobart had seen a coming together of several strangers struck by what the Italians called the 'thunderbolt'. Infatuated with one another, it looked like true love. It was, instead, just another stale one-night stand.

Ian Collins, the wily Carlton chief executive, had thrown his support behind the commission over those two memorable days. Collins had been appointed spokesman for one of the working parties set up during the conference. At the end, he had been extremely vocal and passionate about the national competition. The Game, he'd preached, was bigger than any one club. And if The Game was going anywhere, was going to avoid deteriorating into a series of small-minded and petty squabbles, then the commission had to be given full and total control over the competition. That meant wide-ranging powers and the ability, in some instances, to decide the fate of struggling clubs.

While others had headed straight for the bar during those two days and were never seen or heard from again—it was rumoured one official had somehow ended up in Alice Springs after one too many celebratory drinks—Collins was there throughout the day and night, pressing the flesh, counting the numbers, telling people what they wanted to hear and, as was his wont, sometimes telling them what they didn't want to hear, too.

It was all to no avail. 'I was very pro the commission and about getting it all right,' he would recall. 'I went a lot further than some people expected me to.

'I thought the conference was very encouraging . . . but within two days after all the delegates left the conference, it had all dissipated. The old parochial club feelings came back. It disappeared so quickly it was unbelievable.

'It was,' said Collins, a weary tone emerging in his voice, 'a total and utter waste of time.'

There was, however, one small victory. Within a handful of months, the Victorian Football League was no more. In its place was a new name; the Australian Football League, accompanied by a new logo that would end up being stamped on almost every marketable product in the country, in the same way Jim McKay had taken the old VFL logo and let it loose on the corporate world more than a decade before.

But the task of changing its name was hardly a simple one for the League. While it had examined several name options, including the National Football League and the Australian National Football League, the title AFL had always appealed as the simplest and most marketable.

'If you've got a national competition you could hardly maintain it with a state or local name,' Oakley said. 'It was really a matter of picking the right time. We had to make sure Victorians wouldn't be put off and we also couldn't leave it too late and keep putting off the interstate people.

'One of the philosophies the commission adopted was . . . a national perspective. We wanted to say 'All supporters around Australia are just as valuable. If you adopt that philosophy, you have the right one. You don't hold on to that notion of everything being Victorian.'

But there was a catch. The AFL title had already been registered by a man familiar to the commission and to many of those who knew how football really worked, how its deals were struck in back rooms and who held the real power.

John Adams haunted football's shadows. A former general manager at North Melbourne whose father was one of the club's most historic figures, Adams was quaintly described as a 'suburban solicitor' on the rare occasions his name surfaced in the press. But most of the time he preferred to conduct business away from the glare of publicity.

Adams had plenty of contacts in the game and was used from time to time to help broker a deal. Back in the early 1980s, he had authored a report on behalf of the National

Football League which had recommended the VFL go national and adopt a new name.

Soon after, he registered the title AFL and had held the rights to it since. Most thought him a shrewd operator. Others, however, were not as complimentary.

One member of the commission said: 'We used to admire him early on . . .

'He handled it badly.'

It took a while, but eventually a deal was struck with Adams. Despite the speculation that surrounded the negotiations, Adams was paid less than $10,000 and given a package containing guaranteed tickets to the grand final for years to come as well as two AFL membership passes.

'It was chicken feed,' said Oakley. 'He was looking for acknowledgement that he'd gone out and registered the title and done the right thing . . . there really wasn't a lot of hassle.'

Just business, after all. When John Adams was rung several years later to discuss the events of 1989, he was polite but abrupt. No, he said, he didn't want to talk.

He was far more comfortable back there in the shadows.

They called it the gateway to a new world and for the thousands of immigrants fleeing the turbulence of post-war Europe in the late 1940s and 1950s, Station Pier down in Melbourne's docklands was exactly that.

In 1948, a Rumanian family made its way down the gangplank, glad to be finally off an old rusting, Italian ship called the Luciano Monara. The Columbs had heard the story everyone else had in Europe; Australia beckoned as a wonderful place to hide from the memories of World War II.

Iancu Columb had been classified as a capitalist back home after the war and sent to prison. However, he had smuggled his wife Viorica and three-year-old son Nick out of their homeland to Austria. They made their way from Bucharest to Vienna on a train, with young Nick tucked inside a hidden compartment.

Later, Iancu joined them and they scraped together enough for the passage to Australia. It didn't take long for Iancu Columb (he would soon change his name to John, and his wife to Vicky) to show his entrepreneurial flair and willingness for hard work. By the 1960s, he was working in two jobs; a timber business during the day, a factory worker by night. While the work was hard and he rarely enjoyed the luxury of a good night's sleep, the money enabled young Nick to attend the relatively prestigious Brighton Grammar.

By 1989, Nick Columb's father was dead but the spirit of the man, his flair for a business deal and a decent love of gambling, lived on in his son. Nick had emerged as one of the new men about town in Melbourne. His name regularly surfaced in the social columns of the newspapers, as well as the racing pages. He had become one of racing's most prominent personalities. With two Caulfield Cups to his credit and a growing reputation as an owner and breeder, it seemed he could do no wrong.

But Columb had made a mistake. Like many high-profile businessmen, Columb wanted to head a football club. In early 1989, he finally got that wish when he became president of Footscray. For years he had been associated with the club as a supporter and, later, a board member and director of its football operations. He was the sort of man who seemed to either court publicity, or simply attract it. Reporters went to him automatically because they knew Nick Columb was good for a quote. After all, he had been one of them once. He knew what they needed.

Hadn't he begun signalling the problems ahead for Footscray the year before? 'If we stay at Footscray under the present set-up, we will be broke and out of the competition within two years,' he had cried the year before. And he wasn't even president then.

But everyone knew what he was talking about. The Bulldogs were being sucked into a black hole. Memberships had been dropping, sponsorships were dwindling and the days when the club could proudly proclaim itself as the flag-bearer for Melbourne's depressed western suburbs were long gone.

Footscray had changed since its heyday in the 1950s when Teddy Whitten and his team thundered across the Western Oval, playing a tough and ruthless style of game. Footscray, and particularly Whitten, took no prisoners back then. Opponents were simply put to the sword. Even when Melbourne began growing older and wiser and football began to lose its role as a class war, the Bulldogs carried the torch. Its supporters might have been decent, working-class people who did not enjoy the same sort of privileges those on the other side of the river maintained, but at least they had a football club that stood up for itself.

But like other clubs caught up in the modern era, Footscray had fallen prey to the usual vices. Good players were signed away to other clubs for fat clearance fees and little long-term strategic planning had been carried out. Columb had resigned from the board in 1986 in a bitter public dispute with the then president, Dr Tony Capes, accusing his administration of 'squandering monies'.

Columb's involvement with Footscray had begun in the early 1980s. After years of watching the Bulldogs from the outer, he was talked into helping its cause by another club backer, David Smorgon, a member of one of Melbourne's most prominent families and a former schoolmate at Brighton Grammar. He was soon on the board and given the football portfolio, responsible for overseeing recruiting.

They were good times to recruit because money was flooding the game. The Bulldogs had sold two players, Kelvin Templeton and Ian Dunstan, earning $280,000 in clearance fees for the pair. Soon after they released their hold on Gary Shaw, a Western Australian rover who had attracted the interest of Collingwood. The Magpies gave Footscray $140,000 for

Shaw, who would prove to be a dud, playing just 32 games in three years before being traded to the Brisbane Bears.

There were other sources of income. In one game against Collingwood at the Western Oval, Graeme Allan, a Collingwood defender, committed the ultimate sin of kicking across goal in the dying minutes of the match. The Footscray full-forward, Simon Beasley, marked and goaled to win the match for Footscray. Columb collected a $4000 bet from a Collingwood supporter. Soon after, Columb and coach Michael Malthouse jumped on a plane and flew to Perth to sign up Brad Hardie.

'I put it on the table in a Fremantle hotel on the Sunday, with the money on the table and the saliva gathering in Hardie's mouth,' Columb would recall. Hardie would sign up and go on to win a Brownlow Medal. By 1985 Footscray, through the canny work of Shane O'Sullivan, had built a side that, at last, seemed destined to repeat the glory of the 1950s. But it could only go as far as the preliminary final. The premiers that year, Essendon, had twice been beaten by the Bulldogs during the home and away season.

Columb finally won the presidency in March, 1989, when the president, Barrie Beattie, stepped down from the post for business reasons. Footscray had carried over an operating loss on the previous year of almost $500,000 and was heading toward an even greater loss that season.

The Western Oval, the club's home ground since it joined the League in 1925, was in a sorry state of disrepair. Tucked next to a freeway ramp, the ground was renowned for being one of the worst cold-weather venues in the competition. In the middle of winter a frigid wind blew in from the south and did peculiar things to the ball, lifting it high in the air and dumping it unexpectedly on unsuspecting players. Even those footballers blessed with the much-sought-after gift of reading the play and positioning themselves to the best advantage were often caught unawares.

Various estimates had put the cost of upgrading the venue as

high as $10 million. With the commission hell-bent on its
ground rationalisation scheme and little or no money available
from local councils and businesses, the Bulldogs were a sad
reflection of their former standing.

Morale was ordinary. There were rumours of player unrest.
And Columb, who was fast coming to the view that Footscray
could no longer afford to remain at the Western Oval, was pre-
siding over a club board split down the middle. A rival faction
determined to keep the club at its home ground and in the
Western suburbs was pressuring the board to hold firm.

There was also increasing pressure being put on Footscray
by the commission. 'It became apparent the VFL were not
going to put up with clubs being insolvent,' Columb would say
years later. 'Pressure was brought to bear on us. The VFL had
told us . . .that if, at the end of '89, we couldn't show them we
could financially handle our affairs they would be unlikely to
renew our licence. We were forced into a corner by the VFL.'

By late August, Columb's dreams of returning Footscray to a
position where it could again earn the respect of the other clubs
was in tatters. The energy in his voice had gone, as had the
bluster and bravado. He had feared, even as a young man following the club, that a day would come when the club would
discover 'there would be no more money coming in. The flood-
gates would be turned off.'

'That's what happened,' he said. 'The irony is that I've ended
up the bunny, if you like, with the problem of administering a
club which has no income, no more extraneous income and no
more opportunities for extraneous income.'

The bunny. It would become a description that Columb
would use many times in the following years. He was the
sucker caught holding the bag.

The bunny. Ironically, it was also a word that several of
Columb's critics within thought was appropriate. They
believed Columb and his supporters on the board were behaving just like rabbits.

Stuck in the middle of the road, stunned by the headlights of a car about to mow it down.

Peter Gordon was in Sydney when he heard the news on Tuesday, 3 October. It was over for Footscray. A new club was to be formed, to be known as the Fitzroy Bulldogs. To Gordon, and most of the club's supporters, the announcement sounded more like a takeover than a merger.

Here, finally, was positive proof that football was more than just the game many had supposed it to be. Business had finally triumphed and no amount of passion or loyalty could overturn the bottom line.

Just a few months earlier, on 27 June, shortly before the 1989 finals series began and with Footscray hopelessly floundering in 13th place on the ladder in a 14-team competition, a board meeting of the club had authorised Columb to investigate merger options with a number of clubs.

He made contact with Richmond and North Melbourne but little interest was shown. St Kilda was the first to jump at the bait but their terms constituted an unconditional surrender; any new club would have to be called the South Eastern Saints, be based at Moorabbin, play its home games at Waverley and would remove any vestige of Footscray's links with the Western suburbs.

'I wasn't offering or seeking a merger,' Columb said. 'All I was saying was that we wanted to talk about that option. We wanted to keep a clear head and have a fallback option if the VFL tried to de-licence us.'

The club's board, however, was so split that suspicions about Columb's motives began almost immediately. Footscray's general manager, Dennis Galimberti, a lawyer who had taken on the role just two years before, discovered one night that news of the St Kilda talks had been leaked to a television station.

Furious, Galimberti says he rang the station and spoke to one of its on-air presenters demanding to be told who had given them the story. According to Galimberti, the presenter replied that the story had been fed to them by Columb.

Galimberti believed his president had given up the fight. Just months later, both men would come to loathe one another with a passion and the bitterness would remain for years to come.

'Columb was conditioning the public through the media to get them ready for this merger,' Galimberti would claim later.

At another board meeting, the minutes would record Columb reporting that commissioner Peter Scanlon had told him the commission preferred a presence in the western suburbs, and was keen to see Fitzroy, North Melbourne and Richmond unite into what would become a super-team dubbed 'Melbourne United'.

But finally it had come to Fitzroy. The Lions were not enthusiastic about a merger at first. Club chairman Leon Wiegard had been down this track before and knew the pitfalls. But Columb soon received a call from commissioner Graeme Samuel who said Fitzroy wanted to talk.

Negotiations followed. Besides the combined debts of both clubs being paid off, the new entity would boast an unlimited salary cap for the next two years. It was a sizeable carrot. Here, after all, was a chance to win The Flag.

'It gives us a realistic chance of winning a flag for the first time since 1944,' Wiegard would say.

The events of what would have been Footscray's final week of existence are marked by acrimony and dispute. On September 29 following a meeting with the Footscray council, Columb and Galimberti drafted a letter to Ross Oakley.

The League had just rejected a proposal which had seen the council prepared to loan the club $580,000 subject to its advances being fully secured 'by an irrevocable bank guarantee against the VFL; from the VFL distribution to the clubs in October, 1990'. It was, in effect, an interest-free loan until the club became profitable. It also stipulated the club would have to play at the Western Oval the following season and would abide by a management strategy agreed to by the council. The council was also prepared to consider offering ratepayers a club membership as an inducement for the payment of early rates.

In the letter to Oakley, Columb said: 'We cannot, and will not, give to the Victorian Football League any unrealistic or irresponsible guarantees of the Clubs (sic) financial position at the end of next year. In this regard, however, Footscray is no different from 2 or 3 other Clubs.'

Columb said Footscray believed that the half a million dollar advance from the council would be able to fund the Bulldogs through the 1990 season.

'We believe that the Club has demonstrated that it is doing everything to resolve its problems. There is no justification for any interference by the VFL with Footscray.'

The club sought clarification that its games would be scheduled for the Western Oval the following season. 'If this is not done, the VFL will need to justify why Footscray has been treated differently from other clubs . . .'

Columb would claim that Galimberti by this stage was well aware of the advanced stage of negotiations with Fitzroy as a fallback option and only turned against the move when he discovered that under the proposed merger, he would lose his job. Galimberti would adamantly claim he knew nothing.

According to Galimberti, the first he knew of the merger plan was the following Monday night when the club gathered at the Cadillac Bar for its end-of-season best and fairest presentation. There, he says, he was told by a board member that the merger was signed and delivered.

Disgusted, he left the bar and went straight to his office at the club where he began telephoning every media outlet he could reach to break the news that Footscray was about to be merged.

Over the grand final weekend, talks had continued. Columb

had kept news of much of the negotiations secret from three board members he did not trust and believed were too closely aligned to the 'Save the Dogs' committee, a faction within the club fighting for the Bulldogs to remain at the Western Oval.

By Tuesday morning, thanks to Galimberti, the newspapers were trumpeting the death of the Bulldogs.

That morning, the full Footscray board met Oakley and the commission at VFL House. The news was out and the game was up.

According to Columb, Oakley opened the meeting by saying: 'Gentlemen, this is how it is. You're going to lose your licence unless you merge.'

Oakley then read out the terms of the surrender, reminded the directors they were liable for the club's debts, and the board then met for two hours as the commission moved off to an adjoining room. One board member secretly taped the meeting and found the entire experience traumatic. At one stage, surprised by the aggression shown by Oakley about the club's fate, he began suffering chest pains and thought he was about to suffer a heart attack.

'There was huge debate,' said Columb. 'Some wanted merger. Others didn't . . . Finally, everyone said that in the interests of the club, to save something, let's agree to merge. I don't think there was anyone in that room who wanted to merge.'

The decision had been taken. Key club identities like Teddy Whitten and Charlie Sutton were summoned to VFL House for briefings. And then the decision was announced to a stunned football world.

A pall hung over the western suburbs. Footscray was dead. Even supporters of other clubs in the League were left numb. It had finally come to this. All those newspaper stories that no-one had really believed, all the threats of a dire end for a club on skid row . . . they had all come to pass.

But nowhere was the pain more evident and more keenly felt

than in Footscray itself. People rang the club as the news spread. An old pensioner called, wanting to offer the last $150 in her account if it could be of any help.

Ken Oliver, who had acted as a marketing consultant for the club since August, was another shattered by the news. His father had played for the club for 19 years and captain-coached the team through the war years. His portrait hung on the wall of the social club. When his son heard the news of Footscray's betrayal—and that is how most regarded it—he walked to the social club, removed the painting and took it home with him.

In Sydney, Peter Gordon felt just as bereaved. He had grown up in a house three blocks from the Western Oval. For the past 12 months he had been fighting an apparently unwinnable battle to keep the Dogs at their old home ground. And despite the apparent hopelessness of his position, Gordon relished a decent fight. He had been a thorn in the side of Columb and his board for some time. Years later, when he had become president of the club, he would read the minutes of the 1989 board meetings. 'Most of the board meetings in '89 centred around me,' Gordon would say, still bemused. '(They kept asking) "How do we keep Gordon off the board?"'

Gordon was a pest some of the Footscray board believed they could do without. He was a short man with strong beliefs and to those who ran the game, he seemed to have a naive view of the world. To Gordon, football belonged to the community that supported it, not the businessmen who ran it or the television networks that controlled it.

'We've got a dichotomy here,' he would announce many years later. He was supposed to be eating breakfast and crumbs were spilling down the front of his shirt as he waved his arms around in a small cafe. 'You've got capitalism and egos and money imposed on a game ingrained with working people.'

That, to Gordon, was the fine line football had to tread. It was as though a barbed wire fence separated the essence of the game from its practicalities and too often, football had been caught between with a foot on either side, unsure and sometimes unable to decide which way to step.

The Footscray board had done well to keep Gordon away for so long. A left-wing lawyer who had established a reputation for toughness, Gordon was unaccustomed to finding himself on a losing side. He was rapidly becoming an expert in mass litigation and his work would turn the firm of Slater and Gordon (no relation) into one of the business world's most feared opponents.

He had joined Slaters at the age of 22. It had been a proudly staunch union law firm since the 1920s and it was just the place for someone like Gordon, a young man from the western suburbs with a chip on his shoulder and a healthy dose of cynicism about the business world.

Gordon and the law firm were made for each other. In the mid-1980s, he won the first successful asbestos-cancer case in the country. But the victory that really made the firm came with the Wittenoom miners' case. Slaters took on CSR and eventually won an historic victory against the mining giant, a victory which would cost the company more than $100 million in compensation payouts over the following years.

So when Gordon flew back to Melbourne soon after hearing the news about the death of his club, it was not with the heavy heart many others were burdened with. Here was another fight to be won. And Gordon thought he knew a way it could be done.

Luck was on Gordon's side. Had the League announced the deal somewhere other than VFL House, it might have survived the episode with a lower profile. But by holding a press conference surrounded by its own symbols, it had announced its complicity in the deal. And now there was a target.

Using Irene Chatfield, a stalwart supporter, as a plaintiff, Gordon and the rest of the 'Save the Dogs' committee took the League to court. Within two days, the League had agreed to give the club's supporters little less than three weeks to raise the

$1.5 million it said was required for Footscray to field a side the following season.

A massive outpouring of support followed. And leading it all, too, was Gordon, firing up the troops whenever an opportunity arose, and lambasting the League and Oakley for trying to rid the competition of Footscray. Gordon's attack was simple and effective and it boiled down to this: football was a game of the people and it was now time for the people to take the game back. Oakley, too, was a soft target. Despite his marketing background, he rarely looked comfortable on television or before a press conference; his answers were generally guarded and his demeanour stiff.

How could these men in business suits dare to take the game away from the very people who sustained it, argued Gordon.

On the first weekend of the fightback, a large rally had been organised for the Sunday at the Western Oval. The evening before, Gordon sat at home and debated whether to reveal Oakley's home phone number and address over the public address system the next day.

'I remember sitting there the night before the rally. I had his address and his phone number. Now, it seems almost obscene to me that I would contemplate doing it. But I did contemplate reading it out. I'm glad I didn't. I'm sure it would have turned the debate.'

Thousands turned up to the rally. And in the weeks that followed, the sound of tins rattling for the Footscray cause eventually turned into a cacophony. By 23 October, more than $1.15 million had been raised and it seemed almost everyone in Melbourne who drove a car sported an 'Up Yours Oakley' sticker on their bumper bar.

The chairman of the commission suddenly knew how Allen Aylett had felt several years before, standing alone at the MCG being booed by 100,000 people. Except, in Oakley's case, it seemed like more than a million.

Threats were made to his home in Wheeler's Hill and security guards were employed for around-the-clock surveillance for more than two months. One night, an intruder made his way on to the property.

'He was a Footscray supporter ranting and raving about the merger,' Oakley recalled. 'The security guard said to me the next morning, "Did you hear anything?"'

Oakley replied he had slept soundly. He asked what had happened to the intruder. To Oakley's surprise, the security guard allowed him to leave.

The unprecedented tin-rattling effort saved Footscray and would, in turn, become a textbook example for Richmond soon after as it turned to the public to pull it out of its own financial mire.

But while the Bulldogs had been saved, much bitterness remained. Nick Columb would be dubbed the man who had sold the club out and years later the memories would still rankle.

'It wasn't an easy time,' Columb would say. 'I take full responsibility for what happened, because as president you have to. But the debt wasn't mine, because I wasn't there when it was constructed. The merger I had sought was to create a new team in the western suburbs for the western suburbs. I wanted the Western Bulldogs.

'I still believe a new club in the West would have been terrific. It would have built its own heritage and very quickly would have become a power force. It really turned out to be a takeover and no-one was happy, least of all me. It took considerable guts to make that decision that the board made. It actually forced people out of apathy.

'They had refused to go to games. They refused to support it financially. They refused to become members. Companies had refused to become associated with it. And it was only when it became politically expedient and trendy to become part of that salvation group that people started putting their hands in their pockets.'

Columb paused for a moment. He was angry now and had worked up a head of steam. 'Without us the club wouldn't have lived through the '80s. We kept it alive through that time. There were thousands of hours and many hundreds of thousands of dollars spent trying to save it.

'We were then ostracised. We became pariahs. All these blokes who had put their blood and sweat into it and really worked their guts out . . . we became somehow unacceptable.

'It was costly, emotionally taxing. And I believe that a lot of the people, including Galimberti and Gordon, were opportunists who saw an opportunity to get some kudos for themselves. We were ostracised because it was politically expedient to do so.'

Columb's anger was just about spent. He took a breath.

For a man with such bitter memories, you would expect him to have given up on the club. Not so. Football, as it had done so often, still drew him back. He continued to support Footscray.

But he never went back to the Western Oval.

17
LIKE NO OTHER
BUSINESS THEY KNOW

In late 1979, Bob Ansett had been a leading supporter of North Melbourne for more than six years. As a Gold Pass coterie member, he had gained entry to an exclusive club at Arden Street. The select few who could pay to join Gold Pass were a much-fêted bunch and, like their counterparts at other League clubs, discovered a new world where they could influence how their football club conducted its affairs.

While growing up in the United States, Ansett had played American football for a dozen years and, despite his slight frame, had always been drawn to physical contact sports. When he arrived home in Australia, he was naturally drawn back to League football and North, more than any other club, caught his eye.

It was a club going places. Allen Aylett, Ron Joseph and the rest of the administration had a business-style approach that impressed Ansett. He liked the way they were determined to reverse years of history and turn North into a League power. Plus, North was the closest club located to his burgeoning car rental company, Budget. Supporting local sports and businesses was a trusted and time-honoured business tradition.

For the rest of the 1970s he maintained his Gold Pass credentials until 1979 when Aylett, now at the helm of the League, Joseph and the club's League director, Albert Mantello, who had originally talked Ansett into joining the coterie back in

1973, approached him to stand for the presidency. It was time, they said, for North to embark on another rebuilding era. Two premierships had been won in the 1970s—the club's only flags—and to guide the club into a new decade would require someone with a high business profile and the willingness to make changes.

Ansett wondered whether he would have the time. But it didn't take long for him to make up his mind. The lure of football was simply too strong.

Soon after assuming the chairmanship, Ansett sat down one day with Joseph to assess North's direction and its business philosophy. Joseph had been around the game by then for more than 20 years and knew better than most what a bizarre scene the football world could be. He was still in his 30s, but his experience and tricks over the years had seen him emerge as a veteran administrator in the eyes of many around the competition.

Ansett decided it was time his general manager was given a dose of reality. While he appreciated the enormous advances the game had made over the past 10 years, particularly at North which had spearheaded much of the new business credo in the League, there was still much to be done, he said.

'Footy's a business today,' declared Ansett. 'It's the same as doing business in any other sphere. The same principles apply.'

'Bullshit,' replied Joseph. 'It's not like that at all. I'll give you a few years to think about it and then we'll see whether you still think that way.'

Several years later, as North began experiencing the same financial and on-field problems as many others, Joseph ambled up to Ansett trying to hide a smile.

'So,' he said. 'Is it like a business? Or is it like no other business you know?'

'You were right, pal,' replied Ansett, knowingly. 'You were right.'

While Joseph had embarked on a series of raiding expeditions interstate in the early 1980s, looking to secure several players to boost North's dwindling stocks, it had come at a cost. The club's debt had begun to spiral again and despite a couple of promising appearances in the finals in 1982/83, North slumped to 11th place in 1984. And even though John Kennedy was brought on board, the future had failed to improve.

Joseph, too, was beginning to undergo one of his periodic stages where he grew disillusioned with the game. He was approaching burn-out. He only knew one way to work and that was flat out. 'You know when you are working well,' he would say. 'I work well when I'm out of bed at six in the morning and home at 10 at night and I don't know the day is gone.

'I don't think I will ever enjoy it as I did as a 16-year-old kid watching South Melbourne . . . in those days I was in love with it. Now I could never get the same wonderment from it.'

There were times when the game broke his heart so often he wondered whether it was all worth it. Maybe the old man, Ray, had been right all along. Maybe footy wasn't the sort of occupation out of which one should make a career. These were the personal crises Joseph endured every few years. God, it was a damn hard business. You gave so much of yourself that, at the end of the day, you sometimes wondered how much of yourself was left. He had quit again at the end of a disappointing finals campaign in 1983 but was talked back into the job by the start of the following season.

By the middle of 1986, however, he was growing weary again. There was a national competition due to begin the following season and he could see tough times ahead for North. And other opportunities, ones that would never come to fruition, were on the horizon. They would remain there, forever out of his grasp. John Brown wanted him to become the first general manager of the Brisbane Bears, but the commission's capitulation on the handing of the licence to Paul Cronin's syndicate would end that possibility. Close to Alan

Schwab, Joseph was also contemplating joining the VFL administration in its second most senior position if Schwab won the chief commissioner's role.

'North is not going to get support from anyone else other than itself,' he said in May, 1986, as he stepped down from the general manager's post, to be replaced by John Adams.

'I hope the North members—and there are none more loyal—will take the steps, which I think have to be taken shortly, to position the club in some sort of private ownership concept.'

Private ownership were the new buzz words around the competition. It offered a new form of salvation and it sounded glamorous. After all, weren't all the American professional football clubs privately owned? And look at the way the system operated over there. The turnover was enormous. Secretly, it was the sort of competition many Australian football administrators wanted to copy.

The love affair with the notion of private ownership of a League club showed just how far removed from its roots the game had become. The clubs had been born as suburban tribes, created by the people and the fabric of particular areas of the city. There had always been a sense of public ownership of each club. Everyone was a selector and every decision of a club was examined and analysed with greater scrutiny than that accorded the affairs of the national government.

Now, two clubs—North and Fitzroy, clubs with alarmingly dwindling supporter bases—led the charge toward reversing that historic relationship between supporter and club.

'We'd continued to buy players interstate and that had continued to add to our debt, and that debt had been further exacerbated by a host of other things,' Ansett said. 'We were slipping. We knew that unless we did something dramatic, North's future wasn't bright.'

Under Ansett, North decided to attempt to transfer its

growing debt into equity through a public listing of the club. There was one snag: the commission, while supporting private ownership interstate, was against the idea in Victoria, mainly because it feared it would leave control of a club in the hands of a select few, and could harm that delicate balance between club and supporter.

But a loophole in North's articles of association allowed such a move to go ahead and a meeting of members, warned that North faced an uncertain future unless it changed its direction, gave the move the all-clear.

Finally, it seemed, North Melbourne's future would be assured. It might have been a a weaker club in the scheme of things when it came to supporter bases and revenue, but now it could guarantee its place in the competition.

But like most things in football, the future never quite arrived. Instead, North's dalliance with an ownership structure would turn into a debacle and another lesson for the game on how it was like no other business around.

Ansett had been negotiating with Ian Johns, the general manager of the Victorian merchant bank, Tricontinental, to get Tricontinental to underwrite the proposed $3 million public float in 1987. Johns was well known to Ansett. He was also a director of Budget Transport Industries. But unknown to Ansett and just about everyone else outside the bank, including the Victorian Government, Tricontinental was in deep trouble and facing an imminent collapse. It was a collapse that would, in part, lead to the downfall of the premier, John Cain, one of the League's fiercest opponents in the 1980s.

'There was pressure growing on Tricontinental and none of us knew it at the time,' Ansett would recall. 'After having, in principle, an agreement to underwrite it, Ian pulled out of it at the last minute just as we were about to launch it.'

Ansett met Johns at his office in the city and was told that, while the bank could not underwrite the share issue, it would help fund the launch.

Ansett said Johns, who would spend time in prison a few years later, told him: 'You will not actually personally borrow the money. But we'll set up 10 trusts and each one will have 300,000 shares. And then you'll appoint a person to head up each of those trusts. You'll have to guarantee the repayment of the interest.'

Ansett: 'But he said there'd be no problem. The shares will sell and it will be only for a couple of months and the appreciation on the value of the shares will be such that your interest will be covered.

'We were at that stage so desperate no-one could think of any other way out, so we proceeded with it. We had 300,000 of the shares bought by the general members . . . but the other 90 per cent I had to underwrite instead of Tricontinental.'

After his downfall at the end of the 1980s, when he became one of the many supermen of the decade to fall back to earth, people would often observe that Bob Ansett was a terrific marketing man, perhaps one of the best in the land. But finances . . . when it came to financial matters, they shook their heads.

Within two years, Ansett's Budget Corporation had collapsed with debts of about $60 million and Ansett, a year later on his own petition, would be declared bankrupt.

Under the club's rules, no single shareholder could hold more than a 10 per cent stake in the club. By the time Budget collapsed, Tricontinental emerged with 40 per cent of the issued shares in North as mortgagee in possession, giving it 20 per cent of the voting rights. It attempted to place the shares in order to try to recoup almost $6 million owed to it by Ansett.

The collapse of Ansett and Tricontinental's subsequent recovery of the shares led to a rush of potential investors. Clearly, no-one had learned by the middle of 1991 that football was a business world with laws unto itself. A syndicate headed by a local property consultant, Anthony Zammit, jumped in and made an unsuccessful attempt to buy the shares.

And, as usual, Carlton and that man in the shadows, John Adams, were never far away. By September 1991, Adams was closely associated with the revamped West Coast Eagles board, but his links with Carlton's chief executive, Ian Collins, remained close.

Through Adams, who proved useful because of his past association with North—his father Jack had been given an award for his outstanding 30-year contribution to the club—Carlton moved in on North and bought 10 per cent of the club's voting rights.

North had always interested Carlton and its president, John Elliott, from a predatory point of view. The Blues believed North was vulnerable because of its shaky financial base and its dwindling stocks of talent and support, and believed that if North ever fell, Carlton should be there ready to pick up the leftovers.

Back in 1988, Elliott had secretly approached Ansett with a merger proposal. The new club would be called the Carlton Kangaroos. A new jumper would be designed, and a grandstand used by Carlton's then co-tenant, Hawthorn, would become a haven for North, its honour boards and social club.

'It was a generous deal,' recalled Ansett, who had seen more than one merger proposition for North over the years. 'I thought it deserved discussion with the board, but in the end we were committed to North staying as it was. But obviously, it stayed fresh in Carlton's mind because they tried it again.' This time, though, they used John Adams.

Adams, on behalf of a group of businessmen friendly to the Blues, had successfully negotiated with Tricontinental to secure the shares at a cost of about $140,000. And, predictably, his role hardly enhanced his standing at his old club.

'It was the way it was done that hurt the most,' said Ansett. 'Particularly with the role of John Adams, whose family had been associated with North for God knows how long . . . the whole thing was a joke anyway. They got 10 per cent of the shares. Even if they had got another two packages, it still wouldn't have given them control. There was no risk of it happening.'

Ansett had assumed the role of 'president' after a judge refused to allow him to remain a director of North following his bankruptcy. Alan Johnson, another businessman, was installed as chairman. But when it became clear to the North board that Johnson had been involved in discussions with Carlton about selling his 10 per cent parcel, blood flowed. 'We made it pretty clear to Alan that it wasn't appropriate for him to be around the club anymore,' Ansett stated.

It wasn't long before North Melbourne began feeling the same way about Bob Ansett. In June, 1992, Ansett departed the game after 13 years at the helm in the customary fashion; not at the end of the year, but in a 'surprise decision' in the middle of another struggling season for the club. Several board members had grown tired of his role at the club and believed it was time Ansett was cut. The club, they decided, had to embark on another era.

The new chairman of the club was Ron Casey, the man who, as general manager of Channel 7, had played such a large role in shaping the game it had become in the 1990s.

Casey didn't have Ron Joseph around by then when he announced a day after Ansett's resignation that football was a business 'and in business your end result is your product . . . when your product is not up to the mark, all sorts of stories and innuendos very quickly come to the surface.'

Had Joseph still been at North, he might have pulled Casey aside and given him much the same retort he'd given Ansett all those years ago. Yes, footy was a business. But as North Melbourne and so many other clubs had found, it was like no other business around.

By the time the 1980s were over in football, the League was

too busy putting out fires of its own making, and sweeping up the mess of others, to really notice. If many of the Victorian clubs had one foot in the grave, then two of their brethren interstate were close to receiving the last rites.

Private ownership, despite the commission's optimistic forecasts in the mid-1980s, had proved disastrous in every aspect. The Swans had begun haemorrhaging almost immediately following their sale, when Geoff Edelsten had revealed to a bewildered Bob Pritchard that he didn't have the money he'd claimed he had.

Further north, the Brisbane Bears were hopelessly out of their depth. The collapse of Christopher Skase had only exacerbated a problem that would eventually have come into the open, anyway.

In fact, by the end of the 1980s, if you went outdoors it was best to carry a strong umbrella to avoid all the tycoons falling out of their lofty perches. They were spreadeagled on the ground everywhere and football had more than its fair share. Drawn to the game by its promise of fame and ego-massaging, they were crashing everywhere.

But others continued to line up to replace them. And in Queensland, one would come along just at the right time.

18

THE
BAD BUCK BEARS (II)

He learned to fight down in the Petticoat Lane area of London's tough East End. It was the 1920s. A world-wide depression that would be etched forever in the memories of those who lived through it was about to begin. The East End, a hangout for spivs and other low-lifes, could be a dangerous place. So Reuben Pelerman made the wise move to learn how to use his fists.

There were 15 children in the Pelerman family; six of them died as babies, as meningitis swept through an area the politicians and public servants cared little for. Reuben was the 11th child. He began working fulltime at the age of 13 and drifted through a succession of jobs; he laboured on the wharves, drove taxis, worked hard in factories where workers were sometimes little more than slave labour. And, when he wasn't working, he learned how to box, fighting almost 400 amateur bouts and making a name for himself as a young man who could look after himself in the ring.

It turned out that young Pelerman could look after himself outside the ring, too. He had a canny business sense, of knowing when to gamble and when to fold. After moving for a short time to New Zealand, Pelerman packed his suitcase and decided Australia was the place to make a fortune. It was the 1950s and Australia was a safe, secure and prosperous land. The Lucky Country had it all and the son of a Polish Jew was determined it should share some of it with himself.

He made his fortune, largely through several wise investments and the setting up of a private hospital. He also emerged
as a man with a reputation for philanthropy. Reuben Pelerman
loved Queensland and Queensland loved him.

By the end of the 1980s, the League had decided that it, too,
could love Reuben Pelerman. It needed a benefactor for the
Brisbane Bears and it needed one quickly. The club might as
well have not existed for the previous three years; the only
impact it had made on the competition had been the constant
bad publicity it generated for a national league that had more
holes in it than a fishnet.

At the same time as Paul Cronin was trying to save the club
following the collapse of Christopher Skase's companies, an
approach had already been made to Pelerman to see whether
he was prepared to take over. He had been a key sponsor of the
Bears in their first three years, ploughing up to $1 million into
the club. He seemed to enjoy his association with the game. If
he failed to understand its subtleties, he more than compensated with his enthusiasm and gregarious nature. Pelerman
loved being around people. He could talk the leg off a chair
and loved being the centre of attention.

His passion for the game would, however, dissipate quickly
within a few years as he discovered what many before him had
learned. Football was not a business kind to entreprenuers.

Early one evening several years after he had walked away from
the Bears, his wife called him to the phone. Someone was
telephoning from down south, wanting to talk about his
experiences with the Bears. He sounded gruff at first, his
thickish accent making it hard for the listener to understand
many of his comments.

'I only bought the team to keep them out of trouble . . . to
keep them on the Gold Coast . . . to give the boys a job,' he
explained. 'To be frank, I felt they conned me into it.'

Conned?

'It was a complete failure right from the start. The boys didn't have their heart and soul in the game. They didn't have many good players.

'And I was left holding the bunny. It cost me $50,000 a week for nothing at all.'

All up, Pelerman would estimate the venture had cost him $5 million. He was asked whether he had enjoyed being the owner of the Bears. He asked for the question to be repeated, and then there was silence.

'Send me a fax with some of your questions,' he said.

He replied a week later. 'The enjoyable moments of owning the club were knowing that the boys were employed playing at Carrara, and not Brisbane, and knowing that I rescued the game of football to the Coast,' he wrote.

The Pelerman history of his stint as the Bears' owner is not exactly the same one recorded by the League. He claims he was 'conned' into buying the club. The League says he came running to them with open arms. He says he was unaware of the club's precarious financial nature. The League says he was fully briefed right from the start.

As usual in football, the truth lay somewhere in between.

Ross Oakley almost choked on his breakfast. There it was, splashed across the front page of his morning newspaper in early February, 1990. Reuben Pelerman had bought the Brisbane Bears as a Valentine's Day gift for his wife.

'Oh no,' thought Oakley. Here they go again. First they'd had Geoff Edelsten and his pink helicopters. Now they had a guy well into his 70s buying a club for his wife.

The League would never quite come to terms with Pelerman. It became clear early on that he was the only person likely to put up the hard cash to save the Bears. John Brown, one of the bidders for the original licence back in 1986, had put his hand up once more, joining up with Alan Piper, one of the club's biggest backers and one of its most influential figures behind the scenes.

Piper was a member of the QAFL board and had been instrumental in negotiations to obtain an underwriter for the Bears, back when the club was to be publicly floated. Piper was also one of Brisbane's most prominent businessmen, a wealthy man in his own right and one of the few prepared to put his money where his mouth was.

Brown, Piper and Andrew Ireland had got together one day following the Skase collapse to discuss a rescue plan for the club. At one stage, Piper had written to North Melbourne president Bob Ansett, offering to buy the Kangaroos, who were listed on the second board of the Melbourne stock exchange, and move them north to become a genuine Brisbane-based club in the national competition. A couple of names had been tossed around, including 'The Northerners' and the 'Brisbane Kangaroos'. But Ansett declined the offer.

Brown was prepared to take over the club, but he was not prepared to spend the sort of cash the League required. After Skase's collapse, ANZ McCaughan had become the Bears' largest secured creditor. It had put up the $4 million for the original licence fee. Now it wanted back the $3.5 million it was still owed.

Pelerman was in hospital when he received a visit from an ANZ McCaughan representative, a Qintex receiver and a solicitor. 'I was recovering from a very traumatic operation,' Pelerman said. 'To be frank, they conned me into it. I was sick in bed and the three of them came round and they sat by my bedside talking to me . . .'

The pressure, as Pelerman saw it, continued once he left hospital. On his discharge, he said, one ANZ McCaughan representative 'consistently pestered me that I had an obligation to look after the boys of the club and what I could be doing for the Gold Coast, keeping football at Carrara.'

The commission had agreed with ANZ McCaughan that if it could find a suitable owner to buy the Bears, and the commission decided that person was a fit and proper person to own the club, it would agree to the bank re-selling the licence.

Pelerman was the obvious choice. He had been a sponsor of the Bears during the Skase/Cronin reign, was an identity on the Gold Coast and, most importantly, he was loaded. He certainly fitted the criteria applied by the League.

He was not, however, a man given to small detail. Most of the negotiations over the club he left with his advisers. One afternoon at the Carrara ground, his advisers, an ANZ McCaughan representative, Oakley and Jeff Browne sat around a table throwing numbers back and forth and trying to hammer out a deal that would see Pelerman ride in to save the Bears.

The door swung open. There, standing impatiently dressed in overalls, was Pelerman.

'Well, is it done?' he demanded. 'You got a deal? I've got the bloody toilet maker here. He's going to start digging the holes for the toilets. What do I tell him? Do I tell him to start or not?'

'Give us 10 minutes,' came the reply. Pelerman sauntered off and waited.

While Pelerman became the saviour of the Bears, ensuring payments for players and a much brighter future than what had appeared just months before, the Gold Coast businessman encountered problems from the start.

Pelerman's advisers had approached the Queensland Football League's general manager, Andrew Ireland, to cross to the Bears and assume the role of chief executive. Ireland, a passionate follower of the game who had played with Collingwood for seven years in the 1970s before moving to Queensland in the '80s, was interested.

But having been a strong supporter of a club based in Brisbane, he didn't quite know how he could reconcile that strong belief with a job where he would work for a man who demanded that the Bears remain on the Gold Coast.

He rang Alan Piper, who by now had emerged as one of the

most influential figures in Queensland football. Piper, who was also behind the push for a team in Brisbane, urged Ireland to take the job.

'His position was, "Look, we've been trying from the outside for so long. If you go, I'll get on the board as well." . . . We just weren't going to win from the outside.'

Ireland took the job and Piper won a place on the board. And almost immediately, Ireland saw that Pelerman would not be making money from the venture.

'Reuben was always going to be in trouble from year one,' Ireland recalled. 'As Qintex collapsed, they sold anything they could sell of the 1990 season in advance. In between October and Christmas of 1989, they sold all the memberships, signages and boxes . . . and started offering huge discounts to get paid in advance.

'Everything had gone into this black hole. Reuben arrives at the club with all its operating costs and no revenue. It wasn't unreasonable that he'd lose and lose substantially. I would have thought he'd lost 90 per cent of revenue that year.'

Almost immediately, Pelerman's mood began to sour. He was losing money—$3.3 million of his own fortune would disappear just in the first 12 months—and the team's efforts on the field were also an embarassment. The Bears finished 14th in 1990 and were renowned for poor ball-handling skills and an inability to kick high scores. Sometimes Pelerman, tired of watching his money disappear down the sinkhole, would leave before a game had ended. And as the losses mounted, the commission found him growing more belligerent toward them by the week.

'He has a very simplistic view of life and business,' Oakley said. 'He has a mindset. We'd go up there and he'd say, "Did you bring Tony with you?"

'"Excuse me?"

'"Did you bring Tony with you? Tony Lockett? Where's my bloody full-forward . . . I need some players."'

Pelerman was unimpressed with the AFL's draft system, as well as what he perceived was a lack of assistance from the rest of the League. In that, he was not alone. The commission had allowed the Bears to be poorly conceived from the start and now had a delinquent child on their hands. The clubs back in Victoria moaned constantly every time aid was mentioned for the Bears or the Swans. And what had once been a very promising market for Australian football was shattered. The Brisbane Broncos had entered the expanded NSW Rugby League competition and developed a large and parochial supporter base. They also won matches. The Bears were a laughing stock.

It was inevitable that the Bears would be restructured again. By the end of 1991, Pelerman walked away from the ownership with close to $5 million in losses. He had, in financial terms, become the biggest individual loser the game had seen.

He had saved the Bears, but it was grim recompense for the money he had lost. The team won just three games that season, although its reserves side won the premiership, which led to speculation that the club had all along been playing the wrong team in the senior competition.

The restructure over that summer also guaranteed that, sooner or later, the Bears would finally call Brisbane home. The end of the National Party's dominance in Queensland politics had introduced a Labor government that had begun making the right noises to the League about a redevelopment of the 'Gabba ground. Within 12 months, a multi-million dollar refit of the venue would take place and the Bears, by 1993, would finally relocate to Brisbane, six years after being formed.

But the end of the private ownership era would also spell the end of Shane O'Sullivan's football career in Queensland.

He was the last of the original band of missionaries who had travelled north at the end of 1986 to launch one of the two new expansion teams. Somehow, he had managed to survive all the purges and crises, always emerging with his job and reputation as a shrewd operator intact.

But his time, like everyone's in the game, had run out. His theory, that the longer you were in the game the more likely it was to dump on you, was about to be reinforced once again.

One of O'Sullivan's final acts as football manager of the Bears was to play a role in a complicated three-club deal over Nathan Buckley, one of the brightest prospects to emerge on the playing scene for many years.

The competition was in a lather over Buckley. Having played his first football in the Northern Territory, Buckley had moved to South Australia and become a star with Port Adelaide. He could do just about everything on the field. He was a balanced player who could play both sides of his body and he also boasted that intuition you could only be born with.

He had starred during a state-of-origin carnival and the Bears, with rights over Northern Territorian players, had claimed Buckley. Unfortunately, he was not keen to move. In Victoria interest in him was high, and nowhere was it higher than at North Melbourne. The club's football director, Greg Miller, had flown to Adelaide and met Buckley and his father. After a great deal of smooth talking, he convinced the youngster a move to Arden Street would be in his best interests.

O'Sullivan and Miller struck a deal. The Bears would keep Buckley on their list for the season, thus protecting him from other Melbourne clubs, and then transfer him to North at the end of the year for a lucrative series of trades involving up to three senior North players.

It looked like a good deal all around. And even the AFL seemed to agree. According to several League officials, the AFL was aware of the deal between North and Brisbane and had agreed it could proceed. Buckley, meanwhile, would remain at Port Adelaide for another season.

Halfway through the year, however, rumours began circulating that a deal had been struck between the two clubs. Collingwood's football manager, Graeme Allan, rang O'Sullivan and told him: 'We know what you're up to.'

No-one at that stage, however, knew what Collingwood was up to. Allan, encouraged by his biggest supporter and confidant, the president Allan McAlister, set off in pursuit of Buckley. Bouyed by their premiership victory in 1990, the old Magpie arrogance was back. And the club was prepared to pay whatever it took to get Buckley to Victoria Park and in a black and white guernsey.

The deal between North and Brisbane unravelled quickly after that. Buckley would eventually go on to play a season with Brisbane and then move to Collingwood. Exactly how much the Magpies paid him would be one of those rare things in football that would remain secret. Rumours of under-the-table payments, never confirmed, would constantly swirl through the game.

O'Sullivan's time had run out. One afternoon he received a call from Mike Sheahan, the League's former media director who was now back in the newspaper game. Sheahan had been told O'Sullivan was about to be sacked.

O'Sullivan immediately got on the phone and rang the Bears' administration. 'I rang Andrew Ireland and he denied it and then I rang Noel Gordon (the new chairman) . . . the feedback I get is that the AFL were going to help the club and do things but there would have to be some changes.

'The thing that hurts is . . . no-one's ever sat me down and told me why I was going. I suppose that's what frustrated me. You bend over backwards for them . . . but that's footy.'

According to the Bears, the commission was willing to help the newly restructured club. But at least one of the changes would have to be the axing of O'Sullivan. According to one senior administrator who declined to be named, 'There was some pressure put on us by the League. The AFL had been talking to some of the clubs and concessions for us in the draft and elsewhere would be granted on the basis there would be some changes.'

O'Sullivan packed his bags and his family and headed home to Victoria where, eventually, he would return to his old club, Carlton, in a recruiting role.

'Too many good people were sacked,' he would say about his years with the Brisbane Bears. 'The sad part about it is, if we'd been allowed to run the place and everyone could do their jobs, it could have been fantastic.'

Could have been. Might have been. If. Football was a world filled with unfulfilled possibilities.

19

THE SWANS' SONG (II)

The view from Peter Weinert's office on the 60th floor was breathtaking. The horizon stretched on forever and in the foreground lay the Sydney Harbour, its water glistening. Tiny cars made their way through a maze of streets. It looked like a child's playset.

Weinert, a wiry man with curly greying hair and moustache, looked out of this window each day. For a man whose family had lost more than $1 million in the local Australian rules football club, the view was some sort of compensation.

The loss of the $1 million had hardly sent the Weinert family broke. But it had served as a healthy reminder that some businesses were far more difficult than others. Why had he, along with an assortment of other leading businessmen, ploughed a fortune into a club that, for more than 10 years, had soaked up cash like a sponge and never returned the investment it had promised: a Flag?

'We kept doing it not because we were stupid but because we believed the game needed people like us to see it through that particular period of time,' he said earnestly. 'We never expected to make money out of it. We just wanted to make sure the club survived in Sydney, the game survived in Sydney and the national competition got off the ground.'

Just across town, in another spanking office with a view, Graham Galt leaned back in his chair. Galt was a tall man with thinning silver hair who had moved to Sydney from Victoria for business. A Richmond supporter starved of his favourite sport, he'd welcomed the Swans with open arms when they first moved to Sydney, standing in the outer each Sunday afternoon with a group of friends. Galt, too, had known the frustrations of running the Sydney Swans. And although he had not lost money on the club like many others, he knew only too well its frustrations and problems.

'You know,' he said with a knowing smile, 'John Brown once said to me "Even the most rational of businessmen get irrational when they get involved in sport."'

And when they became involved in the Sydney Swans? The club was enough to send even the most rational person crazy.

If Bob Pritchard and Geoff Edelsten turned the Swans overnight into a glamorous, must-see sporting event, it had come at an enormous cost. In 1986 the League had imposed a salary cap of $1.2 million on the competition's first privately-owned club. But that was effectively doubled as the Swans embarked on their massive spending spree, paying ordinary players star salaries and introducing another round of inflation into the game. Through all this the commission sat silently and, while occasionally slapping Edelsten on the wrist, did little to stem the orgy of spending. Sydney was too important a market and too crucial in the television rights equation to drag it back to the same level on which other clubs were operating.

The cost was quick to be revealed. Powerplay, the club's controlling company that had been floated in June that year, recorded a profit of $8,479. But the licence fees from the Brisbane Bears and West Coast Eagles produced an extraordinary payment of $667,000, camouflaging to some extent the fledgling company's operating loss of $658,000.

Within a season, the average attendances at the Sydney Cricket Ground, buoyed by the hype of Pritchard and Edelsten and a love-struck media, had climbed to a phenomenal 24,000.

Many times, a crowd at a Swans match was larger than the aggregate attendances at a round of NSW rugby league matches.

But in order to get the people through the gate, Pritchard's marketing strategies had cost Powerplay $2.8 million, $400,000 more than what had been raised in total by the company's public listing. Such losses could not, by anyone's reckoning, be sustained over any lengthy period. But what would put the final nail in the coffin for Powerplay was its purchase in late 1986 of the satellite broadcaster Sportsplay.

Sportsplay was a rival to Alan Bond's Sky Channel. It had planned to broadcast a variety of sporting events into the nation's thousands of pubs and clubs via satellite. But Sportsplay was a disaster from day one for Powerplay. Sky Channel had won the rights to most of the available popular sports, leaving Sportsplay with the refuse; trotting and greyhound events became its bread and butter.

John Hodgeman, a businessman-cum-entrepreneur who had sold Sportsplay to Powerplay, had estimated that the satellite broadcaster would lose up to $750,000 a month for the first nine months, before running into profit.

Within six months, however, Sportsplay, in a bid to widen its appeal, agreed to pay the VFL $1.5 million over two years for the 'national satellite broadcast rights.' It also took out a $600,000 sponsorship deal with the League, which itself was struggling to attract corporate support.

Combined with extensive start-up costs and on-going operating requirements, Sportsplay suddenly began costing Powerplay up to $1.2 million a month.

What had been Shane O'Sullivan's theory? The longer you were in the game, the more likely it was to get you. Bob Pritchard had been in it for less than two years. But in that time he had squeezed in more than many administrators managed in a decade. His time was up.

Powerplay was advised from within the VFL commission

that it might be best if Pritchard was sent on his way. For some time, his relationship with the League had been deteriorating.

Oakley would recall: 'We had a few harsh words along the way.'

As usual, he did not go without a cost. Pritchard was paid $100,000, plus the equivalent in shares, to leave the company. After a remarkable period of unhindered spending and media manipulation, he had left his mark for a long time to come.

Powerplay required a new man to replace Pritchard and it didn't have to look very far. Still out there plying his trade and doing deals was Jim McKay, the man who had almost single-handedly changed the way football was presented to the public back in the late 1970s and early 1980s. Now, with a new commission in place that had frozen him out of much of the action on marketing and television rights, McKay was the obvious successor. After all, he knew how football worked. He'd been one of the men behind Edelsten's push for the licence. He'd been there when the Swans first moved to Sydney.

McKay sold his company, Active Marketing, to Powerplay for almost $1 million and a consideration of shares. Years later, he would regret the move as one of the worst of his business career.

'Stupidly and naively, I accepted a lot of my cash and shares on the slate that I would get in periodic payments,' he said. 'It was enough to make me want to sell out . . .

'I should have done a lot more digging. It was in a reasonably bad way when I joined. I just saw it as a good opportunity and everybody's dream of selling out. I should have asked for the money up front and I probably would have got it.'

At about the same time, with Sportsplay draining Powerplay's reserves, the Swans were doing well on the field and just as well off it. An operating profit of $600,000 was recorded for Sydney Rules Ltd, the subsidiary which ran the licence for the club. But the haemorrhaging of the satellite station kept draining money from everywhere. It was then, with

McKay coming on board, that Powerplay went looking for cash.

It found it, with the League commission's knowledge, with the merchant bank Hambros, picking up $1.4 million by using the Swans' licence as security. But nothing, it seemed, could stem the losses of Sportsplay. A planned $14 million float of the broadcaster failed to get off the ground. And in October, 1987, the month when the stockmarket crashed and took with it many of the 1980s high-fliers, Powerplay's shares plummeted and Sportsplay was sold to Alan Bond for $1 after losses of an estimated $17 million.

McKay stayed on for little more than six months but could see the writing on the wall. He resigned and, out of the ashes of Powerplay, would eventually buy back Active Marketing and start again.

'Overall I ended up $200,000 worse off than I had been originally,' McKay would lament later.

'It's difficult. People say you can make money out of football but I don't really think you can. At the end of the day you're not going into football and getting out with a lot of money. One way or another the system works against it. Most of the money I ever made was in real estate.'

In May 1988, the VFL finally stepped in as the Swans' financial crisis worsened. In February, it had begun paying the wages of the players and when Warwick Capper was sold off to Brisbane, its patience had run out. The Taxation Office was chasing $948,000 from Powerplay and the debt to Hambros was now $3.2 million.

Once again, the League was forced to send one of its own men north to run its problem child. Greg Durham, the finance controller, had been ordered to Sydney in April to examine the mess and help the commission flush out new owners for the club.

With the network boasted by Graeme Samuel and Peter

Scanlon, it didn't take long. When the commission bought back
the club for a nominal fee of $10 from Powerplay on 7 May, it
had an interim board ready to go. There was John Gerahty,
chairman of Scanlon's AFP Investments Corporation. Craig
Kimberley, the chairman of Just Jeans and a long-time supporter of the Swans, also joined up, along with the Nine
Network's Mike Willesee. And Alan Schwab would also take a
seat.

The chairman would be Graham Galt, the chief executive of
Aarque Holdings who had made his name in the executive-
placement industry.

'Our role was to stop the rot,' Galt would say. 'We had to
provide credibility in the community and get the club back on
track and create a situation where a new ownership group
could take over.'

The interim board and Durham had their work cut out for
them. As they began sorting through the financial mess, trying
to make sense of the club's accounts, they discovered that the
transfer fees paid by Brisbane to the Swans for the clearance of
Warwick Capper had hardly touched the club's books.

'No-one even bothered with a debit or a credit in the Swans'
books,' Galt would say years later, still amazed by what was
discovered. 'Somebody must have endorsed the cheque . . . and
whipped it straight through to Powerplay . . . there was a lot of
that stuff going on.' The players were experiencing their own
problems. Cars were in the process of being repossessed. For
some, the promise of jobs had not materialised.

On the first night they took over, two of the new directors
wandered down to training to watch the players go through
their paces.

'There's something strange going on here,' one of them said
to his business associate. Out on the ground there was silence.
The normal enthusiastic shouts and rhetoric of a League football training night were absent. The atmosphere was funereal.

One of the new board members thought it was an apt

metaphor for what the club had become.

Two consecutive years of finals appearances without a victory, the uncertainty of when they would be paid and a growing dis-illusionment with the game had combined to send morale at the club to yet another low point. And all was not well between coach Tom Hafey and a faction of senior players, who now resented his hard, uncompromising training methods.

Soon after, several directors would be aghast when they witnessed a near-brawl in the Swans' rooms after a match as a verbal stoush between Hafey and one of his players threatened to escalate into something more serious.

A secret meeting of several senior players followed to discuss what they should do. Soon after the mood changed and to reg-ular match attendees, it looked as though the players had taken charge. Out on the field, veterans like Dennis Carroll and Greg Williams appeared to be directing traffic. The team began to win again, capturing six of its last eight matches to finish seventh.

Hafey's future, however, was sealed. The interim board was regularly consulting with Alan Schwab, who had been encour-aging them to make changes and ensure the club was ready to confront the 1989 season. But when the board unanimously voted to sack Hafey, and a call was made to Schwab, he launched into a scathing condemnation of them, hurling abuse at the directors, claiming they knew nothing about the game.

They were surprised. Hadn't Schwab known this was com-ing and, in fact, been encouraging them to make changes? To the new directors, Schwab was acting irrationally and his response disturbed them. Was this the sort of support the League had been promising them?

By December a new ownership structure was in place. Many of the interim board remained and were joined by several new faces. Many of them, however, were familiar to the VFL com-mission. Among them was Basil Sellers, the unsuccessful bidder for the club back in 1985, John Gerahty, a confidant of Scanlon and John Elliott, and Peter Weinert, a property developer.

Back in June, Weinert had shown interest in putting together his own group of investors to buy the club, but later withdrew, telling Greg Durham he would be prepared to join any future ownership consortium. Later in the year, Weinert received a call from Gerahty, a close friend of Basil Sellers who was, in turn, a close associate of Weinert's. An investment proposal was sent to him showing that the club was looking at a potential profit of $500,000 the following year. But Gerahty cautioned Weinert not to get too excited. Investors, he said, should be happy if the club just broke even.

Weinert signed on, taking a five per cent stake in the club. His father, Jack, would sign up for another five, giving them a 10 per cent stake. On 12th December, Oakley made the announcement in the M.A. Noble stand of the Sydney Cricket Ground. That night, members of the commission and the new ownership group went to a Japanese restaurant in Double Bay called Miyako.

'It was a terrific celebration,' Weinert would recall years later, sitting in that office with a view of the world. 'We all had a few drinks and thought there was a great future.'

But that future would turn out just like the view from Weinert's window. It was fine from above, up there in the soft azure blue sky. But the lower you got to the ground floor, the more grime you encountered.

The new owners—there would be 16 of them in total—agreed to invest a capital sum of $250,000 in the club, pay out existing player contracts of $800,000 and then inject $1 million into the club for immediate funds, much of which was used to pay off debts to many of the Swans' small creditors. A licence fee of $4 million would be paid in regular instalments over five years and, if the ownership syndicate decided not to continue after that five-year term, it would have to pay a termination fee—known as a liquidation settlement—of $635,000.

Within days of taking over, eight of the owners and the League were hit by a statement of claim from Hambros, the merchant bank. Powerplay had borrowed money from Hambros 18 months before and used the club's licence as security.

It was the first inkling many of the owners had that things were not as they appeared. Hambros was claiming the owners and the League had acted in collusion to deny them monies they were owed following an agreement struck between the commission and the bank in May when the VFL bought back the licence for $10 from Powerplay.

The issue would drag on in the Federal Court for a year before a confidential settlement was reached over the $3.2 million Hambros was owed. Graeme Samuel proved pivotal. His knowledge of the law and experience in corporate negotiation enabled him to reach the required settlement.

In the middle of 1989, the owners had issued a cross-claim against the VFL in order to protect themselves. They had agreed not to pick up past debts of the previous owners. And there was no way they were going to be drawn into a dispute that, principly, existed between the League and Hambros.

'During that time it became evident there were agreements the commission had with Hambros . . . which purported to claim certain things,' Weinert said. 'Most of the new owners didn't even know that agreement existed. The majority of us didn't have an idea what had hit our desk at that time.'

If events off the field for the Swans had hardly improved, despite the arrival of some of Sydney's most respected businessmen, the club was struggling on the field as well. With crowds falling, the owners lost close to $1.4 million in their first year. The 1990 season would hardly give rise for optimism, either, with another loss close to $1 million.

During this time, the commission began paying regular visits to Sydney. There, they would discuss strategy with the owners, advising them on potential problems and suggesting ways of improving the club's performance. One of those suggestions would lead to the replacement of Barry Breen, St Kilda's 1966 premiership hero, as general manager for Barry Rogers, a former chief executive of the club back in the early 1980s.

The owners also decided to send a formal SOS signal. In a proposal to the commission, the club asked for formal assistance. The owners wanted help in renegotiating their deal with the Sydney Cricket Ground. They wanted concessions in the national player draft to give them a greater chance of picking up the available talent. And they wanted financial help.

The owners asked the commission to meet any debts over and above $250,000. The request would form the basis of a misunderstanding that would lead, within less than two years, to a bitter falling out between the commission and several of the club's leading figures.

Weinert would be one of those figures and the experience would leave him so embittered that he would decline to comment on the subject. But according to one owner, the club's board believed it had received a guarantee from the commission that it would meet the club's debts over $250,000.

The commission had sent a carefully-worded letter to the board saying it 'reserved the right' to meet those losses.

'We all thought it was a dangerous thing for them to do,' recalled one owner. 'We had no idea how they were going to pay for it and where the money was going to come . . . if some of the other clubs had found out about it, there would have been hell to pay . . .'

According to one owner, the club received money from the League in 1991 that covered its losses over $250,000. But that money was not identified. 'They didn't call it anything. They said we'll let you know. As we went into 1992, we kept asking because our accountants and auditors needed to know.'

By the middle of 1992, the commission was under pressure as a number of clubs put Oakley in their sights and demanded greater accountability from a commission they believed had grown too powerful. The owners were still wanting to know what to call the money in their books.

The club was now being operated on a shoestring. Player contracts had been renegotiated, expenses slashed. To some members of the commission, the club was starting to look like a company winding down its operations. And men like Peter Scanlon were fast forming the view that yet another private ownership experiment was close to failure. The commission was disappointed that men like John Gerahty, who by now was living overseas, were too removed from the running of the club.

The commission told the Swans the monies they had already received were advances on their annual dividends. Advances? The owners had already budgeted for the dividend. 'That immediately threw our budget for 1992 out,' said one owner. 'We had allowed as extraordinary income this money to help us with our losses . . .that was the first sign that the commission was interpreting their words in that letter differently to the board.'

The club's solicitors agreed that the commission was entirely within its rights. It had given the Swans no rigid guarantee to meet its debts. 'That's where the problems began,' recalled an owner.

Money was where all football's problems began.

By the middle of 1992, the commission had begun to suspect it would need a fall-back position in case the owners pulled out and the Swans collapsed. They would need a presence in Sydney. You could not have a national competition without representation in the country's largest capital city.

Talks were initiated with Carlton. While North Melbourne would claim later that it had originally presented the idea to the League, Carlton remained the main target of the commission.

Discussions with Ian Collins and John Elliott had revealed that the Blues were willing to play their 'away' games in Sydney and would co-operate in a plan that would plough millions of dollars into the Sydney market.

Elliott, however, made it conditional. He did not want it to become a fall-back option. 'I said we will not entertain this unless you assure us this will happen.' It was estimated the club could make up to $2 million a year from the move. The Blues would approach Tooheys Brewing, asking for a $3.75 million sponsorship deal spread over five years. With increased television exposure, an influx of new members in Sydney and a better deal on corporate and signage rights at the Sydney Cricket Ground, a $2 million haul would not be out of the question.

Peter Weinert had met privately with Peter Scanlon at the Regent hotel in Sydney in June and painted a less than rosy picture of the club's plight. The owners were getting restless, he told Scanlon, and there was some doubt as to how long some of them would be prepared to continue sustaining the sort of losses they had experienced in the past two and a half years.

Not long after, Scanlon rang a senior member of the Swans' ownership board and outlined the Carlton plan. It would be a scheme that would allow the owners to withdraw honourably and save incurring any future losses. Scanlon's action would annoy Weinert, who believed he had gone behind his back as chairman in an effort to divide the board.

Weinert, Mike Willesee and several other key owners decided to take the fight to the commission. Weinert still believed the Swans could be salvaged, even though annual losses were still around the $600,000 mark.

'Into 1992, certain commitments we believed had been given to us were no longer forthcoming,' Weinert would say. 'That made us stop and look at our position. We had got our expenses under control, we very rarely went a dollar over budget and we were under our salary cap. I will hold my hand up to a Bible. We were under our salary cap. We were in financial trouble but we never went into debt. We always paid everything.'

Willesee and Weinert had drafted an aggressive statement

and released it to *The Sunday Age*, demanding help for the Swans and underlining the club's importance to the national competition. Privately, they believed the commission was starting to lose sight of the national competition.

The push for Carlton would fail to get off the ground. While the clubs had been complaining for years about the Swans and the special attention they always seemed to receive from the commission, there was one thing more unpalatable than helping them out. The prospect of Carlton triumphantly taking over Sydney and making plenty of money was enough to turn their stomachs.

Allan McAlister, the Collingwood president, would lead the charge against the Carlton move. By October, it was clear the commission was on a loser. They then held discussions with Brisbane. The Bears were prepared to play half their games in Sydney, change their colours and rename the club to better describe its role as the only League club north of the Murray River.

By now, Weinert, Willesee and Rogers were out on a tin-rattling campaign through Sydney's corporate world. On 14th October at an emotional meeting, the AFL's board of directors gave the Swans a week to come up with a proposal guaranteeing the club's long-term viability. It was either that, or let Carlton travel north.

'We were busting our guts during that week to save the club,' Weinert would say. 'The commission was going behind our backs and trying to get rid of us.'

By the time the clubs met on 21 October, Weinert was determined to fight it through. As late as 5pm, when the meeting was scheduled to begin, he claims he was still negotiating with Oakley and the commission as they tried to persuade him to accept the Brisbane Bears proposal.

The clubs again found the alternatives too unpalatable. As a compromise, the Swans and the Bears would be granted assistance at the national player draft and the Swans would have $1.95 million in licence fees redirected back to the club.

A restructuring of the club soon began to be put into effect. Plans were initiated to gradually scale down the involvement of the owners and allow Sydney to become a membership-based club.

But to achieve that, some big names were required. Ron Barassi agreed to coach. And Ron Joseph would be installed as Sydney's chief executive.

Football was a game that went in cycles. And now, here he was again, back with the club that he had followed on those wintery Saturday afternoons more than 30 years before. And who knew what sort of great moments and disappointments it held for him?

20

THE END OF THE
COLD WAR

In the late 1970s a small cocktail party took place on the top
floor of the Channel 7 building in Melbourne. The station
had invited many of its most important clients for drinks and
one of them was one of South Australia's leading football
administrators.

The long-running Cold War between Victoria and South
Australia was at one of its periodic intense moments. Both
sides had been watching each other with suspicion and dislike
for years. Nothing much had changed. The South Australians
still distrusted the imperialistic and arrogant way the
Victorians conducted their football. The faces and philosophies
had changed. The feeling had not.

Channel 7 had just premiered the mini-series 'Against The
Wind', one of those sweeping dramas about Australia's convict
past that the country's dramatists so loved depicting on the
small screen.

As the party got under way and the drinks were poured, one
of the station's programming directors walked in and gloated
over the rating figures for 'Against The Wind'. The series had
peaked at a remarkable 50 in all capital cities. Except Adelaide.
There, the show rated a 36, still an extremely healthy showing.
But why was it so far behind the rest of the country?

The South Australian football official quickly pointed out
the reason. He was in Melbourne because, while he had no

345

time for that town's football people, television network chiefs were another thing. Television would be the future of football and it was best to keep them onside. Even if they were Victorians.

As others scratched their heads about the Adelaide figure, he provided a solution. 'Well, it's like this,' he said. 'It was a good show and very well put together. But it's not that surprising. We are, after all, free settlers in Adelaide . . .'

Conversation stopped. Was this a joke? No, the man was extremely serious. South Australia, you see, did not boast a convict past. Unlike some of those other states.

The anecdote would provide a great many laughs in Melbourne for years as it circulated among Channel 7 people and the VFL officials they were so closely aligned with. Here was proof, wasn't it, that South Australians were really the arrogant ones. A cut above the rest. Even with their second-rate 10-team competition they thought they were superior to Victorians.

But across the border, South Australians would view Victorians with far more passion than simply regarding their foes as jokes.

'One Victorian by himself is usually OK . . .' David Hookes, a South Australian and former Test cricket batsman, would muse one day, '. . . but when you get two or three together they can be a pain in the arse.'

Ever since 1860, when the game began taking root in South Australia, the barely-disguised antagonism had been there. By the 1980s it had reached its peak. When the South Australians defeated Victoria in a state-of-origin match it was celebrated with the sort of gusto and pride normally reserved for a gold-medal performance at the Olympic Games. South Australians saw themselves as underdogs when it came to football and, just like WA, were sick and tired of their best players being lured across the border to play in Melbourne.

But while WA would eventually concede defeat and join the expanded VFL in 1987, SA remained defiant. It had not been interested in joining a competition which still boasted the word 'Victorian' in its title and it would only join on its own terms.

By 1990 they still remained defiant. The AFL was interested in expanding but the SANFL was not interested. The main sticking point was the $4 million licence fee—a fee both West Coast and Brisbane had been forced to pay and which the League considered to be non-negotiable. So, too, did the South Australians, led by their president, Max Basheer, and the club presidents. In May that year, the SANFL reiterated its stance by issuing 10 conditions for entry. Having watched West Coast, Brisbane and Sydney suffer enormous financial problems, it claimed there was no justification for a licence fee. And, while it believed a 12-team national competition was the ideal size, it was prepared to join a 14-team league.

Unfortunately, the League was already a 14-club competition. And unless a club soon folded, and with the Footscray-Fitzroy merger having failed, there was little likelihood the stalemate could be broken. The SANFL declared it would not be prepared to consider joining the AFL until at least the end of 1992.

The commission's patience had run out with South Australia. Over the years it had been sounded out by several individual SANFL clubs about breaking away to join the Victorians but the talks never progressed past the initial negotiations. Now, it seemed the League was destined to continue without a South presence. Ross Oakley had hope for more but in public statements played down the importance of SA's rebuff. 'It would be nice to have them, but if they don't come in, so what?' he said.

This was football, after all. And things could change very quickly.

They did about a month after the May declaration and, to no-one's surprise, Ian Collins and John Adams were in the thick of it. The closely-aligned pair flew to Adelaide one day and made a full presentation to the board of Norwood, one of Adelaide's most prominent and successful clubs. Collins had been told Norwood was interested in the possibility of approaching the AFL with a view to joining. Collins and Adams, long-time advocates of a truly national league, believed they could provide the sort of advice Norwood required.

They had also spoken to Port Adelaide, another club which had also shown leanings toward joining the AFL. The pair also floated the possibility of both clubs merging but, as with most football clubs, a strong sense of distrust existed between two of Adelaide's most influential clubs.

By 1990 a sense of desperation was beginning to creep into SA football. Crowds had slipped—by late July only 27,380 would turn up to watch a round of five matches on a Saturday as a preference for watching AFL matches continued to climb—and a general feeling that the local competition was in decline was spreading.

It was Port Adelaide that moved first. On 5 July, Alan Schwab received an invitation to be guest speaker at a Port Adelaide luncheon on 22 August. Schwab, who was in charge at AFL headquarters as Oakley took a short break, agreed. He was then told that Port's president, Bruce Weber, was keen to speak to him. Port might be ready to make the break.

Two days later, on a Saturday morning, the pair met secretly at AFL House and Schwab instantly warmed to Weber and his willingness to compromise in order to get Port into the League. Port was regarded as the Collingwood of SA football back home. It shared a black and white strip and the Magpie motif, along with a rich and controversial history, but it was showing none of the obstinacy and stubbornness its sister club normally displayed in Melbourne.

Two weeks later Weber and a trio of leading Port administrators met Oakley, Schwab, Greg Durham and the League's consultant on interstate clubs, Barry Capuano, for a four-hour meeting that pushed the venture on its way. When the news was broken by Mike Sheahan in *The Sunday Age* on 29 July that Port Adelaide was poised to join the League, all hell broke loose in Adelaide.

The SANFL had been caught sitting on its hands. While it had heard rumours of breakaway clubs before, it had never dared entertain the thought that it might actually happen. No matter what the disenchantment might be locally, it had always believed SA clubs were united on one front; their hatred of Victoria. And that, reasoned the SANFL, was enough to put paid to any talk of rebel clubs.

A day after the news broke, the AFL chiefs worked back late into the night. In Oakley's office on the third floor, Oakley, Schwab, Jeff Browne and several commissioners worked on the wording of a heads of agreement between the League and Port Adelaide. The evening was only lightened by Schwab accidentally dropping pizza all over the floor and staining the carpet forever.

The heads of agreement was finally signed by facsimile. Port Adelaide was in. That is, it was in unless something significant changed the way of thinking at South Australian headquarters.

Bruce Weber had become president of Port Adelaide in 1986 and had always entertained the prospect of entering a team in a national competition. Shortly after taking over the presidency he had floated a plan to merge Port and Norwood and enter a rebel team in the expanded VFL, a plan that went as far as secret talks in an Adelaide hotel between representatives of both clubs, the then federal minister for sport, John Brown, and a League official.

His credentials to run Port Adelaide were impeccable. Weber was a boilermaker who had progressed to running an engineering company that supplied equipment to gasfields in the outback of the state. Port was a working-class suburb and Weber was just the sort of man to run its football club. He was known as a hard and ruthless pragmatist; a man who took decisions and followed them through, no matter what the consequences. And, like his club, he did not take failure lightly.

In 1987 the club lost a semi-final and Weber decided coach Russel Ebert's time was up. Ebert was a living legend in the Port Adelaide district. He had played more games for the club than any other man and had captured four Magarey medals— South Australia's equivalent of the Brownlow. The board, led by Weber, interviewed Ebert about the coaching position during South Australia's grand final week and told him it would talk again with him the following day. But the same morning John Cahill, another favourite Port son, arrived for an interview. Cahill's arrival surprised some board members. As soon as he left, the coaching position was put to a vote. Weber broke a 3-3 deadlock by giving the job to Cahill. Ebert never got another chance to speak to the board.

Weber was a hard man, but hard men were expected to lead Port Adelaide. The club was one of the most successful senior football clubs in the country. Formed in 1870, it had won a record 29 premierships and finished, on average, first or second in the SANFL once every two years.

And Weber would need to be a hard man over the weeks following the revelation that his side had jumped into bed with Victorians. Port Adelaide was about to experience a rare failure.

For a brief time Bruce Weber and his fellow board members at Port Adelaide became the most infamous traitors in South Australian history. 'I feel betrayed,' thundered Max Basheer. *The Adelaide News* ran a photograph of the Port board with a headline 'The men who sold us out' and went on to editorialise that: 'It is hard to believe that one of our finest and most trusted constituents chose betrayal as the lifeboat of survival . . . how does the board of the day justify raping this rich heritage in their brief encounter as trustees of this great club's future?'

Back in Melbourne, a groundswell against the Port inclusion

was also growing. Not surprisingly, it was led by Footscray and Collingwood. The commission, sensing the tide turning against it, decided to try to swing the votes of the 10 of the 14 clubs it required by appealing to the same tried and trusted place; the hip pocket. The League had struck a deal with Port where its $4 million licence fee could be paid over 10 years. Now it was offering the 14 League clubs a $2.8 million sweetener. The commission would take out a $2.8 million loan and provide each AFL club with $200,000. The loan would then be serviced by periodic payments of Port's licence fee.

The leaking of the $2.8 million offer led Oakley to confront the club general managers at a meeting, claiming there was 'a Judas in the ranks'. But this time, not even cash was going to swing the clubs around. Instead of slapping the commission in the face they simply kept deferring a decision on Port Adelaide until September.

By then, legal action had been undertaken in South Australia by several outraged local clubs to prevent Port from any further negotiations with the League for a month. This gave the SANFL valuable time to refine its terms of entry and lobby the most influential AFL clubs to stall Port's entry and support a composite SA side.

The Port Adelaide issue was creating divisions not only in South Australia, but in Melbourne as well. As Port's bid began to founder, a copy of correspondence between Ian Collins, John Adams and Norwood was leaked to the press, with the implication that Norwood, too, had been planning to break away.

Collins was incensed, as was Norwood. And Collins thought he knew who was responsible. 'Alan Schwab leaked some of our papers to the media,' he would recall. 'Norwood then ran scared and accused us of being stooges of the AFL. But they got that wrong.

'John Adams and I have been in the trenches for some time. He's got a good football brain (and) I was very annoyed with Schwabby. We thought about taking legal action at the time.'

They decided against it. Football was already in enough turmoil. On 19 September 1990, the 14 clubs voted 13-1 to give the commisison the power to seal a deal with the SANFL. By early October, a licence agreement was signed and the Adelaide Crows had become the 15th team in the Australian Football League. More significantly, perhaps, the game's longest-running feud was effectively over. South Australians would continue to dislike Victorians. But over time, even that emotion would fade. There was no point blaming the Victorians for everything when you had become one of them.

Down at Port Adelaide there was a sense of bitterness. The club would, however, rebound. And within a few years it would be given the nod to join the League. It would just have to wait until one of the present sides foundered and a new licence was made available. As Port had discovered, things changed very quickly in the game of football.

In 1991, the Adelaide Crows finished ninth on the ladder, a mid-rung position that most observers had thought it would occupy. But more impressive was its off-field performance. Unlike other interstate clubs, the Crows would begin posting a profit immediately. A gross profit of $795,000 was recorded and, after deductions of $305,000 for establishment costs and an agreed distribution of $472,000 to the SANFL, it was still left with a modest net profit of $18,000.

That profit would pale into insignificance in the following years as Adelaide established itself as the wealthiest club in the competition.

Back in Melbourne, the welfare of the interstate clubs was also on the minds of the Victorian clubs. But it was not the well-being of the expansion clubs that concerned clubs like Footscray and Collingwood. Instead, they were growing increasingly worried at how much money, and consequently, how large a power base, clubs like Adelaide and West Coast were nurturing.

The national league had been born out of desperation for cash more than a willingness among the Victorians to expand. And several clubs were now rueing the day it had taken place.

As far as Peter Gordon, the president of Footscray, could see, the debate came down to a philosophical line. The commission and its three key architects—Oakley, Samuel and Scanlon—had been running their own agenda to reduce the number of Victorian teams for several years.

Gordon, along with several presidents, was sceptical of the relationship between the three. While he believed Oakley had drastically improved the marketing of the game and helped create extra revenue, he wondered what the trio were trying to prove.

'It was almost like a competition to show each other how tough they could be when it came to economic rationalism,' Gordon recalled. 'Any sign of moderation was seen as a cop-out.'

By 1992 Gordon was feeling more confident in his role as Footscray president. But he would never forget his first AFL directors' meeting at League headquarters. There were still thousands of cars driving around Melbourne with 'Up Yours Oakley' stickers and he felt partly responsible for the backlash that had hit the commissioner, particularly as the Footscray comeback group had targetted him during its campaign as wanting to get rid of the club.

Gordon walked into that first meeting terrified. 'I remember waging a war within myself saying "I can't let this beat me." You got no briefing, no background papers—nothing. And I'd never been the director of a company before. I spent my first few meetings there absolutely shitting myself. And I believe that was something they knew and understood.'

Within a few months, however, Gordon had gathered the courage to speak up and let his voice be heard. What began frustrating him was Oakley's method of conducting meetings. Oakley would run many of the briefing meetings at breakneck pace. 'Right, anyone got any questions on that issue? No? OK, next item on the agenda is . . .'

Gordon found it remarkable. Where was all the legendary bickering and questioning he had heard went on in the past? It was true. The commission had divided the clubs and now ruled with an iron fist. And the club presidents either didn't understand what was being put forward before them, or were too frightened of getting on the commission's wrong side, to speak up.

'To be able to compete with them you need to be skilful and clever,' one club president would say years later. He prefaced his comments with a request that he be granted anonymity. He didn't want to offend. 'When you look around there's not too many presidents like that are there? They're out of their depth.'

The 1992 year had not been an auspicious one for the League. It had badly handled several issues, including the prospect of a 16th team entering the competition. To the Victorian clubs, more expansion was anathema. The competition had already grown too quickly. The game had changed too fast in too short a time, they argued.

When they discovered that Alan Schwab had written a letter to the West Australian Football Commission agreeing to a list of extraordinary player concessions for a new club based in Fremantle, to begin operating the following year, more questions were asked.

Schwab, who by now was discovering that his old power base was eroding under the impact of the Oakley, Samuel and Scanlon triumvirate, had painted himself into a corner. And the commission couldn't believe its executive commissioner had signed his name to a list that allowed any new Fremantle club access to players from three WAFL clubs, restricted access to other WAFL clubs, up to four SANFL players and access to 10 registered but uncontracted AFL players.

Samuel and Scanlon called in Schwab and gave him a verbal pounding. Scanlon had never been a big Schwab fan from the start and both men had been embroiled in the occasional hostile clash ever since. Scanlon regarded Schwab as a man full of rat cunning, but not the legendary administrator many in the game believed him to be.

Scanlon was always testing him, prodding Schwab to see how far Schwab would argue his own case on issues. If Schwab stuck to his guns, Scanlon would back him. But he believed that only by applying the blowtorch could he discover how well Schwab had thought through an issue.

The commission, too, had reached a dangerous level where power was contained in the hands of three men. Even Scanlon had confided that problem to an associate one day. By then Dick Seddon was long gone, having resigned back in 1988 to go to work in New York. There he renewed the friendship with the basketball commissioner, David Stern, that had set the scene for the salary caps and player drafts of the 1980s. Seddon was replaced by Albert Mantello, Allen Aylett's old right-hand man and a man many clubs believed fitted perfectly the requirement of a commisisoner boasting a strong football background. Peter Nixon had retired, too. Michael Carlile, the former Subiaco president and an influential figure in the birth of the West Coast Eagles, had been appointed in 1991, but his job in Sydney frequently meant he was out of touch with events in Melbourne.

'You're getting people there who have been there from the start,' Scanlon said to a friend, 'and you keep getting the same answer.' Seddon's presence was missed. While some of the other commissioners had not been charmed by his 'hail fellow, well met' personality, they had held him in enormous regard for his contacts at club level. Quite often he was the one who kept the commission's feet on the ground, telling them how their decisions would be interpreted by the clubs.

Without him, Scanlon, Oakley and Samuel had to guess what sort of reaction was in store for them. But when it came to money they could always anticipate the fallout.

In May the commission wrote to the clubs telling them that a shortfall of more than $2 million in revenue would reduce each club's dividend by up to $140,000. It was bitter news. The shortfall had been blamed on a 25 per cent over-estimate on the number of people taking out AFL memberships. Where the clubs had been told to expect a dividend of close to $1.5 million—for many of them it represented almost a third of their revenue—they were now going to be short by $140,000. And even though they would still receive an increase on the $1.03 million of the previous season, it was not enough.

During a briefing of club presidents in the middle of the year, Gordon began firing questions at the commission. When are your contracts up for renewal? Who assesses your performance?

After the meeting, Gordon pulled Allan McAlister, the Collingwood president, aside. The pair spoke about their growing fears and concerns. The commission had become too powerful. There was no accountability.

In the following weeks the pair spoke on the phone about what could be done. McAlister had been a thorn in the commission's side for some time. Encouraged by becoming the president who had finally ended Collingwood's legendary drought of premierships, McAlister was a vocal opponent of the commission and its support for the ailing interstate clubs.

McAlister was quick to remind everyone that he boasted one of the biggest constituencies in football. Wasn't it Collingwood that had the Prime Minister, Paul Keating, as a member? And wasn't it Keating who sometimes rang him on his mobile phone just to talk football?

McAlister had become the saviour of football journalists everywhere. Whenever a quick story was required or a comment needed, he was there to satisfy. But while some believed he was simply a grandstander who enjoyed a high public profile, there was method behind McAlister's mouth. By bashing the AFL, he was on a clear winner and nothing pleased the

Collingwood members more than hearing their chief bravely standing up to the businessmen who ran the game.

There were times when McAlister was almost apologetic in private conversations with the commission about the tone of his comments. Publicly he would criticise them and stand firm against one of their decisions, only to enter a meeting with them and tell them they had his support.

The commission for some time had been encouraging Collingwood to switch most of its home games to the MCG. The idea behind it was obvious. At Victoria Park, Collingwood's capacity for a home game was just under 30,000. At the MCG they could consistently attract crowds of more than 60,000 for big games and this, to the commission, made sense. It boosted overall AFL attendances just where they were needed the most—in Melbourne—and also backed its ground rationalisation program which for years had been encouraging clubs to share facilities and improve spectator comfort.

Essendon had seen the light by leaving its home at Windy Hill and moving its home games to the MCG, a switch which instantly provided sponsorship and other revenue benefits measuring in the hundreds of thousands of dollars.

McAlister knew the benefits such a move would provide Collingwood, but he also knew he had to tread carefully. Magpie supporters were fiercely parochial people who relished the club's rich history. Ghosts walked the boundary line at Victoria Park and no-one wanted to leave them there all alone.

At one stage McAlister made a secret agreement with the commission. Collingwood would move its home matches within a handful of years. Publicly, however, he would have to move slowly and carefully, preparing the membership for the move. He was a canny negotiator. When the Magpies finally made the switch, McAlister had several clauses included. One of them was that Collingwood not play a match at Princes Park, Carlton's home ground. The Magpies' record at the ground was abysmal. They never played well there. In future, they wouldn't have to.

McAlister, however, agreed with Gordon. The commission was not accountable enough. An announcement that Oakley and Schwab would be spending a week at the Barcelona Olympics on board a yacht as guests of the Seven network hardly improved their mood. But both recognised that the two of them were not enough to bring about change.

So McAlister rang Ian Collins, who had also been expressing dissatisfaction with aspects of the commission's performance, particularly its inability to solve the problems of the Bears and the Swans. 'Ian, I'm sick to death of being mucked around,' he told Collins. 'If we join forces they can all go to buggery.'

Collins, however, was not as annoyed as McAlister believed. In a conversation with a commissioner, the Carlton chief executive let it slip there was opposition under way and that the commission faced one of its toughest periods in the coming months.

Gordon had not got involved in the discussions with Carlton. 'Carlton to me were anathema. I always had the preconception that they stood for everything I was against. I think that Elliott has always been an icon for economic rationalism in the competition . . . I think he has played a very important role.'

Joining in the opposition was Fitzroy's president Dyson Hore-Lacy. In the fallout over the failed Fitzroy Bulldogs merger plan, the Lions had come out worst off. Since 1989 their debt had begun spiralling and a summer never passed without a new crisis arising at the club. Could it pay its players? Pay its creditors? While the commission denied it, there was a widespread feeling throughout the League that the commission was doing whatever it could to assist Fitzroy's demise. As it propped up the interstate clubs, it left the Lions to flounder. The merger had left a bitter taste in everyone's mouth. From now on, the commission reasoned, it would not precipitate a merger. But it would do nothing to prevent one, either.

'I think the time has come where the role of the commisison has to be examined, exactly what the responsibilities are and whose interests they are acting in,' said Hore-Lacy. In early July he had asked the League to provide him with details on each club's gate receipts for the past five years.

He was told it was not AFL policy to release the information, even to one of its directors.

Gordon, McAlister and Collins were summoned to a meeting at Peter Scanlon's office, overlooking Collins Street and Melbourne's eastern suburbs. There, with Graeme Samuel also present, the five tried to work out a review of the commission with parameters that would suit everyone. In football, few things were done without a deal and a compromise. The game had always worked that way. By the 1990s it had become an instinctive thing.

Several names were tossed up by Scanlon and Samuel as possible men to conduct a review of the commission's operations, including Sir Roderick Carnegie and Peter Nixon.

And then Graeme Samuel suggested David Crawford, one of the country's leading receivers and the man who had put St Kilda's controversial 22.5 cents-in-the-dollar scheme of arrangement into place. Everyone looked at each other and struggled to come up with a reason why Crawford should not be appointed. Gordon said he would like to meet him and a few days later privately interviewed Crawford, grilling him on his relationship with the commissioners and his views on the game.

There was nothing there, it seemed, to stop his appointment.

'We were outflanked,' McAlister would admit ruefully in hindsight two years later.

'My key error was consenting to Crawford,' Gordon would lament.

They would pay dearly for their mistake.

Crawford delivered his 30-page report, which cost the League $148,000, in March, 1993. It confirmed Gordon and

McAlister's worst fears. It was heavily pro-commission. Ross Oakley, instead of trying to juggle the dual role of chairman of the commission and chief executive, would become the chief executive officer, in reality reinforcing his hold on the game. Had Crawford recommended his powers be cut, Oakley had already decided to quit.

The worst criticism made of the commission was that it had not consulted enough with the clubs. Quarterly briefing meetings would be instituted to compensate.

In effect, Crawford had recommended the final cut be made to football's ties with its past. The board of directors, the men who had argued for almost 100 years long into the night over the most obscure points of order, would be abolished, their role superseded by a new, all-powerful commission expanded to eight members.

The clubs would have their powers reduced even further. Their last remaining influence would be the ability to appoint part-time commissioners and overturn commission decisions to merge, relocate, expel or admit new sides. And they would have to muster 75 per cent support against any such proposal.

In the following months, Crawford was retained to prepare a list of suitable candidates to fill the new commission. Carlile and Mantello were not even interviewed for the role. And in the politicking that followed, many names were proffered to become the new chairman of the commission. At one stage, a push by several clubs to name Scanlon as chairman gained strength. But it faded. John Elliott would claim that Ross Oakley had personally campaigned against Scanlon getting the post. Oakley and his best friend in football, Graeme Samuel, would deny it. But there was no disguising the fact that, while a strong supporter of Oakley, Scanlon was also his strongest internal critic on the commission. He thought it was one of his roles, to critique and oversee the performance of the game's most powerful administrator.

The push faded anyway. Scanlon had stepped down from the

commission at the start of 1993. While he enjoyed the job, it had become a far more demanding position than he had thought it would be back in 1985. He told friends he was also concerned about a battle looming on another front. The National Crime Authority had been investigating, among others, Scanlon and Elliott over their alleged roles in a multi-million dollar transaction. The investigation would ultimately lead to court action and Scanlon did not want football to be harmed by the dispute. He had left a striking legacy.

Without Scanlon as a contender, support swung to John Kennedy. If they were about to have their world turned upside down, then at least it would happen with someone they trusted at the top.

Apart from McAlister, Gordon and Dyson Hore-Lacy, there was also another man who felt disappointed with the Crawford report.

Alan Schwab was retained as executive commissioner under the sweeping overhaul. But he lost his vote on the commission. It had been coming for some time. But it still hurt. Here was another piece of evidence that his career, which eight years before had looked so promising, was going nowhere.

Within a few months, Schwab would be sent to Sydney, a despondent man who now knew with absolute certainty that his career with the League would never advance. He had already realised in the past few years that his chance of ever becoming the chief executive were dimming. Scanlon had made that only too clear.

Now he would return to Sydney for what seemed to be the umpteenth time to get the club out of another crisis. Its long-running and dismal experiment with private ownership was finally over. Schwab would be there to oversee the last rites being performed on one of the League's less memorable performances: private ownership.

He would not come back.

21
FOOTBALL
LTD

In the late 1980s, Alan Schwab sat down in a room at the old VFL House and fidgeted nervously for a moment. In another chair was Mike Williamson, the old doyen of football commentators, the man whose call of the 1966 Grand Final—'I tipped this!'—had become legend.

The League had decided it was time it recorded some of its history for posterity. Unlike many other sports, particularly cricket, Australian football did not boast a rich historical tradition. It was strange, for the game had produced so many colourful characters down the years, and had reflected so much of early Australian life.

The camera work was a bit shaky at the start and Schwab seemed conscious that what he was saying could never be changed. But as he and Williamson laughed over old times, Schwab soon forgot the camera was there.

The years rolled back. He was an office boy starting work at the VFL in 1958. Then he moved to St Kilda as assistant secretary and was there for that club's memorable premiership. Then, in the late 1960s, he moved to Richmond and under his general managership the Tigers would win three flags and establish a reign of rare authority. Like North, they were a progressive club and held enormous influence within the League.

The camera kept rolling and Schwab would launch into a big smile as he relived great moments and old battles. Alan Schwab loved football. Indeed, he loved many things in life. He was known within the League as one of the best lunch partners in town, a man who could go all day and turn a good lunch into a long and funny dinner. Like Jack Hamilton, Schwab was a tough operator.

Williamson wrapped up the interview at the end of Schwab's days as an administrator at Punt Road, just before he moved to the VFL to become assistant general manager to Jack Hamilton. It was a pity. If Alan Schwab had many stories to tell about his days at club level, the yarns would have been twice as long when it came to matters within the League.

He had become acknowledged as football's nuts and bolts man. Schwab had steered through the player drafts, the salary caps, changes to the rules and the fixturing system. He understood better than most the fears and insecurities of the men who ran the 15 clubs that made up the national competition. And despite the disappointments he had suffered, and being damned by the knowledge that his career could never take that final step forward, Schwab had persevered.

The label 'nuts and bolts man' was sometimes seen as a derogatory term by some, but they misread its intentions. Schwab had also been a football visionary in his own way. His handling of the draft and player rules had been designed not with just the present in mind, but the future, too.

They found him dead in his Sydney hotel room on 19 June, 1993, 24 floors above Kings Cross. Alan Schwab was 52 and had failed to keep several appointments scheduled that day as part of his role as interim chairman of the Sydney Swans.

No-one was surprised to discover that his last hours had been typical of the man; a long lunch, followed by more drinks. Toxicology tests would reveal traces of methadone and alcohol in his blood and several personal items, including a mobile phone, were missing from his room.

It would be almost two years before his sudden death was the subject of a coroner's inquiry in New South Wales. His absence left a giant hole in the game. Schwab's contacts and knowledge were irreplacable.

More than a year after his death, Oakley would still miss him, despite the problems the pair had encountered over the years. In that time, Oakley had carefully allowed Schwab to build his own portfolio and ensured he rarely over-ruled him. The pair had rarely crossed words, although Oakley had reprimanded him earlier in the year over a personal relationship Schwab had formed. Oakley believed it was affecting his work and position at the League.

Schwab, said Oakley, would be remembered 'as a passionate, almost obsessed football person who gave everything he had to give'.

There were very few other kinds of people in football, despite what the game managed to do to them sometimes. And when it came time to find a replacement for Schwab, only one candidate fitted the bill. He needed to be a canny operator, a touch ruthless, a man who knew how club administrators thought and felt.

Ian Collins accepted the role.

Just a few months before the climax of the 1994 season, the AFL commission unveiled its long-awaited five-year corporate plan.

Delayed for almost two years as the football landscape kept changing and evolving—the Crawford report had been a major hold-up—the plan was written and published in great secrecy. It had been a long time since anything of such delicacy had been leaked from within the League.

Perhaps it was because everyone had been waiting so long for the plan, but its release was accorded the sort of reverential treatment federal governments awarded their Budget announcements. Several big rooms at the Radisson Hotel in Melbourne's Queens Road were booked for the occasion. The media were 'locked up' and asked by the League not to release information until after 6pm.

Early in the afternoon, about 50 reporters were ushered into a side room. Up on a podium in front of microphones were three men: the chairman of the commission, John Kennedy, a commissioner from Western Australia and former president of the Eagles, Terry O'Connor, and Oakley.

Up there on the podium Kennedy looked like everyone's vision of what a grandfather should be. A kind, weathered face. Those sad eyes, still showing the odd sparkle. He was still a legendary figure in the game, even though he looked out of place in his grey suit, white shirt and fashionable tie. But that big, booming voice was still there, its rich deepness commanding all those in attendance to pay attention.

He looked down at the crowd of scruffy football writers below him. He rarely held anyone's gaze for long. Football had changed a lot since he had first experienced its highs and lows. This day, his eyes were looking just that little bit sadder. Was this what football was all about, a group of suited men sitting before microphones talking about economics and projected revenue sharing methods? What had happened to the game over all those years?

Kennedy looked down again at the assembled press, scanned their faces, and sighed.

'I wish you weren't all so serious,' he said.

Oakley got up and moved to an adjoining podium to present the five-year plan. 'Well, tell 'em a joke, John,' he exhorted Kennedy.

Kennedy looked away, his brow furrowed.

'I would,' he said, before shaking his head slowly. 'But footy has never been a funny occupation to me.'

No-one disagreed.

The five-year plan would set out the commission's objectives for the game up until the end of the millenium. Its biggest surprise was the inclusion of a new 'financial solvency criteria' for clubs; they would have to prove they could operate and meet debts during the following season. It was a tightening of the noose around the necks of several eternally struggling Victorian clubs and, as usual, it met with a heated response.

But most of the reaction was muted. The clubs were no longer in control. A decade had passed and they had gone from being masters of the game's destiny to simple members of a national business generating revenue in excess of $100 million a year.

They only had to look around to see how the game had changed. In 1993 Oakley had renegotiated the existing television contract with the Seven network, engineering a $90 million deal with Seven's Gary Fenton that would last through to 1998.

The deal had largely come about because of the new growth area in communications—Pay television. Home and away matches not covered by the network would soon be screened on cable networks.

And the days of beer companies sponsoring the game were also coming to an end. The League had turned to the giant multinational Coca Cola to provide them with a corporate sponsorship of $30 million until the year 2000, replacing Carlton and United Breweries. Coke was a product that appealed to a younger market and the commission was aware that unless it managed to continue attracting young people to the game, Australian football faced a difficult future. That future, blurred by the rapid developments in global communications, contained a hint that the 21st century would provide the game with an even tougher environment. The media moguls were already eyeing off professional sports as product for their Pay-TV networks and the NSW Rugby League was in turmoil after a lucrative approach by Rupert Murdoch's News Limited to create a 'Superleague' for its cable television ambitions. But what future would there be for Australia's only home-grown sport? After almost a century it had still failed to make a significant impact in Sydney or Brisbane. And now it was expected to compete in the global village against the monetary might of American basketball and football?

The commission seemed to be as perplexed as anyone else.

Its five-year plan contained little on the internationalisation of the game. It was as though the battle to establish an Australia-wide game had sapped everyone's ambitions. Survival was still the name of the game.

In just a decade, the League had hurdled from its suburban Melbourne origins into a national competition generating a turnover of almost $150 million.

What was it Mike Williamson had uttered all those years before, back when the game was broadcast in grainy black and white images on television? It was a great game. A great game.

And now, it was also a business.

In his office at AFL headquarters overlooking the Jolimont rail-yards, Ross Oakley takes a deep breath and shakes his head. Was that a hint of a smile? He is jet-lagged and weary. Forty-eight hours ago he was on a flight home from Europe after attending a sports marketing conference. Some of the world's most influential television executives had been there. It was a chance to press the flesh and let everyone know that Australian football was a commodity and a product that everyone in the global village should be watching.

'Whether we like it or not, this is business,' he says. Then he sighs. 'It's got to be run as a business. Otherwise it's going to fail. Like any business, you have to know how many people have got an interest in your product. And that translates into what sales you make. And that translates into the welfare of the people around the place. And that translates into profit.

'If you look at all those measures of what has happened in the last 10 years, you'd have to say it's been a rip-roaring success.'

The bottom line said football was a success. Increased corporate support and attendances highlighted that. But wasn't something missing, too? A large chunk of the game's fabric had been consigned to history. The days of Ronny Joseph running until his lungs hurt just to see his side go down by five goals were over. Some winter Saturday afternoons in Melbourne were quiet, as supporters mowed their lawns and tended their gardens until it was time to switch on the television and watch a game featuring their club be beamed into their living rooms from the other side of the country.

The bottom line said football had changed forever and that it could never go back to the days and ways of the romantics. But it had at least kept one trait going strong. It could give you a decent kick in the backside just when you least expected it.

'It has a habit of doing that,' says Oakley. 'But they still keep coming back, don't they? The game will always get you and slap you in the face . . . but it hasn't got me . . . yet. The game has tried very hard to get me.'

There was a slight trace of bitterness in Oakley's voice, even given his tiredness. It was as though he felt under-appreciated, that he had not been given the recognition he believed was due to him.

'Football people tend to focus on the trees and the battles. Whether you win the war seems irrelevant. It's the battles they're more interested in.'

He says he is not a vindictive man, that despite the attempts made to oust him over the years, he has not harboured grudges. 'I've heard a lot of stories about Collo and Ron Joseph. And yet, look at it now. Collo's working here in the office next to me and I supported Ron Joseph to become the head of the Swans. My business philosophy has been that if I'm constantly sniping at people, I'll be less effective.'

Collins and Joseph had targeted Oakley during his first months in the job back in late 1986, both men expressing doubts about his ability to last and asking whether someone else more suitable to the role could be found. Eight years later Collins discovered how vulnerable a real Football Man could be.

In September 1994, Collins was strongly criticised by several clubs and the media for cutting a deal with Footscray on the amount of fine it would have to pay after breaking the rules.

The League, conscious of its image, had introduced a rule

fining clubs if their players became involved in melees on the field. But the rule had not taken effect when West Coast and Footscray players became embroiled in an ugly brawl at half-time of a game at Subiaco one Sunday afternoon.

No charges were laid by the umpires and a review of the video replay by the League's investigations officer, Max Croxford, also failed to see players cited for their behaviour. But the commission, under pressure, felt obliged to act.

The finals had arrived and the game's image had been tarnished. Collins paid a visit to Peter Gordon and the pair agreed Footscray would pay a fine of $20,000.

But as the Bulldogs sat down that night to select their side for a final, a fax came through from the League citing several of its players to appear before the League tribunal. Furious, Gordon drove straight to AFL headquarters at the MCG where he found Collins. The man who had replaced Alan Schwab had been rolled by the commission. A fine was not enough. The commission wanted justice to be seen to be done.

The Bulldogs would take the issue to court, seeking an injunction against the tribunal hearing. In the meantime, West Coast decided its players should front the tribunal and all escaped suspension. A week later, Gordon and Galimberti withdrew the court action under pressure from the club's match committee, who claimed their players should not be forced to play in the finals with so much pressure on them.

The episode had capped off another typical season for Oakley and the League. It had introduced its five-year strategy plan and signed a new corporate sponsorship deal. But there had been the usual pitched battles along the way. The commission had had to perform some fancy footwork just to placate CUB when individual clubs signed sponsorship deals with rival brewing companies. And then along came the Collins–Footscray issue that attracted more headlines than anything else that season. There was outrage and condemnation. Didn't it prove, once and for all, that football was now a game played more behind the scenes than out there on the field? Didn't it suggest that football was all about doing deals and then trying to keep them quiet?

'Of course you do deals,' Oakley says impatiently. Then his tone drops and the weariness returns.

'That's what business is all about. Doing deals.'

EPILOGUE

Ron Joseph was tired and frustrated. It was late in 1994 and a sunny day in Sydney was drawing to a close. I found him in his office at the Swans' headquarters, down amid a maze of small alleys and streets at the Royal Showgrounds. He was slumped in an old leather chair, his blue shirt unbuttoned, his eyes weary and half-closed.

He was trying to remember the last decent break he'd had away from football and as he tried to think, he would launch into that familiar scratching of his head, squinting his eyes and face. Maybe there had been a few weekends here and there. And the year before, he'd managed a few days over the Christmas break.

But that was it. Joseph hadn't changed much over the past 30 years. There was too much to do, and the game still consumed him, still kept pulling him in. In the past few weeks he'd just signed up the game's most controversial figure, the former St Kilda full-forward, Tony Lockett, to a multi-year, million-dollar contract. A week later he'd secured another gem; the disgruntled Fitzroy skipper Paul Roos. Slowly, but surely, he was building a new team for the Swans. Once again, there was renewed hope around the club.

But for how long? After a dozen years in Sydney, how long would it be before the Swans collapsed into another crisis? It seemed the club was haunted, forever destined to repeat the past. Still, in football, hope was eternal. Victory was just a kick away. The Flag waited for everyone.

And Joseph had once again shown his shrewdness and stamina when it came to recruiting. Every other club in the League was talking about him again. How had the wily bastard done it? Sure, it seemed he had plenty of money to throw around.

But how was he going to fit all these big-salaried players under the club's salary cap? What sort of tricks had he pulled?

Just a few months later, everyone found out. There were no tricks. The Swans had exceeded their salary cap and, at the internal player draft, would be forced to forfeit choosing a player as penalty. Joseph would go crashing down again, his spirit temporarily broken once more. Typically, he would accept full responsibility, even though some felt others should have shared the blame. 'You know what gets me?' he would ask one evening soon after the debacle. 'We were just starting to get ahead, to really make some gains, and suddenly one stupid thing pulls us right back.'

The game was up to its old tricks. It was as though it was taunting Joseph, doing what it ultimately did to everyone. Here, it said. Taste a little sweet success. Isn't it wonderful? Now experience the bitter side.

Couldn't the game ever let go? Joseph knew it never would. It was his old partner and it would shadow him right until the end.

Still, on a sultry Sydney evening in the dying days of 1994, that was all in the future. He shrugged his shoulders, stood up and tucked the tail of his shirt into his trousers. 'Come on,' he said. 'Let's go and get something to eat.'

We went down to Bondi, to possibly the best seafood restaurant in the country. It had been a beautiful day in Sydney; cloudless skies had warmed the city after a violent electrical storm the previous night. Now it was dusk and a cool wind was coming in off the beach.

On the way down Joseph periodically scratched his head and stared out the window as he drove. Did he enjoy living in Sydney?

'Everyone asks me that,' he said, shrugging once more. 'You know, I don't mind it. It's not a football town but I don't notice it. All I do is go home, sleep, get up in the morning and go back to the office.'

It was the cycle of Ron Joseph's life. He stopped off to get a bottle of wine and when he climbed back into the car he scratched his head again. 'I probably do work too hard,' he said, smiling.

'I've walked away a couple of times through sheer frustration and tiredness. But it's because I just like to get my own way. That's just me, I guess. And I don't think I'm ever going to change now.'

Over fish that melted as soon as it hit your tongue, Joseph travelled back 30 years and talked about the people he'd met. About the characters he'd encountered along the way, the men who'd allowed an obsession with football to overshadow everything else in their lives; the pain the game seemed to enjoy inflicting on those who loved it the most and the great moments it shared with them occasionally as some form of ironic compensation.

Gradually, as the wine seeped in, Joseph relaxed. Sometimes he got excited and, with a mouthful of fish, roared laughing over an anecdote he would dredge up from the sizeable file of memories he had stored away over the years.

When I told him what I had discovered over the past 12 months, that football seemed to be one of the most unforgiving industries anyone could work in, that it could give you the biggest pleasures and then hit you right on the head with a sledgehammer, he nodded slowly.

He cast his mind back many years, back to his days as secretary at North Melbourne. There had been a committee man Joseph had always liked. Monty Millson was a housing developer in the northern suburbs and had been one of the first club committeemen to open his home to the players. They'd enjoyed the opportunity to swim in his pool and to feel comfortable knowing a board member was interested in their welfare.

But Millson's first love was horse racing. He'd won the Caulfield Cup with Taksan in 1978 and was always talking about the nags. One afternoon he rang Joseph and asked him if he was free. 'I want to take you somewhere for a couple of hours,' he told Joseph.

Millson took him to a stud farm he was thinking of buying. On the way there, he turned to Joseph and said: 'I want you to think about managing this property I'm taking you to see. If you put the same amount of time and energy into it and horse racing that you put into the footy club, you'd be a huge success.'

'I'm not interested,' said Joseph.

'Have you heard the statement that racing is the sport of kings?' Millson asked him.

'Yeah, so what?' replied Joseph.

'Well, I've won an event that's a big horse race,' said Millson. 'A big race. I've been on the committee of a footy club when they've won a flag, too. And everyone wants to slap you on the back. They all want to know you. But when you lose, no-one wants to know you. They all turn away. There's no-one there.'

Millson looked at Joseph. 'When I've lost a big race, I'm always the first one to buy the winners a drink. And they are always the first ones to buy me a drink when I've won.

'That's why it's called the Sport of Kings.'

Joseph tucked into another fillet of John Dory. It was left unsaid that football had never earned such a title.

A few months before, Joseph had decided—as part of his mission to create a sense of history and tradition around the Swans—to invite some of the game's biggest names to a Brownlow Medal evening. He cajoled and harried Bobby Skilton, his boyhood hero and on whose front door he had knocked on so many years before to congratulate him on a Brownlow victory and borrow his No. 14 jumper for a day, into surrendering his seat at the Brownlow night in Melbourne to come to Sydney instead.

More than 600 people turned up and when Skilton was introduced to the audience, they stood and clapped for seven minutes. Skilton was visibly affected by the outpouring of emotion. The applause just seemed to last forever. Joseph sat quietly to one side and fought back tears welling in his eyes.

'You know,' Skilton told him later. 'I didn't really want to come up. I like my Brownlow night. But when I got home I told my wife it was one of the greatest nights I'd ever experienced.'

There was hope there, Joseph thought. Sydney could still become a football town.

Back in Melbourne, Justin Madden attempted to curl his long legs around a stool in a small Italian café at the top of the city. After several failed attempts, he surrendered to nature and sat awkwardly as best he could.

'I've always been a cynic,' he said, a cheesy grin appearing again on the face of the president of the players' association. He was waiting for the right time to step down from the post, but first he had to find someone willing to take over.

He remembered back 18 months before, back when he'd been trying to rally the players to get together and fight the League for a minimum pay scale and the rights other workers enjoyed.

'I was out at Carlton and I was trying to get them to sign these forms as part of the battle. One of the old-timers came up to me and said: "Good on you, mate. I hope you get there on this one. I've never known an industry with more narrow-minded and self-centred people than this one."'

Madden reflected on this for a moment.

'Everyone stands on the edge of the precipice,' he said. 'There's no career security. People are constantly covering their arses. And it's at every level and it carries over off the field and into the politics. They're all afraid of being seen to have made a mistake, of being seen to have made the wrong move. No-one wants to take the blame for anything. It's an industry full of frightened people.'

So why did people keep coming back to the game, then? Why was it that, despite what football did to them, they kept being drawn back in? They were all like moths swarming through a darkened room, smashing into one another, hopelessly lost. And then a small light would appear and they would be drawn to it, mesmerised by its glow.

'It's high drama,' said Madden. 'What I like is what it represents. Sports tend to represent the countries we live in. Look at soccer; it's a staid and traditional sport from Europe. US football is filled with strategies and tactics; it's like a war.

'Australian footy on the field is an absolute free-for-all. And that extends to the country we live in.' Here, Madden's background as an architect came in. 'Even the buildings in this country, when you go outside and look around . . . it's a free-for-all.'

He sipped his coffee, raised his eyebrows and smiled that cheesy smile yet again. 'The game,' he announced, 'embodies many things.'

Peter Gordon sat hunched over a table in a small café where every small noise, including the dropping of a teaspoon, clattered and reverberated around the room. He was smiling. The year just finished had been a relatively good one for Footscray. Gordon's relationship with Oakley and the commission had hardly improved, but the Bulldogs had made a profit and things looked good.

Still, he was already thinking about when he would step down as president. The problem was there was no obvious successor and Footscray needed a strong leader. The club had taken a stand over the past five years under Gordon. It was the voice of the little people and the undertrodden, and politically it was a stance that had helped Gordon and the club stay alive in football.

But the issue of when he would step down remained unanswered. 'The club's made a profit, the place is humming and I'm thinking "hey, this is good, I'm enjoying this."

'It pulls you in. And you never want to get out when you're doing well. What happens is that one year we'll go bad, we'll look shithouse on the field and someone will stand up and say the club's got to be about success and I'll get chucked out on my arse.

'And go the way of everyone else.'

By the time he spoke these words, Gordon was fighting a lone battle. Through either necessity or just plain frustration, most of the other clubs had left Gordon to fight the commission and its corporate philosophy on his own. He had still made an impact. One of the commissioners had privately told a Footscray official one day that Gordon was treated with care and caution because he was recognised as a dangerous opponent. 'He's the only one they're really scared of,' the commissioner is supposed to have confided.

Gordon remained defiant. 'The war rages on and I think there are casualties on both sides . . .'

He paused, looked around the café and then smiled.

'. . . most notably, the truth.'

A year before, he had received a call from a journalist at *The Herald-Sun*. The morning tabloid had received a letter from a Mr John Buckley. Mr Buckley was upset with Gordon and wanted him called to account for the way he was running Footscray.

His letter requested an independent investigation into the financial affairs of the Footscray Football Club. The tone of the letter was damning. It was all well and good for Gordon to be calling for the AFL to be more accountable, Mr Buckley said. But what about some of the things that had been happening at Footscray? It went on to cite several instances which it claimed required a closer examination.

Gordon told the newspaper they were welcome to send their best financial journalist down to the club. He would open all the books and they could pore over as many details as they wanted.

The letter was never published. And the paper did not take up Gordon's offer.

A few weeks later, Gordon remain intrigued. Obtaining the address of Mr Buckley, he decided to confront him.

He pulled out his street directory and negotiated his way through the back streets of North Melbourne to the location Mr Buckley had listed as his address.

It was a vacant office. Mr Buckley, it seemed, didn't exist.

'I still wonder where that letter came from,' Gordon said. He wasn't going to hold his breath waiting for an answer.

By the end of 1994, football had embarked on a clear path toward the year 2000. A new team, the Fremantle Dockers, would join the competition the following season. Port Adelaide, its role in delivering South Australia to the League well remembered, had been granted the second licence to field a team in the AFL. It would just have to wait until a Melbourne side folded under the mounting financial pressures.

And the 1994 grand final, played between West Coast and Geelong, seemed to be a perfect example of where the game had gone.

Geelong looked like a team of leftovers from the 1980s. They had always played an open, flowing style of game, taking plenty of risks and sometimes paying the consequences. They had been fortunate to even make the finals, although the introduction of a final eight, designed to increase revenue and enhance the game's public appeal, had helped enormously.

But their strong finish to the season would count for nothing. The Cats might have had flair and daring. But they were about to encounter the 1990s.

If Geelong was a team of entrepreneurs still playing by the old rules, then the West Coast Eagles were the chartered accountants and receivers sent in to clean up and rescue the old, debt-laden companies of the 1980s. Excess was out.

These were the 1990s and to make your way and be successful, you didn't wing it anymore.

You eliminated the variables. You only took a chance when the odds were with you, when the likelihood of success outweighed the pitfalls of failure. West Coast played grim, methodical football. And won by 80 points.

On a cool August day just a few weeks before the grand final, a small, petite figure made her way on to the Melbourne Cricket Ground. Lynn Schwab had come to say goodbye to her husband.

She was sure this was the place Alan Schwab loved more than anything else. He had been a restless man late in his life and many of those around him, including Lynn, his second wife, had helplessly watched as he tried to find a role for himself in football's new world. Like so many men in football, he found it hard to tell people what was really on his mind. Football men were tough, weren't they? But the MCG . . . he always felt comfortable there, always felt at home. How many times had he told Lynn about the memories the stadium stirred within him? He could remember watching the 1956 Olympics there as a boy and those stirring days, when the world was a simpler place and sport still clung grimly to its amateur ideals, had stayed with him forever.

Lyn Schwab was accompanied by her daughter and a couple of officials as they made their way on to the field, down past the towering Great Southern Stand, and into a forward pocket.

It was a private moment and it had been kept secret from most people. There had been a fuss soon after Alan's death when his younger son, Cameron, had wanted to hold a wake for his father in the ground's historic Long Room. The request had been refused and many of those close to Alan Schwab had bitterly viewed it as an affront to a man who had done much to enhance the ground's image.

But some of those wounds were about to be healed. A hole had already been dug in the turf and as the small group looked on sombrely, dwarfed by the cavernous stadium around them, Schwab's ashes were poured into the ground's soil. Lynn said a private prayer, turned and left.

The game had finally taken Alan Schwab back.

Maybe it had a heart, after all.

SOURCES

INTERVIEWS

PROLOGUE: Ross Oakley, Barry Breen

CHAPTER 1: THE END OF INNOCENCE
Interviews: Ron Joseph, Allen Aylett, Greg Durham, Leon Wiegard, John Hennessy, Ralph Lane, Graham Williams, John Holt, Michael Tilley, John Cain, Jim McKay, John Elliott, Dick Seddon, Ranald Macdonald, Ron Cook, David Mandie, Bob Ansett, Lindsay Fox, Kevin Threlfall, Dick Seddon, Ian Collins.

CHAPTER 2: A LEGION OF SWORN ENEMIES
Interviews: John Elliott, Bill Kerr, Ron Joseph, Allen Aylett, Greg Durham, Leon Wiegard, John Hennessy, Ralph Lane, Graham Williams, Michael Tilley, John Cain, Jim McKay, Dick Seddon, Ranald Macdonald, Ron Cook, David Mandie, Bob Ansett, Lindsay Fox, John Holt, Kevin Threlfall, Dick Seddon, Ian Collins.

CHAPTER 3: ALL THE PRESIDENT'S MEN
Interviews: John Cain, Lindsay Fox, Barry Breen, Bob Ansett, Ranald Macdonald, Allan McAlister, Dick Seddon, Ian Collins, Jeff Browne, Greg Durham, Michael Tilley, David Mandie, Ron Cook, Ralph Lane, Ian Crawford, Barry Rogers, Graham Williams, Ron Joseph, Harold Mitchell, John Henessy, Jim McKay, Peter Scanlon, Barry Capuano.

CHAPTER 4: THE POWER OF THE PRESIDENTS
Interviews: John Cain, Bob Ansett, Lindsay Fox, Allen Aylett, Barry Breen, Ron Joseph, Ranald Macdonald, Allan McAlister,

Dick Seddon, John Holt, Greg Durham, Jeff Browne, Barry Capuano, Ian Collins.

CHAPTER 5: THE CHANGING OF THE GUARD
Interviews: Allen Aylett, David Mandie, Bob Ansett, Lindsay Fox, Dick Seddon, Graeme Samuel, Peter Scanlon, Peter Nixon, Ian Collins.

CHAPTER 6: THE SWANS' SONG (I)
Interviews: Barry Lyons, Barry Rogers, Basil Sellers, John Hennessy, Ralph Lane, Peter Bartlett, Creighton Burns, David Wilson, Geoffrey Edelsten, Bob Pritchard, Allen Aylett, Ron Joseph, Peter Scanlon, Graeme Samuel, Ron Cook, Ian Collins, Peter Nixon, Dick Seddon, Doug Sutherland, Bob Ansett, Jeff Browne, Graham Galt, Greg Durham.

CHAPTER 7: PREPARING FOR EXPANSION
Interviews: Michael Tilley, Peter Scanlon, Michael Sheahan, former VFL administrator (anonymous), Dick Seddon, Graeme Samuel, Peter Nixon.

CHAPTER 8: THE BEER WARS
Interviews: Harold Mitchell, Bruce Siney, Greg Durham, Jim McKay, Peter Scanlon, Graeme Samuel, Peter Nixon, Dick Seddon, Ross Oakley, Jeff Browne, Allen Aylett, Ron Cook.

CHAPTER 9: THE NEW FRONTIER
Interviews: Cameron Schwab, Peter Scanlon, Graeme Samuel, Dick Seddon, Peter Nixon, Bob Ansett, Ross Oakley, Michael Sheahan, Greg Hobbs, two former VFL administrators (anonymous), Ron Joseph, Ron Cook, Leon Wiegard, Barry Capuano, John Brown.

CHAPTER 10: THE TELEVISION WARS
Interviews: Ross Oakley, Peter Scanlon, Graeme Samuel, Jim

McKay, Michael McKay, Bob Ansett, John D'Arcy, Gary Fenton, John Elliott, Tim Lane, Drew Morphett, Harold Mitchell, Ted Thomas, Ron Casey, former Channel 7 executive (anonymous), Ron Cook, Peter Nixon.

CHAPTER 11: THE PLAYERS IN THE TRENCHES
Interviews: Cameron Schwab, former Richmond official (anonymous), Graeme Richmond (conversations with the author in the mid-1980s), Ray Jordon, Ron Joseph, Dick Seddon, Ron Cook, Allen Aylett, Geoff Pryor, Justin Madden, Jeff Browne.

CHAPTER 12: THE BAD BUCK BEARS (I)
Interviews: Peter Knights, Shane O'Sullivan, John Brown, Andrew Ireland, Ross Oakley, Reuben Pelerman, Leon Wiegard, Paul Cronin (interviewed by the author in 1986 for an article in *The Times on Sunday*), Allen Aylett, Peter Scanlon, Graeme Samuel, Dick Seddon, Bob Ansett, Tony Grant-Taylor, Ian Collins.

CHAPTER 13: ONCE UPON A TIME IN THE WEST
Interviews: Ron Joseph, Michael Carlisle, Neil Hamilton, Richard Colless, Bob Ansett, Bill Kerr, Peter Scanlon, Graeme Samuel, Ross Oakley, Dick Seddon, Ron Cook, Ian Collins.

CHAPTER 14: THE BATTLE FOR THE CATHEDRAL
Interviews: Jack Hamilton (with the author in September, 1983), Allen Aylett, John Lill, Ross Oakley, Peter Scanlon, Graeme Samuel, John Cain.

CHAPTER 15: GOOD OLD COLLINGWOOD FOREVER
Interviews: Greg Durham, Mark Kleiman, Allan McAlister, Ranald Macdonald, former Collingwood board member (anonymous), Jeff Browne.

CHAPTER 16: MARRIAGES OF INCONVENIENCE
Interviews: Ross Oakley, Graeme Samuel, Peter Scanlon, Nick Columb, Dennis Galimberti, Peter Gordon, John Elliott, Bob Ansett, Leon Wiegard, Ron Joseph, Bill Kerr, Neil Hamilton, Bob Moodie, Ian Collins.

CHAPTER 17: LIKE NO OTHER BUSINESS THEY KNOW
Interviews: Bob Ansett, Ron Joseph, John Brown, Andrew Ireland, John Elliott, Ian Collins, Leon Wiegard.

CHAPTER 18: THE BAD BUCK BEARS (II)
Interviews: Reuben Pelerman, Ross Oakley, Graeme Samuel, Jeff Browne, Shane O'Sullivan, Andrew Ireland, John Brown.

CHAPTER 19: THE SWANS' SONG (II)
Interviews: Peter Weinert, Graham Galt, Basil Sellers, Barry Rogers, former Swans director (anonymous), Greg Durham, Ross Oakley, Peter Scanlon, Graeme Samuel, Bob Pritchard, Jim McKay, John Elliott, Ron Joseph, Barry Breen, Ian Collins, Allan McAlister.

CHAPTER 20: THE END OF THE COLD WAR
Interviews: Ian Collins, Ross Oakley, Graeme Samuel, Peter Scanlon, Jeff Browne, Peter Gordon, Cameron Schwab, Allan McAlister, Michael Carlisle, Ron Joseph.

CHAPTER 21: FOOTBALL LTD
Interviews: Ian Collins, Ross Oakley, Peter Scanlon, Graeme Samuel, John Elliott, John Brown, Peter Gordon, Dennis Galimberti.

EPILOGUE: Ron Joseph, Justin Madden, Peter Gordon.

BIBLIOGRAPHY

NEWSPAPERS

The Age, The Sun, The Herald, The Herald-Sun, The Sunday Age, The Sunday Herald, The Sunday Herald-Sun, The Sydney Morning Herald, The Adelaide Advertiser, The West Australian, The Brisbane Courier-Mail.

I owe a great deal of debt and gratitude to the many football writers who covered the game from 1980 to the present. In particular: Ron Carter, Michael Sheahan, Trevor Grant, Patrick Smithers, Geoff Slattery, Greg Denham, Stephen Linnell, Daryl Timms, Ashley Browne, Peter Simunovich, Jim Main, Michael Stephens, Tony de Bolfo, Michael Davis, Malcolm Conn, Ian Cockerill, Mike Cockerill, Rohan Connolly, Ron Reed, Gerard Wright and Steve Reilly.

REPORTS

VFL/AFL annual reports 1970-94.

Minutes of VFL directors' meetings 1983-86.

Minutes of VFL directors' meetings 1992-93.

'A Proposal for Reconstructing the Existing Competition to Make it Viable for the Longer Term', by John Elliott and Ian Collins.

'Report to the Victorian Football League Directors by Allen J Aylett, president', 1983.

'Establishing the Basis for Future Success: A Report Presented by the VFL Commission to the VFL Clubs', October 1985.

'The Melbourne Cricket Ground: The Last Decade' by John Cain.

'Report on Australian Football in New Zealand: A Study by Alan Schwab and Reg Geary', 1978.

'Report by commission to clubs', 1986.

'AFL Future Playing Structure and the Development of Australian Football Nationally', June 1991.

'Background Information Paper', AFL, 1990.

'Discussion Paper for VFL Directors and Club Presidents from VFL Commission: Restructure of the VFL Competition', July, 1986.

'VFL Task Force Interim Report', 1 August, 1984.

'VFL Task Force, 2nd Report: The decision-making processes', October, 1984.

'VFL Task Force, Final Report', June 1985.

'Background paper: The Fitzroy Bulldogs', 4 October, 1989.

'Discussion Draft: managing the VFL for the long-term success of the Game', Mckinsey and Co., April 1983.

'Industrial relations and professional team sports in Australia', Braham Dabschek, *Journal of Industrial Relations*, Vol 18, No. 1, March 1976.

'Sporting equality: Labour market vs product market control,' Braham Dabschek, *Journal of Industrial Relations*, Vol 17, No.2, 1975.

The Oxford Companion to Australian Sport, the Australian Society for Sports History.

'Victorian Football League Laws of the Game Review Panel Report', October, 1988.

'Channel 7 Television Rights Presentation', October 1981.

'Channel 10 Television Rights Presentation', October 1981.

'AFL Strategic Plan', 1994.

'VFL Search Conference, 1983: Pre-conference Notes', by John Hennessy.

'Proposal for Restructuring the VFL/VFL Club Relationship Relating to Permit Regulations and Payments to Players', by Jack Hamilton, 1983.

'AFL Future Playing Structure and the Development of Australian Football Nationally', June, 1991.

'Restructure of VFL competition: discussion paper for VFL

club directors and presidents', July, 1986.
National Football League annual reports.
'Licenced and Endorsed Merchandise, VFL', 1983.

BOOKS

Aaseng N, *The Locker-Room Mirror: How Sports Reflect Society*, Walker Books.

Aylett A, *My Game*, Sun Books, 1986.

Blainey G, *A Game of our Own*, Information Australia, 1990.

Dunstan K, *The Amber Nectar: A Celebration of Beer and Brewing in Australia*, Viking O'Neil, 1987.

Feinstein J, *Play Ball: The Life and Troubled Times of Major League Baseball*, Villard Books, 1992.

Fitzgerald R and Spillman K (edited by), *The Greatest Game*, William Heinemann Australia, 1988.

Gaumont Football Yearbook, GMG Sport, 1991.

Gorman J and Calhoun K, *The Name of the Game: The Business of Sports*, Wiley, 1994.

Harris D, *The League: The Rise and Decline of the NFL*, Putnam, 1986.

Helyar J, *Lords of the Realm: The Real History of Baseball*, Villard Books, 1994.

Main J and Holmes R, *The Encyclopedia of League Footballers*, Wilkinson Books, 1994.

Mancini A and Hibbins G M, *Running with the Ball*, Lyndoch Publications, 1987.

Rodgers S (compiled by), *Every Game Ever Played: VFL Results 1897-1989*, Viking O'Neil, 1990.

Sandercock L and Turner I, *Up Where Cazaly?*, Granada, 1981.

Spence J with Diles D, *Up Close and Personal*, Atheneum, 1988.

Stremski R, *Kill for Collingwood*.

Taylor K, *The Sydney Swans*, Allen and Unwin, 1987.

Wilson D, with Robinson P, *Big Shots II*, Sun Books, 1987.

Wilson N, *The Sports Business*, Mandarin, 1990.

INDEX

ABC
  broadcast rights 172-3,
  178, 185-91, 192-3
  rigged barrel draw
  189-90
Adams, John 315, 318,
  319, 347, 348, 351
Adelaide Crows 345-52
AFL
  Bears strike threat
  241-2
  club dividends shortfall
  (1992) 356
  clubs question account-
  ability 356-9
  Coca Cola new spon-
  sor 1993 366
  Collingwood move to
  MCG 357-8
  Crawford report
  359-61, 364
  five year corporate
  plan (1994) 364-6
  intervenes with Swans
  335-7, 340-44
  lack of support for
  Fitzroy 358-9
  new commission under
  Kennedy 361
  Players' Association
  and player payment
  211-13
  Schwab dies in Sydney
  361-4
  television deal with
  Channel 7 366
  see also VFL
Alexander, Ron 258
Allan, Graeme 301, 329
Ansett, Bob
  North Melbourne
  President 32, 33,
  59-62, 112-13, 186,
  226, 292, 312-19, 324

on task force 85, 88
attendances 26, 27, 49, 72
Aylett, Allen
  background 5-8
  and Cain 54-5, 269-71,
  275-6
  clubs disenchanted
  15-16, 80-1
  and Elliott conspiracy
  19, 30, 33, 34
  Foschini case 75, 76
  Grand Final at MCG
  263, 266-71, 275-6
  and growth of VFL
  41-2
  and Hamilton 13,
  40-1, 81, 84, 85-6,
  122, 140-1, 225, 281
  management style criti-
  cised 81
  and national competi-
  tion 14, 93, 94, 95
  National Football
  League President 15,
  84, 140-1
  at North Melbourne
  7-9, 61, 180, 312
  recommends new com-
  missions 81-2
  resignation 277
  and Sydney Swans 94,
  95, 96, 104
  and task force recom-
  mendations 83-6, 89
  VFL President 12-17,
  19, 20, 50, 66, 71, 72,
  79, 80-1, 203, 225,
  263, 266-71, 277,
  309-10

Bahen, Peter 286-7
Baldock, Darrel 292
Barassi, Ron
  Melbourne coach 66-9,

137, 144
North Melbourne
  coach 180
Sydney Swans coach
  344
Truth columnist 190
Bartels, Peter 133
Bartlett, Kevin 154
Bartlett, Peter 106-7
Basheer, Max 248-9,
  347, 350
Beattie, Barrie 301
Beitzel, Harry 122
Berry, Kevin 188
Bolte, Henry 264, 270
Bond, Alan 130, 169, 335
brawling 368-9
Breen, Barry 77, 78,
  185, 340
Brisbane Bears
  AFL interferes 241-2
  Aylett's dream 14
  Capper 235-40
  Cronin chairman
  219-25, 227, 229-42
  debts 231-4, 240
  home ground 230-3,
  327
  Knights as coach
  216-20, 235, 236,
  238-9, 240
  Pelerman buys team
  321-7
  restructuring 1991
  327
  Skase buys team
  226-40, 320, 322
  strike threat 241-2
broadcasting
  ABC 172-3, 178,
  85-91, 192-3, 366
  Broadcom 169-72,
  173, 175, 178, 182-7
  Channel 7 162-83, 319

Broadcom 169-72, 173, 175, 178, 182-7

Brown, John 158, 224-5, 314, 323-4, 332

Browne, Jeff 71, 113-14, 115, 136-9, 209, 212, 286, 349

Buckenara, Gary 247, 255

Buckley, Nathan 328-9

Burns, Creighton 106-7

Cahill, John 64, 350

Cain, John (jnr) 40, 53-55, 269-70, 271, 275, 276

Campbell, Kevin 95

Capes, Tony 300

Capper, Warwick
Bears 235-40
Sydney Swans 114-15, 335, 336

Capuano, Barry 348

Carlile, Michael
commissioner 355, 360
with Subiaco 246-7

Carlton Football Club
club reputation 18-19, 20
Collins General Manager 22-3, 211, 341-2
Elliott President 18, 19-22
Grand Final thrashing 155, 173
merger talks with North 318
plan to play away in Sydney 341-3
Rice as President 59-60

Carroll, Dennis 116, 337

Carter, Colin 121, 274

Casey, Ron 162-83, 319

Channel 7 162-83, 319, 366

Chatfield, Irene 309

Clarke, Ern 10

Cloke, David 137

clubs
become businesses 1980s 24-7
businessmen as presidents 59-61
and commission accountability 356-9
disenchanted with Aylett 15-16, 80-1
dividend shortfall 1992 356
and expanded competition 124-6, 152-9, 351, 354
financial problems 118-26
financial solvency criteria 365-6
and Hamilton 40
income from VFL 23
interstate team success 351, 352-3, 354
losing control 366
powers and new commission 360
role in running game 27
VFL task force recommendations 34-5
see also individual clubs

coaches 79-80

Coghill, Bob 111-12

Colless, Richard 246-55

Collingwood Football Club
Buckley deal 328-9
financial problems 120-1, 284
Flag in 1990 282
McAlister as President 287, 329, 343, 356-61
McAlister as Treasurer 64-5, 120, 283, 284
Macdonald as President 21, 23, 30, 62-6, 67, 70, 120-1, 137, 284-8
McLean incident 65-70
move to MCG plan 357-8

New Magpies 63-4, 137, 284-6
player pay dispute 206
ticket-scalping 282-3

Collins, Ian
Carlton General Manager 22-3, 211, 341-2
dissatisfaction with Commission 358-9
and Elliott plan 22-3, 28, 31-5
at Hobart conference 296
queries Oakley's credentials 230
replaces Schwab on commission 369
talks to SA clubs 347-8, 351

Collins, Jon 225

Columb, Nick 293, 298-311

Cook, Ron
critical of VFL over HSV 7 174-5
national competition 158-9, 173-4
US fact-finding trip 201-5

Cordner, Don 273, 274

Cosser, Steve 169-72, 183, 187, 191

Crawford, David 77, 359, 360-4

Crawford Report 359-61, 364

Cronin, Mick 222

Cronin, Paul 219-25, 227, 229-42

Croxford, Max 369

D'Arcy, John 176-8

Dempsey, Gary 186

Dixon, Brian 95, 96

Dixon, Kevin 153-4

Dunn, Ray 195

Durham, Greg 37, 72, 132-4, 282-3, 335, 348

Dyer, Jack 197

Ebert, Russel 350
Edelsten, Geoffrey
97-117, 139, 140, 235,
320, 322, 332, 334
Elliott, John Dorman
and Aylett 84
breakaway competi-
tion 16, 17-33, 34-5,
80
business background
18, 21, 88, 127, 130,
132, 361
Carlton President 18,
19-22, 97, 155, 173,
318, 342-3
merger proposal to
North 318
new commission 360
Sydney Swans 97,
341-2
Essendon Football Club
Flag (1984) 79-80
player pay dispute
206-7
Sheedy as coach
79-80

Fenton, Gary 178-82
Fitzroy Football Club
AFL fails to support
358-9
Hore-Lacy as President
358-9, 361
merger failure
(Footscray) 35, 293,
303-11
merger failure
(Melbourne) 156
move north suggested
223-4
viability 1980s 153,
155-9
Wiegard as Chairman
14,15, 156-9, 223-4,
293, 296, 304
Flannery, Christopher
Dale 102-3, 107
Footscray

brawl with West Coast
369
Columb as president
293, 298-311
Gordon as President
353-4, 369, 375-6
merger talks (Fitzroy)
293, 301-311
Foschini case 69, 73-6,
201, 204
Fosters Cup 128, 132-3,
176-7
Fourex sponsorship
128-36
Fox, Lindsay
Foschini case 73-8
impact on game 59-61,
71-3, 226
impact on VFL 59
St Kilda Chairman
55-9, 86-7, 201
Fremantle Dockers 354-5,
377

Galimberti, Dennis
303-6, 311, 368
Galt, Graham 331-2,
336
Gee, Peter 185, 187
Geelong Football Club
31-2
Gerahty, John 87, 104,
336, 338, 341
Gordon, Peter
and commission
accountability 356,
358, 359-60, 361
and Footscray merger
303, 307-11
Footscray President
353-4, 369, 375-6
Grand Final
at MCG 53-4, 55,
260-76
at Waverley 38, 53-4,
55
Grand Final Breakfast
8
Grimaldi, Phillip 111-12
Grinter, Rodney 198-9

ground rationalisation
43-4

Hafey, Tom 65, 337
Hamilton, Jack
and Aylett 13, 40-1,
81, 84, 85-6, 122,
140-1, 225, 281
and Elliott 19, 30
Fourex sponsorship
128-9, 131-6
full-time VFL commis-
sioner 84-5, 119-20,
121-2, 126, 139,
140-1, 225, 271-2
killed in accident
277-82
management style criti-
cised 81
MCG 260-3, 271-2
national competition
95, 154-5, 158
as player 262-3
retires from commission
144-6, 148, 152, 162
Sydney Swans 95-6,
106-7, 108, 110, 114
TV rights for VFL
162-3, 175
to US re player rules
201-5
VFL General Manager
15, 19, 33, 36-41, 50,
51, 60, 72, 76, 81,
263, 268
Hamilton, Neil 252,
254, 255, 257
Hardie, Brad 232, 238,
301
Harding, Paul 256
Harris, Bernie 157
Harris, George 60
Head, Roger 57, 58
Healy, Gerard 113-14
Hennessy, John 41-4,
92, 93
Hill, David 173, 178,
186-7, 188
Hobart conference
(1989) 289-97

Hobbs, Greg 150-1
Hodgeman, John 333
Holmes à Court, Robert 87, 177, 361
Holt, John 15-16, 71-5
Hore-Lacey, Dyson 358, 359, 361
Huggins, Graham 56, 57, 58, 94, 98

Ireland, Andrew 231-2, 324, 325, 326, 329

Jeans, Allan 56, 78, 154, 217
Jesaulenko, Alex 58, 216
Jess, Peter 209-10
Johns, Ian 316-17
Johnson, Alan 319
Jordon, Ray 197-8
Joseph, Ray 2
Joseph, Ron
  and Aylett 12, 13, 16, 40
  and Elliott plan 32-3
  North Melbourne Committee 8, 9-11, 61, 243-5, 291, 312-15, 319
  queries Oakley's credentials 230, 368
  and Schwab as commissioner 147
  South Melbourne 1-4, 11, 314, 373
  Swans 344, 371-5
  to US re player rules 201-5

Kennedy, John
  as coach 64-5, 291-2, 314
  commission 361, 365
  VFL task force 34, 83
Keogh, John 96
Kerr, Bill 24, 253-8, 294-5
Kimberley, Craig 11, 336
Kleiman, Mark 283

Knights, Peter 216-20, 235, 236, 238-9, 240
Krakouer, Jim 112-13, 243-4
Krakouer, Phil 112-13, 243-4

Lane, Ralph 38, 42, 94
Lane, Tim 172-3, 178, 182, 185-7, 190, 192-3
licence fees 332, 338, 339, 347, 351
Lill, John 273, 274
Lockett, Tony 326, 371
Luke, Kenneth 264-6
Luscombe, Kevin 50, 51
Lyons, Barry 91-3, 96, 97-8, 100, 101, 103

Macdonald, Chesborough Ranald
  Collingwood President 62-6, 67, 70, 120-1, 137, 284-8
  and Elliott plan 21, 23, 30, 84
Macpherson, Keith 14
Madden, Justin 211-15, 374-5
Madden, Simon 211
Malthouse, Michael 259, 301
Mandie, David 34, 83
Mantello, Albert
  on commission 355, 360
  North Melbourne 8, 312
Matthews, Leigh 209, 287
McAlister, Allan
  AFL 356-61
  Collingwood President 287, 329, 343
  Collingwood Treasurer 64-5, 120, 283, 284
McCutchan, Eric 11, 38
MCG
  Collingwood home ground 357-8

for Grand Final 53-4, 55, 260-76
  Great Southern Stand 273-5
  MCC control 263-5
  Sunday sport 53-4
McKay, Jim
  and Swans 101, 104, 104-6, 109-11, 116, 252, 334-5
  VFL marketing 44-52, 94, 128, 297
McKay, Michael 182-3, 185, 187
McKinsey Report 71, 81-3
McLean incident 65-70
McPhee, Neil 201
Melbourne Cricket Club 54, 263-5
Melbourne Football Club
  Barassi as coach 66-9
  Five year Plan 137, 144
  lists players as assets 67
  merger with Fitzroy fails 156
  McLean transfer 65-78
  Moore-Templeton transfer 71, 137-8
  under Seddon 66-70
Menzies, Robert 264
mergers 125-6, 156, 289-3, 318, 358
Merrett, Roger 238
Mickan, Mark 238
Miller, Bob 34
Miller, Greg 328
Millson, Monty 373-4
Mitchell, Harold 127-9, 131, 134
Moncrieff, Michael 200
Moore, Peter 68, 71, 74, 137
Morgan, Paul 228, 229
Morphett, Drew 188-90
Morwood, Paul 76
Moss, Graham 255, 256
Murdoch, Rupert 63, 168, 177

Nathan, Maurice 12-13, 45, 46, 47, 48
national competition
Aylett proposes 14, 93, 94, 95
clubs endorse plan 124-6, 152-9, 351, 354
Cook's views 158-9, 173-4
Elliott conspiracy 17-33
Elliott-Collins proposal 23-4, 34
Hamilton's views 95, 154-5, 158
Oakley's views 290, 291, 293-4, 297, 347, 348-9, 351
problems with interstate teams 221
reasons for wanting 141-2, 154-5
Scanlon views 158, 159, 293, 304, 353, 354
South moves to Sydney 50
National Football League 15, 84, 140
Neagle, Merv 114
Nichevich, Robert 111
Nixon, Peter 86, 87-90, 107, 134, 174, 175, 176, 258, 355, 359
North Melbourne Football Club
Ansett as President 22, 32, 33, 59-62, 186, 226, 292, 312-19, 324
Aylett as President 7-9
Barassi as coach 180
Casey as Chairman 319
first premiership 9, 180
merger talks with Carlton 1988 318
public float 292, 315-18
Swans offer for Krakouers 112-13
Norwood Football Club 351

O'Connor, Terry 365
O'Sullivan, Shane 219, 220, 236-7, 240, 241, 301, 327-9, 333
Oakley, Dennis 149
Oakley, Hector 149, 150, 272
Oakley, Ross
background 148-50, 160-1, 272
Bears home ground 232-3
CEO new commission 148, 150-2, 367-70
and collective bargaining for players 212-13
and Crawford report 359-60
credentials questioned 160, 161-2, 163, 212, 230
expanded competition 290, 291, 293-4, 297, 347, 348-9, 351
five year plan 365-6
Footscray merger 304-6, 309-10, 353, 376
and MCC 272-4
meeting style 353-4
Pelerman buys Bears 323, 326
rigged barrel draw 189-90
rugby 280
SANFL negotiations 347, 348-9, 351
and Schwab 151-2, 364
and Sydney Swans 334, 338,
TV rights 162-3, 166-7, 171-4, 177, 178, 187, 191-2, 366
VFL name change 392-4, 297, 298
West Coast 256
Oliver, Ken 307

Packer, Kerry 63, 99, 100, 169, 267-8

Parkin, David 80
Patterson, Mike 57-9
payment of players 26, 27, 199-201, 206-15
Pelerman, Reuben 321-7
Piper, Alan 323-4, 326
poaching 136-9, 208, 255-6
Port Adelaide Football Club 348-51, 378
Powerplay 332-4, 339
Pratt, Bill 83
Pratt, Richard 104, 105
Pridmore, Alan 187, 190
Pritchard, Bob 98-101, 104-6, 110-11, 113, 116-17, 235, 252, 320, 332-4
private ownership of clubs
attractions to League 315
Bears 226-40, 320, 321-7
Swans 97-117, 235, 337-44, 361
Pryor, Geoff 205-8, 214

Quade, Ricky 98, 100

Raines, Geoff 137, 286
Rantall, John 11
recruiting 194-9
Reid, Wayne 59, 61, 67
Rice, Ian 59-60, 61, 70
Richmond Football Club
Catholic club 4
debts 291
recruiting 195-7
Wilson as President 20
Richmond, Graeme 195-7, 224
Roach, Don 100
Rogers, Barry 340, 343
Roos, Paul 370
Rose, Bob 286, 287, 288
Round, Barry 98, 100
Rozelle, Peter 202-4
Ryan, Phil 12

salary cap 283-4, 332, 372
Samuel, Graeme 86-8, 109, 122, 125, 131, 134, 140, 145, 147-52, 155, 158, 174, 267, 268, 335-6, 353, 354, 355, 359, 360
Scanlon, Peter
  Aylett's criticism 140
  as commissioner 86, 88-9, 106, 108, 121-2, 147, 155, 256, 290, 353, 354-5, 359
  Crawford Report 360-1
  CUB sponsorship 131-2, 134
  and Edelsten and Swans 109
  and Hamilton 122, 145, 147
  and MCG 271-2
  and mergers 125, 141-2
  national competition 158, 159, 293, 304, 353, 354
  and Schwab 147, 151-2, 354-5
  support for Oakley 148, 151, 360
  and Sydney Swans 104, 108, 109, 335-6, 338, 342
  television rights 162, 163, 169, 171, 187-8
Schwab, Alan
  dies in Sydney 361-4, 378
  executive commissioner VFL 151-2, 212, 364
  and Fitzroy move to Brisbane 224
  and MCC 272
  misses chief commissioners job 143-52, 314-15
  negotiates for

Fremantle 354-5
  NFL appointment 140
  and Oakley 151-2, 364
  and Players' Association 212
  and Port Adelaide 348-9, 351
  and Scanlon 147, 151-2, 354-5
  and Sydney Swans 96, 236-7, 336, 337
Schwab, Cameron 143-4, 215, 378
Seddon, Dick
  CUB sponsorship 134-5
  Fourex sponsorship 134-5, 138-9
  and Hamilton 122-3
  Macedon meeting 20, 23
  Melbourne 20, 23, 66-70, 71, 86, 113, 138-9, 144
  part-time VFL commissioner 86, 89, 122-4
  resigns as commissioner 355
  and trading players 75, 113
  to US to look at player rules 201-5
Sellers, Basil 104, 107-9, 337-8
Sewell, Greg 20, 23
Shaw, Gary 300-1
Sheahan, Mike 329, 349
Sheedy, Kevin 79, 80
Shewan, David 137-8
Siney, Bruce 133
Skase, Christopher
  buys Bears 226-40, 320, 322
  HSV 7 owner 191-2, 227
Skilton, Bobby 3, 22, 374-5
Smith, Norm 66
Smorgon, David 300

Snedden, Billy 71, 73
South Australian
  Football League 29, 248-9, 345-51, 352
South Melbourne
  Football Club 1-2, 11, 91-4
Spencer, Stuart 156
sponsorship of League
  Coca Cola 366
  CUB and Bond Brewing 127-36, 366
sports retirement syndrome 214-15
Sportsplay 333, 334-5
St Kilda Football Club
  Baldock as coach 292
  debts 56-7, 76-8, 292-3
  Foschini case 73-6, 201
  Fox as President 55-9, 73-8, 86-7, 201
Stern, David 204, 355
Stewart, Ian 11
Subiaco Football Club 246-7
Sunday sport 53-4, 82
Sutton, Charlie 306
Sydney Swans
  AFL intervenes 335-7, 340-4
  Aylett's dream 14
  Barassi to coach 344
  bid for Krakouers 112-13
  Capper 114-15, 335, 336
  club established 91-117
  early problems 91-7
  Edelsten's ownership 97-117, 235
  Hafey sacked 337
  interim board (1988) 335-7
  Lockett and Roos signed 371-2
  marketing 113-17, 332-3
  new ownership structure 337-44
  Powerplay 332-4, 339

salary cap 332, 371
Sportsplay 333, 334-5

Tandberg, Ron 60-1
television rights 162-93
Templeton, Kelvin 71,
74, 137-8, 300
Testro, Brenda 279
Thomas, Ted 179, 181-2
Thompson, Len 206
Threlfall, Kevin 31-2
ticket scalping 282-3
Tilley, Mike 38-9, 80,
119
Todd, John 258-9
transfer fees 9, 247-8
Tucker, Chester 74
Tuddenham, Des 206

VFL
Aylett as president
12-17, 19, 20, 50, 66,
71, 72, 79, 80-1, 203,
225, 263, 266-71, 277,
308-9
Aylett resigns 79-86
Broadcom deal 169-72,
173, 175, 178-87
Club Development
Fund 72
delegation to US 201-5
discuss Elliott plan 34
early Board meetings 24
Foschini case chal-
lenges rules 69, 73-6,
201, 204
growth under Aylett
41-50
Hamilton as GM 15,
19, 33, 36-41, 50, 51,
60, 72, 76, 81, 263,
268
Hamilton full time
commissioner 84-6

Hamilton retires 144-6
Hennessy as corporate
planner 41-4
Hobart summit 289-97
impact of Fox 59
income to clubs 23
and MCC 54, 263-5,
270, 273-6
McKay and marketing
44-52
McKinsey Report 71,
81-3
Mantello replaces
Seddon 355, 360
name change to AFL
293-5, 297-8
Oakley new chairman
148-52
part-time commission-
ers 86-90
revenue sources 46-50
rigged barrel draw
189-90
role of clubs 27
Schwab executive com-
missioner 151-2, 364
Southern Stand negoti-
ations 273-5
sponsorship of CUB
and Bond Brewing
127-36
Task Force recommen-
dations 34-5
television rights 162-93
Waverley land bought
265
WSC at Waverley rev-
enue 267-8
see also AFL
VFL Players' Association
199, 201, 204, 205-15

Walker, John 250-1,
254, 255

Walls, Robert 80
Waverley 5-6, 38, 53-4,
55, 265-6, 267-8,
269-71
Weber, Bruce 348-50
Weinert, Peter 331,
338-43
Weiss, Don 201-4
West Coast Eagles
brawl with Footscray
194, 369
coaches 258-9
Colless as Chairman
246-55
and Elliott conspiracy
28
formation of club
250-9
Hamilton as chairman
252, 254, 255, 257
Kerr Managing
Director 24, 253-8,
294-5
poaching charges
255-6
relations with League
256-7, 294
Western Australian
Football League 245-8,
354-5
Whitten, Teddy 300, 306
Wiegard, Leon 14, 15,
156-9, 223-4, 293,
295, 304
Willesee, Mike 336,
342-3
Williams, Greg 237, 337
Williamson, Mike 362-3
Wilson, David 106-8
Wilson, Ian 20, 23, 81,
84, 269

Zammit, Anthony 317-18